THE STATE
OF THE
UNIVERSITY

THE STATE
OF THE
UNIVERSITY

Authority and Change

Edited by CARLOS E. KRUYTBOSCH
State University of New York at Buffalo

and SHELDON L. MESSINGER
University of California at Berkeley

 SAGE PUBLICATIONS

Beverly Hills, California

*Chapters 1, 2, 5, 9, 10, 12, and 14, appeared (in earlier versions)
in the May-June, 1968, issue of* The American Behavioral Scientist
(Volume XI, Number 5), published by Sage Publications, Inc.

For information address:

SAGE PUBLICATIONS, INC.
275 South Beverly Drive
Beverly Hills, California 90212

FIRST PRINTING

Standard Book Number 8039-0060-0 (C)
                         8039-0061-9 (P)

Library of Congress Catalog Card No. 70-92356

TO

E. B. K. and M. H. M.

CONTENTS

INTRODUCTION:
AUTHORITY AND CHANGE
IN THE UNIVERSITY

Carlos E. Kruytbosch and Sheldon L. Messinger

Several of the chapters in this volume were published under our editorship in the May–June 1968 issue of *The American Behavioral Scientist*. At that time, we noted that:

> The papers . . . share a concern with the problem of authority in the university—its changing bases, uses, emergent forms, and prospects. On the one hand, the relation of the university to society is changing; on the other hand, the internal constitution, the character of the university, is also changing. The main question is: can a form of authority be found which will at once accommodate these changes and insure the freedom essential to teaching, learning, innovation, and communication? The authors offer no easy answers.

We also noted that each of the papers dealt explicitly or implicitly with the University of California at Berkeley. We suggested two reasons for that focus. First, Berkeley had become since 1964 "the symbol of a university beset by problems of authority." Second, the authors, with one exception, had all been at Berkeley during 1964 and had directly experienced the impact of the Free Speech Movement. "It may be difficult," we added, "for those who were not at Berkeley then to appreciate how profound an experience that was, and how much it affected received conceptions of the university." We expected this to change, however, for Berkeley was held out "as a model and a portent, an early form of what one of the authors calls 'the new university.'"

This last was, of course, a prediction rather than a recommendation. Since that time, Columbia, San Francisco State, even Harvard, to name but three institutions, have experienced major disturbances. In some ways these disturbances—as well as more recent troubles at Berkeley—seem to compare with the Free Speech Movement in the fashion that, say, Viet Nam compares with the Crusades. But in other ways, at least with benefit of hindsight, they raise the same central issue about the university: can forms of authority be found which will both accommodate change and insure freedom? The authors whose studies we have added are at least as puzzled and skeptical as those whose studies made up the original collection. One of the latter—C. Michael Otten—has revised his earlier conclusions and now suggests that "policed managerialism," rather than "private government," may be upon us. The authors of a study we have added—Sheldon Wolin and John Schaar—seek "hope" amidst "despairs." Easy answers were not offered before, and they are not offered now.

One difference, however, is that the prospects of *comforting* answers seem less favorable, as the studies by Otten, Wolin and Schaar, and others suggest. It is clearer in late 1969 than it was in 1964 or early 1968 that problems of authority and freedom on campus anticipate and reflect these problems in the society at large. It is not just that the university has been "injected into politics," for even a cursory examination of the history of universities shows a constant involvement with the goals and functions of contemporary social constituencies. Rather, what is at issue is the basis and balance of university involvement.

Retrospectively, although many appreciated the fact at the time, this was the central issue of the Berkeley Free Speech Movement. The specific question raised was: should the university countenance active concern with changes in the forms and distribution of authority in the community? Would partisan political activity be permitted on campus? The answer at the time, arrived at only after mass disruption and turmoil, was "Yes"—subject only to appropriate regulation of "time, place and manner" to avoid interference with scheduled educational functions. Indeed, the answer seemed better than "Yes," for the question was somehow transformed into whether the university should encourage, and not merely tolerate, this kind of concern. At the time, this positive answer seemed and was liberating.

Today, although the answer may still be "Yes," some of the institutional implications, and some of the obstacles, to the realization of such a norm have become more apparent. Some students and some faculty members are no longer satisfied with yesterday's "Yes"; or perhaps one should say: they are not satisfied with yesterday's question. Yesterday's question seemed to have to do, mostly, with the permissiveness of university authority—would partisan political activity be allowed?—and with what might be called "citizen rights" on campus—would such activity be permitted on campus, say, in Sproul Hall Plaza? Today's question is different and infinitely more troubling. For many, this question is no longer should the university provide a setting for partisan political activities, but rather should it become, itself, a party to and instrument in such activities. It can be argued that this is a distinction without a difference. And it is so argued. On the one side, it is sometimes said that the university is, and always has been, a party to and instrument in political struggles; on the other side, that any political activities by students or faculty members—but particularly if these activities take place on campus—commit the university to a partisan political position. And on both sides, there is a call for a reduction in the permissiveness of university authority—for the elimination of work that supports an evil status quo; for the elimination of talk that challenges it.

The institutional implications of a norm of permissiveness toward partisan politics on campus are clearer; the obstacles to establishment and defense of such a norm are clearer too. The power and depth of societal forces over which the university has little immediate control manifest themselves in a variety of ways—from opinion poll results condemning student "violence" and professorial and administrative "timidity," to the introduction of countless measures in local, state and federal legislatures aimed at "controlling campus disorder." At present, these forces, partly responding to the challenges presented by the university itself, seem to loom more inimical than ever. One would have to be a person of very large faith—with a severe case of myopia—to ignore the urgent possibility that while the university may be radically transformed as a "result" of pressures from students and other internal constituencies, the change may be in directions neither expected nor welcomed by those who have worked so fervently from within the university.

It may seem odd that having conjured up a foreboding vision of the dire effects of societal forces upon the destiny of the institution, we proceed to recommend a collection of papers which focus on matters *internal* to the institution. Little here of demonstrators and police, of the local and national politics of higher education and science—although such studies are badly needed. Instead, the chapters in this expanded collection are mainly concerned with aspects of strain and tension within the university that relate to the capacity of the institution to govern itself.

For the most part, the contributors deal with the character of, and relations between, constituent groupings of the university: trustees, administrators, faculty members, students, and some of those other groupings who carry on the academic work of the university but do not as yet fit easily into any of these categories. Little detailed attention is given to external pressures upon these groupings, except in the paper by Alexander Busch. Instead the effort is to delineate, with the help of specific research in most cases, the make-up of these groupings, their role (or lack of it) in policy making, and their attitudes toward the kinds of issues that have been, and remain, before the university. An effort is made as well to suggest the directions of changes of relations within and among these groupings, and to assess the likely consequences of such changes for the university as a whole.

All but one of the studies—Alexander Busch's again—are primarily concerned with the contemporary university in the United States. Troy Duster's paper uses observations on Swedish universities as a comparative foil for sharper understanding of the U.S. experience. Busch's work deals with the German university and the fate of one category of scholar—the *privatdozent*—within it. The parallels between the experiences of these persons and the situation of teaching assistants, researchers, lecturers, and other partially enfranchised groupings in the U.S. university are close and instructive. They led us to include it. Furthermore, Busch's study is a model for institutional and historical analysis that deserves wider exposure than its original place of publication makes likely. Other than these two usages of comparative analysis, the authors employ a variety of approaches to their subject matters—historical, functional, descriptive, even anecdotal. As selective principles we emphasized a combination of issue relevance, theoretical power and richness of empirical content, for the volume is aimed at bridging the gap between general and specialized audiences. It is one of the ironies of the university that the "specialists" in higher education are not often read by the practitioners—Rodney Hartnett presents some data on this matter.

Whatever one's estimate of the prospects of the university in the United States, given extant pressures and conflicts it is apparent that those who care about the university would do well to become as familiar as possible with the way it works. One way of understanding much of the current turmoil within the university, as well as about it, is to see that constituent groupings are seeking new bases of legitimacy, the old bases having seriously eroded. Put differently, the university is in the midst of a "constitutional" crisis. Reformulation of the university's "constitution" is hindered, among other ways, by a high level of ignorance within it about the activities and functions that are performed within its boundaries or in its name. It may be, as some have suggested,[1] that avoidance, even studied avoidance, of self-knowledge on the part of the very institution dedicated to the discovery of knowledge was once functional for the development of the university. Perhaps. But in any case, the insistent and public demands for definition and justification of the social roles of the university by students and other constituencies within and outside the university—especially from funding sources—have forced self-examination upon the institution.

Our aim in assembling these papers has been to aid the process of institutional self-awareness. Our approach has been eclectic. The contributions do not add up to a "model" of the contemporary U.S. university; neither does any given chapter seriously purport to offer such a model in any detail. In one sense, this collection represents a set of field notes, a group of observations on a subsociety and subculture during a particularly dynamic and stressful period of becoming. It also represents an effort—tentative, uncertain, not entirely explicit—to make sense of, to conceptualize and interpret, these field notes. A more definitive interpretation of what is coming to be remains yet to be undertaken—perhaps by some historian of the next century, if there is one, who is interested in how the university of that time got to be the way it will be then. These notes, empirically based as most of them are, should be of use to that historian. In the meantime, insofar as they capture important aspects of "what is happening" within the university, they will, we hope, contribute to a rational reworking of the university's constitution, one that results in the creation and securing of a humane institution firmly devoted to the enlargement of the dignity of human beings.

NOTE

1. Clark Kerr's suggestion to this effect is well known. See his *The Uses of the University* (1963: especially pp. vii, 18, 38, and 49). Also see Veysey, *The Emergence of the American University* (1966: 337–338).

REFERENCES

KERR, C. (1963) *The Uses of the University*. Cambridge: Harvard University Press.

VEYSEY, L. (1966) *The Emergence of the American University*. Chicago: University of Chicago Press.

PART 1

INSTITUTIONAL
CONSIDERATIONS

CHAPTER 1

THE NEW UNIVERSITY

Burton R. Clark

The American university is becoming an examining and degree-granting institution. In the past, this form of university has developed primarily in European countries and in those societies elsewhere that have followed European models. One extreme instance of this type is the University of Rome, where 70,000 students are listed on the books. Here, the participation of thousands of students centers on two actions: registration and examination. A duly qualified young man in Taranto, 550 kilometers south of Rome, can journey to the university in September to register, return home for the next eight months to do whatever a young man does in Taranto, and journey again to Rome in late June or early July to try his luck in a brief oral examination, sitting for a half hour with one of the professor's assistants. More typically, the student will live in Rome and attend some lectures. Freedom abounds: The professor gives lectures at his discretion, and the student attends lectures at his discretion. The only tyranny for the student is the tyranny of the examination. The goal is the laurea, the degree; *the* means is the examination.

The American university is yet a fair distance from this situation, and we are not likely to go all the way, but the trend toward this form of university participation, with characteristic American adjustments and equivalences, runs strong. The intent of the student is ever more degree-centered, his participation is ever more segmental, the means of graduation are ever more examination results bunched and recorded as course grades. Compared to the Italian university, we give examinations more often, in written and relatively objective forms, with the important consequence that we must have larger dossiers and a larger administrative class to maintain the files. The American genius in the next two decades will be to create a bureaucratic form of the degree university.

Why does the American university tend in this direction? We need to look first at the changing social structure of the university, and then to the

AUTHOR'S NOTE: Revised version of paper given at the annual meeting of the Society for the Study of Social Problems, August 27, 1967, San Francisco.

This chapter is reprinted (in slightly revised form) from *The American Behavioral Scientist*, May–June, 1968 (Volume XI, Number 5).

interests and ideologies of university administrators and faculties that generate the immediate energy for the structural change that is underway.

The Social Structure of the University

The trend in western society toward large size and great complexity in
formal organization is nowhere more apparent than in American higher education. A large college before the Civil War had 500 students, and most
were much smaller. A major university at the turn of the century would
size out at several thousand students. Our large campuses in 1960 ran to
20,000 or so students. Now we are up to 30,000 students, and the rapid
expansion underway will soon bring us a number of campuses with enrollments of 40,000, 50,000, and 60,000. This is not just the case for state
universities; we already have state colleges and junior colleges of 20,000
enrollment, and the private city-oriented universities are serious competi-
tors with the public universities in demonstrating value through scale.
Nearly all grow, and nearly all expand in purpose and duty. "Preserving
truth" covers all the expanding heritage of man, as we quickly find out if
we allow ourselves to roam from the physics professor to the professor of
classical languages. "Creating new knowledge" embraces research in real
estate practice as well as research in the archeology of Peru. "Serving the
needs of man through truth and knowledge"—the third of the commonly
enunciated goals of the university—covers ground that extends from home
economics for the future housewife to R and D work for NASA and the
Department of Defense, and, upon occasion, some serving of the needs of
the CIA. We move to campuses of 75 departments, some of which are 100
faculty members in size; campuses of 50 research institutes, some with
hundreds of Ph.D.'s; campuses of 15 or more professional schools, some of
which in themselves far exceed the resources of the entire university of the
turn of the century.

With these sizes, these purposes, and these duties, the university campus becomes an extremely complicated social arrangement of the relations
of men at work. The formal structure in itself is bound to be full of over-
lap, gap, and contradiction. It becomes somewhat like a confederation of
tribes that have wandered into the same campgrounds. Bureaucracy enforced from the center is, at the level of the professoriate, not fully in control, since the centrifugal forces of profession and discipline are strong. The
professional school and the department are the basic units for organizing
the work, embodying and carrying the diverse expertise of the faculty. The
campus is a setting for a hundred, several hundred, distinctive clusters of
experts. With this as its primary nature, it is fractured rather than integrated by the identification and commitment normal to the occupations that
we call professions.

The campus also undergoes urbanization. The right place to be in Oregon for maximum college-building is Portland, as the University of Oregon
and Oregon State University are finding out, in the face of the growth of

Portland State; in Illinois, it is Chicago, as witness the rapid growth of the publicly supported campuses there; in New York, it is New York City and Buffalo and Binghamton and Albany and Long Island. Expansion is general these days in any location, but new campuses are usually placed where the people are; the city and suburban campuses have high growth rates, and urban growth pushes population out to and around the traditional country places. Higher education moves ever more into the metropolis. This greatly increases the geographic convenience of college and promotes access. It also promotes commuting: Students live with their parents, or they live by themselves or with their own family in an off-campus location, or they pick up a rental with one or two friends. Such students also commonly have a full-time or part-time job. Living and working on the outside, their time on campus is greatly reduced.

With the fracturing of structure and the narrowing of participation, the university campus becomes an "educational city": large, varied, often colorful; sometimes the scene of rebellion and riot; always the home of specialized labor and segmental involvement. We can no longer describe it as a community. Traditional collegial forms of campus governance have lost their efficacy, faculty members go their separate ways, and the student role tends to narrow to formal course work.

The dynamics of this trend toward professional sprawl and narrow involvement are not clear in detail, but we can grasp some broad aspects. The trend does not stem from a traditional view of academia or follow from a new conception of the campus entire that has been enunciated, debated, and widely accepted. The massive, degree-centered university is still an alien vision to many administrators and faculty members. We are getting there by drift—drift that results from major groups pursuing their self-interests, as they define them with the aid of traditional belief and immediate operating ideologies. Many groups outside the university have some leverage on it, but the interest groups that matter most are internal: the administrators and the faculty.

Administrative Interests and Ideologies

The first immediate cause, or set of causes, of the drift to the degree-centered university resides in the bosom of the administration. Each multiversity has a major administrative class with interests and ideologies of its own. Outside groups have more direct effect upon this organizational stratum than upon the faculty, because the top administrative roles, and some of the lower ones of a boundary character (such as public relations), dictate a sensitivity to the outside. From the day-to-day concerns of the administrators there has arisen a logic of growth. What is the central imperative of university administration today? Growth. Growth is necessary to meet the demands of articulate publics, and executive and legislative bodies, for more places for the young. Growth is necessary to satisfy the demands of the many clusters of faculty for more resources and personnel.

Growth is seen as absolutely necessary for strength against other colleges and universities. The institutional stakes are particularly high in this regard in the public systems of the states, where the traditional one-campus state university has given way to six campuses, or to five distinctive universities, and where weak teachers' colleges have become powerful state colleges in the last twenty years. For the administrative class in the multiversities, there is no answer other than expansion. They therefore become possessed by a logic of growth. They can wish for quality, seek quality, and of course always talk about quality; but growth is what motivates them and sets the framework for consideration of quality.

But then there are many ways to handle growth. A state university of 70,000 students can consist of one campus of 70,000, or seventy campuses of 1,000, or many combinations of number of campuses and size of campuses between these two extremes. The administrative class in American universities clearly prefers a small number of large campuses rather than a large number of small ones, a preference dictated by a logic of administrative efficiency. Dollar cost everywhere sits heavy on the mind, and cost analysis everywhere "proves" that it is cheaper to add the next 5,000 students to an existing campus of 20,000 than to start a new campus—grounds, buildings, libraries, and all the rest. The legislature thinks so, the governor's office says so, the whiz kid in the administration, with charts on the wall and pointer in hand, patiently explains to his non-whiz associates why this must be so.

Then, too, a large number of campuses does get messy, especially if they manage to embody diversity rather than being carbon copies of one another. The men who keep the books at headquarters, by training and by demand of role, want standard categories across the system rather than ones so adapted to the individual campus that there would be as many different sets of categories as there are campuses.

So we end up with administrative thought about the nature of the American university very much affected by the connected logics of growth and efficiency. Growth is considered compelling. Then, by applying certain administrative and economic models, growth is made to mean mammoth groupings of educational work. And why not? Working within these modes of thought, one is able to assume that, educationally, a campus of 50,000 is a campus of 5,000 written ten times larger.

Anyone who might want to test the strength of these administrative modes of thought could well begin by examining the dormitories constructed in the last ten years. Dormitory management on the American scene is not usually under the faculty. The dorms are commonly controlled by a business office and the dean of students' office. In many places, the new dorms are cultural disasters, an affront to decency and sensitivity, as well as to the educational process. The business office has defined the dormitory as bedrooms; the dean of students' office adds its *in loco parentis* sense of responsibility for the morality and manners of the young. So out goes the concept of the house master and in comes the house mother, who, in carrying out her assignment, will not only guard the door but will also lock up the coffee cups if the boys leave them dirty. And out goes building design worked up through the ages for student life and in comes the campus Hilton, indistinguishable in exterior appearance from an insurance office or hotel. In come immense lounges a half block long, glass on two sides and functionally furnished; bare hallways decorated only with coke and cigarette machines; and the equally bare cafeteria with music piped in from seven o'clock in the morning until ten o'clock at night. One cannot understand these places, these standarized locations that tear life apart, without understanding the administrative definition of the situation that decides their form. And one cannot understand the unhappiness of students in these places if we continue to think of the dormitory as an educational residence. The modern dormitory is more like a bedroom suburb, with its radical separation of human activity, than it is like a Left Bank. Students flee dormitories for a very simple reason: they cannot live there.

Faculty Interests and Ideologies

The second set of immediate causes of the drift to the degree-centered university is found in the faculty. Teaching is an occupation, and men in the higher occupations have careers. Especially in the professions, men pursue careers according to norms internal to the field. The academic career is strongly defined by disciplines, and the number of distinct career lines in a faculty is even greater than the number of departments, since many departments contain two or more specialties. The clusters of experts that we lump together under the heading of faculty take their cues from a very large number of different reference groups—men in their field—and this is the most important of the fragmenting forces in the university. What all these fields have in common is a logic of career in which a man gets ahead by a combination of personal publication and departmental aggrandizement. The peak of reward is to have published very well and to have the resulting personal prestige enhanced and validated twice over by membership in a prestigeful department. Since at least the turn of the century, men who would have it otherwise, e.g., the general educationalists, have never been able to affect seriously the career orientation that dictates devotion to one's own scholarly labor and to the disciplinary standing of one's own department. As the university has swung ever more toward being a research enterprise, so has the devotion to research and career intensified. There are interesting exceptions, and there is usually a backlash, but this logic of career remains firmly in control.

The career logic is fundamental to the narrowing of faculty participation and perception. Energy and insight flow readily inside the boundaries of the discipline and the department. The corollary is not only a withdrawal of energy from problems of the whole campus but, more important, a trained incapacity to see these problems and to consider them serious. That place is right which enhances career. If it is otherwise so flawed that it becomes a sick organization, then that is only because of administrative ineffectiveness or of students being wrongly oriented. We have long glossed over fundamental differences between faculty interests and student interests. It is comfortable thought, night and morning, that what is good for the faculty is good for the students. Well, sometimes no; and, more and more, as we move toward the degree-centered university, the answer is no.

The trained incapacity of faculty members to understand the nature of the new university is deepened by traditional beliefs that hang fast in the mind. Foremost in this regard are the sentiments that well in the breast when we utter the words, a "community of scholars." This vocabulary has long served academics well in organizational defense and in promoting loyalty and cohesion, so well that it will die hard. But its use, time and again, blinds us to even the simple realities. Take these cherished sentiments, stir them with cocktails and a sunset, and then the internal structure of UCLA in 1968 becomes basically of a piece with that of a turn-of-the-century university or a small college today. All are communities of scholars; one is a little larger, but the social structure is essentially the same.

But the facts are simple: The new university has 1,500 or 2,000 men in the various clusters of faculty who have the rights of full citizenship. This aggregation is politically differentiated into operating elites, attentive public, and apathetic and inattentive public—as witness attendance and participation in normal meetings of the whole. At best, the aggregation is a representative democracy tempered by oligarchy. This already massive core aggregation is surrounded by ever larger aggregations of educational workers who do an ever larger share of the teaching and the research who do not have full rights. In the research centers, there are two non-faculties, one composed of post-doctoral researchers and the other of pre-doctoral research assistants.[1] Back in the departments, there is an army of teaching assistants, an aggregation whose use and abuse has become a scandal on more than one campus;[2] and in the new university, with its metropolitan location, one increasingly finds a fourth-fringe faculty in the person of the lecturer—an elastic category that insures there will be someone at the podium in each classroom. One now finds departments, and indeed campuses, where half of the undergraduate day-session classroom instruction is offered by persons who are on the books as full-time and part-time lecturers and hence do not have a regular faculty position.

Thus, such simple age-old descriptive statements as "professors teach" become inaccurate, and not only because professors do other things, but also because other people do much of the teaching and provide much of the informal instruction that is at the heart of the best research training.

Faculty interests and ideologies are such that the most successful and most powerful professors in the university will tend not to see its defects. Their vision is set on career, they see the campus through the prism of career dividends, and their ideology defines the system as a but-larger version of what universities were like when they were seventeen.

Balance and Discontent

We have also been slow to fix our vision on the problematic features of the new university because of its effectiveness in servicing the economy and in helping various governmental agencies fulfill their missions. Manpower experts, abroad as well as at home, heap applause on the American university and the American differentiated structure of higher training. The new university is a major front of the technological society, and it has the capacity to confer expertise on large numbers of people and to provide expert services for a large number of outside groups. But adjustment to economic and political demands is not the equivalent of social effectiveness, since the university has other social and cultural duties, not the least of which is to assist the young to become educated persons. The multiversity has indeed lost its balance; it has, for many of the best of the young, become an alienating agency of the first order. Despite the assertion of some administrators that balance is all relative, and hence that there really is no such thing as imbalance, we need to work out a balance theory of campus structure, taking into account the services that a university ought to perform at a given stage of social development. If we think of a continuum of "hard" to "soft" social services, at one end there is the development of hardware for the military. We are doing well at this end. At the other end are such emotional qualities of the individual as the desire to stop for a while by the woods, to tarry behind to watch the snow. There is no reason to think that the new university well serves such sensibilities.

The new university is a conflict-prone organization. Its many purposes push and pull in different directions. Its multiple principles of authority and pluralistic power structure make coordination difficult (Clark, 1961; Vollmer and Mills, 1966: 282–291). The faculty, as intellectuals, often think otherwise; as specialists, they think divergently. Above all, the university is increasingly vulnerable to discontent generated in its relation to its participating clientele, the students. The large university has a heterogeneous aggregation of students, and it is not likely to please them all. We now know who will be satisfied and who will be displeased. The university's effective job training and job placement pleases the vocationally-minded students, the ones within the student body who do most to turn the campus into an examination- and degree-centered enterprise. For them, the human touch is sweet, but not required. Others, however—young academics and intellectuals—insist that personal relations with professors and other students are necessary. They even believe they should be a part of academic government. Thus they come with "false" expectations. They dream of participation in a community of scholars as they enter the gates of campuses where no such thing exists. Their hopes for the college years are inflated by both the idealism of the best minds among the young and the traditional images and ideologies of academia that have spilled over into the larger society.

Their desires, time and again, become attached to particularly inappropriate centers of educational work by institutional aura and the claims of competitive advertising. It does not take cocktails and sunsets to induce a university or college to put its pretty features up front and bury its ugly ones in the shadows, and to let outsiders assume that all is golden. Systematic misrepresentation of the institutional self becomes an art form in modern competitive arenas; the truth has long been a captive of romantic illusion in American higher education. To take the most injurious of current deceptions: a university made famous by research will simply not on its own accord broadcast to the young that it offers a mediocre undergraduate education, even if the president of the university believes this to be the case and writes about it as a paradox of greatness (for example, Kerr, 1963: 64–65). Elementary school teachers have to tell lies to little boys in the name of traditional culture; university personnel tell lies to older boys for narrower reasons. Adults who have long taught their young to discount the advertising of the mass media must now also teach them by the age of sixteen to discount educational propaganda.

Thus, for some entering students, expectations will be radically out of alignment with campus realities and there will continue to be discontented minorities in the American educational city. If we take a poll of student satisfaction, perhaps only a small share—say 10 percent—turn up as deeply disappointed; and sensible university men are pleased if they can satisfy or only mildly disappoint 90 percent of the students. Pleased, that is, until we realize that a "mere 10 percent" on a large campus is 3,000 or 4,000 of yours and mine, reflecting an enormous amount of frustration and suffering, and offering more than enough bodies to raise organized hell. Ten percent in smaller places is a number of young people that can be dealt with informally. Faculty members and deans can get to them, to listen, argue, persuade, give in, coopt. But not so in the very large places. The new university, in its commitment to growth and its looseness of internal structure, creates an arena for crowd behavior and for the politics of semi-organized and organized interest groups. Feelings of powerlessness abound; salvation lies in organizing a bloc. The move toward political action will come not only from the student minorities who dissent from the main drift and seek organized voices, especially the graduate students, but also from the fringe educational workers. The assistant professors and instructors, while restive, can usually see promise in the system; but as the ranks of the nonfaculty swell, particularly the post-doctoral researchers and lecturers, discontent over second-class citizenship will become an extensive and powerful phenomenon.

What is missing most in the new university is a sense of the social conditions that promote care and affection. One is tempted to say of the gigantic campus of the near future that there will be no society there. It becomes clearer each year that if there is to be a society there, it must be continuously planned for and worked at. For a long time we have been able to depend on an emergent, unplanned social structure—personal ties generated by students and faculty—to infuse academic campgrounds with saving elements of human caring. But now no longer: students and faculty will occasionally generate a humane social structure in a massive educational enterprise, but we can less and less depend on it. Growth is too fast, specialization is too fragmenting, economic logics of efficient manpower processing are too much in command. The crucial aspect of reform in American higher education is to devise substructures on the large campus that promote informal influence and a sense of personal contact instead of the substructures that build walls of impersonality and formal (and seemingly arbitrary) authority (Clark and Trow, 1966). Given the American setting—particularly parental and student expectations—let us establish several dicta: (a) No campus is effectively organized unless a student can have daily personal contact with a professor. (b) No educational structure is effective that does not put the administrator in those lounges, cafeterias, and hallways where his path will intersect those of the professor and the student. (c) No campus has an appropriate distribution of influence unless students and the various nonfaculties feel themselves among the franchised. Only through personal encounters do we maintain on a campus the sentiments that support order among free individuals. Without the cultivation of the informal situations that build the norms of caring, we turn it all over to the deans, the cops, and the courts.

If we apply a sociological-humanistic model to the modern campus, instead of the current economic and administrative models, we begin to sense that the American educational city may be working its way into a state not unlike that of the American city at large. In the city, we have hoped for the best, while the interplay of major economic and political interests, in a context of weak planning, continues to steer us toward disaster. The social ineffectiveness is staggering. So, too, in higher education, we point to a reform here, a reform there—a Santa Cruz, a Monteith—and hope for the best, while the dominant interests and ideologies lead to structures that insure greater cultural deprivation and social alienation for important minorities. It is time for a new sense of effectiveness in the major universities, one that goes far beyond the annual figures of size and output and far beyond the claims to fame which are the magnified sum of the reputation of individual scholars. If we did not know it before, we know it now—good scholars and good students can make a bad educational system. *Everything depends on how they are put together.* Unless administrators and faculty learn to ask about the quality of interaction on campus, and take that line of inquiry as basic rather than as "interesting," the new university will be an ineffectual social system, following along the trail of the American city in mindlessness and cruelty. What we must promote are the structures of caring that are so necessary to freedom and order in the modern higher learning.

NOTES

1. For information about research workers on one campus, see Carlos E. Kruytbosch and Sheldon L. Messinger (1968); reprinted as Chapter 12 in this volume.

2. Dubin and Beisse have shown that the number of teaching assistants has grown much more rapidly than faculty in recent years in the country as a whole, taking over a larger share of instruction (Dubin and Beisse, 1967; reprinted as Chapter 13 in this volume).

REFERENCES

CLARK, B. R. (1961) "Faculty Authority." *AAUP Bulletin* 47, No. 4 (Winter): 293–302.

—— (1966) "Faculty organization and authority." Pp. 282–291 in H. M. Vollmer and D. L. Mills (eds.) *Professionalization.* Englewood Cliffs: Prentice-Hall.

—— and M. Trow (1966) "The organizational context." Pp. 17–70 in T. M. Newcomb and E. K. Wilson (eds.) *College Peer Groups.* Chicago: Aldine.

Dubin, R. and F. Beisse (1967) "The assistant: academic subaltern." *Administrative Science Quarterly* 11, No. 4 (March): 521–547. Reprinted as Chapter 13 in this volume.

Kerr, C. (1963) *The Uses of the University.* Cambridge: Harvard University Press.

Kruytbosch, C. E. and S. L. Messinger (1968) "Unequal peers: the situation of researchers at Berkeley." *American Behavioral Scientist* 11, No. 5 (May–June): 33–43. Reprinted as Chapter 12 in this volume.

CHAPTER 2

CONCEPTIONS OF THE UNIVERSITY
The Case of Berkeley

Martin Trow

For several years the University of California at Berkeley has been the scene of disturbance and turbulence. This disturbance in its most visible forms has appeared to center on student rights to political action and expression on campus. But the crisis at Berkeley has not been confined to issues of student rights; it has been a crisis involving the basic character and mission of a university, on one hand, and its forms of authority and governance, on the other.

Much has been written about the events at Berkeley; it has been, for reasons that are interesting in themselves, a sort of ink-blot test for the world, which has seen in it the most varied shapes and meaning. But the developments at Berkeley are of sufficient importance for the future of American higher education to warrant this continuing discussion.

One way to approach the matter is chronologically: to try to reconstruct the events, disputes, and issues that have marked the continuing crisis along the way. That, obviously, is impossible in a short essay, and perhaps not even desirable. Instead, I shall attempt to illuminate these matters by directing attention to certain underlying strains and tensions within the University of which these events have, so to speak, been symptoms. I do not want to minimize the importance of the symptoms: men and institutions can die of them. But behind them lie more fundamental problems which the events at Berkeley have thrown into bold relief; issues of considerable relevance, I believe, to other colleges and universities here and abroad.

I would like to turn first to some of the areas of dispute on the Berkeley campus, and the diagnoses and prescriptions for dealing with them, and then focus somewhat more analytically on what I think to be a crucial area: conflicts arising out of differing conceptions of the nature of the university within the faculty and the student body. Lastly, I would like to raise

---

EDITORS' NOTE: This chapter is reprinted (in slightly revised form) from *The American Behavioral Scientist,* May–June, 1968 (Volume XI, Number 5).

the general question of the characteristics of institutions which affect the nature, the forms, and the intensity of the conflicts which arise within them. Here, if anywhere, Berkeley may have some lessons to teach. The issues and disputes at Berkeley are either already present elsewhere, or almost surely soon will be. The problem is not to find ways of escaping these disputes, which may be endemic in great universities, but rather ways of preventing them from assuming forms that are profoundly disruptive to the university, and to its capacity to realize *any* of the many missions which it is assuming in the modern world.

I

Most visible at Berkeley, and certainly the initiating issue in the present crisis, was a demand on the part of a segment of the student body for changes in the rules and regulations which would permit much freer political discussion and organization on campus. Before December, 1964, acting both on principle and out of concern for the larger political environment, the university administration very closely controlled the kinds of political action it would allow on university property. These rules had been gradually liberalized over the preceding few years, so that political speakers of various kinds were permitted on campus, but essentially the effect was to keep day-to-day partisan political activity off the campus. During the fall of 1964, first small groups and then increasingly larger numbers of students rebelled against these restrictions until finally, in December, 1964, as a result both of a student strike and of a faculty resolution carrying with it a very large majority, most of the restrictions on political activity on campus were removed.[1] Since then, broadly, anything legal off campus has been permitted on campus, subject only to rules which address themselves, not to the substance of the political action, but only, as the formula goes, to the "time, place, and manner" of these activities in order that they not interfere with the primary functions of the university.

Many students and faculty thought and hoped that this would end the dispute within the university, allowing activist students to direct their energies outward, toward problems and issues (most notably the civil rights movement and the peace movement) located in the larger society. But this did not occur. The campus has continued to be the scene of disputes, initially over the precise nature of the time, place, and manner rules, then over the role of students in setting those rules (as part of broader student participation in a wide range of university decisions), and increasingly over the basis of authority on campus, the university constitution, and its character and functions in the society. These issues did not simply succeed one another in time; for example, they all still appear in such specific incidents as a student strike of December, 1966. But over time there has been a general broadening and deepening of student demands for more radical reform of the institution, both internally in how it governs itself and externally in how it should act toward the larger society.

This dispute has now become a chronic source of irritation, friction, and sporadic outbursts. Some students will say, and some even believe, that the administration over the past three years has never really accepted the charter granting students the rights of political speech and action on campus, that it has conspired to cripple and then destroy the radical student movement as part of a strategy of counter-revolution aiming at the restoration of the old regime. A slightly more sophisticated version of this viewpoint argues that the administrative officers themselves (at least most of them) are not inherently evil, but that it is in the nature of their office that they be hostile to the student movement, both because of their own special interests and their general identification with the established interests of society which the movement is attacking. Even if the administrators want to be "nice guys" and cooperative, it is said, they are constrained by their offices and interests not to be. Those who hold these views see the university as *necessarily* an arena for conflict, which sometimes takes the form of negotiation, sometimes of more direct confrontation through strikes and sit-ins.

The faculty, during all this, has been rather sharply split along a number of lines. Some have quite consistently supported student demands and positions, some have done so with qualifications, others have supported the administration, while the great majority have tried to get on with their own work, returning to the political arena only at moments of great crisis, when ordinary work on campus was clearly disrupted; and when they did so, they tended to search for some reasonable compromise, some kind of broad consensus that would resolve the immediate conflict, allow the campus to "return to normal" and themselves to return to their unfinished manuscripts and experiments.

Some faculty members, including many who do not share the radical students' view, have criticized the administration for its blunders; for being too punitive, or not firm enough, or both; for creating occasions that could be exploited; and for responding to provocation impulsively, or with poor judgment. A more substantial analysis of this kind suggests that the events of 1964 thrust the faculty into a role, in relation both to the students and the administration, that it traditionally eschewed and did not really mean to play—that of taking a direct interest and part in the regulation of student affairs and conduct on campus (at Berkeley, traditionally an administration function). Since then the faculty has uneasily and without enthusiasm continued from time to time to intervene in student affairs, while at the same time refusing to take the major role in day-to-day administration. It has thus allowed the students to see it as a part-time (and not wholly trustworthy) ally against the administration, encouraging actions designed to strengthen that alliance forged and reforged in moments of crisis.

But while the faculty as a whole has by no means been hostile to the administration during this period, its support has been qualified and erratic. It has thus eroded the authority of the administration, whom it has, in a sense, been able to heckle and second guess between votes of confidence, even while it has disappointed the hopes of the activist students. But an administration whose own authority is insecure, constantly subject to challenge and attack at the same time as its scope and character are in the process of change, is, one might guess, more likely to make mistakes, more likely to be alternatively rigid and yielding, than is a stable and secure one

administering a generally accepted system of legitimate rules and regulations. The problem of a university administration in what might be called a
"situation of moving disequilibrium" is one that may have some lessons for
others, and therefore is one to which I want to return.

Berkeley's continuing crisis has been at least exacerbated by other factors which are remote from the usual concerns of faculty and students.
One, paradoxically, is the very attractiveness and availability of the campus
to nonstudents and to the mass media. The forms that Berkeley's problems
have taken have been in part public and dramatic: mass meetings on public squares, pickets, sit-ins, rather than confined to faculty meetings or
deans' offices. And the media, especially television, have made the most of
it; they come to "cover" a story but stay to define a problem, developing a
kind of vested interest in excitement and confrontation, inherently more
dramatic and interesting than private discussions or faculty meetings.

The effect of this publicity is to transform an enormously complex train
of events and processes into a set of simplified slogans and targets for free-
floating hostilities against intellectual institutions or radicalism or bearded
boys. This does not merely embarrass the university. The publicity enters
very sharply into the situation, as an active exacerbating force. At the very
least, it crystallizes and rigidifies positions, and thus limits the range of discretion and discussion and compromise possible. A university is not a microcosm of the civil society; its activities and relationships, centering
around the creation and transmission of knowledge, are much more delicate and fragile than most of the business of the world outside. Its system
of rules and regulations are not merely civil law applied on a smaller scale;
so, too, its systems of rule enforcement cannot be identical, and this applies
most sharply to the use of police power. But these distinctions, absolutely
vital to the life of a university, though not even fully understood by the university community itself, are quite beyond the powers of television to con-
vey in their ordinary coverage of the latest exciting episode of the Berkeley
story. And this, in turn, generates very strong pressures from alumni, legislators, local district attorneys and police officers, and the general public for
"action" against the rebellious students, without much regard for the effects
of such action, not alone on the students, but on the university as a
community and an institution of higher learning.

Yet another set of difficulties are presented by the "nonstudents," about
whose role in these events there has been much partisan dispute. Whether
they have played a leading or only a supporting role in the drama, there
can be little question that they have complicated the issues and their solutions. Berkeley is a political subdivision of an urban area of some three or
four million people living around San Francisco Bay. The area has for decades been a center of radical political activity and in recent years also
a center for bohemian and non-conformist styles. Berkeley itself, and
the immediate environs of the university, make a convenient focus for
many young (and not so young) people whose chief business is living in a
certain expressive way and developing certain distinctive forms of relationships and behaviors. Some of these people are interested in politics, some

in nonconformist but apolitical forms of expression; many of both groups are, or have been, students at the university. Some of the leadership and part of the easily mobilized support for student protest on campus has been provided by people who are not formally enrolled as students. Ordinarily, the university would not, and still in many ways does not, make sharp distinctions between enrolled students and young people not enrolled who use the campus facilities. This is a characteristic of a public university of varied functions whose boundaries are fuzzy and permeable. For one thing, some of the nonstudents are simply regular students who have not registered for a term or a year to be able to get on with their work without paying fees; others are wives or husbands of registered students; many faculty do not make distinctions between people who are or are not formally registered if they have been students and are, in fact, studying and working as if they were students.

But nonstudents complicate campus problems in several ways. They provide a pool of people to swell the crowds at demonstrations, and thus the public and internal impact of those events. Moreover, they typically have more time than most people to give to student political affairs. In addition, they are not subject to the sanctions of the university when they violate university rules, and thus force, or invite, the use of police on campus, an inherently distasteful and potentially explosive recourse. I do not myself believe the nonstudents are a major cause of Berkeley's difficulties, any more than the TV cameras and the relentless and adverse publicity. But I do not think there is any doubt that in their own way both have made more difficult the creation of new procedures and mechanisms which would enable the university to deal creatively with the new problems that beset it.

If at this point in my narrative the reader finds himself somewhat bewildered by the variety of issues and forces that are involved in the Berkeley affair, somewhat uncertain, and perhaps a bit discouraged about how to deal with them, then he is sharing at least some of the feelings of the Berkeley community. If he can add to these intellectual confusions a set of emotions, including anger, anxiety, fatigue, boredom, excitement, melancholy, and despair, he will have some sense of the climate at Berkeley over the past several years. A prolonged crisis is very different from a short-lived one, and not just in lasting longer. There are resources which academic men can bring to a momentary crisis which are not, so to speak, on tap over prolonged periods. When their institution is in grave and immediate danger, many scholars willingly give weeks, months, even a term or a year of their time and energies to meetings and committees, to the interminable discussions with others, groping for some solutions to immediate problems. But over time there is not only the inevitable frustration and despair: there is also, and not least at Berkeley, the powerful pull of one's work—the unfinished manuscript, the experiment too long postponed, the piles of data awaiting analysis. The problems remain, but there is less readiness on the part of the faculty to give them full attention. Individuals continually appear who give of their time unsparingly, but in the faculty as a whole it seems that its response is more sporadic, distracted, less ready to be responsive to the full difficulties of the issues, more ready to strike a posture, find a form of words or institutions, anything that will promise cessation of the trouble.

II

Let us consider in more detail one aspect of the continuing crisis. During a period of transition, the rules and procedures which served adequately during the earlier stage are suddenly seen to be ineffective: on one hand, their legitimacy is challenged and their authority weakened; on the other, they are confronted with new problems for which the existing procedures do not work well. This has been painfully clear in the realm of student discipline.

Among nearly 30,000 students, a significant number, even though a small proportion, can be found to support almost any social, political, or educational position. Under circumstances of change and uncertainty, a minority position will find latent or potential support among much larger numbers of students and faculty. In the past, the very number and range of activities on a campus like Berkeley's served to dilute the passions of the minority and to muffle its voice. The civil rights movement and the new radicalism associated with it, as well as the protest against the Vietnam war, have created new forms of organization, disseminated political skills, and initiated or adapted forms of political action. These forms of organization and tactics have greatly increased the influence and force of political activists in the student body, and of their demands on the university, with which existing forms of university administration cannot easily cope. For example, university administrators know how to deal with adolescent "misbehavior"—panty raids, vandalism, cheating, and the like. They know much less about how to deal with systematic violations of university regulations by large numbers of students who justify those violations by reference to moral conviction and idealism. Moreover, administrators can cope with infractions of the rules by individuals or small groups of the size, say, of a fraternity; they are singularly ill-prepared to deal with mass infractions of rules. A dean calls a student to his office; two hundred appear, all demanding to be treated like the named offender as a matter of right and justice. Corridors become clogged, it is not possible to take names; the alternatives —the use of force on a large scale, or retreat—are immediately posed.

And apart from the new tactics, the traditional disciplinary machinery is oriented toward the old collegiate culture and infractions that arise out of an excess of youthful high spirits and the perennial pleasures of drink and sex. Deans of students typically have good relations and communications with the communities that give rise to such infractions: student residence halls, fraternities, and sororities. When the familiar forms of trouble arise there is a network of people and institutions that the authorities can call on for information and assistance: housemothers, residence hall officers, student judicial committees, and so forth. But administrators typically have had much less knowledge or understanding of or relation to political activists, or graduate students, or commuters, or students living off campus. And, as at Berkeley, when new forms of disputes arise involving those kinds of students, there is no community of people or institutions that administrators can turn to for advice and help.

Quite apart from its lack of knowledge about, or communication with, large segments of the student body, the administration faces a problem in devising rules that are applicable to and appropriate for quite different kinds of students. Students who cheat on exams or crawl into dorm windows after hours or get drunk on campus are breaking rules, but they are not challenging the legitimacy of the rules, their moral rightness, or the way they are made. In these cases, a conventional student government and judicial system, without too heavy an emphasis on formal legal procedures, may well be the way to enforce the university's rules or to encourage the students' community to make and enforce its own rules. But this machinery does not work so well in the face of political activists who do not accept the legitimacy of that kind of "student government," and who place very heavy emphasis on "due process" for students charged with infractions of university rules. Universities are not really prepared to conduct their relations with students on the model of a democratic state in relation to its citizens. And it is clear that the stance of the new student activists sharply challenges the remaining authority of the university *in loco parentis,* as well as its authority as a community of scholars and students whose members share basic values and purposes to which they can refer in governing the relations among them.

But while we struggle to devise new forms of relationships with student activists, we still have thousands of students for whom the old forms are workable and appropriate. Berkeley has moved toward the creation of a dual system of rules and procedures for governing student conduct, the old system for the traditional student activities and problems, and a new system for political activists and activities. But the distinction is not always easy to make, nor is it being made formally; the old forms continue to exist and operate, but with political disputes getting the immediate attention of the chancellor's office and faculty groups. And this raises new problems: for example, it makes for a more rapid escalation of conflict, since it involves the highest authority on campus almost from the outset of every crisis. But in dealing with actions that directly challenge the authority of the chancellor from the beginning, it is difficult for him to avoid the confrontation through the use of buffer officers and committees.

We still lack adequate analysis of the new student Left—that curious blend of idealism and cynicism, of Utopian fantasies and practical organizational skills, of passionate angers and spontaneous good humor, at once doctrinaire and anti-ideological, with a genuine concern for personal "authenticity" and yet with its eyes toward the TV cameras and the public image. Such an account would be a valuable footnote, perhaps more than a footnote, to the Berkeley story. In that story it has raised the strongest feelings and been the driving force for change, while at the same time quite unassimilable by any forms of university governance, any pattern of campus community, that Berkeley has been able thus far to devise. It may well be that the future of that university depends in large part on how it is able to deal with this most intractable force in university life today.

A central aspect of this force is the conception of some students and faculty of the university as an instrument for the transformation of "a sick society," a conception which calls for "engagement" and involvement in the major social movements of our time—at the moment, the civil rights movement and the movement against American involvement in Vietnam. I must distinguish between people holding strong views about civil rights or the war in Vietnam and those who conceive of the university as an instrument in the political struggles represented by those or comparable movements of protest and radical reform. This latter position, held by relatively few faculty members but a considerably larger number of students, calls for a transformation of the university which would make possible its direct and progressive involvement in the political and social conflicts of the larger society; it calls also for an alliance of students and faculty against the university administration, the regents and other "outside" forces which claim what is, in their view, an illegitimate authority over the university. Moreover, this position argues, quite consistently, that education within the university should reflect the institution's engagement in the central social and political issues of the day. Describing the form this position takes among students, a sympathetic statement observes that:

> Against the professionalism of the insiders, they proclaim the primacy of passion, subjectivity, and openness. Knowledge which is not obviously related to their immediate personal needs and situation is irrelevant. To be relevant, knowledge must speak *now* to *their* needs. The ancient values of detachment and disinterested inquiry are seen as evasions of responsibility; or, worse, as typifying the vice of 'objectivism' which transforms thought and feeling into alienated objects and serves as an ideological fig leaf for a corrupt establishment [Wolin and Schaar, 1967].

The student movement has a number of facets. If passionate involvement is one, idealism is another. The propensity of youth to be radical, and of older people to be Tory, is not solely a matter of left-right shifts. As S. M. Lipset has pointed out:

> Within conservative as well as left-wing groups or parties, youth movements or affiliates tend to give the adult organization trouble by their tendency to demand that the party or church live up to its principles [Lipset, 1966: 41].

> Max Weber, in his great lecture on "Politics as a Vocation," observed that youth has a tendency to follow "a pure ethic of absolute ends," while maturity is associated with "an ethic of responsibility." The advocate of the first fears that any compromise on matters of principles will endanger the "salvation of the soul"; the proponent of the second fears that an unwillingness to confront the complex "realities of life" may result in the goals . . . [being] damaged and discredited for generations because responsibility for *consequences* is lacking [Lipset, 1966: 140].

Thus if some university students are inclined to be irresponsible with respect to the norms of adult society, they also are inclined to be idealistic. And when this idealism is combined with organizational skills and political tactics learned in the civil rights or peace movements, it introduces a political force into the university of a kind with which the existing machinery of university government has great difficulty in coming to terms.

III

There are a number of forces which tend to limit the extent and intensity of disputes within the university, which tend to mute them and press toward compromise and accommodation between differing points of view. One of these is the broad acceptance of the legitimacy of the multiple functions of a university. The practical effect of this conception of the university is to remove from dispute the sharpest and fundamentally irreconcilable issues; disputes then can take the form of arguments about relative emphasis to be given to different views or the relative support allocated to different programs. And even those disputes are further diluted in situations in which there is secular growth and expansion throughout the university, and where disputes then become merely questions of "priority" and time.

Disputes are also softened by a general agreement to conduct them within the regular academic and administrative machinery—the system of committees and meetings through which major universities govern themselves. Disputes are still further softened by the institutional (and often, also, the geographical) insulation of conflicting views. For example, the humanistic scholars are typically centered in a university's college of letters and science, or its equivalent; the service orientations in the professional schools, or in the graduate departments. Historians and engineers may have very different conceptions of the primary functions of the university, but they very rarely have occasion to confront one another in argument.

Conflict between different conceptions of the university is also minimized by making the department, rather than a college or the university, the unit of effective educational decision. The departments, or most of them, are more homogeneous than the faculty as a whole, and they have their own strong mechanisms for compromise and accommodation, not least of which is to minimize the number and importance of issues involving collective decision, allowing what might be called the privatization of intellectual life, a withdrawal to one's own classroom and research. On the graduate level, the university *is,* for all practical purposes, the aggregation of departments and professional schools, their satellite research centers and institutes, and the supporting infrastructure of libraries, labs, buildings, and mostly routine administrative help (though in a university, routines are not all that routine, and many require a considerable level of skill and talent). The departments effectively govern their own appointment and promotion of staff (subject to certain review procedures by extra-departmental committees), admit their own graduate students, and organize their instruction. On the undergraduate level (I am speaking here of the central liberal arts college), with its 12,000 undergraduates at Berkeley, there is, of course, the necessity to organize some structure of education that is not confined to a single department. The form this takes at Berkeley, as in many other institutions, is a set of distribution requirements—so many units required in fields outside one's major, so many in a major field, the remainder electives. This system, whatever its educational justification, has for Berkeley the very substantial virtue of reducing the amount of academic decision-making that is necessary. This reduces the occasions for conflict involving educational values and philosophies, thus letting men get on with their own work. What we see at work there is a spirit of *laissez faire,* within broad administrative constraints set by limitations of space, time, staff, and other resources, that mirrors the broader philosophy of the multiversity as a whole (See Trow, 1968).

This pattern may be seen as an institutional response to the problem of combining higher education offered to very large numbers of students of the most diverse character with the highest standards of scholarly and scientific work. But the events of the past few years have revealed basic weaknesses in the system which are in a sense the defects of its virtues. One of these is the lack of a central widely shared sense of the nature of the institution and a weakness in its capacity to gain the loyalties and devotion of its participants. This means that the institution operates on a relatively thin margin of error. Closely related to this is its tendency to generate both among students and faculty somewhat diffuse resentments, feelings of frustration and alienation from an institution which provides services and facilities but which seems singularly remote from the concerns of individuals, responsive only to pressures and problems that are organized and communicated through the regular channels, and not always even to those.

As two Berkeley faculty members have put it:

> The melancholy truth is there is no widely shared understanding about the meaning and purpose of the institution. Lacking the unifying force which flows spontaneously from common understandings, the system is held together by a bureaucratic organization whose weakness is exposed whenever it is directly challenged [Wolin and Schaar, 1967].

And, indeed, the absence of a common conception of the meaning and purpose of the institution is perhaps inherent in its very plurality of functions, its readiness to turn a hand—one of its many hands—to almost every human enterprise. Clark Kerr (1963: 18–19), in his extraordinarily candid essays on the *Uses of the University,* observed that:

> The multiversity is an inconsistent institution. It is not one community but several—the community of the undergraduate and the community of the graduate; the community of the humanist, the community of the social scientist, and the community of the scientist; the communities of the professional schools; the community of all the nonacademic personnel; the community of the administrators. Its edges are fuzzy—it reaches out to alumni, legislators, farmers, businessmen, who are all related to one or more of these internal communities. . . . A community, like the medieval communities of masters and students, should have common interests; in the multiversity, they are quite varied, even conflicting. A community should have a soul, a single animating principle; the multiversity has several . . . [and] there is much debate on which souls really deserve salvation.

There is considerable agreement between Kerr and his radical critics about the nature of the institution, its diversity and powerful centrifugal forces. And, in a most strongly felt passage, he describes the role of the president of such an institution thus:

> The president of the multiversity is many things [but] he is mostly a mediator. . . . The first task of the mediator is peace . . . peace within the student body, the faculty, the trustees; and peace between and among them . . . peace . . . among all the ideas competing for support. Peace between the internal environment of the academic community and the external society that surrounds and sometimes almost engulfs it. . . . The president becomes the central mediator among the values of the past, the prospects for the future, and the realities of the present. . . . He has no new and bold 'vision of the end.' He is driven more by necessity than by voices in the air.
>
> To make the multiversity work really effectively, the moderates need to be in control of each power center and there needs to be an attitude of tolerance between and among the power centers, with few territorial ambitions. When the extremists get in control of the students, the faculty, or the trustees with class warfare concepts, then the 'delicate balance of interests' becomes an actual war [Kerr, 1963: 36–37, 39].

What are the values expressed in these passages, the values that have in truth governed the working of the institution? They are diversity, pluralism, moderation and compromise, the mediation of conflict. They not only are the values that, as Kerr notes, are necessary for the functioning of the institution; but, as active agents, they also are the values which have shaped the character and organization of the university: the institution *expresses* these values as well as being governed by them. But if these are powerful values, they also are limited and ultimately vulnerable ones as the central common values of a university.

Wherein does their vulnerability lie? First, they do not evoke strong loyalties; they are difficult to defend with passion. They are splendid guides to problems of administration; they are much weaker as the rallying flag, the ultimate justifications for an institution in travail. Second, they do not provide any criteria for determining and justifying the limits of tolerance. They do not tell us which interests are legitimately pressed. All interests seem to have an equally legitimate claim on the institution; conflicting claims are to be mediated, but mediated, of course, with due regard to the relative power of the claimants. But while mediation tempers power, in part by countervailing power and in part by reasoned argument, it deals primarily with power as the basis for negotiated agreements, and thus encourages participants to come to negotiations with as much power as possible. Indeed, Kerr suggests that there are some things that should not be compromised, "like freedom and quality." But this is not helpful when the conceptions of freedom and quality are themselves in dispute. And, third, the multiversity is vulnerable to demands for radical changes because it is broadly inclusive in its functions but still exclusive in its forms of decision-making. The chief political processes of the multiversity are through informed negotiations and mediations between and among administrators and faculty. This form of politics is accepted by those participants who have had access to that machinery and who exercise their power within it (with due regard, of course, to the claims of other parties). It is not accepted by those, chiefly student activists, who feel excluded and want to have influence but do not have access to the machinery of decision-making.

"A multiversity," as Kerr has said, "is inherently a conservative institution but with radical functions" (1963: 37). But its conservatism is a product not of a firm conception of the character of the institution, a statement of the priorities among and limits on its functions that can be morally defended against challenge from whatever quarter; rather, it is the conservatism of an intricate network of understandings and arrangements among participating interest groups. These understandings and arrangements are essentially of two kinds: an elaborate system of rules and regulations emanating from the administration, on the one hand, and from the faculty, on the other hand. Together, these understandings and arrangements provide the framework for the coordination of the multivaried functions of the university. Administration rules largely center on the problems of administering very large numbers of undergraduates: admitting them, organizing their programs, grading and certifying them, housing and counseling them. Side by side with those rules is another large system of activities governed essentially by departments. These are the issues typically closest to faculty members' deepest interests; the content of instruction, the recruitment and promotion of colleagues, the recruitment and training of graduate students, and research. These two forms of governance—the complex administrative apparatus on each campus (and statewide) and the much more flexible departmental structures—exist side by side and make for the faculty member's sense of being at once extremely autonomous and yet constrained, depending on the area of action.

The conception of the multiversity as an enormous diverse network of organized activities and functions, the extent of which is determined almost solely by the availability of money, energy, and interests on the part of some section of the intellectual community, headed by a mediator committed to pluralism and progress, invites a direct analogy between the university and the civil society. And here, perhaps, we come to the heart of the matter: the challenge of radical students and their supporters on the faculty centers on the question of why the forms of governance of the university should not more closely mirror those of the society with which it is so closely intertwined and which it so closely resembles in so many ways.

The challenge takes many forms. On one hand, it is a challenge to extend full rights of citizenship, and the concomitant rights of organization, representation, and participation in decision-making processes, to all the segments of the academic community, most especially the students, the teaching assistants, the professional staffs of research centers who lie outside the regular faculty, and so forth. Second, it invites the development of a much fuller system of formal law governing the behavior of its members, with all the safeguards of due process and adversary proceedings that are the bulwarks of civil liberties in the larger society. And, third, the multiversity, in inviting the analogy with the civil society, is vulnerable to the argument that in order to gain their ends students and others will sometimes be forced to resort to formally illegal procedures—the violation of rules, sit-ins, or strikes—which are also recognized as an aspect of the political struggles in the larger society. The argument on this latter point, for example, holds that these forms of demonstrative action at Berkeley are really no different from comparable actions in the sphere of civil rights and the peace movement, on which, of course, they are modeled. And while people may not approve of them in those spheres, they are widely accepted as part of the democratic process—what we might call "the politics of conscience." And, this argument goes, if indeed the university is a microcosm of the civil society, then some of its members will plunge into the political struggles of that microcosm with both radical demands for institutional change and also, at times, with conceptions of class warfare designed precisely to disrupt the "delicate balance of interests" of which Kerr spoke and to which they are so deeply opposed as conservative and arbitrarily exclusive. The "ethic of absolute ends" and the politics of compromise in the service of "a delicate balance of interests" are profoundly antithetical, at Berkeley as in the larger society.

Now I have put the matter more sharply than it usually appears to the faculty, though not more sharply than it is put in the documents of the student movement. But even among those faculty members who deplore strikes, violent language, and coercive threats and demonstrations, many share an underlying sympathy with the thrust of the demands. Many faculty do not see why students should not have wider representation in the decision-making processes that affect them; many support the extension to the students of the safeguards of academic freedom and due process as a safeguard against arbitrary administrative authority. Many also observe that even the illegal nonviolent forms of protest are occasioned by deeply felt principles regarding the necessity for reform of the university or arise out of other strongly held social and political views; they are not just another kind of panty raid but represent the deepest concerns of some of the best and most serious students, and therefore deserve the respect and sympathy of the faculty, rather than a coercive repression which violates the spirit of academic life more fundamentally than do student demonstrations guided by high principles.

Thus, there is among the faculty itself more than a little sympathy for the motives of the student activities, and also for their goals and purposes, if less for their forms of action. And here the faculty is moved by their own experience with the government of the university and their experience of its capacity to ignore sentiments and feeling when they are not organized and strenuously advanced, and sometimes even then. At the same time, there is a deep concern for the effect of student action on the "normal functions of the university," a concern which for some suggests the need to devise some new arrangements that will remove the sources of disruption, the necessity for illegal protest, essentially by incorporating the new interest group into the "delicate balance of interests" whose peaceful accommodation is the guiding principle of the university's governance.

This has, thus far, not happened and disturbances continue. It has not happened because some student demands are quite sharply at variance with university traditions and the sentiments of many of the existing interest groups, the faculty no less than the administration or the regents. It has not happened because it is not completely clear that these new interests want to be absorbed into the established institutions. It has not happened because to accede to these demands is to accept more fully than many wish the analogy of the university with the civil society, and with it the legitimacy of the ordinary political processes that go on in the larger society.

Not many students press these demands in a systematic and comprehensive fashion, and even fewer faculty members would support all those demands. But many would accept parts of this program, and many more respond negatively to administrative actions which essentially resist or reject these demands, and also appear uncompromising, arbitrary, and coercive. A university is by its nature committed to reason and compromise, and hostile to arbitrary acts of power, so there is continual pressure from other members of the university, and from outside the university, for it not to accede to these demands. And so we get sporadic crisis, centering usually on the enforcement of some rule, sometimes a trivial one, which calls out a larger and illegal form of demonstrative action, which, in turn, calls forth a more substantial disciplinary action, sometimes involving the police, which, in turn, evokes much more widespread outrage, a strike, and another effort by the faculty and administrators to find a short-run solution and a long-run accommodation. And of this there is, as yet, no end.

If authority is to be accepted as legitimate, justice not only must be done, but also must be seen to be done. But where good will and a basic trust are lacking, there is no way to demonstrate, beyond cavil, that authority is exercised justly, since it is by definition an unjust and illegitimate authority. For a section of the student movement, the basic structure and character of the university is wrong and illegitimate. And in the multiversity, as I have suggested, it is very difficult to find more general principles arising out of a widely shared conception of the nature of the institution which can be used as a basis and guide in the search for viable and acceptable procedures. A very great deal of effort and intelligence has been and is being directed toward such procedures. But in the absence of general principles, the procedures we invent are *ad hoc* and reflect temporary political situations: there is always the anxious concern over how much support they can gain and whether, in the next crisis, they will be "discredited" and discarded.

IV

To sum up: What we see at Berkeley are different conceptions of the university, existing side by side within the framework of the all-embracing doctrine of pluralism, yet finding themselves in conflict in time of crisis when the treaties of peace are broken. One, the more traditional conception, sees the university as a corporate body governed through complex arrangements among the permanent members of the community; that is to say, the faculty, administrative officers, and the representatives of the larger society which provides the resources of the institution and whom that society holds ultimately responsible for the actions of the university—that is, the trustees or regents. In this conception, the students play a distinctly subordinate part, justified by their youth, their lack of competence, and the shortness of their relationship to the institution.

For various reasons, this traditional conception of the government of the university, and especially of the place of the student in that government, has been under attack. In part this is due to growing numbers of graduate students, who with families and children of their own are in no sense children; in part because of the presence on campus of well-organized groups of students who are hostile to the major social institutions of our society; in part due to a secular trend toward more direct participation in the government of organizations by all kinds and classes of participants. The call for more genuine and effective forms of democratic government and participation in decision-making in private organizations, as in civil governments, has deep roots in liberal and democratic values: it is widely felt that it is right that men should have a share in the government of the institutions that shape their lives. And this doctrine, turned against the modern mass university, has appeal both to the activist students, who clearly are excluded from many decisions that affect them, and also to many of their teachers, who do not see why the students should not play more of a part in the life of the university than they now do.

This conception of the university informs the majority report of a Berkeley faculty-student Study Commission on University Governance (1968). This Report, which recommends major changes in the structure of the university, as well as in its procedures for making rules and policies, calls for a university in which politics and political participation are much more central to the life of the institution.

> When we acknowledge the student's membership in the university by asking him to share responsibility for governing it, we express the hope that such participation will enrich the relationships and reinvigorate the intellectual fellowship that have been dessicated in the process of maintaining an efficient system of mass education and training. We hope that such participation and the new relationships it creates will help promote the growth of human communities, and thus transform an environment which has become fragmented, confining, and impersonal into one which is liberating [Study Commission on University Governance, 1968: 33].

The Report sees widespread student participation in university government as desirable in itself, as an extension of citizenship, and also as a way of involving students more deeply in their own education. And the Report also recommends a decentralization of decision-making to involve more students in more aspects of university government, from educational policy-making to the enactment and enforcement of rules governing student conduct.

The Report is in part a response to, in part an expression of, the demands of student activists. It poses a Utopian vision of small communitarian educational units built on participation and consensus against the anti-Utopia of the mass impersonal, conflictful, and interest-ridden multiversity full of apathetic, alienated, sullen students teetering on the edge of full-scale rebellion. But this, as some critics of the Report have noted, is an expression of faith and ideology rather than a description of reality, one which dismisses the very large numbers of faculty and students who are reasonably satisfied with the multiversity and who even prefer it to the realities of small participatory educational communities as they exist elsewhere. Berkeley has shown a remarkable capacity to retain its faculty, and even to attract other distinguished scholars, despite the disturbances of the past several years; nor has the quality of its students declined. Moreover, in surveys and polls students persistently, and in very large majorities, express their general satisfaction with the education they get at Berkeley. The discontent expressed by the Report is felt strongly by a relatively small proportion of students and faculty—though even 10 per cent of 28,000 students is nearly 3,000 people.

The Report (Study Commission on University Governance, 1968: 41) envisions a much higher level of faculty as well as student participation:

> If the faculty is to achieve genuine participation in governance, as distinguished from more effective faculty power, it must organize itself in ways which promote wider participation, more informed deliberation, and closer integration with other elements of the campus. These ends cannot be achieved by the reform of Faculty committees or Senate procedures alone. They require not an improved and more powerful central forum for the expression . . . of faculty interests, but a multiplication of forums at lower levels. We foresee senates at the level of colleges, schools, and small clusters of departments where issues are more comprehensible, more manageable, and more likely to evoke spontaneous participation.

The assumption that the faculty wants even more opportunities to sit on committees than they now have, that they "require . . . a multiplication of forums," reflects not merely an ideology of communitarian fellowship but, in the Berkeley context, a fantasy at great distance from the realities. Whatever may be true of a small section of student activists and an even smaller group of faculty sympathizers and communitarians, the bulk of faculty and students have other priorities, other concerns besides politics. For the majority on the Commission, this is seen as apathy, a perennial problem (really a kind of moral failing) to be fought by exhortation and the proliferation of forums and senates that somehow will make people better, more politically involved. But there is no evidence, certainly not the tiny numbers who attend the public meetings on campus governance or curriculum reform, which carries weight against the evangelical spirit. If a campus crisis involves 1,000 students or so in a mill-in, that is taken as evidence of widespread discontent; if a meeting on the Commission Report is attended by 100 students out of the nearly 30,000, it is evidence that its recommendations for increasing participation are needed.

The Commission's conception of the university as an "intellectual fellowship" of students and teachers continuously involved in both learning and self-governance (and to a high degree of learning through self-governance) has the attractive appeal of all arcadian Utopias which hark back to largely imaginary pre-industrial forms of life and work. The notion that men were freer, more creative, and happier before the Industrial Revolution and the rise of large organizations is a recurrent theme in modern social thought, though it is more commonly linked to reactionary rather than radical political doctrines and movements. At Berkeley the development of the multiversity at an accelerating pace since World War II has engendered very real problems, both in the relation of the university to the larger society and in its internal processes. But it is the essence of the multiversity rather than its problems that offends its radical critics—its enormous multiplicity of functions and relationships, without a common overriding conception of its own character and purpose; its government by committees and administrators that coordinate rather than inspire; its reluctance to make of politics (both internal and external) its chief instrument and focus of attention; its strange, stubborn refusal to see itself as an agency for radical social reform.

The students and faculty who see in the university an instrument for the radical transformation of man and society are relatively few in number but full of energy and passion, and occasionally well organized. They are strengthened by more widely held feelings of uneasiness and discontent with existing social institutions that arise out of the nation's international and domestic troubles, as well as by dissatisfaction with the way the university performs the variety of functions it has taken on. There is also the difficulty of articulating a philosophy of the multiversity that can command not merely rational assent but also strong loyalties. Add to this the vulnerability of a university to disruption and the threat of disruption by passionate minorities, and we have the essential ingredients of Berkeley's current difficulties. These are likely to persist. It remains to be seen whether they can be contained and harnessed to the causes of educational reform, or whether they will continue to be a source of the cycle of confrontation, rule violation, punishment, and confrontation that only the most committed and nihilistic ideologues can welcome.

NOTE

1. The events at Berkeley during the fall and winter of 1964 to 1965 have been discussed at great length. See, for example, the essays in S. M. Lipset and S. S. Wolin (1965).

REFERENCES

KERR, C. (1963) *The Uses of the University*. Cambridge: Harvard University Press.
LIPSET, S. M. (1966) "University students and politics in under-developed countries." *Comparative Education Review* 10 (June).
—— and S. S. WOLIN (1965) *The Berkeley Student Revolt: Facts and Interpretations*. New York: Anchor Books.
Study Commission on University Governance (1968) "The culture of the university: governance and education." Report of the Study Commission on University Governance. Berkeley: University of California (January 15). Also published as Caleb Foote, Henry Mayer, and Associates (1968) *The*

Culture of the University: Governance and Education. San Francisco: Jossey-Bass Inc., Publishers.

TROW, M. (1968) "Bell, book and Berkeley." *American Behavioral Scientist* 11 No. 5 (May–June): 43–48. Reprinted as Chapter 14 in this volume.

WOLIN, S. S. and J. H. SCHAAR (1967) "Berkeley and the university revolution." *New York Review of Books* (February 9).

PART II

ADMINISTRATORS AND TRUSTEES

CHAPTER 3

COLLEGE AND UNIVERSITY TRUSTEES
Their Backgrounds, Roles, and Educational Attitudes

Rodney T. Hartnett

In the center of the many current attacks on American colleges and universities, and demands for their reform, stands the trustee. For years ultimately responsible for charting the course of his college, his role is now becoming uncertain. As greater demand is made for student and faculty involvement in college and university governance, the authority of the trustee is being challenged and his suitability as legal head of the institution's affairs disputed.

Some may argue, of course, that the trustee's influence has never been substantial and that the faculty has always controlled most matters of significance in the educational community. Without rejecting or conceding this argument, the point remains that, during what may prove to be the most important period in the history of American higher education, the trustee's vested importance remains great, his legal authority substantial. As Algo D. Henderson (1967: 2) has said, "Governing boards of colleges and universities derive their authority from the law and, legally, the full and final control for an institution lies with the board."

Given these circumstances, it is somewhat remarkable that so little is known about who trustees are, what they do in their roles as trustees, and how they feel about current issues in American higher education. Except for a now outdated and somewhat limited survey by Beck (1947), a more recent survey by Duster (1966) and a statewide study in New York (Regents' Advisory Committee, 1966), practically nothing in the way of empirically gathered information has been accumulated for this rather elite group of people. In order to diminish our ignorance, an eight-page questionnaire was mailed in February, 1968 to over 10,000 college and university trus-

EDITORS' NOTE: This is a modified and abridged version of a report published by Educational Testing Service, the copyright holder. See *College and University Trustees: Their Backgrounds, Roles, and Educational Attitudes,* ETS (1969), Princeton, New Jersey.

tees, representing the voting members of the governing board of 536 colleges and universities. With individual and institutional anonymity assured, complete usable responses were received from over 4,200 trustees. This report represents an attempt to briefly summarize these data.[1]

Biographical Characteristics

Data regarding the biographical characteristics of college and university trustees conform to previous findings. In general, trustees are male, in their fifties (though, nationally more than a third are over 60), white (fewer than two percent in our sample are Negro), well-educated, and financially well-off (more than half have annual incomes exceeding $30,000). They have occupations of prestige, frequently in medicine, law, or education, but, even more often, they are business executives. In the total sample, over 35 percent are executives of manufacturing, merchandising, or investment firms and, at private universities, nearly 50 percent hold such positions; fewer than one percent are writers, artists, or musicians. As a group, then, they personify success, in the usual American sense of that word.

Most are Protestants, with only four percent being Jewish and 17 percent Catholic, the majority of the latter serving on boards of Catholic institutions. Trustees also tend to identify themselves as Republicans (approximately 58 percent overall) and, most often, regard themselves as politically moderate (61 percent) rather than conservative (21 percent) or liberal (15 percent). Many of them—nearly 40 percent overall and well over half at certain types of institutions—are alumni of the institutions on whose boards they serve. Of considerable interest is the fact that, for the great majority (85 percent), their current board membership, whether with their alma mater or not, is their only college or university trustee commitment.

In considering some of these facts, however, the reader should keep in mind their very general nature. There is considerable diversity on these characteristics, especially among trustees at different types of institutions. Table 1 suggests the danger of describing college and university trustees as if they were interchangeable among institutions. Note, for example, that 46 percent of the trustees at private universities are over age sixty, whereas, only 24 percent of trustees at public colleges are of this age. Further, nearly 40 percent of the private university trustees have annual incomes in excess of $100,000, over four times the percentage of public college trustees at this income level. This is, admittedly, a carefully drawn comparison, chosen to make a point: trustees, like students and faculty (and probably administrators too, though the evidence is not so clear), differ markedly across institutions. Whether describing demographic characteristics or (as we shall see later) attitudes, variety is conspicuous. Though such a statement may seem like another case of science revealing what has long been known, it would seem to be worth emphasizing here. Much of what has been said or written about trustees suggests the naive impression of trustees

TABLE 1
AGE AND INCOME OF TRUSTEES IN TOTAL SAMPLE AND
AT TWO TYPES OF INSTITUTIONS (IN PERCENTAGES) [a]

	Total Sample	Private University	Public College
Age			
39 or under	5	1	4
40–49	21	14	28
50–59	37	37	43
60–69	27	36	20
over 70	9	10	4
Income			
Less than $10,000	8	2	4
$10,000–$19,999	18	5	27
$20,000–$29,999	15	9	20
$30,000–$49,999	19	16	27
$50,000–$74,999	13	17	10
$75,000–$99,999	7	10	3
$100,000 or more	16	39	9

a. Percentages have been rounded to whole numbers. Also, throughout this paper, the word "college" refers to a senior but non-Ph.D.-awarding institution (Levels II and III by U.S. Office of Education definition) and "universities" to only those which grant the Ph.D. (U.S. Office, Level IV).

as a sort of large, homogeneous fraternity. Our data clearly dispel this notion.

On the other hand, it is well to note that the diversity of the trustees is only relative. For example, women, persons under forty years of age, Negroes, and persons with incomes of less than $10,000 a year are but lightly represented, compared to their proportions in the population at large or among the clientele of the institutions of higher learning. And the almost complete exclusion of artists, musicians, and writers from the governing boards of institutions, who claim interest in the liberal arts, is also noteworthy.

Educational and Social Attitudes

The relevance of information about occupation, income, and the like is its presumed relationship to attitudes about education. Traditionally, this relationship has been taken for granted. Some have drawn the rather reckless conclusions that, because the trustee is seldom young, his educational attitudes are old-fashioned, that, because he is frequently a business executive, he will urge that his institution be run like a business, and so on. (Of course, an opposite, and perhaps more dangerous, assumption has also been frequently made: that, because one is a successful businessman, attorney, dentist, or whatever, he will, therefore, be a competent overseer of a higher educational institution.) One of our intentions in developing the questionnaire was to replace suppositions with facts, to replace easy generalities with "hard" data. To our knowledge, information regarding trustees' opinions, on most of these matters has never before been systematically gathered on a national scale.

ACADEMIC FREEDOM

One of the prime areas of interest is that of academic freedom. A number of items in the attitude section of the questionnaire were directed at this issue. These items and the trustees' responses are summarized in Table 2.

TABLE 2

EXTENT TO WHICH TRUSTEES AGREE WITH STATEMENTS
REGARDING ACADEMIC FREEDOM [a]

	Percentage Agreeing or Strongly Agreeing	Percentage Disagreeing or Strongly Disagreeing
Faculty members have right to free expression of opinions	67	27
Administration should control contents of student newspaper	40	51
Campus speakers should be screened	69	25
Students punished by local authorities for off-campus matter should also be subject to discipline by the college	49	38
It is reasonable to require loyalty oath from members of faculty	53	38

a. Statements in all tables in this report are slightly abbreviated; also, percentages do not add to 100 because of rounding and those responding "unable to say."

Though the great majority of trustees favor the right to free expression by faculty in various channels of college communication, the general impression one gets from these data is that the trustees, by and large, are somewhat reluctant to accept a wider notion of academic freedom. For example, over two-thirds of these people favor a screening process for all campus speakers; nearly half feel that students already punished by local authorities for involvement in matters of civil disobedience *off the campus* should be subject to further discipline by the college.[2] These attitudes clearly are relevant to campus problems today. Those who would argue that the trustee holds no authority or influence need only to examine, against a backdrop of trustee-faculty conflicts, some of the trustee attitudes regarding academic freedom. In the fall of 1968, for example, the Regents of the University of California voted to withhold regular college credits for a series of lectures by Eldridge Cleaver (Minister of Information for the Black Panthers, an Oakland-based black militant group, and author of *Soul on Ice*) at the Berkeley campus. The Academic Senate at Berkeley has recorded its opposition to the Regents' encroachment in curricular matters, but, at the time of this writing, the trustees' decision stands.[3] There are many cases similar to this one, and none should come as a surprise in view of trustee attitudes.

As with the biographical characteristics discussed earlier, trustee opinions about these matters vary considerably, not only across types of institutions, as already suggested, but across other dimensions, as well. Analyzing the Table 2 data by geographic region, for example, reveals that over half of the trustees of institutions located in the South agree that the contents of the student newspaper should be controlled by the institution, whereas, only about 30 percent of the trustees of New England and Mid-Atlantic institutions hold similar views. Similar comparisons suggest that, in general, trustees of southern and Rocky Mountain institutions are most cautious in these matters, whereas, trustees of institutions located in the New England and Mid-Atlantic regions appear to be the most liberal.

There is another interesting sidelight on the academic freedom data which is not presented in Table 2. That is, trustees of public junior colleges appear to be the least freedom oriented in terms of their responses to these items. Specifically, 45 percent of the public junior college trustees agree that the administration should control contents of the student newspaper; 76 percent think that all campus speakers should be subject to some official screening process; and 64 percent feel that it is reasonable to require loyalty oaths from members of the faculty. The percentage of public junior college trustees endorsing these statements is higher than the percentage of trustees at any other type of institution. At the same time, our data indicate that 42 percent of the trustees of public junior colleges are elected by the general public. This led us to wonder if publicly elected trustees, in general, may not be somewhat more conservative in matters of academic freedom than trustees gaining board membership via some other route. Our interest in examining such a possibility was stimulated partly by a recent opinion offered by Jencks and Riesman (1968: 269) that, "Publicly elected or appointed boards of trustees seem in many ways to cause more trouble than they are worth." This opinion apparently stemmed from their belief that "budgetary support and review are the only forms of public control that make much sense" and that these functions could, just as easily and more efficiently, be performed by already existing groups (for example, the legislature). As suggested by comments of these same authors (1962: 109) in another source, however, we may wonder if their opinion wasn't also influenced by the numerous cases in which trustees have campaigned for a position on an institution's governing board on a plank opposed to academic freedom. In any event, with these considerations in mind, we decided to compare the academic freedom attitudes of trustees at public junior colleges who had become trustees in different ways.[4] These data are presented in Table 3 and provide little support for the hypothesis that publicly elected trustees have more conservative educational attitudes. The data, in fact, are hard to interpret. For example, a higher percentage of publicly elected trustees favor free expression of faculty opinions, yet over two thirds of them feel that it is reasonable to require loyalty oaths (as opposed to 58 percent and 56 percent for the other two groups), and 77 percent favor a speaker screening policy. By and large, there appears to be very little relationship between these attitudes and method of attaining board membership.

TABLE 3

ACADEMIC FREEDOM ATTITUDES OF PUBLIC JUNIOR COLLEGE TRUSTEES
WHO ATTAINED BOARD MEMBERSHIP VIA THREE DIFFERENT ROUTES

Percentage agreeing or strongly agreeing

	Elected (N = 109)	Appointed by Governor (N = 90)	Selected by Board (N = 22)
Faculty members have right to free expression of opinions	69	62	61
Administration should control contents of student newspaper	41	51	39
Campus speakers should be screened	77	76	70
Students punished by local authorities for off-campus matter should also be subject to discipline by the college	43	42	52
It is reasonable to require loyalty oath from members of the faculty	67	58	56

Note: These three avenues of membership account for 85 percent of the public junior college trustees. Other means (e.g., elected by alumni, appointed by the president) were too few to be considered separately.

Thus, it would suggest that publicly elected trustees are confronted with the long-standing dilemma facing other governing board members, that is, whether to adopt the role of protector of the public interest or that of insulator between the public and the institution. The publicly elected trustee, simply by virtue of being elected rather than appointed, appears to have no special commitment to the former position.[5]

EDUCATION FOR WHOM?

Another topic of recent concern to American higher education has to do with the question of "education for whom?" Until fairly recently, American higher education was restricted to those of demonstrated academic ability who could afford the high costs that earning a degree required. More recently, however, we have seen a trend toward more flexible selection criteria and an "open-door" philosophy, perhaps best exemplified by the growing number of junior colleges throughout the country. Trustee attitudes toward this phenomenon are summarized in Table 4.

TABLE 4
TRUSTEES' VIEWS REGARDING WHO SHOULD BE
SERVED BY HIGHER EDUCATION

	Percentage Agreeing or Strongly Agreeing	Percentage Disagreeing or Strongly Disagreeing
Attendance a privilege, not a right	92	6
Aptitude most important admissions criterion	70	24
Curriculum designed to accommodate diverse student body	63	27
Opportunity for higher education for anyone who desires it	85	11
College should admit socially disadvantaged who do not meet normal requirements	66	22

Note: Percentages do not add to 100 because of rounding and those responding "unable to say."

For the national sample taken together, there appears to be general sympathy for the broader-access trend just discussed. Slightly more than 85 percent agree (with almost one-third strongly agreeing) that there should be opportunities for higher education available to anyone who seeks education beyond secondary school; two-thirds agree that colleges should admit socially disadvantaged students who appear to have the potential, even when these students do not meet the normal entrance requirements. Nevertheless, over 90 percent still regard attendance at their college to be a privilege, not a right. In fact, 68 percent of the trustees of public junior colleges, open-door institutions, if you will, also share the privilege-not-a-right sentiment. In view of the other responses indicating acceptance of the concept of wide accessibility of higher education opportunity, these latter figures seem inconsistent. Several explanations seem plausible, however. It may mean that even trustees of nonselective institutions cling to the elitist model, perhaps thinking that, while *other* colleges should employ flexible admissions criteria, their own institution must maintain high standards. To put it another way, trustees seem to be saying, "It is a privilege to attend *my* institution, but a right to attend *yours!*" But this, of course, is by no means certain, and other explanations are plausible. Perhaps most trustees simply interpreted the statement somewhat differently, wishing only to indicate their feeling that students should not *expect* to be in college but, rather, should feel *grateful* for the opportunity. Or, finally, it could mean that trustees favor extending the opportunity for college *admission* to more and more students but, in order to protect themselves and their institutions against unacceptable student conduct, feel the institutions must retain the authority to decide who will *remain*.

But, whichever of these explanations is accurate (if any) in explaining the inconsistency, the point is that the inconsistency exists. And, while we have no data to support such a claim, it would be surprising if this same pattern did not occur among most members of the faculty and administra-

TABLE 5

TRUSTEE RESPONSES TO ITEMS INDICATIVE OF THEIR BUSINESS-MODEL ORIENTATION FOR COLLEGES AND UNIVERSITIES (IN PERCENTAGES)

	Regard themselves as executives of manufacturing, merchandising or banking firm (col. 1)	Agree that running a college is basically like running a business		Regard experience in high-level business management as important quality for new president	
		(col. 2) Business Executives [a]	(col. 3) Others	(col. 4) Business Executives	(col. 5) Others
TOTAL SAMPLE	35	49	31	49	44
Public junior colleges	33 (7) [b]	56 (2)	49	45 (6)	46
Public colleges	39 (3)	56 (2)	42	55 (1)	40
Public universities	36 (5)	45 (6)	28	51 (4)	43
Private colleges	36 (5)	48 (4)	29	49 (5)	45
Private universities	49 (1)	42 (7)	23	41 (7)	38
Catholic colleges and universities [c]	22 (8)	56 (2)	31	54 (2)	43
Selective public [d]	36 (5)	47 (5)	30	53 (3)	38
Selective private	43 (2)	30 (8)	14	31 (8)	25

a. "Business executives" includes all those in first column, determined on the basis of their response to the occupation item (#16) in first part of questionnaire.

b. Numbers in parentheses alongside percentages in columns 1, 2, and 4 are within-column ranks (excluding total sample). Rank-order correlations (ρ) between columns are as follows:
$\rho_{12} = -.62$ (p. $< .05$), $\rho_{14} = -.40$ (n.s.), $\rho_{24} = +.69$ (p. $< .05$).

c. Catholic institutions were classified separately and throughout this report are not included in the private college or private university categories.

d. Selective colleges and universities were chosen on the basis of selectivity indices in Cass and Birnbaum's *Comparative Guide to American Colleges* (Harper & Row, 1965), or the selectivity index in Alexander Astin's *Who Goes Where to College* (Science Research Associates, 1965).

tion as well. Maintaining high standards and being exclusive have a long history of being interpreted synonymously in American higher education.

There are some signs of change, however. Recently, Rutgers, the state university of New Jersey, has launched a new experimental program of open admission. Though the program has been only vaguely defined and is still too early in its infancy for feedback, the mere fact that the effort is being made would appear to signal some positive changes in higher education's stance in this area.

BUSINESS ORIENTATION OF TRUSTEES

One frequently hears the criticism that trustees tend to think colleges and universities can best function by imitating the corporation or big business model (the assumption being that such a model is inappropriate and, in the long run, damaging to higher education). Whether such a model is appropriate or not cannot be answered by these data, but we can, at least, get some idea of whether or not it is a model preferred by the trustees.

It has already been indicated that trustees are frequently business executives. Two indices were used to tap what might be called a business orientation: first, whether trustees endorse the statement that "running a college is basically like running a business," and, second, the extent to which they feel experience in high-level business management is an important quality to consider in the selection of a new president. These data are presented in Table 5.

Inspection of this table makes it clear that trustees who are business executives definitely have a stronger business orientation toward the university than trustees with other occupations. For the total sample, of the 35 percent who are business executives nearly half (49 percent) agree that running a college is basically like running a business, whereas, fewer than one-third (31 percent) of the nonexecutives accept this view. In fact, of the 16 possible business executives versus other comparisons (eight institutional types by two attitude items), there is only one case in which trustees who are business executives are not also more business oriented. The exception is for public junior colleges, where a slightly higher proportion of nonbusiness executives regard business management experience as an important quality for a new president. Thus, there appears to be validity to the often heard claim that because governing boards are made up of businessmen, the decisions they make about the institutions will reflect this business outlook.

Another finding emerging from the data in Table 5, however, suggests that the business outlook hypothesis is not so simple. Note that the group having the second greatest proportion of trustees who are business executives (selective private universities) is the group which has the smallest percentage of those executives agreeing that running a college is like running a business and also the smallest proportion regarding high-level business management experience as an important criterion for a new president. Contrast this with trustees of public junior colleges, where a nearly opposite pattern occurs. In fact, the rank-order correlations between columns indicates that, across all types, the proportion of trustees holding business executive positions is *negatively* correlated with the proportion of those executives endorsing the attitude statements in Table 6; that is, the greater the proportion of business executives on the governing board, the *smaller* the proportion of executives who feel that "running a college is like running a business," and that high-level business management experience is an important quality to consider in choosing a new president. Consequently, even though the business orientation is distinctly more prevalent among business executives, generally, it would be a mistake to jump to the conclusion that on boards where the proportion of business executives is high, the business orientation will be strongest.

What is the explanation for this befuddling situation? One is at first tempted to speculate about the influence of the nonbusiness trustees on their colleagues' attitudes. While such a possibility should not be lightly dismissed, a more convincing interpretation might consider the varying levels of "executiveness" represented on the boards. We suspect, for example, that the types of institutions having the greatest proportion of business executives (the private universities and selective private institutions), generally, have men who are a much different kind of executive than those who serve on boards with the smallest proportion of businessmen (the junior colleges and Catholic institutions). This is probably a case of men simply not being cut from the same cloth, regardless of what may be suggested by the mutual occupational perception of "business executive." This difference, in turn, is reflected in their attitudes about running a college, and the high-level executive appears to be more inclined to see it as a nonbusiness undertaking when compared to his, probably, less prestigious executive counterpart serving on some of the other boards.

THE DECISION-MAKING PROCESS

One of the complaints most frequently made about higher education, by disenchanted members of the academic community is that the wrong people are making the decisions. Many of the campus demonstrators have been claiming, in one way or another, that the university should be run by the faculty and students, not by administrators and trustees. The following quotation, taken from a newspaper article (Kramer, 1968) summarizing some of the events at Columbia in the spring of 1968, is not atypical: "Speakers in buildings and on the lawn . . . called for the 'reconstruction of this university,' with students and faculty assuming the power now exercised by the president and trustees."

Though the extent to which faculty and students across the country actually feel they should run the campus is not known, there are some indications that it is not just a radical minority who desire more participation in the decision-making process. In a survey of faculty opinion regarding participation in academic decision-making at one institution, for example, 51 percent of the faculty included in the survey felt that "the faculty has too little influence on decisions; more of the decision-making power should rest with the faculty," and another 44 percent agreed that "the faculty's role is not what it should be ideally, but, it is about what one can realistically expect." Furthermore, 63 percent indicated that they were either dissatisfied or very dissatisfied with this situation (Dykes, 1968). And a recent survey of college trustees, administrators, faculty members, and students, conducted by the American Council on Education (Caffrey, 1968) tells us that faculty are almost unanimous in wanting a larger share in academic rule, including greater participation in the selection of their president. Though the former study was done at one university in the Midwest, and the faculty sample in the A.C.E. study consisted only of American Association of University Professors chapter heads (thus, making neither sample "representative" in any sense), together they provide some empirical support for the claim that there is dissatisfaction with the perceived way in which decisions are reached.

With this information in mind, let us examine the trustees' views of who should have major involvement in deciding various campus issues. Several things are made quite clear by these data, which are presented in Tables 6 and 7.

First, trustees generally favor a hierarchical system in which decisions are made at the top and passed down. For example, over 50 percent of the total sample of trustees believe that faculty and students should *not* have major authority in half of the sixteen decisions listed (that is, eight column-one percentage figures exceed 50 percent in Table 6). The proportion feeling that trustees and/or administrators alone should have major authority in making the decision exceeds 40 percent in 12 of the 16 decisions. Some of these are particularly interesting. For example, 63 percent say that the appointment of an academic dean should be made with only the administrators and trustees having major authority, or, to say it another way, 63 percent feel that the faculty should *not* have major authority in the appointment of their dean. Similarly, 57 percent would exclude the faculty from major authority in the awarding of honorary degrees, and 58 percent would exclude them from major authority in policies regarding faculty leaves. To many, of course, these findings come as no surprise. But, surprising or not, they do help underscore some of the very wide differences of opinion among members of the academic community as to who should govern.

Second, there is a perceptible difference in the kinds of decisions trustees feel should and should not involve other groups having substantial authority. For example, the areas that should have greatest faculty authority are seen to be, by and large, academic matters, such as whether or not to add or delete specific courses, or what criteria should be employed in admitting students. Student authority is judged relevant in matters of student life, such as housing, student cheating, fraternities and sororities, and the like.

Third, though the trustees, generally, prefer an arrangement in which the faculty and students do not have major authority, neither do they want to rule by themselves. Notice in Table 6, for example, that, with the excep-

TABLE 6

Percentage of Trustees Who Think that Certain Campus Groups Should Have Major Authority in Making Various Decisions

	Decision should be made by administrators alone (A), trustees alone (T) or trustees and administrators together (TA) (col. 1)				Decision should be made by faculty alone or in conjunction with administrators, trustees or both (col. 2)	Decision should be made by students alone or in conjunction with faculty and/or trustees and/or A and/or T (col. 3)
	A	T	TA	Total [a]		
Add or delete courses	11	1	4	16	65	14
Add or delete degree programs	9	6	18	33	57	3
Rules re student housing	32	2	13	47	6	37
Commencement speaker	29	4	13	46	25	22
Presidential appointment	1	64	5	70	8	1
Determine tuition	10	17	64	91	2	1
Professor's immoral conduct	29	7	28	64	27	2
Tenure decisions	27	7	30	64	30	1
Student cheating	20	0	1	21	39	37
Policy re student protests	16	6	30	52	18	22
Appoint academic dean	22	8	33	63	30	1
Policy re faculty leaves	19	8	31	58	37	0
Admission criteria	17	3	16	36	59	1
Honorary degrees	7	19	31	57	34	1
Athletic program	17	4	22	43	22	24
Fraternities and sororities	18	5	21	44	10	31

a. Column 1, which is simply a total of columns A, T, and TA, can be interpreted as the percentage of trustees who feel that faculty and/or students should *not* have major authority in deciding the various issues.

tion of presidential appointments, they prefer major authority for decisions to rest with the administration alone or with the administration and trustees conjointly. Thus, the power-at-the-top model must be modified. Trustees prefer their own power to be singularly authoritative only when it comes to choosing the president of the institution. Having selected him, however, they like to lean heavily on him (and his administrative colleagues) for making the decisions.

It should be remembered that these data refer to how trustees think decisions *should* be made, not how they *are* made. They are trustee preferences. As noted above, many claim that the trustee's real authority has diminished substantially over the years to a point where the gap between "paper" power and actual power is large indeed.[6] Also, they probably reflect trustee preferences for a *most-of-the-time* framework for making decisions. Whether trustees would feel the same way about the question of who calls the shots during a time of crisis (again, see note 3) is not known.

Finally, as seen in Table 7, there is a great deal of variation from group to group on these matters. It would appear that trustees of selective private institutions are most inclined to include other members of the academic community in the decision-making process, while trustees of nonselective public institutions are more inclined toward a power-at-the-top sort of arrangement. Notice, for example, that 50 percent or more of the trustees feel that administrators and/or trustees alone should have major authority in deciding 13 of the 16 issues at public junior colleges, but only 4 of the 16 issues at selective private institutions. The concept of democratic governance, or shared authority, clearly has a more receptive audience among trustees at the latter type of institution. In fact, the ordering of institutions in Table 7 would correspond very closely to an ordering of institutional types by educational prestige. That is, where prestige is defined by the usual (but not, necessarily, reasonable) indices of student ability, faculty prominence, and the like, it would appear that the greater the prestige of the institutional type, the more likely the trustees are to favor student and faculty involvement in decision-making.[7] It can also be seen that, with the exception of the selective public universities, there is public-private division on this question.

Several speculative interpretations are compelling in attempting to account for these phenomena. The most basic reason for the public-private difference probably comes from the sources of financial support. Because they do not have to answer to a public constituency, trustees of private institutions may be more willing to maintain a looser hold on the reins. Though accountable to the alumni, parents, and "friends" of the institution, such groups are basically *for* the institution and are seldom as concerned about its actions as the general public might be of colleges supported by tax money. Thus, trustees of private institutions are less hesitant to involve the faculty and students.

The reason for the prestige difference is not as straightforward, but, certainly, no less important. There is a relationship between institutional prestige and trustee affluence. More specifically, the greater the prestige of the institution, the higher the trustees' income, level of education, occupa-

TABLE 7

PERCENTAGE OF TRUSTEES BY TYPE OF INSTITUTION FEELING THAT VARIOUS DECISIONS SHOULD BE MADE WITH ADMINISTRATORS AND/OR TRUSTEES HAVING THE ONLY MAJOR AUTHORITY

Decision	Total	Public J.C.	Public Colleges	Public Univ.	Private Colleges	Private Univ.	Catholic C's & U's	Selective Public	Selective Private
Add or delete courses	16	31	21	17	14	10	13	13	6
Add or delete degree programs	33	56	42	32	31	25	31	26	18
Rules re student housing	47	54	55	53	46	47	37	48	40
Commencement speaker	46	52	49	46	46	48	44	39	44
Presidential appointment	70	85	72	60	69	70	70	61	63
Determine tuition	91	91	87	88	93	93	88	88	95
Professor's immoral conduct	64	74	70	67	65	60	56	63	54
Tenure decisions	64	79	67	61	67	55	54	63	44
Student cheating	21	26	27	24	19	20	20	14	19
Policy re student protests	52	64	60	61	51	54	45	63	49
Appoint academic dean	63	81	68	57	64	61	61	48	54
Policy re faculty leaves	58	70	65	60	59	54	46	57	48
Admissions criteria	36	56	50	41	33	27	33	47	25
Honorary degrees	57	64	62	48	55	51	60	43	45
Athletic programs	43	49	58	50	41	42	41	48	37
Fraternities and sororities	44	95	48	47	45	47	38	43	44
Number of issues with 50% or more trustees feeling trustees and/or administrators alone should have major authority	8	13	11	9	8	8	6	6	4

tional status, etc.[8] Such people are probably more inclined to delegate authority and to be less concerned personally about maintaining control. Trustees of the more prestigious institutions, by virtue of the characteristics that led to their being selected for such boards, are simply more inclined to a laissez-faire attitude regarding student and faculty involvement in campus governance.

The question of who shall govern is obviously very complex. Many faculty who complain about lack of participation in academic governance are actually unwilling to participate themselves and suspicious of other members of the faculty who do get involved. Furthermore, it is, sometimes, members of the faculty who would prefer to keep authority out of the hands of their colleagues. As one recent example of this, at an institution which is moving from a teachers' college to a large state university, one department chairman opposed efforts to give greater authority to faculty members on the grounds that there were still far too many holdovers on the faculty from the teacher-training days who were not at all interested in research and, presumably, would have slowed the institution's emergence as a first-rate institution (Rourke and Brooks, 1966: 117).[9]

Nevertheless, it seems safe to conclude that, by and large, faculty members tend to favor a horizontal, as opposed to vertical, form of authority, whereas, trustees prefer a hierarchical arrangement, or system of graded authority, imitating, it would seem, the bureaucratic management model. Though neither of these forms of government actually exist in any pure sense, they still represent, what would appear to be, rather basic ideological differences between trustees and faculty.

POLITICAL PREFERENCE AND IDEOLOGY

A summary of the trustees' political party affiliations, political ideologies, and the relationship between these two variables is presented in Table 8. Of the trustees who indicated both their party preference and ideology, over 60 percent described themselves as Republican, and slightly less than 35 percent as Democrat. The majority regard themselves as moderates, 21.6 percent as conservatives, and 15.9 percent liberals. Furthermore, there was an interaction or correlation between these characteristics. We note the tendency for Republicans to regard themselves more often as conservative than liberal (approximately 17 percent vs. 4 percent) and for Democrats to view themselves more often as liberals than conservatives (10.5 percent vs. 3.7 percent).

Contrast this profile of the trustee with that of the college faculty member. In general, one gets a much different picture, with most reports indicating that the majority of college faculty members are Democrats.[10] Furthermore, though we can cite no research evidence for this claim, it is extremely unlikely that as many as 22 percent of the faculty would regard themselves as conservatives (though we do suspect that conservative trustees tend to be at the same institutions as conservative faculty). With such a gap in the political orientations of these two groups, then, it should

TABLE 8

CLASSIFICATION OF TRUSTEES BY POLITICAL PARTY
PREFERENCE AND IDEOLOGY (IN PERCENTAGES)

	Conservative	Moderate	Liberal	Total [a]
Republican	16.95	39.53	4.06	60.54
Democrat	3.74	20.32	10.50	34.56
Other	0.91	2.69	1.31	4.91
TOTAL	21.60	62.54	15.87	100%

Note: The correlation (contingency coefficient) between party affiliation and political ideology is .32 (p < .01), i.e., there is a tendency for those who are Republicans to also be conservative, etc.

a. The data in this table include only those trustees who indicated both their party preference *and* ideology. Therefore, it differs slightly from the data reported above in the opening section on biographical characteristics.

hardly come as a surprise to find disagreement over educational matters, for both party affiliation and political ideology are related to the attitude items already discussed. On the basis of correlational data, for example, we note a definite tendency for trustees who regard themselves as conservatives to endorse such statements (see Table 2) as "the administration should exercise control over the contents of the student newspaper" (r = .37), and "the requirement that a professor sign a loyalty oath is reasonable" (r = .47).

Most academicians would probably attach a negative value to such facts, but it should be pointed out that, as with most situations of this kind, there are two sides to the coin. Jencks and Riesman (1968: 277–279), for example, offer cogent arguments that, at least until quite recently, it has been the Republican moderates, not the Democrats, who have led the struggle for more generous university appropriations. These are obviously not simple matters.

Activities as a Trustee

Having sketched an outline of who trustees are and what opinions they have about important educational matters, let us turn now to a consideration of what they do in their roles as trustees.

First, most boards meet three or four times a year, and most trustees attend these meetings rather faithfully. Furthermore, attending board meetings was the single activity requiring the most time from trustees, with nearly half of them spending over 20 hours (including travel) attending these meetings during the year. Aside from the general board meetings, the most time-consuming activities of trustees appear to be attending committee meetings, having conferences with college personnel, soliciting contributions (for the private institutions but not the public), and meeting various ad hoc college groups.[11]

TRUSTEES AND THE "LITERATURE" OF HIGHER EDUCATION

One activity *not* engaged in by most trustees is reading about college and university activities. Included on our questionnaire was a list of relevant books and journals, and the trustees were asked to indicate the extent of their familiarity with these references. The data clearly indicate that, as a group, trustees are barely familiar with the major books and periodicals of relevance to American higher education. In terms of books, for example, only Ruml and Morrison's *Memo to a College Trustee*—a book now some nine years old—has been read completely by more than ten percent of the trustees. In fact, of the fifteen books listed, only four have been completely read by more than five percent of the trustees, and, in most cases, the trustees have never even heard of the books, most of which are now regarded as "classics" in the higher education field. The same story holds for educational periodicals. Only the *EPE 15-Minute Newsletter* is read regularly by more than ten percent of the trustees, and, again, the majority of trustees are not even familiar with most of the journals listed. A partial summary of these data is presented in Table 9.

One might argue, of course, that this lack of familiarity with higher education books and journals is understandable because trustees are extremely busy men, caught up in the activities that led to their selection as trustees in the first place. While this is undoubtedly true, the trustees' lack of familiarity with the literature serves to underscore the peripheral nature of the trusteeship for most of the board members. It also suggests that the institutions are not doing enough in the way of keeping their trustees abreast of current thinking. Though there is strength to the lack-of-time argument as an explanation of why trustees do not read these materials, it would seem that some of the blame for their not even being familiar with such publications can be directed to poor communications from the officers of the institutions.

The seriousness of this situation, like so many others already touched upon, depends on the role of the trustee at a particular institution. If the board is regarded primarily as window dressing, and the only expected function is to rubber stamp decisions reached by others, their lack of familiarity with the relevant literature is, perhaps, not important. But, to the extent they are expected to be more than this, the shortcoming takes on new meaning. To be serving in a major, influential seat in higher education, without any familiarity with its history (Rudolph), methods or systems of governance (Corson), students (Sanford), current goings-on (the *Chronicle*), and the like, is truly a serious indictment of the way higher education is conducted.

TABLE 9

EXTENT OF TRUSTEES' FAMILIARITY WITH SELECTED BOOKS
AND JOURNALS ON AMERICAN HIGHER EDUCATION (IN PERCENTAGES)

Books	Have Read Completely	Have Read Portions	Have Briefly Examined but Not Read	Know of the Book but Haven't Seen it	Have Never Heard of it
Corson, The Governance of Colleges & Universities	5	7	6	14	54
Kerr, The Uses of the University	6	8	7	20	45
Millett, The Academic Community	2	5	7	15	57
Perkins, The University in Transition	5	6	7	16	52
Rudolph, The American College and University	2	6	7	14	58
Ruml & Morrison, Memo to a College Trustee	17	11	7	11	43

Journals	Read Regularly	Read but Not Regularly	Have Read Several Articles from this Periodical	Familiar with this Journal but Have Never Read it	Not Familiar with this Periodical
Chronicle of Higher Education	6	4	6	9	62
College Management	4	6	8	11	58
Education Record	3	5	7	10	61
EPE 15-Minute Trustee Newsletter	20	10	7	6	47
Journal of Higher Education	4	10	12	13	50

Note: The lists of books and journals in this table are incomplete. The questionnaire listed 15 books and 12 periodicals.

TO MAKE DECISIONS OR OFFER ADVICE

We have already seen that, as a general rule, trustees feel that the major authority for many institutional decisions should reside with the trustees and/or administrators of the institution. The delicate balance between deciding and advising, however, remains unclear, at least as it pertains to the way the trustees and the administration together reach decisions. The trustees were, therefore, asked to indicate their perception of their action in terms of the decide-advise-confirm model for topics commonly considered by trustees.

Responses to this section of the questionnaire make it clear that the trustees perceive their responsibility to lie most clearly in the areas of finance, physical plant, and external affairs. In matters of personnel, student life, and the educational program, the trustees' preferred role would appear to be one of approving or confirming a decision already made by some other, presumably better qualified, group. It is true, of course, that the distinction between making a decision and approving one already made is far from clear. Since the reverse of the approve or confirm option is, obviously, disapprove or veto, even this latter level of involvement is (or could be), essentially, a decision-making function. Nevertheless, there are clearly many "rubber stamp" activities required of trustees, and our purpose here was to attempt to learn how trustees perceived their role in these terms.

In Table 10, the percentage of trustees feeling they have *decided* on a course of action in six areas (personnel, student life, finance, plant, educational program, and external affairs) has been converted to ranks. Thus, we see that the percentage of the total trustee sample who have made a decision is highest in the area of long-range financial plans, second in the area of fund raising, and so on. It would appear that trustees make most decisions in the fiscal areas, followed by physical plant, and external affairs, in that order. (The selection of the president was not included in this list of topics.) Across all types of institutions, the five topics about which trustees most often make decisions are in the three major areas of finance, plant, and external affairs, with only two exceptions: the area of personnel (wage scales for nonfaculty) for junior college trustees, and student life (policies on student-invited speakers) for trustees of selective public universities. It is interesting to note that, of the topics listed, the one about which most trustee decisions were made in three types of institutions was *the selection of new trustees.*

Table 10 also includes an indication of the total number of topics (out of twenty listed in the questionnaire) about which twenty percent or more of the trustees have made a decision. From this listing, it would appear that trustees of public junior colleges make the largest number of decisions, while, at the other extreme, trustees of selective public institutions more often advise or confirm the decisions of others, since twenty percent (or more) of their trustees actually made a decision in only four areas.

TABLE 10

RANKING OF TOPICS IN WHICH TRUSTEES WERE DIRECTLY INVOLVED IN THE DECISION-MAKING PROCESS

	Total Sample	Public JC's	Public Colleges	Public U's	Private Colleges	Private U's	Cath. C's & U's	Selective Public	Selective Private
Finance:									
Investments	5		5	2	5	4		3	4
Budget analysis		4 [a]	4	4		5	4	5	5
Long-range plans	1	2	1	1	2	3	3	2 [b]	3
Plant:									
Master plan	4	3	2	3	4	4	5	4	
Select architect		1	3	5					
External Affairs:									
Fund raising plans	2				1	2	2		2
Select new trustees	3				3	1	1		1
Total number of topics in which 20% or more of the trustees have been directly involved in making a decision (out of 20 topics listed):	8	11	6	6	8	6	7	4	8

Note: The ranks are based on within-type percentages and should be interpreted carefully. Thus, for example, the area of investments is ranked second at public universities (i.e., the second highest proportion of trustees made one or more decisions in this area) and fifth at private four-year colleges, yet the proportion of trustees at each type actually making a decision in this area is very close (36.8 vs. 32.3 per-cent).

a. Fifth rank for public junior colleges was in the area of personnel.
b. First rank for selective public institutions was in the area of student life.

Summary and Conclusions

This chapter has attempted to summarize questionnaire data gathered from more than 5,000 college and university trustees. Of greatest importance, perhaps, have been the findings (or confirmation, in some cases, of impressions already held) that:

(1) It is naive to speak of the college trustee as if he could be easily and accurately described and the description thus provided were generalizable to all trustees. Though summaries of the data yield modal patterns, it is also important to see that there is a great deal of diversity—in terms of backgrounds—between and among trustees serving on boards of different types of institutions.

(2) This disclaimer notwithstanding, the modal trustee can be described as white, male, in his late fifties, well-educated, and, financially, very successful. His current college or university board membership is his first, and he serves on only the one board.

(3) Trustees are, generally, somewhat cautious regarding the notion of academic freedom. Further, junior college trustees appear to be somewhat more guarded in this respect than trustees of other types of institutions, but the speculation that this is due primarily to the fact that junior college trustees are often elected cannot be substantiated.

(4) Some of the assumptions held about the relationship between biographical characteristics of trustees and their style of operation as governing board members appear to be accurate, generally, but run the risk of being over-simplified. For example, trustees who are business executives consistently favor running a college like a business more than trustees with other occupations. At the same time, however, trustees who serve on boards at the types of institutions having the greatest proportion of business executives are the *least* likely to espouse a business orientation for the institution.

(5) In general, trustees prefer a modified "top-down" form of institutional government, often preferring to exclude members of the faculty even from those decisions having to do with the academic program of the institution. Yet, the trustees themselves shy away from direct decision-making except when it comes to selection of the president and matters of finance, the physical plant, and external affairs. In other cases, they prefer that the college officials make the decisions.

(6) Trustees appear to differ markedly from those occupying the academic positions beneath them. In terms of political party affiliation and ideology, and attitudes about higher education, the trustees are, generally, more conservative than the faculty.

(7) Trustees do not read—indeed, have, generally, never even heard of—the more relevant higher education books and journals.

These, then, are the basic results of our study. Some of the findings provide no more than an empirical base for beliefs already held about those who govern our colleges and universities, while others may have disclosed information previously unknown. But, in either case, we need to learn much more. It is helpful to know that trustees are often business executives and Republicans, that the majority think it is reasonable for faculty members to sign loyalty oaths, and so on. But the full benefit of this knowledge will not be realized until we learn how these facts relate to substantial issues. For example, what is the relationship between a trustee's occupation and his educational attitudes and behavior as a trustee? How do trustees who are alumni of an institution differ from board members who are not? Is there any relationship between a trustee's familiarity with the higher education "literature" and his educational attitudes? Does the better-read (and presumably more informed) trustee hold different views about the higher education scene?

Answers to these questions—and many more like them—will hopefully emerge from further sifting of the information available, and, indeed, will have to be answered before one can pretend to have more than a superficial understanding of the complex role trustees play in our colleges and universities. For though many argue that the trustee's role has diminished, there is evidence that his influence continues to be strong. Whether it should be strong cannot be answered by data presented in this report or, perhaps, by any data, for, in the last analysis, these are questions of values. Survey data, no matter how well it is gathered and analyzed, will not tell us what the governing structure should be. But, surely, a better understanding of some of the more basic educational attitudes of the major groups involved should point to more reasoned and mutually satisfying purposes and procedures for our colleges and universities.

Trustees, as we have seen, often prefer to exclude faculty and students from the process of appointing academic deans, and, almost always, to exclude them from the deliberations involved in selecting a new president. Doesn't this contribute to faculty resentment toward the administration, an unnecessary hostility which, perhaps, could be avoided if the faculty had been involved in these appointments?

Faculty members often complain that trustees have no logical role at all, and governing boards should be abandoned altogether. But isn't this, perhaps, due to overemphasis on the concept of *authority* and not enough on *communication?* Has there been sufficient understanding of the trustee role as a liaison between the ivory tower and the larger society? In Corson's words, "What responsibility should trustees assume for interpreting to the faculty the evolving needs of the society . . . ?" (Corson, 1960:58)

If this latter approach is adopted—i.e., regarding trustees as a liaison group—then it is clear that drastic changes in the procedure for selecting trustees are necessary. As things stand, trustees, as a group, are not *representative* of a very large segment of American society. They were never meant to be. But as our ideas about the basic nature and purposes of higher education change, so must our notions about the men who govern these activities. For openers, a far broader range of occupational and economic backgrounds would seem to be in order. But this would be just a beginning, and many other modifications would seem to be appropriate: more women, more who are familiar with some of the problems that black collegians and other disadvantaged students are likely to face, etc. In other words, more people whose background, training, and skills are relevant to the functions and programs of higher education.

Eventually, the question of attitudes must also be considered. Though it is not unlikely that some of the changes already suggested will result in attitudinal shifts as well, we must be very tentative, for, as already noted, much more needs to be learned about the relationship between these characteristics. Furthermore, it is hard to see what would be gained by intentionally searching for trustees whose educational attitudes parallel those of the faculty and administration. Such a practice would result in a board no more representative than those of today. Nevertheless, we must somehow combat the difficulties which arise when groups with markedly different educational philosophies try to work together. Differences of opinion must be present; without them, progress is doubtful. But great gaps in ideology will get us nowhere, and to the extent that ideological differences among these groups remain (or increase), we might expect greater conflicts and disruption of the academic program, a deeper entrenchment of the ideas of competing factions, and, worst of all, an aimless, confusing collegiate experience, where the students' program is a result of arbitration rather than mutual determination of goals and purposes.

NOTES

1. For full details regarding development of the questionnaire, selection of the sample, and procedure for obtaining the names and addresses of the trustees, see the original report (Hartnett, 1969).

2. This particular item, dealing with off-campus civil disobedience, is probably more a matter of *in loco parentis* than academic freedom. Nevertheless, it is included here since freedom (though perhaps not academic freedom) *is* involved, and the item does correlate with the other four in this table.

3. Cases like this have led some observers to conjecture that in tranquil times the trustees are content to maintain a safe distance from the affairs of the campus, but in times of crisis and turmoil move in the direction of assuming greater power and control, largely in response to various pressure groups.

4. Such a comparison had to be made separately, by type of control and level of institution, owing to the very different patterns of becoming a board member at the public vs. private institutions. Obviously, trustees of private institutions are not elected by the public. But, even within public institutions, the pattern varies by level of offering. For example, as already mentioned, 42 percent of the public junior college trustees were elected, yet at the public four-year institutions, fewer than 1 percent were elected (85 percent were appointed by the governor or some other government official), and at public universities fewer than 10 percent gained board membership in this way. Clearly, then, a comparison of attitudes by method of obtaining board membership had to be done *within* junior colleges in order to draw any meaningful conclusions.

5. For a more detailed discussion of these roles at both public and private institutions, see John D. Millett (1962).

6. For example, see Ernest L. Boyer (1968).

7. There is corroborating data for this assertion. In other research currently

under way in the Higher Education Research Group at ETS, scores on the Democratic Governance scale of an experimental *Institutional Functioning Inventory* (an instrument which asks for faculty perceptions of their own institutions) have been found to correlate significantly with selectivity, income per student, proportion of faculty holding a doctorate, and average faculty compensation.

8. Much of our data supports this. As one indication, look again at Table 1 of this chapter.

9. Readers interested in more detailed discussions of this problem should see *Faculty Participation in Academic Governance,* a report of the AAHE Task Force on Faculty Representation and Academic Negotiations, Campus Governance Program (1967), and a report of a study by Archie R. Dykes (1968).

10. However, there is variation across academic fields. Charles G. McClintock, Charles B. Spaulding, and Henry A. Turner, who have reported on the political orientations of academic psychologists (1965), political scientists (1963), and sociologists (1963), report that over two thirds of the social scientists regard themselves as Democrats. But a recent multidiscipline study (Spaulding and Turner, 1968) indicates that political preference differences are associated with different orientations of the disciplines toward social criticism or toward the applications of knowledge in business and industry. Thus, they found engineers and mathematicians, for example, to lean toward the Republican party. See also an older source, Lazarsfeld and Thielens (1958).

11. Again, for more complete details the reader is urged to consult the larger report (Hartnett, 1969).

REFERENCES

BECK, H. P. (1947) *Men Who Control Our Universities.* New York: King's Crown Press.

BOYER, E. L. (1968) "A fresh look at the college trustee." *Educational Record* (Summer): 274–279.

CAFFREY, J. (1968) "Predications for higher education in the 1960s." Pp. 123–152 in *The Future Academic Community: Continuity and Change.* Background papers for participants in the 51st annual meeting of the American Council on Education.

CORSON, J. J. (1960) *Governance of Colleges and Universities.* New York: McGraw-Hill.

DUSTER, T. (1966) "The aims of higher learning and the control of the universities." Berkeley: University of California (unpub.).

DYKES, A. R. (1968) *Faculty Participation in Academic Decision-Making.* American Council on Education.

HARTNETT, R. T. (1969) *College and University Trustees: Their Backgrounds, Roles, and Educational Attitudes.* Princeton: Educational Testing Service.

HENDERSON, A. D. (1967) *The Role of the Governing Board.* Association of Governing Boards of Universities and Colleges, Report 10.

JENCKS, C. and D. RIESMAN (1968) *The Academic Revolution.* New York: Doubleday.

KRAMER, J. (1968) "Does student power mean: rocking the boat? running the university?" *New York Times* (May 26): sec. 4, p. 32.

LAZARSFELD, P. F. and W. THIELENS (1958) *The Academic Mind.* New York: The Free Press.

McCLINTOCK, C. G., C. B. SPAULDING, and H. A. TURNER (1963) *Sociology and Social Research* 47.

—— (1963) *Western Political Quarterly* 16.

—— (1965) *American Psychologist* 20.

MILLETT, J. D. (1962) *The Academic Community: An Essay on Organization.* New York: McGraw-Hill.

New York State Regents Advisory Committee on Educational Leadership— James Perkins, chairman (1966) *College and University Trustees and Trusteeship.*

RIESMAN, DAVID, and CHRISTOPHER JENCKS (1962) "The Viability of the American College." In N. Sanford (ed.) *The American College.* New York: John Wiley.

ROURKE, F. and G. BROOKS (1966) *The Managerial Revolution in Higher Education.* Baltimore: The Johns Hopkins Press.

RUDOLPH, F. (1962) *The American College and University.* New York: Alfred A. Knopf.

CHAPTER 4

PREDICAMENTS IN THE CAREER OF THE COLLEGE PRESIDENT

David Riesman

At the Minnesota Conference on Higher Education in 1962, Meredith Wilson declared:

> If you have almost limitless numbers seeking education, and you begin by saying that the numbers are in themselves a tragedy, then you are already defeated. If you begin by thinking that these numbers are beyond our capacity, then you have accepted the assumption that education is some sort of finite reservoir that can serve only limited numbers. This is not true.
>
> While excellence in education is dependent on exciting minds among teachers, it is really an active consequence of the minds and the expectations which students bring to it. Finding a way to maximize these expectations, while not reducing the influence of the teachers, is what we really need to discover. If, for example, you begin with the assumption that there are in the University of Minnesota not 2,000 professors, but rather, 30,000 students, then you have multiplied by 15 the number of active agents. If you then ask how you can make certain that each student is being stimulated toward spontaneous, enthusiastic study, you have almost no danger of being a failure [Beck and McClure, 1962].

There are, in fact, many dangers of failure in American higher education today. The small private college has no assurance of success, either financially or educationally. The large public universities which, like Meredith Wilson himself, reject the slogan Kingsley Amis made popular in England that "more means worse," ordinarily do very badly vis-a-vis students at the lower division level, however distinguished their graduate and professional programs. Yet comparison of institutions operating under rather similar conditions leads one to conclude that their quality, their degree of success or failure, while heavily dependent on history and on local conditions, also reflects the talent and energy of their top academic administrators.

Many of the great state universities have concluded that they must be huge at the undergraduate level to support financially and politically their

---

EDITORS' NOTE: Revised version of a talk delivered at the dedication of the O. Meredith Wilson Library, University of Minnesota, May 13, 1969.

expensive graduate and professional programs. Some of their presidents have defended this expansion on democratic and egalitarian grounds; I think here of such men as Fred Harrington at Wisconsin, David Henry at Illinois, and Meredith Wilson, formerly at Minnesota. I respect their judgment and accomplishments, and I hope I do not speak simply out of an elitist bias when I express my own sense that universities, like other human groups, can grow too large. Some single campuses seem to me to have more than enough students—logistically if not always politically—to support the full range of departments and specialties, a first-rate library, and foreign students from New York, Japan, Africa, and everywhere else. Beyond a certain indeterminate point of size, it takes a superhuman individual to keep the institution in touch with itself, with all its inner and outer constituencies.

This paper focuses on this sometimes superhuman individual, how he is recruited, what his career lines look like, and describes some of the aspects of the on-the-job training that he may receive. Finally, I turn to what I regard as the almost impossible situation of having responsibility without commensurate power, especially in the eminent universities where the faculty, organized in departments, have held the major power, and where students and outside publics are now also visibly contending to increase their formal power (they have always had a great deal of informal influence). To maintain what is distinctive about American higher education—its unique contributions to research, to the transmission of culture, to the training and further development of both its students and its faculty—seems to me increasingly difficult in an age of polarized politics, when new demands are coming into the universities, even while public support may be diminishing, relatively if not absolutely. I have watched in the last several years what I have come to call the collision course of higher education: There are angry student and faculty militants, white and black, asking that the university do more against the war, against poverty and racism, while taxpayers and other citizens see the universities as coddling the young and egging them on (See Riesman, 1969).[1]

Neither small colleges nor great universities are mobile units, geared to respond instantly to the new demands for expanded urban studies and better medical care in poverty areas, for legal aid and pollution control, for black and other nonwhite recruitment and for black studies—the many intense and diverse idealisms which add to the pressures on the universities, ordinarily without adding to their resources. In fact, these demands incur costs. However, it seems to me unlikely that faculty salaries will be cut in order to respond to the new demands; they may even have to be increased because these demands have a price in faculty exhaustion and endless committee meetings, so that the troubled activist university may have to pay more to stay in the academic competition. Student scholarships are not likely to be cut either. Cutting the athletic budget will not save much money, and it may antagonize some alumni who are already restless. Indeed, for some time I have feared that the great research libraries will be among the first casualties since some new activists and old philistines regard them as luxuries, and in time their growth and maintenance may suffer. I feel passionately that the autonomous and scholarly functions of the university must be preserved, even against the newer demands for meeting contemporary challenges (Trow, 1969).

In 1955, I spoke at the dedication of the Kettering Library at Antioch College (Riesman, 1964). I was defending books against what was, at that time, the somewhat special culture of Antioch with the desire of many of its students for immediate relevance in workaday jobs. Today, almost every great campus is where Antioch was then. The demand for relevance obviously has its positive side in asking students and faculty constantly to re-examine the worth and meaning of what they do. But there is also the temptation to pull down the heights of culture to fill up the abysses of our time in a drastic leveling operation demanded both by well-educated and often idealistic activists, and by the more collegiate or mindless students for whom any excuse for avoiding study will do. And the danger is perhaps greatest in the ambivalence of many faculty members who, when challenged by radical students and colleagues, reveal the doubts they have always had about the legitimacy of scholarship when long-range, well-tempered work appears to compete with the imperatives of a desperately troubled country.

In this situation, the model of the university president as arbitrator and negotiator, presented by Clark Kerr in *The Uses of the University* (1963), seems to many constituents insufficiently inspiring. Arbitrators and negotiators are needed as much as, or more than, ever. However, in major universities the long-range task of defending against moral attack the legitimacy of the traditional pursuits of the university requires talents of leadership and conviction that are not always coupled with those of the mediator. Those faculty members and students who are presently on the defensive, look to the president for a sense of rightness and of validation. The president must find ways to help provide this while also finding resources and, if need be, validation for plunging the university into some of the newer areas of contemporary concern, where the risks of failure are not only very great but highly visible.[2]

When, in 1964, Frederick Bolman did a study of how college presidents are chosen, he found that trustee and faculty committees began with criteria that could only be met by someone who could walk on water (See Bolman, 1965). He observed what many have noticed, namely, that there is no career line which one can embark upon in the hope of becoming a college president. It is true that if one wants to become the president of a community college, one can get a doctorate in higher education at Teachers College, Columbia, or at some of the centers for the study of higher education, but that is not a route toward leadership of an eminent university. In the past, the closest thing we have had to a career line is through the ministry. Yet I doubt if people entered the Lutheran ministry in an earlier day in order to head St. Olaf or Gustavus Adolphus, or if people entered the novitiate of the Sisters of St. Joseph of Carondolet or a Benedictine seminary to have a chance to run the College of St. Catherine or St. John's University in Collegeville. Even in what was once called the Bible Belt, it is hard to find a Protestant minister at the head of a Protestant college; the only exceptions might be in some of the black denominational colleges, and here such men are fast giving way to men with regular academic training. Among the Catholic religious, the spirit I sense is anti-organizational, if not antivocational, and the young people entering the religious life seem to me not to have the kind of personal force which an older generation in the Catholic leadership sometimes possessed. Such personal force seems among young people to be regarded almost as unfair—there is a great confusion of the authoritative and the authoritarian; the young seminarians I see want to work one by one as Lone Rangers on the ghetto frontier, and the last thing they want is the budgetary headaches and organizational networks of academic administration.

A few years ago, a group of students from the Harvard Graduate School of Business Administration came to see me, saying that they wanted to enter upon careers as university administrators, and how could they begin? I told them that I saw very little chance for them in beginning with a Master's in Business Administration, for even if they could get jobs as comptrollers or budget officers in universities, and perhaps work themselves up to become Vice-Presidents of Finance, I thought that they would very seldom have a chance for the top job. Further, if they did reach it, they would always be on the defensive because they would seem too professional with their business school training; what is wanted is a Ph.D. who temporarily gives up his profession to become a part-time amateur manager, and either actually hates such work or appears to despise it.

Indeed, the cult of the amateur characterizes American academic life in many of its aspects. The college professor is supposed to know how to teach because he has once been taught. There is no on-the-job training for him as there is for school teachers. Rarely does he believe that he needs to learn anything in a systematic way about the field of higher education or about the social psychology of learning or teaching. He leaves that to those uncultured fellows over in the college of education. One way of looking at this is to see that aristocracy has been democratized in America, along with everything else, so that the cult of the gentleman who despises the professional is widely available. Indeed, this is even more evident in the case of administration. There is a Populist element in the American academic's scorn for the specialized understandings and tasks of administration, reminiscent of the attitude toward high civil servants in the Jacksonian era, and part of an old American tradition which makes us assume that a Senator, who has never run anything larger than his own office, can become an instant executive.[3]

Our aversion to bureaucracy and even to organization (which unites the Right and the Left in America) sees to it that college administrators are desperately understaffed. Let a new administration building go up on campus, and faculty members are sure to denigrate it as needless, while demanding an additional faculty member for their own department who will want an office, a secretary, a travel budget, a parking space, fellowships for his graduate students, and all the other prerequisites whose provision adds to the tasks of administration. My own impression over the years in these matters has recently been confirmed by a study, *The Mirror of Brass,*

which examined the working conditions of college and university administrators the country over. I emerged from reading the book with the feeling
that the job of the college president is to provide professors and other staff
with fringe benefits such as sabbaticals and long vacations that he dare not
take himself (See Ingraham, 1968).

This is a situation ripe for scapegoating. The college president is visible
and seems important, while, in fact, he has limited power, and if he loses
the support of his faculty, he is finished, even if he retains the support of
other backers. In a good college or university, it has been the faculty which
has held power on the campus, able to enforce its desires by its ability or
threat to move elsewhere. Yet a recent study confirms the common impression that faculty members *believe* that the president or perhaps the trustees
hold the power (See Gross, 1968; Gross and Grambsch, 1968). Many faculty members, in my own observation, have little appreciation of the contribution administrators made toward their productivity. In this, they appear
to resemble Texas oilmen or devotees of Ayn Rand, who believe there can
be such a thing as a completely self-made man. College presidents are
often in the position of helping men who resent having to be helped, and
who find it convenient to regard the administrator as a failed academic
rather than as a generous one.

Indeed, in most good universities the president must have a Ph.D., and
he often comes from the ranks of the faculty.[4] If one includes history
among the humanities, the majority of presidents are still drawn from the
humanities. Such men are apt to have greater loyalty to the institution than
are the somewhat more favored natural scientists, who are oriented to their
guilds and to their graduate students and postdoctoral fellows, whom, if
they leave the institution, they can carry with them like the tail of a comet.
Social scientists are the second most-likely cadre from which presidents are
chosen, possibly under the mistaken impression that a degree in political
science, public administration, or psychology offers some guarantee of an
ability to work with people. In the future, I rather expect that we may see
more men chosen from the natural sciences. Even before recent cuts in federal budgets for science, some natural scientists were realizing that their
half-life as researchers was short, and that they might discover a second career as administrators, whether of a laboratory or of a university, while still
chronologically young. Medical school physician-presidents are rare; law
professor-presidents are becoming more usual, it seems to me, perhaps with
the belief that they can handle student contentiousness. Men from the
world of business are not entirely excluded—witness Wesleyan's new president, a devoted alumnus and a scholar *manqué,* or the unusual new president of Sarah Lawrence, who was Vice-President for Research at IBM. I
do not know whether the leading institutions will ever be willing to turn to
colleges of education for top administrators. Edmund Williamson at Minnesota seems to have trained most of the deans of students and student personnel people in the country—the antitrust laws notwithstanding. The
deans of students are even more unpopular than university presidents,
being regarded as finks by the students and as double agents by everybody
else. And in the hundred and fifty or so colleges and universities which,

having been teachers colleges, have become four-year liberal arts colleges and now want to become major, graduate-oriented universities, a man with a background in education or student personnel work is unlikely to be made president when the place hopes to become distinguished enough to believe it can afford amateur administrators drawn from the more traditional disciplines (See Dunham, 1969).

In spite of what I have said, we can see the rudiments of a career line when men who have been department chairmen are made academic deans or provosts with the thought of grooming them for the presidency. Moreover, the American Council on Education five years ago set up a program of academic internships, which provide a year in the office of an administrator, or perhaps in a smaller administrative position, for a young man who has some interest in entering on a career in academic administration (See Astin, 1966).[5] There are also several institutes which run from three to five days for college presidents or academic deans—in one of these the man must have been on the job five years or less—and they study cases in the Harvard Business School manner and have a chance to take part in workshops with other men and women in the same line of work. So diverse are the institutions of higher education and so diverse are the trajectories which bring men and women into college presidencies, that when I have visited such institutes, I felt their members to be suffering from culture shock on discovering each other, much as can happen to Peace Corps trainees when they meet their fellow volunteers. However, a Peace Corps training program, although far too short, lasts from eight to eleven intensive weeks, while in-service programs for management—for example, the Sloan School at MIT—run for periods from three months up to a year.

The even more difficult job of a college president is only rarely taken by a man who has been president somewhere else. It is true that one can move from Lawrence College to Harvard or Duke or from Oregon to Minnesota, but of 1200 presidents recently surveyed, less than one-eighth had been president somewhere else.[6] Furthermore, while a study by the American Council on Education a few years ago showed that the average president lasted eight years on the job, now the figure is down to less than six among the members of the Association of American Universities.[7]

The career of the president seems to be a ladder with almost no rungs; and in this respect, as in the lack of training, it seems to me to resemble the leadership of our labor unions. One does not move from Local 482 of the Packing House Workers to Local 3 of the Electricians, although one might move from the latter to the presidency of the AF of L. Indeed, I suspect that one reason for the tyranny of some union leaders, such as James Hoffa, is this absence of a career line, and the abysmal alternative that, if unseated by an election, one must return to driving a truck or to the assembly line (See Lipset, Trow, and Coleman, 1956).

The professor turned president can, of course, return to his research and teaching, and a goodly number have made that transition successfully. Indeed, a few academic deans of large places and presidents of smaller ones have managed to continue teaching a course and to do some reading in their field. But, for most of them, their situation resembles that of women who have been excellently educated and then have left the labor force to raise a family: they feel a lack of self-confidence when they want to return to work if they do not have the benefit of some program of continuing education. Only rarely is the college president seen as an administrator who can run another institution—although this does happen, as with the President's present Secretary of Agriculture and the new director of the AID program, or with some foundation presidents. There is no genuine career line, either in preparing for the role or in creating a rhythm of movement within it and, eventually, out of it again.

This is the more problematic because it is a position of remarkable aloneness. Some presidents (like Franklin Murphy, when he was at UCLA) find friends in the local business community, and thus do not appear to the faculty to play favorites among them. But, of course, such friendships do not help with radical students and faculty. Presidents do talk to each other, and today the talk is often of casualties, and who is resigning and who would like to resign if he thought the local Regents would appoint anybody half-decent to take his place or if anyone at all would be persuaded to take his place. But the meetings at which presidents can do this are short and far between, and, in recent months, men sometimes do not dare to leave their institutions, lest something explode in their absence. The things they need to know on the job are of such detail and intricacy anyway that the two- or three-day meetings, for example, of the American Council on Education, cannot do much for them. They cannot learn, in such a forum, how to handle police and the different types of police, and what sorts of force can be counted on from local and state patrolmen, the National Guard, and student guerrillas and community vigilantes. Indeed, people do not enter graduate work in history or in physics, or enter the seminary, in order one day to have to be expert in the use of controlled force. To be sure, many Americans have in wartime discovered new resources and adaptabilities that they never dreamed they had; but it is somehow different to be involved in a common enterprise shared by millions (as in World Wars I and II) as against the situation of enduring seemingly adventitious, yet relentless, pressures, when most of one's friends and colleagues are going about academic business more or less as usual.

These new hazards created by student activism have not eliminated more traditional ones, as when the president is asked to look into the freshman grades of a legislator's nephew or favored constituent, or to see whether he can get football tickets for important alumni. I know the president of one state university who was accustomed to being called vile names at hearings of the state legislature long before he was called "Honky" by angry blacks or "Fascist" by radical whites.[8] Presidents are apt to be criticized by faculty members, both for being insufficiently scholarly and for handling their public relations in the mass media with something less than professional aplomb. Describing his job to the *Wall Street Journal,* Chancellor Charles Young of UCLA declared: "Sometimes I feel as if I'm being picked apart slowly but surely by a big flock of birds." Alexander Meiklejohn, a not untroubled college president forty years ago, came to talk to the Harvard Liberal Club when I was an undergraduate. I asked him what he would talk about; he replied that he had but one speech, which he gave innumerable times a year. Unlike the presidents of today, he could be inspirational over and over again without fear that he would be overheard by the instant exposure of television.

The university presidency would seem to be a job for celibates. If the wives had had private lives before their husbands' new roles, they will often find themselves trapped, and they too will face loneliness, often without the satisfactions the husbands get simply from being on the go. Indeed, a study of university governance being conducted by Harold Hodgkinson at the Center for Research and Development in Higher Education at Berkeley turned up the fact that organization charts did not include two groups who sometimes played an important role, namely, presidents' wives, and also the network of secretaries. When wives do play a role other than that of support, it is seldom, in my observation, considered a benign one.

Thus, to marry a potential college president is not a way for a career-minded woman to get ahead in the world. Nor, in my observation, does it help to marry a college president's daughter. Yet I remember when I talked with students about the play, *Who's Afraid of Virginia Woolf?,* that they took it for granted, as the play does, that somebody might marry the daughter of a college president in order to get ahead. It is hard to imagine a less helpful match, or a weirder sense of the division of power between the academic guilds, which give a man visibility and, therefore, power in his institution, and the president, whose chief power over his faculty is that of persuasion, and who can only exploit his faculty if they are so dedicated to the institution as to have lost mobility. Even in the denominational Negro colleges, or in other small denominational colleges, today one hardly finds anyone like Dr. Bledsoe, of Ralph Ellison's *Invisible Man.* Rather, the presidents of such institutions are torn by the conflict between the local mores and the national styles and values, which are spread by all the media, by newly-arrived faculty, and by the mobile students.

The national style and values have always had a more or less democratic component, which denied to academic and other leaders the deference traditionally given them in Europe and in other parts of the world. Presently, however, there is an insistent demand for the redistribution of dignity, so that students should have dignity—and presidents should not be pompous or overbearing. Their manner should be informal, their decisions consensual. If, as so often happens, the president *believes* in democracy, as well as professing it for public relations reasons, he may find himself paralyzed in responding to his multiple constituencies. In a benighted institution, faculty members and students may need protection against arbitrary action by presidents and trustees; they are apt to seek this protection by formally democratic procedures, since it appears natural to bring into voluntary associations the "one man, one vote" formula applicable to the larger political sphere. Yet at other levels of the academic enterprise, such a transfer may have quite unhappy consequences. Increasingly, students and faculty alike insist that no one else can speak for them or commit them to a program; representative government tends to give way to plebiscitary arrangements, and these tend to transfer power to those students and faculty members who choose campus politics over other forms of involvement. Students frequently regard such involvement as profoundly educative, as well as profoundly moral, perhaps failing to appreciate the degree to which they will give much of the rest of their lives to meetings and committee work; whereas their college years provide an often nonrepeatable opportunity to learn difficult new skills and to have some surcease from the pressures of vocational and political commitment.[9] In less contentious academic settings, faculty power vis-a-vis the administration tends to produce the regimen that prevailed, until recently, at Berkeley, where all pedagogic innovations needed the approval of faculty committees whose leadership tended to gravitate into the hands of home-guard men whose vested interests were often provincial. Even at more hierarchical institutions, it has been my personal experience that experiments in undergraduate education have found more support from administrators and outside foundations than from faculty; indeed, my colleagues had a capacity through committee supervision to veto experiments in education.[10] Furthermore, a faculty member who cares about such issues as disarmament and foreign policy, who has scholarly interests and educational ones, ought to be glad that the President does the hard work of keeping the place going, and seeing to it that the payroll is met, and that growth occurs in manageable rather than cancerous ways.[11]

My own preference for more hierarchical university structures offers only the not-always-available remedy of transiency in dealing with a narrow-minded or otherwise incompetent administrator. Yet, it seems to me that more often than not the university president tends to gain a broader horizon about higher education than most individual faculty members, simply because he must be concerned with the whole institution, and not with any single part of it. Still, faculty members who have paid no attention to the institution in the past, often rush in when there is a crisis to attack the president with self-righteousness and instant wisdom. The constraints on his actions are seldom appreciated by any one of his innumerable constituencies.

One irony of the president's position is this: the more attractive he makes the institution to talented faculty and, hence, the more distinguished, the less power he will have to continue to innovate because the faculty will take charge. One can watch this happening in many institutions, which might be called the "Avis" or second institutions of their respective states, at Michigan State or Southern Illinois or Buffalo, or many other places where dynamic presidents have built the place up, only to lose momentum and room for maneuver to their new faculty.

Because a faculty is a collectivity rather than a hierarchy, the ordinary canons of business or governmental management do not apply. Academic men are, on the whole, men who want to do their own thing. Yet one's own thing is, generally, also someone else's thing, or, indeed, the fashion of the whole peer group. It takes the awesome self-confidence and, perhaps, the private fortune of a Jeremy Bentham to believe in one's own thing, if one is not crazy and if others find it valueless. In the past, faculty members have looked to members of their own guild or discipline to test the value of their work, rather than to colleagues at the university where they happen, at the moment, to teach. But today, both inside the guild and outside it, there are fierce attacks on the supposed irrelevance of what many of us do. Such attacks come most poignantly from those we have previously considered our fondest allies, namely our young disciples and students. It is they who tell us that what we are doing and what our institutions are doing is, if not actively immoral, at least beside the point. If we are engaged in work which tempts fate by risking failure, we ourselves harbor such doubts from the very outset. Our radical critics are thus an echo of part of ourselves. In the past at many universities, the president has had to defend faculty members against right-wing attacks upon them as subversive. This more traditional requirement remains. More contemporary is the requirement that the president help to define the relation of the university vis-a-vis military and other governmental demands or temptations for classified research, military training, and other chauvinistic (or allegedly defensive) uses of knowledge. The moral and tactical questions involved here can be of extraordinary intricacy, with some presidents easily tempted into allying themselves with outspoken, antimilitarist students and faculty, whereas others feel that the moral course is not to put the weight of their own ethical and partisan judgments behind any particular position.[12] Whatever else he does, the president may increasingly be required to defend the esoteric against the popular, the long-run against the short-run, the uses of history, as well as the uses of sociology and political science.

For such intricate tasks, the resources at the disposal of the president are more his personal persuasiveness, vision, and occasional power to inspire, than his limited institutional armory. As I have said, faculty and students, as well as outside constituencies, tend greatly to overestimate the power of the president. Businessmen with little academic experience assume that the president exists in a more hierarchical, and less collegial, situation than is, in fact, the case. Some politicians know better, but make that assumption because it simplifies things or allows them to appeal to constituencies who see the whole world as more authoritarian and less fluid than it is. Students interested enough to notice or care, see the president as someone who can grant their demands or on whom they can bring pressure. The whole egalitarian, anti-elitist, and nonhierarchical style of contemporary America may see the president as a symbol of formal structure, perhaps personally decent but inevitably compromised.

The president has some power over the budget, but not much. In a private university, wealthy alumni may decide that they would rather give money for a dormitory or a gym than for a library; or they may prefer a hospital, which, until recently, was pretty uncontroversial. Some rich cognoscenti may help support the esoteric against the demands of the immediate. Occasionally, the president may have marginal power to influence the direction of such donations. But the Board of Trustees in a private university, and perhaps in a public one, often have more influence; and they must be allowed some occupational therapy, else they will mess with the curriculum or with appointments, or with buildings and grounds, thinking that the latter are outside the competence of faculty, soon discovering that faculty (and students) think otherwise. There are enormous differences among institutions in the degree to which the president has an opportunity to influence the selection of trustees or, at any rate, to help educate them over a long span of years. The appointed Regents of the University of California, with their sixteen-year terms, probably take a more dispassionate attitude toward the University than is the case with regents or trustees elected on partisan slates for shorter terms.[13] The University of North Carolina has something like one hundred trustees, each owing his appointment to a particular state legislator; yet magnetic leadership, such as the University of North Carolina has had, can rally members, even of so large a body, behind the University when it is under local attack.

State funds come generally to the institution, but, in the eminent universities, the major grants come directly to faculty members individually or in groups to support their research, or their institutes, or other enterprises. Much of this money comes from different agencies of the federal government, some from private philanthropy. Some university presidents, and many outside critics, complain that direct grants to faculty, over which the institution has no control, destroy cohesiveness and make it impossible for the administration to help shape the institution's priorities. Many of these critics are, in fact, hostile to all research which does not meet what they regard as a moral payroll, just as earlier unsophisticated businessmen have opposed research which appeared not to meet a pragmatic payroll. In my own view it is important, especially for the great state universities, to have the largest possible diversity of sources of support, including the vast and disorganized array of federal agencies. For I believe that freedom survives in the interstices of diversified sources of support, no one of which can be cut off instantly on the basis of a single political reaction to what is happening in universities in general, or in this one in particular. Under such circumstances, presidents will indeed have the very limited control Clark Kerr described in *The Uses of the University,* but this also means that no one outside group can quickly take control either. And, here, what the president and other administrators may be able to do is to help faculty members decide what they really want to do, what their priorities are, so that their own work, and that of the institution, does not grow simply by accretion but, in a measure, by conscious choice.[14]

The powers of the administrator are, indeed, marginal and peripheral. They are, at best, incremental, slow to become visible, undramatic, often frustrated. A president may find that, in defending the academic freedom of his most intemperate critic, he must lose the library for which he had hoped, the new chairs of which he had dreamed, or the scholarship fund promised but not yet delivered for underprivileged students. Not all presidents have to make such hard decisions as to what their ultimate convictions are; but I think that, in the times that lie ahead, there will be more such choices, as universities and communities become more polarized. The consequences of this polarization will be different for different institutions, depending on the local situation as well as on the national tides. If Meredith Wilson is to be proved right in his belief that education is not some sort of finite reservoir that can serve only limited numbers, then a college president needs to ask himself which among those numbers is presently most beleaguered and, therefore, most needs his support. In those institutions where the pressure is on to help the cities, to help the society, to help what is contemporary, the president may need to use his limited freedom of maneuver, and his limited budgetary leeway, so as to serve those not yet born, as well as those now alive. A library is as good a symbol as any of that not yet existent and, hence, voiceless constituency.

NOTES

1. For a penetrating discussion of the rivalries within universities as heightened by rivalries over sources of local and federal funding, see Betz, Kruytbosch, and Stimson (1969).

2. See the discussion in Herbert A. Simon (1967) from which I have profited greatly.

3. Carlos Kruytbosch reminds me that this scorn is not traditionally extended to management, at least of large and supposedly efficient corporations. Presently this seems to be changing, and all corporate leaders are presumed guilty of being organizational men in the invidious sense unless proven otherwise. Compare with my foreword to Stimson Bullitt (1960).

4. In addition to the Bolman study cited above, see an as yet unpublished report of research done by Harold Hodgkinson of the Center for Research and Development in Higher Education at Berkeley. Data on the background of college presidents is also reported in Algo D. Henderson (1960).

5. A number of men in the program have since become presidents, provosts, and deans.

6. See the Hodgkinson survey previously mentioned.

7. Personal communication from Alexander W. Astin, Research Director of the American Council on Education.

8. For a proposal that there be a Bill of Rights for administrators as well as for faculty and students, see Logan Wilson (1967).

9. These are obviously complex issues which cannot be done justice in the brief statement in the text. For discussion of some of the problems of undergraduate learning, see Riesman (1969b).

10. For fuller discussion of why it is easier to pioneer in research than in pedagogy because of the veto power of one's fellow academics, see Christopher Jencks (1965).

11. The study of governance undertaken by Harold Hodgkinson and others at the Center for Research and Development in Higher Education at Berkeley has found that faculty members feel happier and more fulfilled in more hierarchical settings in comparison with "flatter," more apparently democratic ones. This conforms to my own more limited observation.

12. Compare the addresses by the Berkeley Chancellor Roger Heyns and President Harris Wofford of the State College of New York at Old Westbury given at the 10th Institute on College Self-Study (See Heyns, Wofford, 1968).

13. To be sure, the ex-officio Regents (including the Governor, the Lieutenant-Governor, the State Superintendent of Public Instruction, and the President of the State Board of Agriculture of California) have, especially since Governor Reagan's inauguration, taken an active hand and tilted the Regents in the direction of those State Boards more traditionally vulnerable to Populist pressures.

14. See the discussion of this theme in the essay by Betz, Kruytbosch, and Stimson (1969); see also, Carl Kaysen (1969).

REFERENCES

Astin, A. W. (1966) "Research findings on the academic administration internship program." *The Educational Record* (Spring): 173–184.

Beck, R. H. and R. C. McClure (1962) "A university looks to the future: The Minnesota Conference on Higher Education." *Journal of Higher Education:* 496–502.

Betz, F., C. E. Kruytbosch and D. Stimson (1969) "Funds, fragmentation, and the separation of functions in the state university." *Social Science Information,* 8 (February): 131–148.

Bolman, F. de W. (1965) *How College Presidents are Chosen.* American Council on Education.

Bullitt, S. (1960) *To Be a Politician.* New York: Doubleday.

Dunham, E. A. (1969) *Colleges of the Forgotten Americans: A Profile of State Colleges and Regional Universities.* New York: McGraw-Hill.

Gross, E. (1968) "Universities as organizations: a research approach." *American Sociological Review,* 32: 518–534.

—— and P. V. Grambsch (1968) *University Goals and Academic Power.* Washington, D. C.: American Council on Education.

Henderson, A. D. (1960) "Finding and training academic administrators." *Public Administration Review,* 26 (Winter): 17–22.

Heyns, R. (1968) *"The university as an instrument of social action." Colleges and Universities as Agents of Social Change.* Boulder, Colorado: Joint publication of the Center for Research and Development in Higher Education (Berkeley: University of California) and the Western Interstate Commission on Higher Education (November).

Ingraham, M. (1968) *The Mirror of Brass: The Compensation and Working Conditions of College and University Administrators.* Madison: University of Wisconsin Press.

Jencks, C. (1965) "A new breed of B.A.'s." *The New Republic* (October 23).

Kaysen, C. (1969) *Higher Learning: The Universities and the Public.* Princeton: Princeton University Press.

Kerr, C. (1963) *The Uses of the University.* Cambridge: Harvard University Press.

Lipset, S. M., M. Trow and J. Coleman (1956) *Union Democracy.* New York: The Free Press.

Riesman, D. (1969a) "The collision course of higher education." *Journal of the American College Personnel Association,* 11.

—— (1969b) "The search for alternative models in education." *The American Scholar,* 38, 3 (Summer): 377–388.

—— (1964) "The oral tradition, the written word, and the screen image." Pp. 418–442 in *Abundance for What and Other Essays.* New York: Doubleday.

Simon, H. A. (1967) "The job of the college president." *The Educational Record,* 48 (Winter): 68–78.

Trow, M. (1969) Address at All University of California Conference. Riverside (March).

Wilson, L. (1967) "A few kind words for academic administrators." *Educational Record* (Winter): 9–11.

WOFFORD, H. (1968) *"Agents of whom?" Colleges and Universities as Agents of Social Change.* Boulder, Colorado: Joint publication of the Center for Research and Development in Higher Education (Berkeley: University of California) and the Western Interstate Commission on Higher Education (November).

CHAPTER 5

AUTHORITY AND IDEOLOGY IN THE ADMINISTERED UNIVERSITY

Terry F. Lunsford

To a degree perhaps unparalleled in history, the American university is marked by administration. The colorful "giants" who built the great universities early in this century are gone, and with them the simple cry of "presidential autocracy" (Cattell, 1913; Kerr, 1963: 29–36). But the presidents, vice-presidents, and executive deans who head "the administration" today do not find their actions or authority unchallenged. Indeed, they confront a more complex predicament than their predecessors. They stand as highly visible representatives of formal authority in a community long suspicious of hierarchy. The growth in size and importance of universities, together with increasing specialization, has sharpened the separateness of administrators from the rest of university life. Their authority is consequently mixed and precarious, combining strong imperatives to both legality and expediency. And they are compelled to elaborate ideologies where ideology is anathema.

The intent of this chapter is to examine some features of the situation of these new university "executives," their attempts to establish a legitimate basis for their authority, and some consequences of these attempts for the conflict that now racks many large campuses.

AUTHOR'S NOTE: This chapter reports preliminary results of research on the special situation of the large-university "executive" in the United States today. Its conclusions are based on (1) study of the literature on university administration, (2) direct observation of university "administrative councils" in several universities, and (3) preliminary interviews with a number of large-university administrators, designed to explore the issues raised here. I am indebted to a number of persons for criticism over the last several years, including Reinhard Bendix, Harland Bloland, Burton R. Clark, Troy Duster, T. R. McConnell, Sheldon Messinger, Philip Selznick, and Martin Trow. This work is supported currently by the U.S. Office of Education, Department of Health, Education, and Welfare, under Contract No. OE-6-10-106, Cooperative Research Project No. C-07, to the Center for Research and Development in Higher Education, University of California, Berkeley.

This chapter is reprinted (in slightly revised form) from *The American Behavioral Scientist,* May–June, 1968 (Volume XI, Number 5).

First, let us examine some of the conditions which have led to the current period of crisis. Bureaucratic, rule-based authority has long been insecure in the academic setting, due to its competition with a complex interplay of professional and consensual principles.

EXPERTISE AND ACADEMIC FREEDOM

Much has been written about the conflict of "professional and bureaucratic" bases of authority in organizations that use high expertise (Blau and Scott, 1962: 60–64, 244–247; Etzioni, 1964: 75–87). Universities are, in some ways, extreme cases of such "professionalized" organizations, since the acquisition and selective transmission of esoteric knowledge are the very essence of their mission. One consequence is that standards of scholarship and methods of instruction are the almost exclusive province of specialized academic disciplines, which expect and tolerate relatively few intrusions from "higher" officials or managers (Clark, 1963; Etzioni, 1964: 75–87).

Interlaced with the esoteric qualities of specialized research are traditions of "academic freedom," which tend to be especially strong in the major centers of research. These traditions cast a halo of uncertain scope over much of academic life. They provide an added reason for administrators to avoid trying to supervise research or teaching in any direct way—lest the detached perspective of the scholar be subordinated to official orthodoxy.

CONSENSUAL FORMS AND TRADITIONS

Faculty orientations to consensual government also influence university authority, and consensual forms constrain the acceptance of hierarchic, rule-based authority in administrators. The formal responsibility of faculties for curriculum, degree requirements, and standards of work is a collective one, held by the faculty as a whole and typically exercised through its elected "senate" and/or standing committees. Consensual, even explicitly political, processes are inescapably involved here. It is true that genuine faculty participation in campuswide academic policy is sorely attenuated in the large universities (where faculties may number 1,500 or more), and that much policy is being taken over by the separate academic departments. Still, collegiality survives in decision-making within departments. And, although the academic rank of the participants introduces a hierarchic element that is not without force, it is widely *believed* that the professional ideal of content-oriented discussion among formally equal professional colleagues (Kornhauser, 1962; Marcson, 1961) is dominant in many departmental decisions.

These present-day practices and beliefs are enhanced by long-standing images of the university as a "community of scholars," a "body of equals" without managers or even permanent executives. Such "democratic" models, drawn (with some idealization) from the experience of prestigious European universities, had considerable force during the confrontations of presidents and faculties a half century ago (Cattell, 1913; Laski, 1948: 348–360; West, 1906). They have not entirely lost their impact today (Daiches, 1957; Presthus, 1965).

"MIXT" AND UNCLEAR JURISDICTIONS

One classic response to conflicts between specialties is a separation of powers and jurisdictions. As suggested, this device is firmly entrenched in the university setting, causing some observers to refer to its "unique dualism" of controls (Corson, 1960: 43–46). But the problem of administrative authority is not solved thereby.

For despite their formal separation, "academic" and "nonacademic" spheres inescapably impinge upon one another, so that their borders and interrelations become blurred. Many years ago, President Eliot (1911: 443) of Harvard made note of those "mixt questions" involving *both* "science" and "a right proportioning of expenditures" in the university's budget. Samuel B. Gould, Chancellor of the State University of New York, has more recently pointed to this area—where budgets and institutional forms affect substantive programs—as the critical point of ambiguity and conflict between universities and government officials (Minter, 1966: 6). His remarks might well have been applied to the relations between faculty members and administrators (Etzioni, 1964: 87).

The problem is augmented by the very *absence* of a clear technical separation between faculty and administration in the processes of governance. The "academic senate" and the administrative hierarchy have their formal and separate existences on most major campuses, hence their "symbolic" separation as well. But frequently there is no simple and understandable division of specific responsibilities. A classic statement of this fact was provided by the *Byrne Report* (1965) on the University of California at Berkeley, an institution where both administration and faculty participation in governance are well-advanced:

> In some areas the [Academic] Senate is a legislative body making basic policy, which the administration then carries out. In other areas, the administration makes basic policy, and the responsibility for implementing it is left to faculty committees, either appointed by the administration, appointed by the administration with the advice of the Senate, or appointed by the Senate itself. In still other areas, the administration makes policy and also attends to the problems of implementing it.

SPECIALIZATION WITHOUT A SPECIALITY

Attempts to separate "administrative" and "academic" spheres of control also bring other problems. As his tasks become more specialized, the university executive must face the question of his own expertise in his own specialty. He can legitimately claim information and experience that his faculty colleagues do not share about the typical problems and specific exigencies of institutional management. And this is important for his authority in faculty eyes, because "competence" in one's job is what the faculty specialist honors above most other things.[1]

But the special competence of the academic administrator is highly precarious and contingent. In the first place, there is no esoteric specialty of "higher education" as an activity that academic men generally will acknowledge today and in which university administrators might claim a trained and systematic "competence" akin to that of an academic discipline. Second, no expertise in governance (or administration, or management) is accepted by most academic men as a specialty that might undergird the special functions that administrators have come to perform. Thus university specialists in administration today cannot convincingly claim, *as a group,* any distinctive expertise which might clothe their bare, formal positions with "professional" legitimacy. In the highly professionalized organization that is a university, this alone means that their very authority is always more or less precarious.

These facts lend credence to a fond faculty view (lately adopted by students) (*New York Times,* 1965) that administrators in a university properly should not "manage" at all but should simply act as "caretakers"— charged to provide the conditions that academics need for their work but which they do not wish to spend time maintaining. The implied lack of respect can reinforce prevalent prejudices against administrators' competence in general. Every campus has heard faculty members comment that the only academics who turn to administration are those who were not fully "competent" in their scholarly work or those who are motivated by desires for personal power and prestige (Petry, 1958: 15). Such ideas form important parts of academic mythology, and they take their toll of administrative authority.

These dimensions of the faculty orientation to formal authority have not changed dramatically over the years. But major changes in the social context of university administration have intensified the difficulties of the university executive.

THE IMPACT OF GROWTH

The rapid growth of student enrollments and faculty research contracts has brought in its train a vast expansion of the numbers of university faculty members and university administrators. Large *numbers of persons* are now involved in each of the two specialized types of tasks and positions.[2]

NEW DEMANDS FOR ACCOUNTABILITY

Moreover, universities are so highly visible today, so much more costly than before, and so dependent on state and federal funds, that they are coming under ever-closer scrutiny by government officials. This means greater pressures to justify drains on the public purse—to "cut the fat" out of campus budgets, to set "formulas" for state appropriations, to require that faculty members carefully allot their time among projects differently funded, to emphasize "efficiency" through "cost-benefit" analyses of university programs. Where once academic bookkeeping approached a happy chaos, today it begins to approach a business model. Where fiscal rules once could be treated as "mock bureaucracy," today many of them must be taken seriously.[3]

Administrators become the conduits of these newly felt demands to the academic practitioner, and they must search for ways of transmitting them in a form appropriate to the flexible and informal traditions of academic work.[4]

COMPLEX ADMINISTRATIVE SPECIALIZATION

These changes have helped to advance the division of labor within the administration and to sharpen the separation between "administrative" and "academic" tasks on the large campus. Faculty members tend more to be concerned with, and effectively control, the university's "substantive" or directly goal-oriented activities: teaching, research, and professional consultation. More and more, administrators find themselves excluded from such work. "Academic" vice-presidents, provosts, and even the deans of large campus units, although customarily recruited from the academic ranks, find that they must give up trying to teach or to remain current in their academic specialties, and must devote their energies *exclusively* to the problems of institutional support and coordination.[5] Other administrators lack the experience of faculty membership and bear "nonacademic" responsibilities entirely. An increasing number of university executives spend most of their time coordinating the work of other administrators and have little official reason for direct contact with either faculty members or students.

These forces have produced two related developments that are critical for university authority. One is the emergence of new patterns of association, and hence new group perspectives, within and between university campuses. The other is a symbolic separation of "the Administration" from the rest of the university.

DIVERGING SOCIAL WORLDS

University executives and faculty members are increasingly isolated from each other in their daily lives, while each is encouraged toward contacts mainly with his own "kind." The administrator, especially a "high-level" executive of a prestigious and fast-growing institution, is a chronically busy man. The sheer volume of the demands upon him, and the number of faculty members on his campus, make it effectively impossible for a vice-president or "executive dean" to meet regularly with any significant portion of the institution's faculty. Much less can he get to know many of them personally, forming lasting ties. Often, an administrator's duties require him to make official judgments about competing faculty interests, and he can no longer expect the free and collegial interaction he may have enjoyed with his colleagues when he was primarily a faculty member.

> He must cut the bridges between him and the scholarly community when
> he accepts the new post. . . . He no longer can sit with them in judgment
> to determine the fate of students; he will now sit in judgment on them.[6]

As a consequence, association with his fellow administrators not only is
necessary because of impinging work problems but also, in many cases, is
more comfortable.

On many large campuses, a dozen or so high-level administrators meet
regularly in an "administrative council," sharing perspectives on specific
problems of university management. Not infrequently, personal ties are
formed from these associations, and these may be explicitly encouraged to
help create a working "team." This group is routinely talked of as "the
Central Administration" by its members on some campuses.

High-ranking university executives also find themselves "marginal
men," (Park, 1950) destined to associate frequently with university trustees, state legislators, alumni delegates, federal bureaucrats, and other community leaders. Some accommodation to these groups' ways of thought becomes almost inevitable. Indeed, university administrators typically find
that they share with these groups common concerns for institutional "responsibility" that are frequently far less salient among their faculty "colleagues." Honest conviction thus helps to solidify the contacts begun in ritual courtesy and institutional ceremony. For some administrators the
respect and even awe accorded them when they meet the outside world as
spokesmen of the university contrasts pleasurably with their lower prestige
as administrators inside academe. These contacts therefore add their bit to
shaping the administrator's perspective on university life; he becomes more
aware of the "reasonableness" of many nonacademics' views.

Increasingly, also, university officials meet their opposite numbers in
other institutions away from their campuses, at meetings of the many regional and national boards, commissions, advisory councils, interuniversity
groups, and "professional" associations of administrative specialties. Literally scores of voluntary groups are peopled principally by campus administrators. Their meetings are at once Rotary conventions and "scholarly"
conferences for the participants. Some of the administrative specialty
groups work deliberately in these sessions to develop "professional" identities, and foster self-conscious sharing of "expertise" or "viewpoints" on
problems typically met by their members (See, for example, Nygreen,
1966). At other meetings, deans or presidents "represent" their universities, and the focus is more general. Here one hears speeches on "educational policy" problems, business-like discussions of relations with the federal government, and more or less rueful jokes about the problems of being
"hated by everyone" back home. At both types of meetings, corridor talk
and after-meeting conversations over drinks usually turn to the "politics"
of campus, inter-campus, or support-source relations and to the characteristic, persistent dilemmas faced by the administrative group to which the
speakers belong.

Through such interactions, confidences are exchanged and perspectives
compared. The participants come to realize (often with some relief) that

others face problems similar to their own, and that they, too, have haltingly approached similar "solutions." Thus the range of alternative administrative actions and postures is defined and shaped for future reference. *Group* processes and identities are established and, later, are maintained by long-distance phone calls, jet trips, and correspondence.

SYMBOLIC SEPARATENESS

The specialization of tasks, the restriction of associations, the visibility of executive status, the unwelcome burden of conveying accountability—all of these conspire to accentuate the separateness of "the Administration" as a distinct and even alien segment of the university. Significantly, this segment is peculiarly identifiable with a classic ill of bureaucracy: displacement of organizational goals by "the organization" itself (Merton, 1967: 199). Not only are the demands of the formal organization now greater, and "the Administration" distinctively associated with them; this often appears its *only* domain. Thus it becomes easy for faculty members and students to blame "the Administration" for all bureaucratic excesses, such as "red tape" or the constraints due to general rules. "The Administration" becomes prominently associated with growing "outside" pressures on the university, in many academics' minds. The symbolic gap dividing "the Administration" from the substance and authenticity of daily academic life is thereby widened, and this has its force in making the gap a real one.

A major effect of these changes has been to erode the informal relationships between administrators and faculty members, relationships which engendered and sustained the trust necessary for an easy exercise of administrative authority, and which muted the potential conflict between administrators and academics in the university of an earlier day. Radical shrinkage of informal contacts has also reduced the actual knowledge that administrators have of faculty and students—and vice versa. How have university administrators attempted to cope with their predicament? Several kinds of responses are typical.

BUILDING NEW CHANNELS OF "COMMUNICATION" AND SUPPORT

First, they have tried to overcome their separation from "academic" affairs by getting better information, "communicating" more "personally" with students and faculty, trying to remain involved in their academic specialties, even teaching a course occasionally. These devices help to re-immerse the academic executive in the activities and ways of thinking typical of the non-executive life, renewing his sense of the academic subcultures. But the pressures of time and of more clearly "administrative" work are strong obstacles. Overwork is one answer: A large-university president stated with evident pride during an interview that he spends most of his evenings and many of his weekends at "informal" social gatherings with faculty and students from his campus for the *specific purpose* of "keeping

in touch" and "finding out what people are thinking." Others actively cultivate personal friendships with representatives of influential faculty groups
—hoping that these will not be seen as "palace cliques" by those who are
not included.

More acceptably, dozens of advisory groups and "administrative committees" of faculty members are created to give assurances that administrative actions will not stray too far from "representative" faculty opinions. A
related device is the cultivation of oligarchy and bureaucracy within the
faculty itself through the proliferation of academic senate committees—
aided, where possible, by key faculty members of the committee on committees (Clark, 1961: 297–298). But these tactics also have their limitations. They must be handled delicately and with great skill, lest they backfire
in resentment against administrative "manipulation" of faculty government.
A safer technique is gaining much currency lately: the appointment of respected faculty members as part-time "special assistants" to the chief executive. These men help him keep in touch with the special problems of the
day and speak his piece from a vantage point closer to the "pure" academic status. This tactic is especially inviting where administrative "arbitrariness" and the legitimacy of authority are specifically at issue, as in the
"student affairs" area today.[7]

ATTACKING "DIVISIVE" VIEWS OF THE UNIVERSITY

A second response, complementary to the first, is to attack directly the
notion that there are serious divisions or social bases of conflict in university life. As Roger Heyns, Chancellor at Berkeley, has put it:

> There are in American higher education today many different competing
> conceptions of what a University should be. Let me list just three of these:
>
> (1) *The University consists of three power blocs.* These are—the admin-
> istration (including the Board of Regents), the faculty, and the students.
> The essential processes that go on in the University are those of power
> confrontations, of bargaining, and temporary coalitions.
> (2) *The University is an instrument of direct, social action.*
> (3) *The University is a public utility, existing to serve the needs of tax-
> payers.* . . .
>
> None of these conceptions of the University is adequate. If any one were
> to be given a dominant role, serious harm could be done to our free aca-
> demic institutions.
>
> I would like to urge upon you the advantages of considering the Uni-
> versity as a Center of Learning. . . .[8]

A variant of this approach emphasizes the *relative* closeness of university administration and faculty, as contrasted with the wide gulfs between
the university and those outside it, who may "intervene" if a common front
is not maintained. James A. Perkins (1965: 11) former president of Cornell University, has put this argument colorfully:

The administration and faculty must learn that they have at least one over-lapping mission, which is the internal integrity of the university—and the president and faculty that forget this mission will see their university become a gigantic intellectual mobile—put in motion only by the chance currents of air generated by the opening and closing of distant doors.

Another approach admits the existence of administrative "separateness," and the fact that it has consequences, but insists that its effects are good. Administrators are seen as academics who, by taking on themselves the problems of institutional governance, learn greater "responsibility." Subject to "accountability" that is "spread more widely," (Wilson, 1958: 4) they must "work through others, with others, and for others," while the faculty member has the luxury of being "primarily responsible for his own individual efforts and duties" (Sullivan, 1965: 314; see also Strong, 1963: 110–112). Thus the effects of "changing occupations" from academic to administrator are all wholesome ones, bringing some lessening of individual power and free initiative, but broadening one's sense of responsibility for the institution within which he works.[9]

When attacking "divisiveness" within the university, administrators sometimes use a style reminiscent of earlier philosophers of moral and social order, intertwining descriptive or analytic statements with normative prescriptions, so that "is" and "ought" become almost indistinguishable to the unpracticed eye. For example:

> Fortunately for educators who have administrative functions, however, most professors are dedicated both to their jobs and to the institutions they serve. There is no real antithesis of interests, as is sometimes found elsewhere between employers and employees. All who serve the college or university directly are employees bound together by many kindred interests in a high calling. In the final analysis, it may be seen that collegiate administration is essentially a teamwork function . . . [Wilson, 1955: 692].

Here is a blend of empirical assertions about the things to which professors "are dedicated" and normative prescriptions for the "real" interests of these groups, capped by a conclusion as to what kind of "function" college administration "is." Thus right reason and the opinion of "most professors" coincide to show both the moral and rational validity of faculty-administration "teamwork." Put another way, the implicit premise of such a statement is this: Since separate administrations are necessary for the university to do its job "properly," the "real" interests of all members will be served best if both faculty and administration try to *act as if* the separation created no gulfs between them.[10]

A somewhat older formulation was blunter about the argument for teamwork. The following description of "a proper division of labor" for the university, signed by "One of the Guild," has been ascribed to David Starr Jordan, first president of Stanford University:

> If we are to accomplish even a fair part of all that is easily possible, educationally, in the next century, we must separate quite sharply the work of

instruction and the work of administration. The prime duty of the occu-
pant of every college chair, and of those who are his assistants, is to give
themselves unreservedly to research, to investigation, and to instruction.
. . . Hence, the general policy of the institution, its relations to the outside world, its connection with secondary or preparatory schools, the requirements for admission, the requirements for degrees, the discipline of
students—all properly fall within the executive department, to be determined by the president and by the trustees; and a wise faculty will be glad
to have these burdens taken from their shoulders . . . [*The Atlantic
Monthly,* 1900; see also Brubacher and Rudy, 1958: 357 and n. 96].

BUILDING MYTHS OF WHOLLY "RATIONAL" DECISION

It is a short step from such a sense of "teamwork" to the conviction
that the administrator's decisions are always "rational" by criteria that
everyone in his many constituencies can share. This notion is prominent in
administrative myth today.

Rationality through "consultation." "Consultation" and "communication" come close to being absolute "goods" in administrative myth. Academic executives are acutely aware that they cannot determine the university's course by any grand "vision" of the future or by giving orders to
subordinates (Kerr, 1963: 37). But it is through "the consultative process"
that the administrator regains his confidence in the substantive rationality of
policies he determines. Harold W. Dodds (1962) has made this clear in a
well-known book.

> The goals of the consultative process are a wiser decision than the presi-
> dent alone is equipped to make, a wider sense of ownership in the decision,
> and a more direct responsibility for carrying it out. To treat it as a ma-
> nipulative tool for securing one's way is treason to the principle. It is also
> foolish, because the fraud is soon found out. The consultative process must
> be open and free. The knowledgeable president will see that all views are
> fully explored, particularly those that run counter to his own. This he does,
> not only as a matter of intellectual integrity and to save time in reaching
> a decision, but for the vital reason that, as discussion proceeds, his own
> views may be altered. . . . For once the president feels that all elements
> have been adequately explored, his duty is to decide and make his decision
> known [Dodds, 1962: 73].

Here is a "judicial" role for the university executive. After hearing all the
arguments, he must judge the outcome. But as official representative of the
university he is also an explicit party to the debate upon which he must decide. As Dodds makes explicit, a vital premise of this conception of decision-making is the notion that the consultation significantly affects the decision that the president (in this case) would otherwise have made. It is this
premise that tends to break down when administrators are seen by others
as carriers of a systematic "organizational" bias.[11]

"The institution" as an ideal. A second myth that has great meaning
for academic executives, and which serves to support the image of "rational" administration, is the concept of "the institution." Like the "public

interest" against which political leaders purport to measure their actions, it is "the best interests of the institution" that provide a "basis" or "criterion" for the decisions of the university executive. This imagery lends the unexamined judgment of the administrator a color of rationality, since there *is* a standard for his decision—even if it cannot be defined.[12]

The concept of "the institution" also effectively covers both "the organization" and "its goals," thus helping to re-integrate those two in the public rhetoric. After all, the argument runs, the organization is not really a separate "thing," but instead is a necessary prerequisite to "its goals." Any abstract distinction that obscures this fact irresponsibly ignores the hard practicalities of social life. The idea that "the organization" may "become an end in itself" by "displacing its goals" is thus dealt with (Merton, 1967: 199).

Consensus and shared interests. Often combined with "the institution" as a criterion is the suggestion that universities operate largely by "consensus" rather than by "hierarchy" (Millett, 1962). The implication is that strongly shared and well-understood values unite most members of the "academic community," providing guides to the difficult decisions that must be made.[13] While a university administrator often must make a final decision without awaiting a complete consensus, he does so within this value-framework, as the benevolent representative of "the institution." Implicitly, "its" interests are also the "true" interests of all its participants.

It is important to realize that the myth of "no hierarchy" and of unselfish concern for "the institution" is no simple conspiratorial fabrication: administrators tend to become convinced that it is true. Bendix (1963: 254–319) has documented the uses of the "human relations" ideology by industrial managers in manipulating workers. Direct observation of several university "administrative councils" in action suggests that this ideology is *implicitly* accepted by most administrators who participate in them. The importance of this fact is that it legitimates highly manipulative "maneuvering" (Sullivan, 1965: 316) by institutional executives vis à vis groups of faculty, students, or outsiders. As long as the end being sought is a way to make things "serve the best interests of the institution," whose welfare the administrators feel that *they* represent in a unique way, both legalistic maneuvers and openly adversary strategies against expressions of faculty or student opinion are felt to be justified.[14]

This innocence of motivation is related to the indignation which many administrators feel on hearing that their discretionary authority should be limited by "due process" requirements or by removing certain questions from their jurisdictions. From the university executive's point of view, he is the last person on the campus who needs "restraining," since the recalcitrant forces of human inertia and the halo of academic privilege already block the way to "getting things done" in his area of responsibility. He sees the administrative position as carrying a greater awareness of responsibility —meaning responsibility to "the institution." But he does not see it as creating a narrow perspective of its own or any special powers that might be misused. Much current student-administration conflict turns upon this fact.

No "politics" in administration. A frequent insistence of academic executives, especially when under the fire of radical student activists, is that the university is and must remain "nonpolitical." Thus it is denied that controversial matters of university policy—such as whether Communist speakers are to be allowed on campus, or whether discipline should be meted out to student radicals who have openly flouted campus rules—are at all affected by "pressures" from the outside community or from the students and faculty themselves (Williamson, 1965: 36).

Such arguments are supported by the apparently honest belief of many university officials that they have very little power—indeed, that they are not involved with "power" at all in making decisions about the affairs of others. As one state university vice-president said during an interview: "I really don't think of myself as dealing in power. My work is largely human relations." Another executive, this time a university president, said:

> Is administration a kind of politics? You know, I never thought of it that way. . . . No, in my experience it has very little to do with that boot-licking sort of business, or whatever you would call politics. As I've said many times, administration is the art of compromise.[15]

A number of explanations may be given for this refusal of administrators to affirm that "power" and "pressures" affect their decisions or university life in general (Mannheim, 1936: 118). However, one explanation is applicable to all high positions of formal authority. As we have suggested, the university president or vice-president is a highly visible speaker. He learns to expect that his pronouncements on the dynamics of university life will tend to influence others' views. Thus statements emphasizing the role of power in administration may return to haunt him if they encourage a belief that decisions can be affected by bringing "pressures" to bear. He may, in other words, produce a self-fulfilling prophecy (Merton, 1967: 421–436) about the role of power in administration, helping to bring greater pressures on *himself* from groups which ordinarily rely mainly on respectful requests.[16]

The uses of law and order. A companion element in the rhetoric is that university administration concerns itself with the impartial maintenance of "law and order" on the campus, without concern for broader political or moral implications of its rule-enforcement activity. For example:

> The University of California assumes responsibility for the preservation of law and order upon its campuses. The University deplores disrespect for the law on the part of any citizen, whatever his organizational ties [Lunsford, 1965: 67].

The implication of such rhetoric is that "law and order" are parts of a single concept, not meaningfully to be treated in separation. Administrative officials who mete out punishment to rule-breaking students, for example, are depicted as impartially determining what existing rules require in light of the "relevant circumstances."

Such theories of law enforcement have, of course, a long history. Whether judges "find" or "make" law when they apply and interpret rules is not likely to be settled soon; arguably, they usually do both, in varying mixtures (See Llewellyn, 1960; Cardozo, 1960; Friedmann, 1959). As to "circumstances," it is probable that every legal system has somewhere in it a conception of the "reasonable man," whose normal, "prudent" judgment provides an ideal standard against which the legal order may judge its members (Cardozo, 1960; Gluckmann, 1967). However, in the Anglo-American legal tradition such uncertainties are hedged around by requirements of due process, including a heavy burden of proof upon the rule-breaker's accuser and final decision by a tribunal that is institutionally independent of the dispute. These safeguards of individual liberty against the interests of order are typically absent in university "judicial" procedures.[17]

More importantly, university rules on many issues are very broad, and university administrators tend personally to be "rule skeptics."[18] Interviews clearly reveal the latter fact: university executives quite generally express a belief that rules should properly enter university life only as broad "guidelines," setting approximate limits within which most issues are determined by informed discretion and by the many rough compromises of "human relations." Rules rarely help the "major" university executive in solving the institutional problems he faces; accordingly, it is not surprising if he places little faith or reliance on them.

In fact, of course, even "middle-level" executives break, or "make exceptions to," formal rules every day—often in the interest of justice to the individual. For example, a student may be allowed to register late without a penalty fee if a family crisis has created "extenuating circumstances." Such judgments, not the rules themselves, are what administrators learn to rely on. Again, the conscious criterion is what will serve the "institution," that complex whole of individuals, groups, goals, and relationships. Rules are routinely to be *used,* as necessary, in the service of that entity.[19] And so are slogans like "law and order."

In the balance between "law" and "order," then, university executives tend to rely heavily on the latter—on that symbolic harmony of activities and rationales that is thought necessary to serve institutional objectives and the "interests" that they dictate. The broad, judgmental latitude provided by the *in loco parentis* doctrine fits easily within this orientation, as do current rules forbidding "conduct unbecoming to a student." Thus emphasis on "the rule of law" is primarily an appeal for "voluntary" conformity to broad understandings of the internal harmony that "the institution" needs to survive and prosper. This conformity is given the name "responsibility."

Two related strains may be seen in the university administrator's situation, shaping his responses to it. These are strains toward pragmatism and toward ideology. Both stem from his central problem: the inability to expect *implicit* acceptance of his authority based on his organizational position.

The university executive cannot expect that "suspension of judgment" which some analysts (Simon, 1965: 125–128) have considered the hallmark of authority. He must expect frequently to *justify* his decisions to important segments of the organization he represents and to its critical out-side publics. Moreover, he will rarely be able to point to a simple and clearly applicable rule covering the case that requires justification. Even the clarity of his "jurisdiction" to make the particular decision may be in doubt, because of vague formal authority relations on the campus.

THE STRAIN TO PRAGMATISM

One consequence is that strong "pragmatic" demands are placed upon the university executive to "make things come out right" for his organiza-tion in the eyes of its constituents or to step down (compare with Harrison, 1960: 234–235). He is forced to be "personal" and "political," rather than authoritative, in seeking to gain acceptance of his decisions, or even to remain in office. He must see to it that he makes few "mistakes" which will raise the issue of his competence and legitimacy to public view. And, when the inevitable mistakes occur, he must convince the majority in each of his "constituencies" that his policies *in general* are in the interests of all.

By themselves, these demands are a strong check on arbitrary executive action, requiring that the decision-maker take into account needs experi-enced by his constituents and their views of proper policy. But the univer-sity executive is under special handicaps in trying to stay informed of those needs and views. His constituencies are many and diverse. Like other "high" hierarchic officials, the university official is subject to defects and distortions of information due to his position itself (Wilensky, 1967: 43–44). But the forces that underlie the social and symbolic "separate-ness" of "the Administration" create more serious obstacles to a free flow of information. The restricted associations of administrators tend to bring them only certain information about university life and to shape the princi-ples by which they assign importance to what they learn.

Thus a premium often is placed on what may be called "political" in-formation: the executive's informal knowledge of his constituents' attitudes and of the shifting patterns of interpersonal influence within the faculty and student bodies. In a crisis, this information may comprise little more than an expediential reading of "what the traffic will bear." It is knowledge of what each influential group of individuals will accept if and when reasoned discussion breaks down and "political" stances become salient. The univer-sity executive needs it because he must be able to predict with some suc-cess what policies can be justified to his diverse constituencies before he announces them.

Such information also may be difficult for the executive to obtain just when he most needs it. His knowledge of the academic subcultures based on his personal experience as a former student and faculty member often is a major source. But these subcultures may have changed considerably since his last intimate acquaintance with them—especially the subculture of stu-dents, from which he is farthest removed. And his interpretation of those subcultures will be highly colored by the degree that he is involved in ad-ministrative tasks and immersed in an "administrative" subculture. During a time of campus crisis, when "political" attitudes are being sharply affected by events, the executive's isolation may be increased and its effects overwhelming.

By contrast, as noted above, the university executive can claim special access to some "information" by virtue of his position—the "overview" which allows him to see the total "relevance" for the university of scattered courses of action. As members of the official administrative "team," university executives will also be given specific information denied to others, including both complaints and expressions of support. But this information, precisely because it often expresses "political" viewpoints, also is limited in its use, because the administrator can rarely discuss it openly. Instead of helping the administrator, it may actually hamper him by emphasizing the very real but covert "political" strains in his position (See Knorr and Minter, 1965: 41–57, esp. 52).

THE STRAIN TO IDEOLOGY

University executives also find themselves compelled to become specialists in creating and spreading official ideologies. As visible, official representatives of an increasingly "public" institution, they are regularly called on to explain that institution—even to define it—to its many publics through speeches, through policy statements, through reasoned explanations for decisions made. Working with broad, vague goals and ambiguous formal relationships, university officials have greater need of the "normative power" of shared ideals and purposes than do the leaders of other organizations, such as business firms or prisons (Etzioni, 1964: 59–63). They have *special* needs for those "socially integrating myths" that help to hold the loosely coordinated organization together and give its members "a sense of mission." [20]

By focusing attention on such unifying myths of common purpose, the executive can help his institution to pursue "its" ideals more effectively. He also may shore up his own authority, emerging as a "leader" who expresses a sense of the enterprise genuinely shared by his followers (Selznick, 1957; see also Etzioni, 1964: 61–67). But this task is a difficult one. The university official shares with other busy executives the overwhelming mass of detail, of specific decisions and technical information, that continually threaten to overwhelm his working life (Corson, 1960: 60–61; Dodds, 1962: 59–60). He lacks the time for reflective thought, for "philosophizing" about university structure and purpose. His isolation from faculty and students reduces his knowledge of the problems that concern the "audiences" who will read his message.

The internal looseness and diversity of the large university, which make the job of the university ideologist so important, also make it more difficult. Only the broadest abstractions will reconcile the diversity of orientations among scientists and humanists, "applied" and "basic" researchers, those oriented to teaching and to research, political activists and political quietists—and the many other quite genuine divisions common to the large campus. Thus ennobling references to "the search for truth," to "liberal education," and to similar broad objectives have a strong place in traditional university rhetoric. Their very abstractness lends them the virtue of many possible meanings, which is no small asset in the complex modern university. But it necessarily detracts from their usefulness in setting institutional priorities. For example: *Which* department (among those searching for the truth) shall be given the two new professorships it asks this year? Which student "political" activities, if any, are incompatible with such university "purposes?"

Where myths will not "do work," will not help to assign priority among values and persons and actions, they are likely to inspire more affectionate or indulgent skepticism than solid respect and support. Where the issue at hand is controversial, and thus potentially divisive, there is always the danger that the latent ideological character of such myths will become dominant. They will then be seen widely as serving *only* to rationalize decisions made on other grounds, or to express the narrow interests of the decision-making group. These myths, too, may then become suspect as merely further devices to gird up incumbent officials' authority.

For the university executive, then, the two faces of pragmatism are paralleled by the two faces of ideology. In each case, a dilemma is posed by the inherently "political" dimensions of the university administrator's task. It is in this context that we can understand much otherwise puzzling administrative rhetoric, which treats "communication" as if it were a bland passing of technical information between specialists, and which denigrates the importance of brute opinion, doctrinal preferences, and existing relations of power. By substituting the *ideal* of rational discussion for the more complex reality of institutional decision-making, the executive often describes his own genuine *attempts* to find an apolitical consensus and his *hope* of encouraging others in that direction. But he is doomed to failure in every case where the stakes are high and the consultation is less than "open and free." Such cases occur frequently today, especially where the university's affairs touch upon the government and the controversies of the larger society. When they do, the rhetorical use of ideal-as-reality serves another, subtler, purpose—to draw a mask of rationality over the inescapably "political" decisions of the executive.

Some administrators, it appears, are unable or unwilling to face their situation in all its complexities. Many appear to believe their own rhetoric (Wilensky, 1967: 22–24) of impartial "rationality." When that rationality is questioned, when it is suggested that power relations and group pressures do influence their decisions, their response may be indignation. Some feel obligated to reassert their "non-negotiable" authority as living symbols of "the institution" they serve. Denial of conflict and affirmation of their own "good will" and rationality may seem the only course of action. In this posture itself there is much potential for conflict: during times of stress, the clear inconsistency of myth and political reality may make "that very myth" of unquestionable authority "one of the most passionately hated objects of attack." [21]

There are others, including many administrators, who believe that the large, impersonal American university must move toward firmer institutional bases, evolving a more humane internal legal structure and a more realistic involvement of both faculty members and students in governing the institution where they spend important years of their lives. If these things come about, they will powerfully affect the position and perspectives of the academic "executive," holder of precarious formal authority in today's administered university.

NOTES

1. Much of the large literature on professionals in bureaucratic settings has emphasized this fact. Official "faculty" statements have made it explicit: "The responsibilities of each group should depend on its own particular competence for the functions it undertakes." (See American Association of University Professors, 1962: 321.)

2. A recent study of university administrative growth concluded that contrary to popular conception on many campuses, the *proportion* of administrators to total faculty members has not increased notably, varying between 16.3 and 17.2 per cent over a sample of ninety-seven diverse institutions. (See A. H. Hawley, et al., "Population Size and Administration in Institutions of Higher Education," *American Sociological Review,* XXX, No. 2 [April, 1965], pp. 252–255.) Using a somewhat different set of definitions, the U.S. Office of Education has reported figures similarly suggesting a relatively stable proportion of "general administrators" to "faculty and professional staff." (See U.S. Department of Health, Education, and Welfare, Office of Education, *Faculty and Other Professional Staff in Institutions of Higher Education,* 1963–64 [Washington, D.C.: U.S. Government Printing Office, 1964]). However, the *number* of administrators on any large campus involves scores of persons at the least, and may run to several hundreds.

3. See Gouldner, 1964: 181–228. Gouldner used the term "mock bureaucracy" to describe those areas of organization in which rules formally exist, but are not regularly followed or enforced.

4. See Rourke and Brooks, 1966. For an example of the time and effort involved in such matters, see also the discussion and policy recommendations on accounting for "contributed faculty effort" in federal research contracts, Association of American Universities, 1966: 66, 80–81.

5. Some persons still play intermediate roles, of course. The academic dean of a college within the university may still actively teach, as will most department chairmen. Research institute directors, immersed daily in substantive problems and determined to keep their administrative duties to a minimum, are an emerging group called "managerial scholars" by some. (See Sieber with Lazarsfeld, 1966: 151–208; also see Etzioni, 1959.) Many senior faculty members find themselves becoming inveterate committeemen, doing "administrative" work much of the time, and leavening their "faculty" loyalties with strong doses of executive responsibility. From these ranks come many a dean or vice-president; from the faculty-committee "oligarchy" comes much support for policies of "the Administration" in times of crisis. (See Clark, 1961: 298.) But substantial groups of persons in every major university either are full time in administrative work and are effectively committed to it, or do as little of it as possible and have little sense of responsibility for it.

6. Address by O. Meredith Wilson, then president of the University of Min-

nesota, at inauguration of Ivan Hinderaker as chancellor of the University of California, Riverside, Calif., May 21, 1965. Dittoed text, p. 8. See also, Dodds, 1962: 25.

7. Even here there are hazards. One popular philosophy teacher, who was among those closest to local student activist leaders, later became his campus' prime symbol of the "cooptation" that "inevitably" occurs when one enters administration—thereby "proving" to the activists that "responsible cooperation" with administrators was incompatible with independent judgment.

8. R. Heyns, chancellor's remarks at a university meeting, October 12, 1966, University of California, Berkeley, Calif. Dittoed text, pp. 6, 7.

9. Dodds' discussion suggests one source of the urge for institutional aggrandizement described so colorfully by Veblen. For the administrator, Dodds says, "self-realization is attained in, and through, an organization. For previous reliance on himself as his chief source of ideas and center of action, he substitutes faith in the principle of organization as a 'conscious planned order of relations between men.' " (See Dodds, 1962: 71; see also Veblen, 1957: 167 ff.)

10. The relevance of Durkheim's (1933: 227) point about the interdependence of functional parts is obvious.

11. The assignment of systematic biases to administrative positions is not foreign to administrative theorists. So rationalistic and individualistic a writer as Herbert Simon (1965: 204–218) has pointed to the narrow "identifications" and "focus of attention" of sub-unit administrators, which tend to be "determined by their position in the structure." He urges trying to "transfer allegiance from the smaller to the larger organizational units, and from the narrower to broader objectives." What Simon does not consider is that a special, narrow "focus of attention" might attach to the position of the administrator whose concern is the "larger organizational unit" as such.

12. See Lynd, 1939: 188–189. See also Weber's comment on the "by no means unambiguous ideal" embodied in the bureaucrat's canon: "reasons of state," in Gerth and Mills, 1958: 220.

13. Goss (1963: 170–194) points to the importance of such shared standards of judgment in making possible "advisory" relations between physicians of high and low formal rank when discussing "professional" matters. This commonality of assumptions is largely absent among the diverse disciplines within a university as a whole, and between administrators and faculty members in many areas of decision.

14. Apparent examples of such manipulation for "institutional" purposes occasionally come to light, with what may be publicly damaging effects. For such an instance, see The Daily Californian, University of California, Berkeley, Calif., January 3, 1968, pp. 1, 16.

15. See also Kerr's (1963: 39) interesting formulation: "Power is not necessary to the task, though there must be a consciousness of power. The president must police its use by the constituent groups, so that none will have too much or too little or use it too unwisely."

16. A striking example of this may be seen in the use made of Clark Kerr's insightful book The Uses of the University (1963) by student protest leaders during the Free Speech Movement at Berkeley. While Kerr, as university president, was arguing his own good will and reasonableness, student leaders enhanced their arguments with his famous passages on the president as "mostly a mediator" among "power centers." Kerr may be the first prominent university president to state so bluntly and compellingly the degree of dissensus and power

orientation found in the modern university—*while still in office,* where he could be held to share heavily in the responsibility for it.

17. See the useful symposium on "Student Rights and Campus Rules," 54 *California Law Review,* I (1966), with a bibliography.

18. H. L. A. Hart, *The Concept of Law* (Fairlawn, N. J.: Oxford, 1961), pp. 11–13, 121–150. Compare Merton's famous essay on bureaucratic formalism in Merton, 1967: 195–206.

19. Michel Crozier (1964: 156–157) has emphasized the managerial "use" of rules and the desire of each group to create rules for the other while keeping its own sphere free to operate by "rule-of-thumb" skills. (See also Cahn, 1963.)

20. See Selznick, 1957: 152. Selznick emphasizes that such myths not only may help to preserve an organizational status quo, but also may help the organization to achieve its goals. His discussion of the relation between an "organization" and an "institution" is germane here.

21. See Rheinstein, 1954: 335–336, translated edition of *Max Weber on Law in Economy and Society.* Weber here referred more broadly to the myth put forth by "every highly privileged group" that its advantages are "deserved." The formulation is found, however, in his discussion of organized "domination," or authority.

REFERENCES

American Association of University Professors (1962) "Faculty participation in college and university government." *AAUP Bulletin* 48, No. 4 (December).

Association of American Universities (1966) Journal of the Proceedings and Addresses of the Annual Conference of the Association of Graduate Schools.

Atlantic Monthly, The (1900) "The perplexities of a college president." Vol. 85 (April).

BENDIX, R. (1963) *Work and Authority in Industry.* New York: Harper & Row.

BLAU, P. and W. R. SCOTT (1962) *Formal Organizations.* San Francisco: Chandler Publishing.

BRUBACHER, J. S. and W. RUDY (1958) *Higher Education in Transition.* New York: Harper & Row.

BYRNE, J. C. (1965) "Report on the University of California and recommendations to the special committee of the Regents of the University of California." May 7. Reprinted in the *Los Angeles Times,* May 12, and distributed as a reprint.

CAHN, E. (1963) "Law in the consumer perspective." *University of Pennsylvania Law Review* 112, No. 1.

California Law Review (1966) "Student rights and campus rules." Vol. 54, No. 1.

CARDOZO, B. N. (1960) *The Nature of the Judicial Process.* New Haven: Yale University Press.

CATTELL, J. M. (1913) *University Control.* New York: Science Press.

CLARK, B. R. (1963) "Faculty organization and authority." In T. Lunsford (ed.) *The Study of Academic Administration.* Boulder, Colorado: Western Interstate Commission for Higher Education.

—— (1961) "Faculty authority." *AAUP Bulletin* 47, No. 4 (Winter).

CORSON, J. (1960) *Governance of Colleges and Universities.* New York: McGraw-Hill.

DAICHES, D. (1957) "Education in democratic society: the U. S. and Britain compared." *Commentary* 23, No. 4 (April).

DODDS, H. W. (1962) *The Academic President: Educator or Caretaker?* New York: McGraw-Hill.

DURKHEIM, E. (1933) *The Division of Labor in Society.* New York: The Free Press.

ELIOT, C. W. (1911) "The university president in the American commonwealth." *Educational Review* (December).

ETZIONI, A. (1964) *Modern Organizations.* Englewood Cliffs: Prentice-Hall.

—— (1959) "Authority structure and organizational effectiveness." *Administrative Science Quarterly* (June).

FRIEDMANN, W. (1959) *Law in a Changing Society.* Berkeley: University of California Press.

GERTH, H. H. and C. W. MILLS, Eds. (1958) *From Max Weber: Essays in Sociology.* Fairlawn, N. J.: Oxford.

GLUCKMAN, M. (1967) *The Judicial Process Among the Barotse of Northern Rhodesia.* 2nd Edition. Manchester: Manchester University Press.

GOSS, M. E. W. (1963) "Patterns of bureaucracy among hospital staff physicians." Pp. 170–194 in E. Friedson (ed.) *The Hospital in Modern Society.* New York: The Free Press.

GOULDNER, A. W. (1964) *Patterns of Industrial Bureaucracy.* New York: The Free Press.

HARRISON, P. M. (1960) "Weber's categories of authority and voluntary association." *American Sociological Review* 25, No. 2 (April): 234–235.

HART, H. L. A. (1961) *The Concept of Law.* Fairlawn, N. J.: Oxford.

HAWLEY, A. H. (1965) "Population size and administration in institutions of higher education." *American Sociological Review* 30, No. 2 (April): 252–255.

KERR, C. (1963) *The Uses of the University.* Cambridge: Harvard University Press.

KNORR, O. A. and W. J. MINTER, Eds. (1965) "The Berkeley case." In O. A. Knorr and W. J. Minter (eds.) *Order and Freedom on the Campus.* Boulder, Colorado: Western Interstate Commission for Higher Education.

KORNHAUSER, W. (1962) *Scientists in Industry.* Berkeley: University of California Press.

LASKI, H. J. (1948) *The American Democracy.* New York: Viking Press.

LLEWELLYN, K. N. (1960) *The Common Law Tradition.* Boston: Little, Brown.

LUNSFORD, T. F. (1965) The "Free Speech" Crises at Berkeley, 1964–1965: Some Issues for Social and Legal Research. Berkeley: Center for Research and Development in Higher Education and Center for the Study of Law and Society.

LYND, R. S. (1939) *Knowledge for What?* New York: Grove Press.

MANNHEIM, K. (1936) *Ideology and Utopia.* New York: Harcourt, Brace.

MARCSON, S. (1961) "Organization and authority in industrial research." *Social Forces* 40, No. 1 (October).

MERTON, R. K. (1967) *Social Theory and Social Structure.* New York: The Free Press.

MILLETT, J. D. (1962) *The Academic Community.* New York: McGraw-Hill.

MINTER, W. J., Ed. (1966) *Campus and Capitol.* Boulder, Colorado: Western Interstate Commission for Higher Education.

New York Times (1965) "Collegians adopt a 'Bill of Rights,' say administrators should be campus housekeepers." March 29.

NYGREEN, G. T. (1966) "Professional status for student personnel administrators?" Pp. 125–137 in *Proceedings,* National Association of Student Personnel Administrators.

PARK, R. E. (1950) *Race and Culture.* New York: The Free Press.

PERKINS, J. A. (1965) "The new conditions of autonomy." In L. Wilson (ed.) *Emerging Patterns in Higher Education.* Washington, D.C.: American Council on Education.

PETRY, L. C. (1958) "A faculty view." In F. C. Abbott (ed.) *Faculty-Administration Relationships.* Washington, D.C.: American Council on Education.

PRESTHUS, R. (1965) "University bosses; the executive conquest of academe." *The New Republic,* February 20: 20–24.

RHEINSTEIN, M. Ed. (1954) *Max Weber on Law in Economy and Society* (E. Shils and M. Rheinstein, trans.). Cambridge: Harvard University Press.

ROURKE, F. E. and G. E. BROOKS (1966) *The Managerial Revolution in Higher Education.* Baltimore: Johns Hopkins Press.

SELZNICK, P. (1957) *Leadership in Administration.* New York: Harper & Row.

SIEBER, S. D. with P. F. LAZARSFELD (1966) *The Organization of Educational Research.* New York: Bureau of Applied Social Research, Columbia University.

SIMON, H. A. (1965) *Administrative Behavior.* New York: The Free Press.

STRONG, E. (1963) "Shared responsibility." *AAUP Bulletin* (Summer): 110–112.

SULLIVAN, R. M. (1965) "Administrative-faculty relationships in colleges and universities." *Journal of Higher Education* 27, No. 6 (June).

U.S. Department of Health, Education, and Welfare, Office of Education (1964) *Faculty and Other Professional Staff in Institutions of Higher Education.* Washington, D.C.: U.S. Government Printing Office.

VEBLEN, T. (1957) *The Higher Learning in America.* "American Century Series." New York: Hill & Wang.

WEST, A. F. (1906) "The changing conception of 'the faculty' in American universities." *AAU Proceedings* 7: 65–73 (March).

WILENSKY, H. L. (1967) *Organizational Intelligence.* New York: Basic Books.

WILLIAMSON, E. G. (1965) "Rights and responsibilities of students." In O. A. Knorr and W. J. Minter (eds.) *Order and Freedom on the Campus.* Boulder, Colorado: Western Interstate Commission for Higher Education.

WILSON, L. (1958) "A president's perspective." In F. C. Abbott (ed.) *Faculty-Administration Relationships.* Washington, D.C.: American Council on Education.

PART III

PROFESSORS

CHAPTER 6

FACULTY PARTICIPATION IN UNIVERSITY GOVERNANCE

Kenneth P. Mortimer and T. R. McConnell

American colleges and universities are under mounting pressure to increase democratic participation in their governance. "Democratic participation" is not a precise term; in practice it covers a wide range of beliefs about the relative roles of the individuals and of the groups and subgroups which comprise the academic society.

On the one hand, there is the principle of collegiality stressing community and consensual government. A member of an Oxford College, standing with one of the writers in a small quadrangle, remarked that "this is where the Fellows meet to settle most of the affairs of the college." That college had about two hundred students at the time. But in the United States, size, specialization, professionalism, outward reference, and a host of other complexities and divisive influences stand in the way of communal relationships. It has been said that collegiality survives in departmental decision-making (Lunsford, 1968: 6), but this is doubtful in a large institution in which the department may have as large a faculty as a liberal arts college —and a faculty split into many specialties and ideologies. Even small liberal arts colleges, with their increasing administrative specialization, are now seldom communities in any organic sense.

On the other hand, there is the proposal to assign areas of exclusive, and in some cases, overlapping authority to the principal components of an institution. For example, the student-faculty Study Commission on University Governance, established by the Berkeley Division of the University of California Academic Senate and the Senate of the Associated Students, was given the mandate to define "the 'areas' in which policy-making and administration 'should be delegated wholly to students or wholly to faculty or administrative officers'; and the 'areas' in which either students or 'faculty members and administrative officers' should have 'primary responsibility' with 'appropriate participation' by the other segments" (Foote, Mayer, and Associates, 1968: 1–2).

EDITORS' NOTE: This chapter was especially prepared for this volume. It is based on studies conducted at the Center for Research and Development in Higher Education, University of California, Berkeley.

There is a variety of intermediate positions. One of the principal ones has been proposed by the American Association of University Professors, together with the American Council on Education and the Association of Governing Boards of Colleges and Universities. These agencies have recommended that institutions should be administered through a system of shared authority in which all parties—students, faculty, administration, and governing board—participate, in varying degrees, in decision-making (AAUP, 1966). This system leaves open the opportunity for administrative leadership. (See a discussion of administrative leadership in McConnell, 1968.)

Whatever the particular and relative roles of the members of the academic organization, power has become widely dispersed. This diffusion has led to a situation in which, according to Mooney, neither the faculty nor the administration feels that it can take command. He asserted that the myth of communal governance conflicts with the harsh reality that the assembled faculty is no longer an adequate governing mechanism (Mooney, 1963: 49, 51). Faculty members turned administrators, on the other hand, often attempt to perpetuate another myth, namely, that they have no inherent administrative power, but are simply representing their colleagues in the decision-making and administrative processes. Attempts by students to infiltrate the power structure or to seize power in varying degrees compound the confusion. In practice, the governance of the university is a *pattern* of authority and influence wielded by a large number of groups or agencies both within and outside the institution. It is evident that the pattern is changing.

This chapter is an attempt to relate faculty self-governance and faculty participation in institutional governance to certain general organizational characteristics and to certain processes of democratic government in non-academic institutions. First, the nature and practices of governance in university organizations are briefly examined. This is followed by an account of the theory and practice of participation in democratic government in the polity. A discussion of governance in professional organizations and in industrial research laboratories follows. The chapter continues with a discussion of the conflicting roles of faculty members against the background of problems of governance in other kinds of organizations. A discussion of the effects of crisis on normal academic governance patterns is next. The chapter concludes with a brief discussion on models of university governance.

University Organization

Although most college and university governing boards have full legal authority over both the fiscal and educational affairs of their institutions, in practice this authority has become widely dispersed. A board may delegate a large measure of authority to its own officers and committees, to the president of the institution, and to the faculty. Diffusion may also take place informally; administrative officers and faculty may assume responsibility and authority with the tacit approval of the governors.

It has become customary to contrast the monocratic hierarchical authority structure of the business corporation with the collegial character of colleges and universities, although there is a trend in business organizations toward greater participation. Millett has said that in spite of superficial similarities in such matters as apparent hierarchical structure, specialized function, and administrative efforts to improve economy and efficiency, colleges and universities have little resemblance to business and governmental administrative agencies (Millett, 1962: 4, 27). He refers to the academic organization as a community. College presidents or deans profess to serve dual roles by retaining faculty membership while in administrative positions, and are expected to represent the faculty point of view to the board of trustees and the public. Millett and others hold that it is unfortunate and inappropriate when a faculty comes to regard these officers as administrators rather than as faculty representatives, or functionaries set apart from the teaching and research staffs. Lunsford, on the other hand, believes that administrators comprise not just a distinct and separate, but even an "alien" part of the university (Lunsford, 1968: 7).

In most large non-academic organizations, according to Caplow and McGee, the authority structure generally conforms to a hierarchical arrangement which is supported by a formal assumption that rank and capability are closely correlated. In a university, however, such correspondence does not frequently obtain. There a double system of ranking operates; the university confers the academic rank, but external agencies (the man's peers or his scholarly society) bestow what Caplow and McGee call "disciplinary prestige" (Caplow and McGee, 1963: 176–178). Power cannot, therefore, be tied to specific positions in the form of specified authority because this would result in the establishment of superior-subordinate relationships inconsistent with professional associations and peer relationships. The point is not that no hierarchical relationships exist in academe, but rather that an attempt to specify them formally would conflict with the informal conditions of authority and influence which in practice characterize academic organizations.

The result of this loose or informal authority structure is described by Caplow and McGee as follows:

> The system works, then, by distributing power in such a way that anyone who is able to exercise it may do so if he chooses. The product of this system is the university "strong man"—dean, chairman or professor—who converts his prestige, either disciplinary or local, into authority by enlisting the support of the men around him [Caplow and McGee, 1963: 178].

The concept of academic strong man runs counter to a traditional and widely accepted ideal of communal, consensual, or collegial relations in the academy. Millett has declared that consensus *ought* to exist between the several chambers—students, faculty, administrators, and trustees—of the academic community (Millett, 1962). Gustad points out, however, that

each of these "estates" is a conglomerate of subgroups, and that role conflicts within groups and subgroups make consensus in the community as a
whole very difficult to achieve (Gustad, 1966: 440). He argues that in the
absence of consensus within smaller groups, no effective consensus can be
achieved among them, or in the larger community which encompasses them.

The wide dispersion of power and a presumed—but mythical—norm of
consensual administration seem to replicate the conditions under which, in
other organizations, oligarchies arise. "Oligarchy becomes a problem only
in organizations which assume as part of their public value system the absence of oligarchy, that is, democracy. In societies where self-perpetuation
of the governing elite is the norm, few people will raise questions regarding
the determinance or consequences of oligarchy" (Lipset, et al., 1962: 3).
According to Lipset, et al., Michels regarded oligarchies as an *unintended
consequence* of democratic organization whose importance stemmed from
the lack of deliberate design rather than from any inherent value of the
elites (Lipset, et al., 1962: 2–13).

One might ask, then, whether the presence of academic oligarchies, if
documented, should be regarded as an unintended, but, nevertheless, ex-
pectable accompaniment of academic organization. The emergence of oligarchies would seem to require a revision of the concepts of community
and consensus which many academics, and such scholars as Millett, favor,
or assume to characterize academic government.

At this point some examination of the structure, the needs and the operation of democratic government is needed. The discussion will proceed
from certain theories of political participation and accountability to the
governance and/or administration of voluntary professional organizations.
In each case, the parallel with research or practice in academic governance
will be discussed.

Political Participation in Democratic Government

Research in political behavior has indicated that political participation
on the part of the general populace falls into three categories (Milbrath,
1965: 5–38). About one-third of the adult population are *apathetics* who
do not even vote. Another 60 percent are classified as political *spectators*.
Spectators usually vote, expose themselves to political stimuli, engage in
political discussion, and perhaps try to convince others of their political
views. Finally, the political *gladiators,* or activists, comprise less than ten
percent of the population. They take part in such activities as contributing
time and money to a political campaign, attending caucus meetings, soliciting funds, and standing for office. Participation in these three types of activities, according to Milbrath, constitutes a hierarchy of political involvement. Persons who are engaged in gladiatorial activities (see Table 1) are
very likely to perform spectator activities also. On the other hand, partici-

pation in spectator activities may or may not lead to greater eventual involvement.

TABLE 1

HIERARCHY OF POLITICAL INVOLVEMENT

Spectator Activities	*Transitional Activities*	*Gladiatorial Activities*
Wearing a button or putting a sticker on the car	Attending a political meeting or rally	Holding public and party office
Attemping to talk another into voting a certain way	Making a monetary contribution to a party or candidate	Being a candidate for office
Initiating a political discussion	Contacting a public official or a leader	Soliciting political funds
Exposing oneself to political stimuli		Attending a caucus or strategy meeting
		Becoming an active member in a political party
		Contributing time in a political campaign

Source: Milbrath, 1965:18.

Clark takes the position that the structure of faculty participation in academic governance parallels that of society at large and is apparently normal to a representative mass democracy (Clark, 1963a). Thus, the academic community is comprised of a few actives or gladiators who participate a great deal and who comprise a political elite;[1] a considerably larger group, the spectators, which constitutes an alert and informed public which participates modestly; and, finally, a large apathetic group which ordinarily does not participate at all, but which may under certain conditions become more active.

Eckert's study of appointments to Academic Senate committees at the University of Minnesota confirmed this structure of academic self-governance (Eckert, 1959). During a thirteen-year period, only 20 percent of staff members eligible to serve on Senate committees actually did so. Of those who did serve, 64 percent served on only one committee, 24 percent were members of two, and the remaining 12 percent were on from three to seven committees.

This general confirmation of the broad comparability of governance structures in the polity and in the university justifies a more comprehensive analysis of two of the groups: gladiators and spectators.

GLADIATORS

As indicated above, the existence of a relatively small core of political professionals seems to be an empirical fact of democratic government. There appear to be both organizational and personal reasons for this. Theorists have argued that the organization needs the capacity to make decisions and to act. However, the organization *as a whole,* especially if it is large and complex, lacks this capacity. At the same time there are *individuals* who are oriented towards the problems, positions, and rewards that governmental or administrative activity offers. This relatively small number of persons may coalesce into a ruling, or at least an influential, minority. Monsen and Cannon have summarized the factors which support the minority control groups as follows: (a) large size, which necessitates smaller, more workable groups for making decisions; (b) a monopoly over political and managerial skills; (c) control over sources of revenue; (d) the ability to spend time on the group's activities (Monsen and Cannon, 1965: 18).

The problem of size is an obvious impediment to decision-making by all the parties who might possibly be interested in the decision. Similarly, the control of sources of revenue, and the mountain of specified budgetary information that goes with it, constitute an important source of actual or potential control over the internal allocation of financial resources. Control over information and resources is one of the more commonly recognized factors that favor organizational control by minorities. For example, when writing about political parties of the early 1900s, Michels maintained that the masses are mechanically and technically incapable of governing themselves due to their large numbers, and that because of this

> . . . we are led to conclude that the principal cause of oligarchy in the democratic parties is to be found in the technical indispensability of leadership. Initially these leaders arise spontaneously and have accessory and gratuitous functions. Soon they become professional leaders and in this second stage they are stable and irremovable. . . . Who says organization says oligarchy [Michels, 1959: 400–401].

As the size of faculty bodies increases, so does the trend toward bureaucratization of the activities in which they engage. An example of increased faculty bureaucratization is the elaborate system of committees which characterizes the organization of faculty self-government. Another area of prime faculty activity which is becoming increasingly bureaucratized is organized research. Rossi believes that the large-scale research which predominates today requires more hierarchy of command and division of labor than departmental organization provides (Rossi, 1964). Interdisciplinary research institutes have evolved as an organizational answer to the department's emphasis on teaching and to the necessity for collaboration among scholars in more than one discipline.

Since a large faculty cannot operate as a collegium, it delegates, on the bureaucratic model, most of its work to committees. Serving on committees is time-consuming, and it would be instructive on any campus to discover what members of a busy faculty actually do the work. Is a very large part of the committee work performed by a few faculty members who make this their primary activity and consequently do little research or scholarly writing? At many universities this would be a violation of the institutional ethic —research productivity is the scholarly model and, consequently, the principal qualification for promotion. Since committees at most institutions constitute one of the major channels through which faculty participate in governance, and since committees and committee members often dabble in administration, it is possible that a study of committees would uncover a fairly large number of what might be called "professional amateur administrators," or "professional faculty administrators."

Some faculty members, after doing enough research to secure promotion to a tolerably high rank and salary, may turn from scholarship to committee activity at a later stage of their career. Nisbet has said that ". . . at the present time not less than 60 percent of all academics in the universities in this country have so profound a distaste for the classroom and for the pains of genuine scholarship or creative thought that they will seize upon anything—curriculum iconography, faculty politics, bureaucratized research, anything—to exempt themselves respectably from each" (Nisbet, 1965).

The important point to note is that the emergence of well-defined oligarchies leads to the creation of a class of professional *leaders*. The study of community governance in New Haven revealed that these professionals used their political potential at a high level and in the process acquired a great deal of skill and efficiency (Dahl, 1962: 305–310). Perhaps the most important resource of the professional leader is available time for political activity. He often has an occupation which leaves him freer than most to engage in political affairs, and is likely to acquire political skill both because he is motivated to do so and because he spends more time at it. In the case of faculty members, it seems almost tautological to expect that the "professional" committeemen will have gained the time for heavy involvement at the expense of some other activity, be it research or teaching.

The basis for faculty oligarchies is interest in faculty and institutional problems and the time to devote to them, experience in the processes of faculty government, and skill in working effectively through committees.[2] As the academic oligarchy takes over essential control of the faculty organization, it is likely to develop its own peculiar forms of irresponsibility, lack of accountability, and even oligarchic dictatorship. Once in power, an oligarchy ordinarily strives to perpetuate itself, or at least to perpetuate its dominant ideology. Some of the means of sustaining an academic oligarchy may be secrecy of operation, usually in the name of confidentiality; mastery of the formal documents and structures of faculty organizations; failure to report activities and decisions to the faculty as a whole (which, except in times of crisis, may be expected to accept this apathetically); and mediation of jurisdictional conflicts among faculty committees.

Although they may acquire varying degrees of power, the minorities which control the governance of democratic organizations are not entirely free to operate as they please. Political spectators act as an important restraint on their freedom of action.

SPECTATORS: THE POTENTIALLY ACTIVE

There are gaps between the actual and potential political influence of a citizen in a democracy, which has been referred to as slack in the system

(Dahl, 1962: 301). The existence and nature of these gaps is explained in the Almond and Verba study of the political culture of five different countries.

> These two gaps—between a high perception of potential influence and a lower level of actual influence, and between a high frequency of expressed obligation to participate and the actual importance and amount of participation—help explain how a democratic political culture can act to maintain a balance between governmental elite power and governmental elite responsiveness (or its complement, a balance between non-elite activity and influence and non-elite passivity and non-influence). The comparative infrequency of political participation, its relative lack of importance for the individuals, and the objective weakness of the ordinary man allow governmental elites to act. . . .
>
>   The citizen is not a constant political actor . . . he is the potentially active citizen. . . .
>
>   . . . the balance between citizen influence and citizen passivity *depends upon the inconsistencies* between political norms and perceptions on the one hand, and political behavior on the other [Almond and Verba, 1965: 346–348].

Political spectators comprise an important part of the democratic structure, and their *potential* activity in the policy-making process is one of the distinguishing features of a democracy. Characteristically, they feel obliged in principle to participate in governance and they perceive themselves as able to achieve results by such activity. However, under ordinary conditions, they do not test their actual influence by political participation, but are content with their assumed potency. It is in periods of crisis, great tension, or provocative challenge that they may enter the political arena (Almond and Verba, 1965: 350; Campbell et al., 1964: 288).[3] Furthermore, they may organize groups roughly comparable to political parties to promote their interests. This happened at Berkeley at the time of the FSM controversy.

The model of democratic government which emerges as a result of the existence of a core of professionals and a larger group of potentially active participants is called *cycles of involvement*. The model is based on the balance between the need for elite power and the need for an elite responsive to the populace (Almond and Verba, 1965: 305). For example, those who operate the government need to have enough freedom (or discretion) to act in behalf of the electorate in order to make decisions and to carry on the work of the organization with at least a minimum degree of efficiency. (See Boyer, 1964: 155 et seq., for a discussion of the need for administrative discretion in a bureaucracy.) However, the elite who lead in a democracy must be reasonably responsive to the expressed will or the unexpressed interests of the populace, or at least of the spectators. These conflicting organizational requisites are met by the cyclical involvement of the potentially active citizen in the governmental process.

Studies of political behavior in the polity have shown that in the absence of crises political issues have low salience and those who rule are able to make their decisions relatively free from popular interference

(Campbell, 1964: 288). When the situation arises in which a significant number of people are motivated to test their perceptions of their own political influence, the governmental leaders must respond or face the uncertain consequences of an aroused and participating populace. Theoretically, a policy adjustment is made on the issue in question, and the now active citizen can return to his previous position as a *potential* activist. This permits the government to regain its relative freedom to make decisions until another critical situation arises and calls again for accommodation.

POLITICAL ACCOUNTABILITY

Theoretically, the government in a democracy is elected by the people and is held broadly accountable to them through the electoral process. In practice, such accountability is operative only in that small minority of cases in which the rules of the political game have obviously been breached or the national welfare has been threatened. In the absence of such crises, the lines of accountability of the executive and of the legislature to the electorate at large become relatively vague and may be largely replaced by accountability to constituent interest groups which supposedly act in behalf of their membership.

Groups, rather than individuals, comprise the major part of the constituency of both elected and bureaucratic officials in democratic government. Congressmen are "lobbied" by representatives of groups who are interested in pending legislation. Long-time association with the programs of an organization or group of organizations has led to the development of specialized constituencies such as the "labor" unions, the drug companies, or the agricultural interests. Administrative agencies, as well as legislators, develop their specialized constituencies. The highly favorable public image acquired by the Federal Bureau of Investigation under J. Edgar Hoover is a case in point. Legislative attempts to restrict or redirect the activities of this agency almost invariably lead to protest from the Bureau's public and private constituencies. Perhaps the only federal executive department without a fairly well-defined supporting set of political interest groups is the Department of State.

In practice then, the citizen in a democracy either explicitly or implicitly delegates the protection of his individual interests to the various formal and informal groups of which he is a member. Governmental accountability is essential to these groups, which represent the collective interests of their membership. The point to be stressed is that in the absence of crisis, policy is made not by consultation with all possible parties but rather with that minority directly affected by the decisions. This view of the workings of democratic government has been summarized as follows in Monsen and Cannon (1965: 327):

(1) The threat of serious damage to the interests of a group provoke extraordinarily intense political activity which, coupled with widespread apathy, would vastly multiply the political influence of the group in question.
(2) Because American society is characterized by overlapping group member-

ships, a threatened group can multiply its influence through utilization of these affiliations to gain support for its cause.

(3) In most issues, there are many groups which do not become involved at all.

In the university the individual faculty member either directly or implicitly delegates the protection of his interest to some of his colleagues. The problem in applying an interest group rationale to faculty government is one of identifying the potential groups, both formal and informal, which operate in behalf of faculty members or which comprise the various faculty constituencies.

The formal academic structure of most universities is, of course, based on groups of faculty with similar *academic* interests. Departments, schools and/or colleges, faculty senates, interdisciplinary curriculum committees and research institutes are examples of formal internal interest groups organized to attain stated or unstated purposes. Informal groups and groups external to the university are confounding factors. Some faculty members belong to groups which, though external to the university, provide significant contacts with certain colleagues. Such groups would include the local chapter of the American Civil Liberties Union, a local AFT affiliate, a church, a political party or a professional association.

In the university, as in the polity, multiple group memberships tend to increase the *potential* influence of any one group. For example a faculty member may be simultaneously a member of the following internal groups: an academic department, a school or college within the university, an interdisciplinary research institute, a committee of the academic senate, and the AAUP or the AFT. All these bodies may be involved in a single issue, such as a curricular proposal, or in several issues at the same time, such as those concerning personnel policies, curriculum, and educational policy.

The pattern of accountability exhibited by a faculty member in such situations is a complex one. An individual serving on a senate committee is presumably accountable to his colleagues. In practice, most of the latter are not much interested in the committee's work, and the effective accountability of the committee is toward the minority group of faculty members whose personal, professional, departmental, or other interests are directly involved. Or, the committee may in fact be accountable to the administrative officer whose responsibility it is to make the final decision. In either situation, the committee may make only a perfunctory report to its parent body, the senate, which may accept the report just as perfunctorily. In committee action involving confidential matters no report may be made, or the decision may be conveyed without supporting data or rationale.

While faculty interest groups are likely to be more informal than those in the general political sphere, the patterns of accountability may be somewhat similar. The argument here is that, in the absence of crisis, a faculty committee, while it formally "represents" the entire body, exercises its accountability, in its day by day activities, only to the particular group with a specialized interest in the committee's assignment and activities.

When an issue before a committee becomes critically important to a larger segment of the faculty, or when a crisis or conflict breaks, the accountability sphere broadens. Generally, the more severe the crisis, the broader the area of accountability. But since such disruptions in normal operation occur infrequently, a relatively small group ordinarily holds governance in its hands. The same phenomenon appears in the governance of professional organizations.

Governance in Professional Organizations

Research on professional organizations appears to be relevant to the salience of specialized interest groups in organizational behavior and to minority rule in the absence of crisis. The relevance of professional to university governance is based on the assumption that faculty members are professionals, and that whether the term refers to professional academics or to professional chemists, engineers or sociologists does not make an appreciable difference in this analysis. Some of the data on governance in professional associations are briefly summarized below.

THE AMERICAN BAR ASSOCIATION (ABA)

Ladinsky and Grossman were interested in discovering the conditions in an organized profession that legitimate the actions of the association on public policy issues (Ladinsky and Grossman, 1966). They studied the role of the ABA, the principal organization of the legal profession, in the selection of federal judges and sought to measure the membership's acceptance of the actions of the Association's committee on the federal judiciary. The investigators found that there was a high degree of consensus (about 95 percent) on general questions of public policy, but progressively less agreement as issues became more specific; the same relationship has been documented by students of political behavior. They also confirmed the existence of an oligarchic pattern of organization similar to that described by Lipset, with two important qualifications (Lipset, et al., 1962: 452–453). In the ABA, the oligarchy's monopoly over political skills and the large gap in status between officials and members do not appear to be of great importance. As a matter of fact, most professional organizations are characterized by one-party rule and seldom attribute a great deal of status to their office holders. One might argue that, while it may be more prestigious to be a union officer than a steelworker, not much more distinction attaches to being an officer in the ABA than to being an attorney.

THE AMERICAN MEDICAL ASSOCIATION (AMA)

That part of Garceau's study of the AMA which deals with its internal politics is also relevant to the subject of minority rule in professional organizations. Garceau examined the characteristics of physicians who comprised the active minority governing the Association. Tenure in office in the Association was related positively to such variables as urban origin and status as specialists. Long-term AMA committeemen were *exclusively* from cities of over 100,000 inhabitants ($N = 20$ with terms of 6 to 31 years); 78.4 percent of the AMA Trustees and 75 percent of the members of the Judicial Council were from urban centers. The national AMA officers were drawn *exclusively* from the ranks of medical specialists ($N = 18$), as were long-term committeemen. The percentages of specialists on the Judicial Council and the Trustees were 93 and 90 respectively (Garceau, 1941: 43, 52, 57). These data reveal a remarkable degree of control of key Association officers by big city medical specialists.

Data on the governance of professional associations would suggest that if faculty are professionals, their associations (e.g., academic senates) should exhibit the following characteristics: (a) minority or oligarchic control of the governance structure, (b) one-party rule, (c) relatively little status attached to offices, and (d) homogeneity in the characteristics of the governing minority. These conditions, however, may not obtain during periods of crisis or strong controversy, or when a faculty becomes sharply divided over strongly-felt issues, or when the faculty becomes highly polarized politically or ideologically. In such cases the faculty is likely to organize into formal and/or informal groups in order to achieve political or ideological goals.

An important point to be stressed is that as a professional continues to devote his energy to the administrative activity of the organization, he becomes a *less competent professional*. Garceau, quoting Michels, says that the activist professional becomes *progressively unfitted* for any other occupation (Garceau, 1941: 64). Etzioni's statement is worth summarizing on this point:

> Most successful professionals are not motivated to become administrators.
> . . . Those "academicians" who are willing to accept administrative roles
> are often less committed to professional values than their colleagues. . . .
> From other studies, especially those of state mental hospitals, it appears
> that those who stay are often less competent and less committed to professional values than those who leave [Etzioni, 1964: 83].

The fact is, of course, that not all professionals become administrators, but that those who do develop an interesting pattern of accommodation to bureaucratic pressures. Such patterns are discussed in the following brief account of professional behavior in industrial research laboratories.

Professionals in Industrial Research Organizations

Professional authority is usually contrasted with administrative authority. After a review of the relevant literature, Peabody divided the bases of authority into formal and functional ones which correspond to the commonly held dichotomy of administrative-professional authority (Peabody,

1962). Formal administrative (bureaucratic) authority is based on hierarchical and legal position, while functional (professional) authority depends on competence, technical expertise, or charisma. Professionals rely on their peers for evaluation. The former value competence and consider it as their prime means of control. They stress individuality and autonomy in organizational relationships. Almost inevitably this leads to strains and conflicts among those who esteem professional but are in fact subject to administrative authority. These conflicts have been summarized in Table 2.

TABLE 2
SOURCES OF PROFESSIONAL-ORGANIZATIONAL CONFLICT

Scott [a]	Kornhauser [b]	Marcson [c]
1. Professional resistance to bureaucratic rules	1. The goals of the professional versus those of the organization	1. Goal conflict
2. Professional rejection of bureaucratic standards	2. Locus of control (hierarchy versus colleagues)	2. Role conflict due to different norms
3. Professional resistance to bureaucratic supervision	3. Incentives as professional rewards versus the organization's values	3. Uncertainties of research
4. Professionals' conditional loyalty to the bureaucracy	4. External versus internal influence	

Sources:
a. Scott, 1966.
b. Kornhauser, 1962: 12–13.
c. Marcson, 1960: 147–149.

While Scott's classification (Table 2) has general theoretical applicability, the ones offered by Kornhauser and Marcson have specific relevance to scientific professionals who work in industrial research laboratories. The latter agree that the goals of the professional scientist are different from those of the laboratory administrator. Kornhauser states that the issue of basic versus applied research expresses the underlying tension between professional science and industrial organization. Management usually attempts to quantify and measure progress in economic terms, like product development and return on investment, and this is offensive to the professional research staff because, among other things, management embraces a different set of goals. According to Marcson, the "other things" include role conflict which results from the fact that the corporation and the scientist have different norms. Essentially this conflict is one between the economic values of the firm and the needs of the scientist for professional recognition, equality in professional relations, and self-realization. Marcson's role conflict, then, incorporates much of Kornhauser's categories of locus of control, nature of incentives, and sources of influence. Marcson's "uncertainties of research" refers to the organization's need for predictability in contrast to the professional's need for freedom and risk-taking in investigation.

The conflicts sketched above lead some professionals to adopt organizational goals and control mechanisms and to begin thinking about moving up in the *organization* rather than in their profession. Scientists who become managers are more concerned with administrative considerations than with professional ones. *They become professional administrators of scientific professionals.*

One might argue that as faculty members desert their academic profession for administrative positions, they, too, become quasi- or professional administrators. They come to adopt a different viewpoint from that of "pure" or "professional" faculty members; thus role conflicts arise in the academic community (Lunsford, 1968: 9). These conflicts comprise the next topic of discussion.

Conflicting Academic Roles

There are full-time or nearly full-time university administrators, and also faculty members who do some administrative work but who are not "full-fledged" members of the administrative cadre. But such quasi-administrators are not representative of the faculty as a whole. This small but significant proportion of faculty share administrative values of power and prestige which include career aspirations strongly tied to their home base, loyalty to their institution, and a propensity to compromise. Administratively-oriented faculty members rarely include persons who are productive academically, and therefore their professional marketability is limited and they are closely bound to their administrative masters. Consequently, they specialize in acquiring political and administrative skills and in enhancing their own organizational status (Presthus, 1965).

It is important to note that in Millett's view, academic administrators are *colleagues* of faculty members (Millett, 1962). This implies that the two groups have the same value systems, e.g., the same regard for academic freedom, and a propensity to regard organizational questions from a similar point of view. Presthus, on the other hand, asserts that academic administrators, erstwhile faculty members, have become organization men. They no longer are free to follow their conscience and to protect individual autonomy in organizational relationships. The faculty's assumption is that those who become part of the administration change their academic reference group from faculty colleagues to administrative masters; in any event, this is what their former colleagues usually assume. Writers on faculty-administrative tensions have examined this assumption in some detail.

A former university president has summarized the varying tensions between faculty members and administrators as follows:

> The differences in the approach of the administrator and the teacher to the educational effort are due much less to variations in philosophy or conception of function than they are to divergences in vantage point from which the task is viewed and the responsibilities which must be assumed in each case [Newburn, 1964].

A faculty member has suggested three factors to take into account in examining faculty-administrative tensions: (a) background, training and interests, (b) personal characteristics, and (c) responsibilities (Petry, in Abbott, 1958). He concluded that faculty and *nonacademic* administrators have little in common in background and personal characteristics. However, the significant difference between faculty members and *academic* administrators is in the responsibilities of the positions they occupy. Academic administrators "like to manage," and this also makes them different from scholars. De Baum says that faculty members distrust administrators simply because "they are not like us" and they do not understand the true purposes of a college or university (De Baum, 1962).

Gustad found his explanation of tensions between faculty and academic administrators in role conflict. He observed that faculty members tend to assume diverse roles, a disparity which makes it difficult to achieve consensus in the faculty community (Gustad, 1966: 441–443). He classified faculty reference groups as being primarily oriented toward students, toward faculty colleagues, or toward administrators. He went on to classify faculty members into six different groups presented in Table 3.

A faculty member as *scholar* is primarily a man of learning who regards himself not as an employee but as an enfranchised citizen of the academic community. A faculty member may play the role of *curriculum adviser,* while still another may become an individual *entrepreneur* who is capable of a great deal of independence in organizational relationships because of outside sources of support. Some faculty members are continually off-campus serving as *consultants.* Others are primarily *administrators,* and still others are *cosmopolitans* who are oriented to a professional reference group mainly external to the institution.

Gouldner stressed the importance of three organizationally relevant variables in his examination of faculty orientations: (a) loyalty to the employing organization, (b) commitment to specialized or professional skills, (c) reference group orientation (Gouldner, 1957, 1958). His typologies are also presented in Table 3.

TABLE 3
A SUMMARY OF FACULTY ORIENTATIONS

Cultures [a]	*Orientations* [b]	*Roles* [c]
1. The teacher	1. Locals	1. Scholar
2. The scholar-researcher	a. the dedicated	2. Curriculum adviser
3. The demonstrator	b. the true bureaucrat	3. Entrepreneur
4. The consultant	c. the homeguard	4. Consultant
	d. the elders	5. Administrator
	2. Cosmopolitans	6. Cosmopolitan
	a. the outsiders	
	b. the empire builders	

Sources:
a. Clark, 1963.
b. Gouldner, 1958.
c. Gustad, 1966, 441–443.

Cosmopolitans are likely to be low on loyalty to the organization, high on commitment to specialized professional skills, and more likely to identify with external than with internal groups. The outsiders are not personally close either to faculty or students, and participate very little in the formal structure of the college. The empire builders are committed to specific academic departments, but retain a sense of economic independence. They are somewhat integrated into the formal structure of the college or university. Locals, when compared to cosmopolitans, are likely to be high on loyalty to the institution, low on commitment to specialized or professional skills, and more oriented toward an inner reference group. The dedicated have a stronger commitment to the institution and its values than to specialized professional or scholarly roles within it. For example, they are more likely to support interdisciplinary studies than their colleagues who have a strong attachment to a specialized discipline. The true bureaucrat tends to emphasize formal regulations and to be formally oriented to the college per se, rather than to the inherent values it represents. The homeguard are the least occupationally specialized, have only limited advanced scholarly training, and tend to be second-rung administrators. The elders are the oldest members of the community in age and service and are oriented primarily to an informal peer group, i.e., other elders.

Table 3 also refers to Clark's identification of four subcultures in the general body of a university faculty (Clark, 1963b). The concept of faculty subcultures is one which also embodies the idea of varying reference groups or orientations to academic life. The teacher refers to the stereotypic Mr. Chips who is devoted to his students and general education. The scholar-researcher is the chemist or biologist who is totally involved in his laboratory. The demonstrator is the vocationally oriented faculty member who shows his students how to acquire a specific set of vocational skills. He is often a part-time practitioner as well. The consultant is the faculty member with a national reputation who spends half his time in airplanes rather than in residence on the campus.

What roles do cosmopolitans and locals play in the operation of the institution? To which group or subgroup do administrators belong? Gouldner (1957, 1958) found that in the college he studied (a) the outsiders were least likely to be administrators; (b) empire builders were as likely to be researchers as teachers, and less likely to be administrators; (c) the dedicated, the true bureaucrats, the homeguard were most likely to be administrators and least likely to be researchers. These findings suggest that locals are likely to participate more frequently than cosmopolitans in faculty and campus governance; for example, to spend a large amount of time in committee work (not only because they may have more time for such activity, but because they differ in personal characteristics and orientations from those who are more committed to their disciplines, their research, or their professional societies). These participants may engage in minor administrative activities, or become "faculty administrators." While professing still to be scholars, they may in fact become what were referred to above as "professional amateur administrators." Some of them probably end up with administrative titles.

Summary

The rise of oligarchies or ruling elites is a normal phenomenon in democratic politics, in professional associations, and in academe. Oligarchies are encouraged and sustained by the increasing size and complexity of academic organizations, minority control over information and resources, general political apathy in the absence of crisis, wide dispersal of authority and/or power, conflicting roles and interests of groups and subgroups, and orientation to external reference groups.

The emergence of ruling elites, together with the necessity of decision-making on a day-to-day or long-term basis, favors the creation of a class of professional leaders who either become the ubiquitous committeemen, faculty-administrators, or full-time administrators.

The oligarchs walk a tight line between their constituencies (often special interest groups or subcultures rather than the faculty membership as a whole) and their administrative superiors. Except in periods of crisis, the "rulers" may pay little attention to the principle of general accountability and may be able to operate in relative secrecy.

In academic organizations, as in industrial research laboratories, tension or even conflict between those who esteem professional or scholarly competence and those who exercise administrative authority is the normal expectation. This conflict is the product of such factors as disparate roles and values, different reference groups, and different personal orientations. While the myth of colleagueship persists in universities and in some other kinds of organizations, there is almost inevitable tension between professionals and administrators.

EFFECTS OF CRISIS ON THE NORMAL PATTERN OF GOVERNANCE

The normal pattern of academic governance described in this chapter is severely strained in times of crisis. Both the Free Speech Movement (FSM) at Berkeley and the Columbia sit-ins temporarily jolted the faculty majority out of their apathy towards university affairs. At Berkeley attendance at Academic Senate meetings skyrocketed during crises, and at Columbia, where there was no central faculty Senate, an Ad Hoc Faculty Group (AHFG) began to hold meetings (Cox Commission, 1968).

The faculty at large began to seek new and direct powers to settle these crises. The Emergency Executive Committee of the Academic Senate at Berkeley was directed to negotiate between all parties to the dispute. The AHFG at Columbia sought to insert itself between the administration and the students. These new relationships and groupings were not independent of oligarchic and seniority patterns which existed before the crisis. At Columbia junior faculty were allowed to attend and vote at AHFG meetings, a privilege which was not a part of faculty government in the constituent colleges at Columbia, but negotiations were still handled by the senior faculty. The Committee of 200, which emerged during the FSM at Berkeley, did not win control of the Emergency Executive Committee from the moderates.

Crisis is also likely to increase the amount of formal and informal political activity that goes on in the faculty community. Conflicts will tend to heighten the tension involved in these political relationships. One could expect that the gladiators would continue to be intensively involved and that some of the political spectators would also be motivated to move into the arena. Some of the leading intellectual figures on any campus will probably leave their laboratories and begin to test the responsiveness of the system and their own ability to influence the course of events through increased participation.

As pointed out in this paper, one can expect that the ruling elite or oligarchy which controls faculty governance will operate relatively free of detailed requirements of accountability to the general faculty and will develop its own limited constituencies. In times of crisis, oligarchies will respond in some fashion to the demands expressed by those who precipitate the crisis or form the opposition. Depending on the severity of the crisis, new people will become involved in the governance process and some of them may even become a permanent part of a new oligarchy. However, although the faces may change, the dominant ideology is likely to survive. In the meantime, most of the political spectators will not remain permanently knowledgeable about or involved in the controversial issues but will return to their formal state of partial or potential political awareness.

It is important to note that there is little practical or theoretical reason to expect changes in the value structures or priorities in a pluralist political system or in the ruling elite as a result of crises which fall short of a revolution or coup. Pluralist political theory, such as that described in this paper, does not predict that crises will substantially change the value priorities of the system, but rather it does predict that the ruling elite will be sensitive to some of the dissent expressed in crises and that some adjustments will be made when these conflicts occur. A central question becomes what model of governance will best ensure that the ruling elite will be responsive to the broad community of interests over which it reigns?

WHAT MODEL OF THE UNIVERSITY?

The debate over competing models of the university, such as those cited earlier on separate jurisdictions as opposed to shared authority, should be conducted in the light of administrative-political "realities." There are competing needs in a multiversity which require a governance structure which provides for an acceptable degree of administrative efficiency together with a degree of responsiveness to constituent groupings, be they either majoritarian or minority based. The advantages of oligarchic control of faculty governance structures tend to be in the area of administrative efficiency. Its disadvantages are likely to be its unresponsiveness to the wide range of faculty groupings and values which permeate academe. The presence of academic conformity and the reality of academic self-interests are likely to result in a governing elite which is not representative of the divergent minority viewpoints present in the system as a whole.

Given these "realities," it is difficult to see how the maintenance of strictly separate faculty and administrative areas of jurisdiction will do anything but perpetuate control of faculty governance by the ruling elite. Furthermore, exclusion or mere "token" inclusion of minority viewpoints from faculty decision-making structures sets the stage for faculty-administrative relationships based on an adversary principle. A system of separate areas or jurisdictions also does not appear to take into consideration the need for administrative efficiency which is necessary to the management of a large bureaucracy.

On the other hand, attempts to create consensus and communal feelings based on majoritarian values which do not reflect the basically different values of articulate and well-informed minorities make it "necessary" for the minorities to precipitate incidents if their views are to gain adequate consideration. As stated earlier, communal or consensual organization is no longer, if it ever was, an adequate response to the conditions of size, scale and diversity of values which confront contemporary multiversities.

A more promising model of university governance is the one embodied in the principle of shared authority between faculty, administrative officers and, where appropriate, students. The concept of shared authority provides for full participation in policy matters by all parties involved in the decision-making process.

The requisites of shared authority are not satisfied by mere discussion between the administration and a faculty oligarchy. Whatever accommodations are to be made in a given situation must be made through formal or informal processes which are representative of as many constituent groupings as possible. The opposition to the faculty majority must be involved in the resolution of the problem and the problem must be considered on its *educational* merits as well as on its administrative, budgetary and political feasibility. There are also some structural mechanisms which should be a part of the system of shared authority.

First, decision-making structures in both the faculty and administrative bureaucracies should be as open as possible. If committees are appointed, care should be taken to ensure that they reflect a wide range of *viewpoints*. In personnel cases the individual should always be told why he is not being retained or promoted. There should be periodic, open and substantive discussions of the criteria on which such personnel and other educational policy decisions are based.

Second, the existence of conflict within the faculty and between the faculty and the administration on any issue should be acknowledged and the *educational* relevance of these differences should be the basis of broad substantive discussions. The model of democratic governance which was discussed in this paper assumes that there will be conflict, or at least, vigorous controversy in the faculty. Some of this conflict will be over what a university should do, some over conflicting academic roles or different orientations to academic life. These conflicts should be overt ones directed towards the substance of the educational issues involved, not covert discussions among a small cadre of ruling faculty elders.

Thirdly, it is difficult to overstate the need for increased sensitivity on the part of the ruling faculty elders and the administration towards the views and the divergent values which exist in a multiversity. Those in positions of power must respond *visibly* to the internal pressures of various groupings if the legitimacy and viability of existing governance structures are to be sustained and if change is to be orderly rather than precipitous.

NOTES

1. The terms "leader," "oligarchy," "political elite," or "ruling minority," as used in this chapter, are for descriptive purposes only. No evaluative overtones are intended.

2. Dykes' research identified three reasons for greater faculty participation: (1) special competence, (2) protection of special interests, and (3) special ties with the administration (Dykes, 1968: 20–21).

3. The Campbell reference is to the low salience of most political issues to the general public.

REFERENCES

AAUP (1966) "Statement on Government of Colleges and Universities," by American Association of University Professors, American Council on Education, and Association of Governing Boards of Colleges and Universities. *AAUP Bulletin* 52 (December): 375–379.

ALMOND, GABRIEL A., and SIDNEY VERBA (1965) *The Civic Culture.* Boston: Little, Brown.

BOYER, WILLIAM W. (1964) *Bureaucracy on Trial.* Indianapolis: Bobbs-Merrill.

CAMPBELL, ANGUS, et al. (1964) *The American Voter.* New York: John Wiley.

CAPLOW, THEODORE, and REECE J. McGEE (1963) *The Academic Marketplace.* Garden City, New York: Anchor Books.

CLARK, BURTON R. (1963a) "Faculty organization and authority." Pp. 37–51 in T. F. Lunsford (ed.) *The Study of Academic Administration.* Boulder, Colorado: Western Interstate Commission for Higher Education.

—— (1963b) "Faculty culture." In *The Study of Campus Cultures.* Boulder, Colorado: Western Interstate Commission for Higher Education.

Cox Commission Report (1968) *Crisis at Columbia.* New York: Vintage Books.

DAHL, ROBERT A. (1962) *Who Governs?* New Haven, Connecticut: Yale University Press.

DE BAUM, VINCENT C. (1962) "The faculty as administrative seedbed." *The Educational Record* 43 (April): 158–162.

DYKES, ARCHIE R. (1968) *Faculty Participation in Academic Decision Making.* Washington, D.C.: American Council on Education.

ECKERT, RUTH (1959) "The share of the teaching faculty in university policymaking." *AAUP Bulletin* 45 (Autumn): 346–351.

ETZIONI, AMITAI (1964) *Modern Organizations.* Englewood Cliffs: Prentice-Hall.

FOOTE, CALEB, HENRY MAYER, et al. (1968) *The Culture of the University: Governance and Education.* San Francisco: Jossey-Bass.

GARCEAU, OLIVER (1941) *The Political Life of the American Medical Association.* Cambridge: Harvard University Press.

GOULDNER, ALVIN W. (1957) "Cosmopolitans and locals: toward an analysis of latent social rules." Part I. *Administrative Science Quarterly* 2 (December): 281–307.

—— (1958) "Cosmopolitans and locals: toward an analysis of latent social rules." Part II. *Administrative Science Quarterly* 2 (March): 444–480.

GUSTAD, JOHN W. (1966) "Community consensus and conflict." *The Educational Record* 47 (Fall).

KORNHAUSER, W. (1962) *Scientists in Industry.* Berkeley: University of California Press.

LADINSKY, JACK, and JOEL B. GROSSMAN (1966) "Organizational consequences of professional consensus: lawyers and selection of judges." *Administrative Science Quarterly* 11 (June): 78–106.

LIPSET, SEYMOUR M. et al. (1962) *Union Democracy.* Garden City, New York: Anchor Books.

LUNSFORD, TERRY, Ed. (1963) *The Study of Academic Administration.* Boulder, Colorado: Western Interstate Commission on Higher Education.

—— (1968) "Authority and ideology in the administered university." *American Behavioral Scientist* 11 (May–June).

MCCONNELL, T. R. (1968) "The function of leadership in academic institutions." *The Educational Record* 49 (Spring): 145–153.

MARCSON, S. (1960) *The Scientist in American Industry.* Princeton: Department of Economics.

MICHELS, ROBERT (1959) *Political Parties.* New York: Dover Publications.

MILBRATH, LESTER W. (1965) *Political Participation.* Chicago: Rand McNally.

MILLETT, JOHN D. (1962) *The Academic Community.* New York: McGraw-Hill.

MONSEN, R. JOSEPH, and MARK W. CANNON (1965) *The Makers of Public Policy.* New York: McGraw-Hill.

MOONEY, ROSS L. (1963) "The problem of leadership in the university." *Harvard Educational Review* 33 (Winter).

NEWBURN, H. K. (1964) "Faculty and administration in the governance of the university." *The Educational Record* 45 (Summer): 258.

NISBET, R. A. (1965) "What is an intellectual?" *Commentary* 40 (March): 93–101.

PEABODY, ROBERT (1962) "Perceptions of organizational authority: a comparative analysis." *Administrative Science Quarterly* 6 (March): 463–482.

PETRY, LOREN C. (1958) "A faculty view." Pp. 12–20 in Frank C. Abbott (ed.) *Faculty-Administration Relationships.* Washington, D.C.: American Council on Education.

PRESTHUS, ROBERT (1965) "University bosses: the executive conquest of academe." *The New Republic* 152 (February 20): 20–24.

ROSSI, PETER (1964) "Researchers, scholars and policy makers—the politics of large scale research." *Daedalus* 93 (Fall): 1142–1161.

SCOTT, R. R. (1966) "Professional and complex organizations." Pp. 265–275 in Vollmer and Mills (eds.) *Professionalization.* Englewood Cliffs: Prentice-Hall.

CHAPTER 7

DECISION-MAKING IN THE ACADEMIC SYSTEM
Influence and Power Exchange

Gerald M. Platt and Talcott Parsons

This chapter presents a theoretical orientation toward, and an empirical view of, the decision-making process in the American academic system. The data reported here were gathered in the spring of 1965. Originally these materials were part of a larger but limitedly circulated report on the pilot phase of our research on higher education.[1] That report was written in 1966–1967 after the Free Speech Movement at Berkeley, but before the more recent events of Columbia, San Francisco State, Cornell, and Harvard.

We believe that the theoretical orientation developed at that time is still essentially correct and that the character of decision-making in academia follows the main theoretical and empirical lines we have described. However, because of strains and pressures on the academic system from students, faculties, administrations, trustees, and various outside political and economic sectors of the society, the character of the academic decision-making process has been under extreme stress. The attendant re-evaluation has led, at least temporarily, to the emergence of some altered forms. While some of these structural changes will remain, others will not; the degree of durability of these alternations is, however, of special interest to us. Harvard University makes an excellent case along these lines, one with which we are most familiar. Later in this chapter we will have more to say about Harvard and some recent changes.

A recent modification of the decision-making process, which we have witnessed at Harvard and to a degree at Columbia as a result of the student disturbances, has been that faculty have gained greater influence over the governing of their universities. There is a point, however, where continuous disturbance tends to actualize previously alleged degrees of schism and political power machinations. This has been the case to a greater degree at San Francisco State and to some degree at Berkeley. In other

EDITORS' NOTE: This chapter, especially prepared for this volume, is partly based on materials collected for the report mentioned in note 1, below.

words, while the radical students may initially believe that they perceive an *alleged* polarization between them and the university or between the university and external political forces, it is their actions over a course of time which exacerbate any fissures to the point where *real* schisms, reactions, political attacks, and political polarization do occur. It is at that point when external bases of political and financial support, such as state and federal governments, alumni, and the general population, become strained and frequently the awesome power of these institutions and sectors of society are turned against the relatively powerless academic world. When this condition comes to full fruition, the radical fantasy is fulfilled and it can be reported that "we were forewarned all along that these were the political realities of the distribution of power in America."

Radical students have tended to view the academic system internally and externally in relation to an "establishment," as one of power relationships and in terms of a struggle for control over a limited quantity of power. While power is to some degree involved in these processes, describing the academic system itself in these terms is at best a caricature; at worst, grossly erroneous. In the course of this discussion we will indicate how and why this is the case.

This should not imply, however, that there is no value to the critiques of the radical students and their moderate allies, or that there will be no potentially positive consequences forthcoming from their demands. Quite the opposite might well be true if appropriate changes are made without submerging the academic, scholarly, and instructional functions and values of the university. Indeed, out of this era of strife we may well witness the emergence of a more inclusive and vital academic community.

Rationale and Methods for the Study of Academic Men

The American academic system, particularly the organization of the faculty, is frequently on a large scale with a high division of labor and a variegated number of tasks; yet it is not "bureaucratic" in the classical Weberian formulation. In academia, there is little line hierarchy of authority of command from president to deans to chairmen through full professors, associates, assistants and finally to instructors. Each faculty member has his domain of teaching and research authority over which there is little or no control by other faculty members, the administration, trustees, alumni, and so on. If for no other reason, this organizational "anomaly" should draw the attention of any student of society to the American academic system.

There remain, however, other reasons for our interest in this social phenomenon. Perhaps most startling has been the tremendous growth of the American academic system since the turn of the century. This growth was accomplished before the practical consequences of higher education were visible, and despite the relative "nonutilitarian" or "nonimmediately accountable" character of academic values and products.

Furthermore, higher education has other special organizational features. Specific problems of the university, such as the recruiting and coordinating of large numbers of professionals, the university's incapacity to independently generate the bulk of its own financial resources, its administrative problems and their articulation with the professional corps, and the socialization function the university performs for on-coming generations also drew our attention.

Thus a rather broad gauged survey of the academic profession was undertaken to investigate some of these issues. The material reported herein refers only to the decision-making processes in the academic system and not to the many other areas examined by our research. This area, however, is crucial for reviewing organizational arrangements, mechanisms of integration, the distribution of authority, and the variations of these features throughout the system.

We selected for analysis a sample of eight institutions of higher education. These were stratified by three levels of size and two of quality.[2] The parameters of size and quality were selected following the work of Lazarsfeld and Thielens (1958). For the large- and medium-size institutions with high and low quality cells, one institution was selected as representative for each. For the small-size institutions with high and low quality cells, two schools were selected for each cell in order to insure a sufficient number of faculty respondents. Six departments in each institution were consistently and totally sampled: two departments in the physical and biological sciences, two in the social sciences, and two in the humanities.

The institutions were chosen on the basis of convenience and with an eye to our own financial limitations. All schools were four-year accredited liberal arts universities and colleges; technical, vocational and junior or community colleges were not included in the universe from which our sample was drawn. Our sample institutions tend to have larger faculties, to be of higher quality and to be about equal in research orientation when compared with the average figures for all four year liberal arts institutions in the United States.[3] In spite of these biases, comparisons with early analyses of our subsequent national sample of academic men (1967) indicates that the general response patterns of the national study are similar to those reported herein from the pilot research.

Six hundred and thirty-nine faculty members were mailed questionnaires; 420 (66 percent) returned them. Of the 420, a sub-sample of 160 were personally interviewed. The findings reported in this chapter are taken from responses to both survey instruments.

Early analysis of these data, using the size-quality matrix, proved disappointing in eliciting trends. Since research orientation and levels of differentiation played so large a part in our thinking, however, we decided to construct a linear scale combining size, quality, and research orientation and to define this scale as measuring degrees of institutional differentiation.

This scale of institutional differentiation (SID) was constructed by an analysis of institutional characteristics of 127 colleges and universities randomly selected from Cartter (1964). The eight sample institutions were ranked using the criteria established for the 127 schools. Three of the institutions were then categorized as manifesting a "high" degree of differentiation, the next three by a "medium" degree and the last two a "low" degree. These three classes of differentiation constitute the main analytic "independent" variable.[4]

This scale of institutional differentiation attempts to describe the degree of preoccupation with intellectual values and research activity. Institutions at the top of the scale are strongly oriented to research. The second group is slightly less intensely oriented to intellectual standards, and tends to have a balanced plurality of goals, e.g., research, scholarship, and general education. Finally, the institutions at the lowest levels put the least emphasis on intellectual values, and are primarily oriented to the creation of an educated citizenry and to the vocational training of their students.

This scale remains problematic in the sense that there is some flaccidness in the degree to which the theory and its application mesh. But in spite of this problem, it still intuitively approximates the theory and, even more important, it is extremely effective in analyzing our data.[5]

What must be kept in mind while reading these materials, however, is that findings should be considered *indicative* rather than demonstrative of our theoretical position. We say this not because of sampling, methodological, or technical difficulties, but rather because we have been working with a complex set of analytic distinctions and categories which are systematically related. These are difficult to operationalize, and it it difficult to use the methods presently available in social science to examine and verify them. At best, we can only obtain approximations and indications which tend to validate the way we theorize the workings of the system. This is by no means an apology for our data, for by present day social scientific standards our findings are "good." Rather, we are suggesting that the chapter be read as a whole rather than taking each finding separately on its own merit. If the chapter is approached in this way, it becomes a convincing argument for our theoretical description of one aspect of the academic system.

A Brief Theoretical Overview

Perhaps the most manifest features of the American higher educational system have been its rapid growth and rise to international prominence since the Civil War. During this period, the United States developed what has come to be called a "university" system. Prior to the Civil War, American colleges were small, sectarian, classical in their teaching, and traditional in their orientations (Earnest, 1953). The emerging university system, however, did not displace the older colleges, nor did it impede the development of new institutions. What occurred was the transformation of the old and the new into a uniquely American system of higher education.

What developed was a secularized and exceedingly extensive and variegated system of higher educational institutions. This system included technical and vocational schools, junior and community colleges, elite small liberal arts colleges, state public teachers' colleges, undergraduate, graduate and professional schools, and large private and public research oriented universities. These latter institutions, the "full" universities, which are at the highest prestige level of this variegated system have, somewhat paradoxically, tended to integrate and fuse, rather than split off, diverse academic functions.

For example, the ideal type of the American full university has tended to include the whole spectrum of disciplines, and to maintain both undergraduate and graduate schools. A balance between the teaching and research functions is also attempted with certain checks used to insure that neither function totally dominates faculty activities. The full universities have, for the most part, refrained from developing research institutes or professorships that may exclude or down-grade the teaching function among the rest of its faculty. They have instead related and intertwined the two functions. Further, the full universities have tended to bring their professional schools closer into the organization of the university, to a degree integrating and shading off the arts and science faculties into the professional, rather than having the professional schools break off into completely separate and independent units.

All of this has been accompanied by an enormous growth in the size of faculties, particularly at the level of the full universities. In spite of this growth, academic *faculties* have characteristically remained associational, collegial, and conspicuously decentralized rather than becoming bureaucratized. The basic rule in academia is equality among full members. This is an outgrowth of the historical tradition of collegiality in academia and of the necessity for highly trained professionals to have sufficient autonomy to implement their acquired value-commitments.

A special and differentiated value pattern has, since the turn of the century, been institutionalized in the American higher educational system. This value pattern has significant meaning for every aspect of the academic man's attitudes and role configurations, for the organization of his occupational environment, and for the character of the decision-making process itself in academia.

The American Academic Value System

A discussion of the interpretation of attitudes, the commitment to values, the capacity for mutual influence, and the distribution of authority, power, and decision-making in academia necessitates elaboration, definition and analysis of the American academic value system. The definition and analysis of the academic value system and the ways in which it articulates with concrete social structures constitutes an important locus for the analysis of our data.

We treat the American academic value system as a specified sub-system of a more generalized societal value system—that of instrumental activism (Parsons and White, 1961; reprinted in Parsons, 1964). The general value orientation has its roots in the religious heritage of American society, especially in what Weber has called "ascetic" Protestantism. An essential feature of this value pattern is the balance between, and combination of, individualistic and collective emphases. The maintenance of the value pattern itself is the collective responsibility of the society. Its implementation, however, is largely the responsibility of discrete units, ultimately the individual. The value pattern of instrumental activism thus focuses on the opportunity (freedom) and responsibility (obligation) for contributions to implementation. (See, in this connection, Parsons, 1960; reprinted in Parsons, 1967.)

The opportunities and responsibilities focused on by the value pattern must be specified at relevant levels and in relevant institutions of the particular environment. Insofar as instrumental activism is institutionalized in a particular realm it defines, among other things, a particular mode of rationality or approach to implementation. The most familiar of these modes is *economic rationality* (Parsons and Smelser, 1956). In the academic realm, we suggest that the relevant mode is *cognitive rationality* which, because of the special nature of academia, focuses on the boundary between cultural and social systems in the value pattern.[6]

The reference is to the concern for the state of knowledge; hence the term *cognitive*. The *rationality* consists of the value pattern's codification of knowledge in terms of logical categories and propositions, and in terms of empirically valid observations. Perhaps the most direct and concrete expression of this cultural value pattern is that of scholarly research. The other academic functions—the transmission and application of knowledge —presume relatively deeper involvement in more general *societal* value patterns, and therefore to a degree, a "dilution" of the value pattern of cognitive rationality.

This most concretely describes the cognitive rationality value pattern in the academic context. Commitment to this value constitutes a mandate to give objects of knowledge, along with a particular mode of their manipulation, a priority in the academic man's life. The realistic conditions of academic life, the way in which the value is variantly institutionalized at different schools, the particular exigencies faced, the specific commitments that an academic may make over a temporal course are not defined for the individual by his commitment to this value. These are conditions, realities, and circumstances that the academic man must face and about which he must make choices as he moves through time and into varying contexts, and consequently is faced with different and changing opportunities and responsibilities.

We suggest that there are two correlative aspects of the instrumental activism value pattern which form the major normative premises for more specified levels. These are opportunity (freedom) and responsibility (obligation) for contribution. Among men in the *institutional* system of higher education, these should be interpreted, respectively, as *academic freedom* (the normative condition for opportunity) and the *obligation* (responsibility) to *contribute to the advancement, transmission, application of knowledge,* and to become involved in other relevant and related activities. Hence, these value patterns in higher education tend to give precedence to research, though by no means to displace obligations to contribute to the effective transmission, practical application of knowledge, and so on.

Two things should be kept in mind regarding this pattern. First, academic freedom does not imply freedom from all imperatives toward value implementation (Weber, 1946). Quite the contrary is true. This value formulation should be understood as a means of legitimating those freedoms as necessary conditions for effectively performing the unique obligations imposed by the value pattern of cognitive rationality. Second, cognitive rationality, as part of the general value system, belongs at the cultural level. To the degree that it is institutionalized in social structures in its "purest" form, e.g., scholarly research, it has cultural primacy. To the degree that it is institutionalized in other social structures, e.g., teaching and practical application, less emphasis will be given to cultural concerns and more to socially involved interests.

Social Organization of American Academic Collectivities

The institutionalization of the cognitive rationality value pattern, with its cultural primacy and normative emphasis on protective freedoms and obligations to contribute, has influenced the development of a particular type of academic collectivity structure. In the discussion that follows, we will emphasize the collegial character of academic collectivities over their *bureaucratic* aspects.

There has been a tendency, although sometimes loosely formulated, to equate growth, change, and largeness of scale with bureaucratization. We hold, following Weber, that the primary hallmark of bureaucracy is *hierarchy of authority,* independent of scale. This means that the chief executive or the top management has a relative maximum of control over all the situations and performances in offices lower on the hierarchical scale. Such a formulation does not adequately describe academic collectivities, nor would such a pattern permit the freedom to implement the value of cognitive rationality that academic men must and do entertain.

As is the case with most realms where the "operatives" are professionals of high technical competence, there are, in the academic sphere, circumstances of social structure which, on the one hand, foster the institutionalization of cognitive rationality and, on the other hand, prohibit radical bureaucratization. The first of these circumstances is the very simple fact that an organizational superior cannot, except coincidentally, be equal in technical competence to his "inferiors" in their individual fields. It is therefore out of the question for an administrator, e.g., a dean or a department chairman, to tell his "subordinate" what to do, except in the most general sense of saying what he (the "superior") wants to get done, not *how* to do it, which is the essence of supervision (Parsons, 1968a). Second, it is difficult, if not impossible, for administrators to assess the *quality* of a staff member's research or contributions, his standing in his discipline, or even his capacity to teach and train students in his particular discipline. Third, it is difficult and sometimes injurious to evaluate in detail the "short-run" activities of academic men, or to expect immediate accomplishments from them, a necessity that is paramount in a bureaucratic system.

These factors, combined with the long-standing traditions that faculties are "companies of equals," have produced a real freedom for individuals, departments, and faculties. This has engendered and sustained the norms of academic freedom and tenure, two structures which have been institutionalized in the American system of higher education simultaneously with the growing emphasis on research, both of which are calculated to give the individual faculty member a maximum range of autonomy to do his job in his own way free from administrative directives.[7]

Thus, the main tendency of departmental and faculty organization is in the *associational* direction. This tendency, however, is not the equivalent of associational membership, for example citizenship or membership in a voluntary association. This is the case because a faculty or departmental position is also a full-time job; that is, it is also an *occupational* role for the incumbent. We have called this type of social structure *collegial*. We have done this in order to distinguish this tendency toward the associational combined with occupational structures from either of these two types taken individually. This structural tendency toward the combination of association with occupation, a tendency toward collegial structure, has in general been related to the modern professional world. (Demerath, Stephens, and Taylor, 1967, and Stinchcombe, 1965, have suggested a social organizational type similar to the one being delineated here.)

The main tendency of faculty organization is, therefore, to preserve and strengthen the collegial pattern which should be contrasted with the bureaucratic. In terms of social structure it is closely tied to and involved in the implementation of the cultural pattern of cognitive rationality. Nonetheless, it should not be overlooked that academic institutions do have a bureaucratic side in their administration. However, the administration is more closely related to social than to cultural values. Academic administrations have grown in recent times, but their functions have differentiated from the more academic teaching and research, and tend to be more readily involved in administering and recruiting finances and students, overseeing the construction of libraries, laboratories, and so on.[8]

Although there are important points of interpenetration between the faculty, departments, and administration, they have tended to remain relatively involved only in their own endeavors and functions. Such a collective organization of faculties has, however, had particularly important implications for the mechanisms of integration and control. Individuals, departments, and faculties with relative degrees of autonomy, if not integrated through the power of hierarchical authority, as is the ordinary custom, must be controlled by other means. We have, in light of this premise, em-

phasized commitment to the academic value pattern and exchange of influence as the centrally important mechanisms of integration. Technically defined, these are media of exchange.[9] Suffice it to say that we have
hypothesized that in a whole range of attitudinal data, academic men have
shown that they would prefer the influential capacity rather than positions
of formal power. Such attitudes are an outgrowth of commitment to the
academic value pattern, the desire to implement it, and the realization of
and the willingness to employ the uniquely effective mechanisms of social
structural organization found in academic collectivities, as well as the trust
that others will respect these noncoercive mechanisms.

Media of Exchange and Integration in Academia: Value-Commitments and Influence

In contrast to the political and economic spheres, the academic system
is not powerful, nor does it generate more than a fraction of its own financial resources. Both internally and externally, it is a system of reputations
and prestige that relies on its capacity to mobilize commitments and to utilize its influence on other collective units to bring money and power to itself. This process operates on both the individual and institutional levels.
Further, this works through a ramified and pluralistic interpenetrating system of environing collectivities. As a result, academia can tap a wide range
of possible resources open to it in a multiple collectivity environment.

The effective functioning of this differentiated academic system, inter-
penetrated with its variegated environment, could not occur without generalized media of exchange used in common throughout the system of
academic collectivities and those of the public beyond it. We have referred
to these generalized media of exchange as *influence* and *value commitment;*
they have properties analogous to money and power. While we suggest that
influence and value commitments have a certain degree of primacy in academia, the other two media are also operative in this realm.

Initially, we should note that value commitments to cognitive rationality must be specified in particular contexts, and at levels where they can be
utilized to command the essential resources for their concrete implementation. It is through the progressive involvement in various levels of the academic system that the individual (or the institution) gains a reputation for
the integrity of his value commitment and his level of competence to implement it. This generalized "fund" of reputation for implementing commitments can be "spent" by using it to facilitate the acquisition of enhanced
opportunities for further and higher level contributions to knowledge transmission and application. The conditions of effective implementation are
mediated through a variety of "valued associations." Perhaps the most
basic "valued association" to the individual is departmental and faculty
membership, but there are certainly others, e.g., disciplinary associations,
honorary associations, participation in administrative affairs in the academic

institution, work in industry, government, other consulting, and lecturing to and writing for lay audiences.

Value commitments predispose an individual to seek or accept participation in valued forms of association. The more this is done in properly valued ways, the higher the professional prestige, because such participation facilitates value implementation. However, the associational structure of the academic system and its interpenetrating environment involve another level of generalized mediation through what we call, in a technical sense, *influence*. By influence we mean the *generalized capacity to persuade* by use of the prestige of a position in a valued associational system. By using influence, the actor is calling upon the reputational backing of the relevant part of the associational reference system, as for example when a high prestige department tries to convince outstanding undergraduates to become graduate students there by citing its high standing in the disciplinary community.

In explaining our pilot study findings, we have attempted to show the combined functioning of value commitments and influence as primary media of exchange in academia. Therefore, although we cannot work out here all the relationships involved, it is obvious that empirically we could expect value commitments and influence to be most saliently operative (in the relative sense) among those collectivities where the value of cognitive rationality is most highly institutionalized. The scholarly communities, the disciplinary associations, and those academic faculties in full universities interpenetrate extensively in the sense that a high proportion of members of such institutions are also participants in these more cultural collectivities. Therefore, we would expect that in the "full" university, we would find greater preference for influence over power, as compared with the lower differentiated institutions where there is not such an extensive degree of interpenetration.

The Structure of Decision-Making in Academia: An Empirical View

We have given only the most sketchy outline of our theoretical framework in order to make our empirical analysis intelligible. Our expectations are twofold: first, that value-commitments and influence will have greater salience than power and money among academics and second, that faculties at more highly differentiated institutions will manifest this trend to a greater degree than those at lesser differentiated institutions.

In this discussion, our focus will be more on power and influence than on value commitments and money. Simply put, power is defined as the ability to make binding decisions on, or for, collectivities. Influence is the capacity to persuade. The term "differentiated units" refers to functionally specific, bounded units integrated within a larger system; such a formulation makes explicit what is meant by higher and lower levels of institutional differentiation from a structural point of view.

SOURCES OF INFLUENCE ON ACADEMIC MEN

The pattern of collective influences on the individual in academia is not constant, but depends on the issue involved. This applies both to the extent of influence admitted and to the particular influential agents. The issues we asked respondents to consider included questions regarding general educational policy, departmental issues, course content, and the issue of controversial speakers on campus. On each issue, the respondents reported how much they were influenced by the administration, department chairmen, junior and senior men, and so on.

Several general findings emerge. First, respondents at high- and medium-differentiated schools make a clearer distinction between people within and outside of their department than do respondents at low-differentiated schools. Second, tenured men report a wider range of influential agents than nontenured men. Third, different types of collectivities are influential at various levels of differentiation; in general, collectivities with a bureaucratic emphasis have more influence at lower levels of differentiation. Fourth, issues involving the more central values and norms of academia, e.g., questions of course content or controversial speakers, are less open to negotiation for men at high- than for those at low-differentiated schools.

TABLES 1–3
SOME SOURCES OF INFLUENCE ON ACADEMIC MEN REGARDING
SHAPING DEPARTMENTAL ISSUES, BY SID

	1. *Administration*			2. *Senior Men*			3. *Junior Men*		
	Levels of Differentiation								
Degree of Influence	*High*	*Medium*	*Low*	*High*	*Medium*	*Low*	*High*	*Medium*	*Low*
Much	3%	9%	23%	44%	40%	37%	30%	31%	15%
Some	16	17	20	35	31	26	43	35	29
Little	81	74	57	21	29	37	27	34	56
TOTAL	100%	100%	100%	100%	100%	100%	100%	100%	100%
	(179)	(179)	(35)	(182)	(178)	(35)	(182)	(172)	(34)

These trends may be seen in Tables 1–3. Respondents at low-differentiated schools are influenced more by the administration than those at high-differentiated schools, while they report relatively less influence by senior and junior men. These findings suggest greater departmental control over its own affairs with increasing differentiation.

The responses to the question on controversial speakers present some interesting differences among the sample schools. Men at high- and medium-differentiated schools indicate a greater unwillingness to be influenced on this issue than did men at low-differentiated schools. For example, while 83 and 73 percent of the respondents at high- and medium-differentiated schools, respectively, ruled out any influence by the administration, only 48 percent of those at low-differentiated schools did so. Similarly, for the department chairmen the figures were 80, 76, and 50 percent respectively; for alumni, 95, 90, and 77 percent. Clearly this issue was perceived at the high- and medium-differentiated schools in terms of the norm of academic freedom, which was felt to be relatively unnegotiable. To the extent that influence was admitted, the variations are interesting. For high- and medium-differentiated schools, the two most influential agents were reported to be the *students* and the *general faculty,* while at low-differentiated schools, the *administration* was reported as having the same influence as the *general faculty* while the student body ranked far behind these. A similar response pattern was reported for the question on course content.

We also posed a few questions to our respondents about the basis for accepting suggestions, bringing about compliance or agreement between themselves and their department chairmen. When we asked whether their chairmen tried to influence them, about 50 percent of all the academic men indicated either "sometimes," "often," or "always." When asked whether they were actually influenced by their chairman, however, we found that the chairman had greater success in influencing his colleagues with increasing level of differentiation. The differences were not great, but they are in accord with other evidence we have which suggests that the chairman is perceived differently at the various types of schools.

At low-differentiated schools, the chairman is seen more as a representative of the administration than of the department. In contrast, with increasing levels of differentiation the chairman is viewed more as a colleague and the relationship with him is more strictly based on *influence exchange.* We explored this exchange by asking the respondent to rank in importance several concrete examples of factors which *might* be involved as the basis for this exchange and in mutual acceptance of suggestions or "orders" between the chairman and faculty. We expected that at higher differentiated schools there would be a tendency to use influence as the mechanism for achieving consensus, while at the lower levels there would be a greater tendency to employ powers such as negative sanctions, coercions, threats, etc., and inducements, such as positive sanctions, gifts, favors, and money. Influence should be activated by persuasion, through respect or recognition of the initiator as a member in the collectivity, through activating commitments to commonly shared collective values, etc. Statements A and B (Table 4) reflect the uses of shared values and the uses of membership in a common solidarity as the bases for employing influence. Statements D and E refer to the uses of power and inducement in exchange. Statement C refers to the personality level exchange dealing with collective affective exchange—it will not be dealt with at length herein. Finally, statements F through J follow this same pattern (as indicated in Table 4), but the initiator in this case is the member of the department and not the chairman; that is, the initiator of the act is the respondent. (These statements were loosely derived from the "Technical Notes" to Parsons, 1963b, and from Parsons, forthcoming.)

These factors are listed below in Table 4 along with their rank in relation to each other and the percentage of respondents at each level of differentiation who ranked each factor *first;* the same rank order was obtained by calculating mean scores for each factor. Table 4 shows a fairly high degree of consensus across the board. The rank order of factors involved in the chairman's influence on the respondent was the same for each level of differentiation, and the discrepancies in rank order for the respondent's influence on the chairman were not large. In general, the results may be said to agree with our conception of academia as a system which operates on bases of commitment to common values and influence exchanges among members related to each other in common solidarities and the loyalties that can be accrued from these. Factors suggesting the use of power and inducement in order to bring about mutual compliance, consensus and agreement tended, in general, to be ranked substantially below those suggesting influence as a basis for achieving consensus. (See Freidson and Rhea, 1963.)

In spite of these general trends, some variations occurred which point to certain discriminable patterns within the academic system. The pattern for low-differentiated schools may indicate that the line between influence and power is less clear-cut at these institutions than at medium- and high-differentiated ones. Likewise (although not reported in Table 4), respondents at lower differentiated schools tend to rank higher the two statements most clearly suggestive of power and inducements than their colleagues at higher differentiated schools. For the statement, "He can apply pressure or penalize those who do not cooperate," 71 percent of the respondents at high-differentiated schools ranked it least important, while 63 and 43 percent did so at medium- and low-differentiated institutions. Similarly, in the case of the statement, "The chairman knows that I could exert pressure and make his work more difficult," 85 percent at high-differentiated institutions ranked it last, while 79 and 67 percent did so at medium- and low-differentiated schools.

The percentage trends for statements A and F in particular present an interesting line of conjecture concerning the perceived bases of influence exchange between the respondent and his chairman. At first glance, the trend for statement A seems to imply that with increasing differentiation, the chairman takes greater leadership responsibility in shaping policy through his capacity to influence departmental members. However, when this trend is considered at higher differentiated schools in light of trends found for statement F, we can suggest that it is not an usurpation or inflation of influence on the part of the chairman that we are witnessing, but a greater willingness to accept the chairman's influence and, in turn, a greater willingness to influence him. Perhaps faculty are more willing to be persuaded, and to persuade the chairman at this level because they do view him as a colleague and feel he is closer to their value orientations than those, for example, who are more closely perceived as part of the administration. In contrast, according to our respondents at lower levels of differentiation, consensus is to a degree based slightly more on influence exchanges and is slightly more dependent upon particularistic relationships between the chairman and faculty (see percentage trends for statements C and H), and also slightly more upon positive and negative sanctions.

Table 4
POTENTIAL BASES FOR BRINGING ABOUT CONSENSUS BETWEEN
CHAIRMAN AND FACULTY BY SID

Description or Statement	Rank Order and Percent by Level of Institutional Differentiation		
Influence on Respondent by Chairman	High	Medium	Low
A. "I respect his competence and judgment about things with which he is more experienced than I." (Leadership responsibility, influence)	1 (46%)	1 (42%)	2–3 (24%)
B. "Considering his position, he expects that his suggestions will be carried out." (Value-based claims to loyalties, influence)	2 (34%)	2 (32%)	1 (31%)
C. "I respect him personally, and want to act in a way that merits his respect and admiration." (Collective-affective exchange)	3 (14%)	3 (14%)	2–3 (24%)
D. "He can apply pressure or penalize those who do not cooperate." (Negative sanction, power, coercion, etc.)	4–5 (3%)	4 (7%)	4 (18%)
E. "He can give special help and benefits to those who cooperate with him." (Positive sanction, inducement, gifts, money, etc.)	4–5 (3%)	5 (5%)	5 (3%)
TOTAL	155	140	31
Influence on Chairman by Respondent	High	Medium	Low
F. "The chairman feels that his job properly includes an obligation to consider and act upon my suggestions as a faculty member." (Value-based claims to loyalties, influence)	1 (59%)	1 (51%)	1 (48%)
G. "The chairman respects my competence and judgment about things with which I am more experienced than he." (Commitment to common value, value commitment)	2 (30%)	2 (30%)	2 (24%)
H. "The chairman respects me personally and wants to act in a way that merits my respect and admiration." (Collective affective exchange)	3 (7%)	3 (11%)	3 (14%)
I. "The chairman knows that I can give assistance and support in return for acceptance of my ideas." (Positive sanction, inducement, gifts, money, etc.)	4 (3%)	4–5 (4%)	4 (10%)
J. "The chairman knows that I could exert pressure and make his work more difficult." (Negative sanction, power, coercion, etc.)	5 (1%)	4–5 (4%)	5 (4%)
TOTAL	(154)	(143)	(29)

This line of thinking is especially consistent with our findings related to the possession of tenure. Tenure acts to protect academic men from administrative and other forms of outside pressure. In those systems which diverge most from the ideal model of the influence system, i.e., the low-differentiated institutions, nontenured men are particularly unprotected against bureaucratic power. Analyzing the questions on influence exchange between respondent and chairman by tenure, we find no differences in rank order for either tenured or nontenured men at high- and medium-differentiated schools. In striking contrast to this are the replies from the low-differentiated schools. Tenured men at these schools did not diverge much from the respondents at high- and medium-differentiated schools, but the nontenured men at low-differentiated institutions ranked statement D as of first importance in explaining why the chairman was able to influence them: "He can apply pressure or penalize those who do not cooperate." Certainly this statement ascribes a far greater importance to power relations than to influence exchange, and they thus apparently perceive the department chairman as a potentially powerful representative of the college administration.

INFLUENCE OF RESPONDENT ON OTHERS

We asked respondents a series of questions about the exercise of both power and influence in the following areas of academic decisions: general educational policy, hiring, broad financial policy, and course content. The major finding was that tenured men in all cases rated their influence on others significantly higher than did nontenured men. Table 5 shows the percentages of respondents rating themselves as having *little* influence on three types of decision-making processes. These figures indicate a sharp distinction between tenured and nontenured men. They also reveal some interesting and unexpected trends.

For example, the figures show that for educational and financial policy, respondents at lower differentiated schools feel they have more influence than do those at higher differentiated schools. This situation is probably a

TABLE 5

PERCENTAGE OF RESPONDENTS RATING THEMSELVES AS HAVING LITTLE
INFLUENCE IN AREAS OF ACADEMIC DECISION-MAKING BY SID

| | Level of Differentiation | | | | | |
| | High | | Medium | | Low | |
Area	Tenure	Non-tenure	Tenure	Non-tenure	Tenure	Non-tenure
General Educational Policy	45%	76%	41%	80%	16%	60%
Broad Financial Policy	82	94	70	84	53	80
Hiring Faculty	15	64	23	70	42	73
TOTAL [a]	(114)	(67)	(101)	(74)	(17)	(15)

a. These are the approximate totals for each of these three areas separately.

function of both size and differentiation. The fact that it is not merely a matter of size is demonstrated by the reverse trend in the case of hiring. In the process of differentiation, broad questions of educational and financial policy are relegated more to specialized parts of the administrative structure and to special committees, while hiring is to a considerable extent decentralized and placed in the hands of the departments where there is greater competence for assessing faculty. Certainly, these results suggest that increasing size does not *per se* reduce the individual's sphere of influence over institutional decisions.

COLLECTIVE INFLUENCE EXCHANGE

In the interviews, we inquired about the legitimate scope of influence on departmental issues for various collectivities. We found that at all schools there was widespread agreement on the legitimacy of the various types of collective influence, but the mode of this influence sometimes varied. For example, in coding we found that distinctions were frequently made between types of influence which might be labelled "opinion-giving" or "information-giving" as opposed to more active types of influence which would allow for the initiation of proposals, discussion, etc. (Goss, 1961). Interestingly, no important variations by tenure occurred.

On the whole, influence by the board of trustees was rejected as inappropriate. There was considerable variation on this question by schools, but to the extent that influence was considered legitimate, it tended to be limited to opinion- and information-giving at high-differentiated schools while more active forms of influence were permissible at low-differentiated institutions.

Between 50 and 60 percent of the interviewees said that administrative influence regarding departmental affairs was appropriate. In general, active influence was felt to be legitimate. This finding held by levels of differentiation. As for members from departments other than the respondent's, about 50 percent across the board said that the use of influence was appropriate, but its mode varied. At high-differentiated schools there was an emphasis on opinion- and information-giving, while more active types of influence were accepted at low-differentiated schools. It is thus observed that where departments are less differentiated, both from the administration and from each other, there is greater involvement in the affairs of other departments. There was also widespread agreement at all levels of differentiation that student influence was legitimate, although it was almost universally limited to opinion- and information-giving.

Turning to specific cases of collective influence exchange, we again find that the extent and type of influence varies with the issue involved. Table 6 lists the percentage of respondents rating the trustees, administration, department chairmen, and the senior faculty as "highly influential" in three types of decision-making processes on campus.

In the case of educational and financial policy, the most important collectivities are the trustees and the administration. The relative greater importance of the trustees at the low-differentiated schools, particularly in the case of financial policy, involves some decrease in the influence of the administration. At medium- and high-differentiated institutions, the administration is seen as least subordinate to the board of trustees. Variations in the amount of influence of department chairman and senior faculty on these issues along the SID are not great.

The data in Table 6 on hiring policy support our earlier statements about the decentralization of hiring policy as differentiation occurs. The trustees and administration retain greater influence on hiring policy at low-differentiated schools than at high. The department chairman plays an important role at all schools, but the influence of senior faculty increases directly with differentiation. At high-differentiated schools, 81 percent of the respondents reported that the senior faculty had either a "great deal" or "considerable" influence, 66 percent at medium-differentiated schools, and only 14 percent at low-differentiated schools. Similarly, respondents re-

TABLE 6

AGENTS OF INFLUENCE IN AREAS OF ACADEMIC DECISION; PERCENTAGES OF
RESPONDENTS RATING AGENT AS "HIGHLY INFLUENTIAL," BY SID

Agent	Educational Policy			Financial Policy			Hiring Policy		
	High	Medium	Low	High	Medium	Low	High	Medium	Low
Trustees	24%	33%	48%	75%	95%	86%	1%	3%	30%
Administration	77	78	80	89	90	64	44	40	83
Department Chairmen	50	38	58	12	18	14	89	85	81
Senior Faculty	41	32	37	3	6	3	81	66	14
TOTAL	(174)	(177)	(36)	(178)	(176)	(36)	(172)	(174)	(34)

ported far greater use of departmental committees at medium- and high-differentiated schools than at low.

In conclusion, it appears that our data contradict the popular belief that increasing institutional size inevitably leads to loss of faculty control and to the concentration of power and influence in the hands of the administration. We find that increasing differentiation enhances departmental autonomy and control over policies directly related to its own operation, although on important policy issues such as educational and particularly financial policy, the administration and the trustees play a very influential role.

Before turning to the role of power in academia, however, we shall briefly consider two other aspects of influence. The first concerns the correlation between influence and reputation of specific departments, while the second concerns factors in personal prestige.

DEPARTMENTAL REPUTATION AND INFLUENCE

The department is both the locus of the main interplay of influence and power among its members and an influential collectivity in institutional decision-making processes. We probed several aspects of departmental reputation and influence which would tend to coincide. This hypothesis was only partially borne out by the data.

We asked respondents to rank departments according to: (a) reputation of the department; (b) degree of influence of the department on the general faculty; and (c) degree of influence of the department on students. These three indices did not prove to be highly related for the total sample. At highly differentiated schools, departmental reputation for excellence and capacity to influence the general faculty and students were not closely related. At the two lowest differentiated schools, on the other hand, all three factors were found to correlate with the *history* departments. These empirical findings have led us to suggest temporarily that reputation and influence is more likely to coincide at low levels of differentiation and perhaps also at those institutions oriented towards a specific type of educational program.

TABLE 7
DISCIPLINARY REPUTATION BY SID

	Level of Differentiation		
Discipline	*High*	*Medium*	*Low*
Natural Science	64%	35%	22%
Humanities	17	36	66
Social Science	10	15	6
Misc. Responses	9	14	6
TOTAL	100%	100%	100%
	(168)	(160)	(25)

Certain unexpected trends arose concerning reputation and influence when departments were grouped by discipline. When asked to identify the departments with the highest reputations at their schools, over 50 percent of the respondents at each school agreed on departments in one discipline. For the whole sample, 53 percent constituting majorities at four schools, named a department in the natural sciences, while 32 percent and 13 percent, respectively, named a department in the humanities and the social sciences. An interesting breakdown by level of differentiation is shown in Table 7. The percentages given represent the percentage of respondents at each level of differentiation listing a department in that discipline first. Natural science tends to be accorded higher prestige with increasing level of differentiation, while humanities departments have higher reputation with decreasing differentiation.

A large number of respondents (about 50 percent) failed to reply to the question about departmental influence on faculty and students. This may indicate a diffusion of influence among departments, but it may also be tied up with the perception and feeling from a common-sense point of view that departments do not act as units. In our interviews, several college administrators observed that individuals in departments generally acted more on their own than as members of departments. Thus, the figures which we did get may be indicative not of departmental influence as such, but of a concentration of influential individuals in certain departments.

Of the respondents who did reply, 58 percent said that social science departments influence *students* the most, while 50 percent said that humanities departments influence *faculty members* the most. This latter finding is especially clear at medium- and low-differentiated schools, reflecting their orientation toward the humanities. In the schools placing greatest emphasis on the importance of the humanities in a liberal arts education, both reputation and influence tend to be concentrated in humanities departments. These departments are not only the guardians of the humanistic values of the institution, but are also generally the largest in size.

FACTORS IN PERSONAL PRESTIGE AND INFLUENCE

In this section, we shall briefly consider some factors related to "professional prestige" and "local campus influence." Based on "objective" and "subjective" data reported by the respondents, indices of "professional prestige" and "campus influentials" were constructed.[10] By use of *eta* correlation coefficients, the degree of relationship between several status, attitudinal, and background variables were related to the indices.[11] The *eta* coefficients for the eight variables are reported in Table 8.

TABLE 8
SELECTED VARIABLES RELATED TO GENERAL PROFESSIONAL PRESTIGE
AND LOCAL INFLUENCE OF ACADEMIC MEN

| | Eta Coefficients | |
Status, Attitudinal and Background Variables	Professional Prestige	Local Influential
Current institution	.408 +	.221 +
Job satisfaction	.216 +	.145 +
Discipline	.206 +	.144 +
Preference for teaching-research balance	.189 +	.098
A.B. institution	.135 +	.077
Religious preference	.083	.151 +
Social origin	.058	.067
Ethnic origin	.064	.156 +
TOTAL	(393)	(395)

+ significant at or beyond the .05 level.

Considering the theoretical formulation described earlier, it is not surprising that the respondent's current institutional position is correlated most closely with general professional prestige. The relatively lower relationship of ascriptive background variables such as social origin, religion, and ethnicity with general professional prestige underlines the *achievement* base of prestige. In contrast to this, background variables appear to have a greater relationship with local influence. An achieved status, such as "current institution" (see Table 8), although significantly related to local influence, is of less magnitude than the relationship between achieved status and professional prestige.

Exercise and Distribution of Power in Academia

Although we should characterize the academic system, in contrast to other systems, as primarily reliant upon the exchanges of influence, it too *must* also exchange power and money in order to sustain itself through time. At certain critical points, in order to continue to function, the academic unit must make binding commitments to other systems; this entails the exercise of power.

We assume that the extent of the use of power is inversely related to level of differentiation. Thus at highly differentiated institutions, we expect to find the use of influence dominant; at low-differentiated institutions, power will be more evident. To help our respondents distinguish between power and influence, we asked them to consider the latter in terms of "informal influence . . . in helping to formulate or shape the issues *prior to decision*," and the former in terms of "actual formal or binding decisions." As with influence, we found that the tendency to use power, and the particular collectivities using it, varied not only along the SID, but also according to the issue involved.

In analyzing our data on power, we encountered two methodological problems. First, our questionnaire operationalized a too-limited concept of power. We asked the respondent to indicate the one person or group making the formal decision in regard to educational, financial, and hiring policy and the question of course content; we realized only afterwards that the exercise of power should in most cases be conceived as being located at a *series* of temporally related points in the decision-making process rather than in a single body. At successive points, different collectivities make binding decisions which take the process further, concluding at some higher level or terminating the process prior to going further.

The effect of the approach we took was to orient responses toward the *final* decision or decision-making body. Because the question was to a degree ambiguous, however, there was considerable variation in response, presumably because some respondents chose to concentrate on different points in the decision-making process. Thus this variation may be interpreted as providing clues to other centers of power, and it is by studying this variation that we shall proceed in this section.

The second methodological problem is not limited to this particular section, but comes clearly into focus in the process of analyzing the data on power. This is the problem of maintaining an institutional focus when using individual questionnaires as our primary research tool. One possible procedure for achieving this is to assign a score for each school on the basis of the aggregate individual responses, and thus to create a new sample of schools and work with the data at this level. The sample of eight schools in this pilot study was too small, however, to make this kind of analysis feasible.

Even with these reservations, several general trends may be noted. First, there is a wider diffusion of both power and influence as a function of increasing differentiation among various campus collectivities. Since high- and medium-differentiated schools are consistently larger than the low-differentiated schools, it appears that the greater size need not lead to the concentration of power and influence in fewer hands. Second, the same trends hold in regard to collectivities as held for our discussion of influence in the previous sections. Collectivities with bureaucratic emphasis have greater power in low-differentiated systems; those with collegial emphasis gain in power with increasing differentiation.

TABLE 9
AGENTS OF POWER IN VARIOUS AREAS OF ACADEMIC DECISION BY SID

Type of Decision

| | Educational | | | Financial | | | Hiring | | |
Agent	High	Medium	Low	High	Medium	Low	High	Medium	Low
Trustees	2%	5%	20%	46%	29%	72%	2%	1%	31%
Administration	59	61	46	42	60	14	42	42	56
Department chairman	1	6	0	0	1	0	34	44	6
Senior faculty	7	1	3	0	0	0	19	8	0
Faculty in general	25	21	23	0	0	0	1	2	0
Misc., don't know	6	6	8	12	10	14	2	3	7
TOTAL	100%	100%	100%	100%	100%	100%	100%	100%	100%
	(176)	(174)	(36)	(181)	(178)	(36)	(178)	(179)	(36)

Table 9 shows that most respondents report that the administration generally holds the most power concerning educational issues in the sense of making formal or binding decisions for the institutions. On financial issues, the tendency of the trustees to hold more power, particularly at low-differentiated schools, becomes evident. This entails a lessening of administrative power relative to the medium- and high-differentiated institutions. It is important to remember, however, that respondents were allowed to check only one person or group, and thus the scattered percentage in the case of educational policy is probably indicative of active participation by the faculty.

As in the case of collective influence, the case of hiring differentiates most strikingly along the SID. Whereas a majority of respondents located the formal decision in faculty hands at high- and medium-differentiated institutions, the trustees and administration received 87 percent of the responses at low-differentiated schools. Power was much more diffused with increasing differentiation.

Keeping in mind our operational error which prevented respondents from indicating the degree of dispersion of power, if any, we must conclude that formal power is more readily in the hands of the administration and trustees than with the faculty. On two of the three issues, financial and educational policy, the majority of the respondents perceived the sum of formal power in the hands of the trustees and the administration combined. It is only on hiring policy at high- and medium-differentiated schools that the majority of the power is perceived as lying with the faculty.

RELATIONSHIP OF POWER TO INFLUENCE

In actual practice, power and influence must be intertwined.[12] The fact that power and influence are more widely diffused with increasing levels of differentiation means that for the approach we used, there was greater discrepancy between positive influence and positive power. This was no doubt partly a result of the relative inability of our power question to indicate the degree of diffusion of power, compared with the question on influence. However, there are some theoretical considerations which suggest that this trend is related to the process of differentiation as well.

We conceive of high-differentiated academic systems as more likely to be influence systems, where influence is the emphasized medium of exchange and where power, while relatively diffused, is limited. The limitations on power and the preference for influence should thus lead to greater discrepancies between power and influence with increasing differentiation.

Our discussion of power and influence, while demonstrating the usefulness of our SID scale in conceiving of academia as a differentiated system, has also shown certain uniformities throughout the academic system which distinguish it from other societal subsystems, e.g., the more generally occupational. For example, we have reported elsewhere that although the preference for influence over power bore a linear relation to differentiation, a majority at every level of differentiation preferred influence over power. (See Parsons and Platt, 1968a.) Similarly, certain uniformities emerged in connection with decision processes on specific issues. Financial policy questions are in the hands of the administration and trustees at all schools. On educational policy, the administration tends to hold power, but department chairmen and senior faculty are seen as highly influential. On the whole, the academic system appears far more collegial than hierarchical.

Significant variations within the system do exist, however, and they coincide with our differentiation scale. These variations support our contention that increasing differentiation is related to increasing departmental and faculty autonomy and involvement in the institutional decision-making process. The relative decline of administrative power and influence for the issue of hiring policy may be seen in Tables 10–12.

Clearly, the administration is both more influential and more powerful at low-differentiated schools. Moreover, the cases of positive power combined with negative influence at high- and medium-differentiated schools (19 and 12 percent respectively) suggest that in these cases a small number of respondents perceive that the administration, while making the formal or binding decisions, has been essentially a rubber stamp body on this matter. In contrast with this pattern is the increasing power and influence of collegial associational collectives with increasing levels of differentiation.

TABLES 10–12
ADMINISTRATION POWER AND INFLUENCE ON HIRING POLICY BY SID

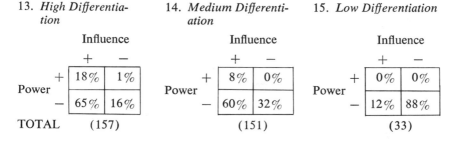

10. *High Differentia-tion*

	Influence	
	+	−
Power +	22%	19%
Power −	25%	34%

TOTAL   (156)

11. *Medium Differentiation*

	Influence	
	+	−
Power +	31%	12%
Power −	13%	44%

(156)

12. *Low Differentiation*

	Influence	
	+	−
Power +	58%	0%
Power −	29%	13%

(31)

This may be seen in Tables 13–15 for the issue of hiring policy in the case of the senior faculty. The pattern may be discerned most clearly by focusing on the percentage of respondents who assigned senior faculty both negative power and negative influence. At high-differentiated institutions, this figure is only 16 percent. It rises to 32 percent at medium-differentiated in-

TABLES 13–15
SENIOR FACULTY POWER AND INFLUENCE ON HIRING POLICY BY SID

13. *High Differentia-tion*

	Influence	
	+	−
Power +	18%	1%
Power −	65%	16%

TOTAL   (157)

14. *Medium Differentiation*

	Influence	
	+	−
Power +	8%	0%
Power −	60%	32%

(151)

15. *Low Differentiation*

	Influence	
	+	−
Power +	0%	0%
Power −	12%	88%

(33)

stitutions, and to 88 percent at low. Clearly hiring policy in terms of influence and power is to a greater degree in the hands of the senior faculty at the more highly differentiated schools. But what our data shows most clearly is that faculty at medium- and high-differentiated institutions are either influential or powerful concerning hiring, while faculty at low-differentiated schools are neither powerful nor influential.

DECISION-MAKING IN PROCESS

With regard to hiring policy in particular, but also in other areas of decision-making, we must keep in mind that the decision of the faculty to hire is most frequently tantamount to the power to hire. Rarely, at least to date, have administrations or trustees over-ridden departments' suggested candidates. Thus, while formal decision to hire (and on occasion, other policy) may lie elsewhere, the influence of the faculty on this issue is exceedingly important for describing and understanding the structure of academic decision-making.

We have attempted to put the decision-making processes in a more dynamic perspective. By an analysis of data drawn from our interview materials, we constructed a general picture of the decision-making process at the departmental level. In order to do this, we examined six facets of the decision-making process, as perceived by the respondents. The first section deals with the *different types of problems* which necessitated a decision; the second concerns the *condition which brought about* the situation; the third involves the person or collectivity *initiating action* on the problem; the fourth deals with the person or collectivity *dealing with the problem* in the stages after the problem is initiated and prior to the final decision; the fifth involves the *actual decision* made; and the sixth section concerns the person or collectivity making this final decision.

We have found that in each of these sections, differences in the character of action taken and in the collectivities involved can be observed among the three levels of differentiation.

(*1*) *Types of Departmental Problems.* The respondents in the interviews described six major types of departmental incidents which required the initiation of the decision-making machinery. They were (in frequency of occurrence for the whole sample): (1) curriculum revision; (2) undergraduate program change; (3) graduate program change; (4) policy change (salary, tenure, etc.); (5) need for a new department chairman; and (6) need for a new faculty member.

Curriculum revision was mentioned most frequently at all levels of differentiation, but the second choice of problems varied: at high-differentiated schools, it concerned the graduate program; at low-differentiated schools, the undergraduate program. General policy questions ranked second for medium-differentiated institutions, perhaps a reflection of the strains produced by the processes of differentiation. Similarly, at the medium-differentiated schools, there was a disproportionate number of cases dealing with the need for new faculty members and department chairmen.

(*2*) *Origin of the Problem.* Four main conditions brought about the need for the initiation of the decision-making process. The first was a state of dissatisfaction among faculty members in the department; the second was a concern on the part of the administration; the third was the need for additional faculty members; and the fourth was the need for expansion in teaching or research facilities. Table 16 indicates the frequency of occur-

TABLE 16
ORIGIN OF THE PROBLEM BY SID

	Level of Differentiation		
Origin	*High*	*Medium*	*Low*
Dissatisfied members of department	70%	38%	41%
Administrative concern	3	25	46
Need for new faculty	10	21	0
Need for expansion	12	8	4
Misc. responses	5	8	9
TOTAL	100%	100%	100%
	(60)	(65)	(22)

rence of each response by level of differentiation. The existence of "dissatisfied members of the department" was seen as the primary source of recognition of a problem at high-differentiated schools. In contrast was the high incidence of "administrative concern" at low-differentiated institutions.

(3) *Initiation of the Issue.* There were three main categories of initiators reported by our respondents: first, a faculty member; second, the chairman of the department; third, a member of the administration. The percentage of respondents identifying each of these initiators is listed in Table 17.

The findings concerning "departmental faculty member" and the "administration" parallel those observed above. With regard to the "chairman" category, it is interesting to note that this position seems to carry the most power of initiation at the middle-differentiated institutions. It is perhaps surprising that the chairman is not mentioned more often at lower differentiated schools, but, as we noted earlier, it is most likely that he is subsumed

TABLE 17
INITIATION OF ACTION BY SID

	Level of Differentiation		
Agent	*High*	*Medium*	*Low*
Faculty member	69%	43%	32%
Department Chairman	18	27	14
Administration	3	21	45
Misc. responses	10	9	9
TOTAL	100%	100%	100%
	(60)	(66)	(22)

under the category of "administration" by the respondents at these institutions.

(4) *Handling of the Problem.* There were six main categories of persons or collectivities who handled the incidents that were reported. In terms of frequency of occurrence there was first the entire department itself; next a specially-appointed committee of members of the department; third, the department chairman; fourth, the administration; fifth, a standing committee made up of faculty members not necessarily in the department; and sixth, "concerned" members of the department meeting on their own initiative. Table 18 shows the distribution of responses for these six alternatives. Handling of the problem by the entire department was greatest at high- and medium-differentiated institutions, reflecting the increased departmental collegiality and autonomy that comes with increasing differentiation. Particularly at high-differentiated schools, specially appointed committees were used, which accounts for the slightly smaller percentage of responses to the entire department category compared to that at medium-differentiated schools. In contrast, the administration and department chairmen play a greater role in problem-handling as the level of differentiation decreases.

(5) *The Action Taken.* Five main forms of action taken to arrive at decisions were mentioned. These were: meetings of the entire department; formal committee meetings of some department members; informal com-

TABLE 18
HANDLING OF THE PROBLEM BY SID

Agent	Level of Differentiation		
	High	Medium	Low
Entire department	38%	44%	24%
Special committee	34	9	5
Chairman	2	13	19
Administration	5	19	43
Standing committee	9	9	9
Concerned members	9	6	0
Misc. responses	3	0	0
TOTAL	100%	100%	100%
	(58)	(65)	(22)

mittee meetings of department members; advancement of proposals by one or more faculty members; and administrative rulings. The distribution of responses for these forms of action is reported in Table 19.

Table 19 indicates that with increasing differentiation the trend is toward "meetings of the entire department" and "formal committee meetings" of department members. "Informal committee meetings," "individual proposals," and "administrative rulings" all increase in frequency with decreasing level of differentiation.

It is our suggestion, although this has not as yet been empirically substantiated, that such forms of action as "individual proposals" and "in-

TABLE 19
FORM OF ACTION BY SID

Action	Level of Differentiation		
	High	Medium	Low
Meeting of entire department	34%	22%	9%
Formal committee meeting	43	15	5
Informal committee meetings	7	24	33
Individual proposals	12	19	29
Administrative ruling	4	9	24
Misc. responses	0	11	0
TOTAL	100%	100%	100%
	(56)	(60)	(21)

formal committee meetings" perform the informal collegial associational function where the more formal organization tends to be organized more bureaucratically and hierarchically.

In an effort to measure the tendency to differentiate and integrate the mechanisms of the decision-making process, we asked the respondents to specify whether or not committees were used to act upon the issues in question. Since this was a pilot study and since we were interested in finding out the relative function of committees in the decision-making process, we explicitly asked this question in our series of probes; we could not be sure *a priori* that the previous questions would elicit the trends that were subsequently discovered. The findings are presented in Table 20 and they underline the fact that greater reliance on committee action is clearly an important aspect of the differentiation process.

We explicitly asked whether the administration was involved in any part of the decision-making process and if so, whether the role of the administration involved the use of influence or the making of binding deci-

TABLE 20
PERCENTAGE OF RESPONDENTS REPORTING THE USE OF COMMITTEES
BY SID

	Level of Differentiation		
Use of Committee	High	Medium	Low
Yes	81%	60%	40%
No	19	40	60
TOTAL	100%	100%	100%
	(57)	(60)	(20)

sions (power). The replies fell into four categories: the administration played no role at all; the administration exercised power; the administration used influence; and the administration was influenced. The findings may be seen in Table 21.

In 81 percent of the incidents reported at high-differentiated schools, the administration was said to play no role at all. At medium-differentiated

TABLE 21
ROLE OF THE ADMINISTRATION BY SID

	Level of Differentiation		
Role	High	Medium	Low
None	81%	52%	11%
Influence	9	23	16
Power	5	24	63
Was influenced	5	1	10
TOTAL	100%	100%	100%
	(60)	(63)	(19)

institutions the use of administrative power and influence was reported with about equal frequency as cases in which the administration played no role. At low-differentiated institutions, 63 percent of the respondents reported that the administration used power in settling the departmental incident.

(6) Settlement of the Problem. Similar trends may be seen in Table 22, which presents the percentage of respondents identifying various means of final settlement.

Department vote is the mechanism most often used at high- and medium-differentiated schools. The chairman seems to make binding decisions more frequently at medium-differentiated schools, a result in line with the findings on initiation of action on problems reported in Table 17. Standing committees and special committees are not the major agents of settlement anywhere, but they do not occur at all at low-differentiated schools, reflecting again the greater emphasis on committees and collegiality with increased differentiation. Finally, there is a clear tendency for the administration to decide issues at low-differentiated schools.

It may thus be said that the study of departmental decision-making processes shows that with an increase in the level of differentiation there follows: (a) an increase in departmental autonomy and involvement in decision-making in every phase of the process; and (b) a curtailment of relative administrative power and influence over departmental affairs and policy. With decreasing level of differentiation and therefore, interestingly, smaller sized institutions, the administration comes to dominate almost all aspects of the decision-making process.

TABLE 22
MEANS OF FINAL SETTLEMENT BY SID

	Level of Differentiation		
Means	*High*	*Medium*	*Low*
Department vote	78%	41%	10%
Decision by chairman	0	14	10
Standing committee	5	8	0
Special committee	7	8	0
Administrative ruling	5	22	60
Administrative approval	5	5	20
Misc. responses	0	2	0
TOTAL	100%	100%	100%
	(57)	(63)	(20)

These findings interweave with our previous remarks that formal binding power may lie with the administration or the trustees, but a great deal of policy is initiated, formed, suggested or more generally influenced by the faculty. We have shown that this is very much the case for hiring, but we can now see from these immediately previous sections and from "types of departmental problems" that faculty have a great deal of control and influence over curriculum, graduate and undergraduate programs, and even tenure and salary, where these issues impinge on their departmental affairs. Further, these results also seem to negate the hypothesis that with growing size academia becomes, in every aspect, more bureaucratized. Certainly this does not appear to be the case for the decision-making process on the issues reviewed here.

However, it must be kept in mind that such remarks and findings refer to only one aspect of the academic system, i.e., faculty and administrative decisions: they have little implication for others, as for example, the often alleged depersonalization of the teacher-student relationship with an increased growth in faculty and student size.

CONTROL OF MEMBERSHIP: HIRING AND PROMOTION

One of the central areas of academic decision concerns the control of membership in the faculty association. The reasons for the importance of professional control are obvious, and involve a wide range of processes, including professional socialization. In this section, however, we shall limit ourselves to a consideration of two institutional processes of importance: hiring and promotion.

More than the legal and medical professions, the academic profession lacks formal control over membership in the faculty association. Formally, at least, academic appointments are made by *institutions*. Placed in the context of the interplay of power and influence, hiring and promotion processes illustrate several important aspects of the American academic system. Moreover, having reviewed the general dynamics of the decision-making processes in the previous section, the case of membership control offers a useful, specific example to follow through in greater depth.

THE HIRING PROCESS

The operative collectivity in the hiring process appears to be directly related to differentiation. At low-differentiated institutions, collectivities with a bureaucratic emphasis have the greatest control over hiring, while more collegial decision-making in this area is most important at high-differentiated institutions.

In the questionnaire, we examined some of the criteria used by these collectivities in making decisions about hiring full and assistant professors by asking respondents to consider certain factors. Tables 23–24 present the percentages, by level of differentiation, of respondents rating each of these factors as most important.

TABLES 23–24
IMPORTANT FACTORS IN HIRING FACULTY BY SID

23. *Full professors*				24. *Assistant professors*		
High	*Medium*	*Low*		*High*	*Medium*	*Low*
2%	3%	16%	Personality	4%	5%	21%
3	17	55	Teaching ability	7	30	61
43	40	26	Disciplinary reputation	29	24	15
29	29	3	Reputation as specialist	8	7	3
23	11	0	Research promise	52	34	0
100%	100%	100%	TOTAL	100%	100%	100%
(179)	(152)	(31)		(184)	(175)	(33)

A striking difference in the evaluation of teaching ability and research is evident. Undoubtedly this difference is related to varying orientations and modes of implementing values of cognitive rationality. Teaching is the primary mode of implementing values at the social system level. Teaching is also of central importance due to the greater emphasis given to "occupational" components involved in hiring at low-differentiated schools. At high-differentiated institutions, research capacity assumed a far greater importance. In hiring assistant professors, research promise is the major criterion, while reputation in general (based to a large degree on past research) is the most important factor for full professors.

THE PROMOTION PROCESS

Examination of promotion processes was undertaken in the interviews through a series of questions dealing first with the bases of promotion and then with the promotion processes themselves. On the whole, the findings parallel the questionnaire results on hiring. Table 25 presents the percentage of respondents rating teaching ability, or research and publication as either of first importance or as unimportant.

The variations are again clear. While 57 percent of the respondents at low-differentiated institutions rated teaching ability first, only 12 percent did so at high. At medium-differentiated schools, an equal number rated each as first. The fact that only 12 percent rated teaching ability first at high-differentiated institutions should not be interpreted to imply a total neglect of the teaching function: 50 percent rated it as second (not reported in Table 25).

TABLE 25
IMPORTANT FACTORS IN PROMOTION BY SID

	Teaching Ability			Research Ability		
	High	Medium	Low	High	Medium	Low
First importance	12%	40%	57%	71%	40%	0%
Unimportant	9%	8%	10%	2%	11%	34%
TOTAL	(65)	(62)	(30)	(65)	(62)	(30)

While the lower differentiated schools put the greatest emphasis on *teaching* in recruitment and promotion, and the higher differentiated schools emphasize *research,* it is somewhat amazing to find that those institutions in the middle tend to emphasize both more equally. This is a trend that we had not predicted, but it is one that can be deduced given the structural middle position of such institutions and the simultaneous cultural and social demands put upon such institutions.

Turning to the promotion process itself, we find a familiar pattern of systematic variation along the SID. Respondents were first asked to indicate the person or persons who assess the qualifications of a candidate for promotion. A breakdown of the responses by level of differentiation appears in Table 26.

In promotion, the power of the chairman at low-differentiated schools is striking: all those who replied named him alone. At high- and medium-dif-

TABLE 26
ASSESSMENT OF CANDIDATE'S QUALIFICATIONS FOR PROMOTION BY SID

	Level of Differentiation		
Agent	*High*	*Medium*	*Low*
Department	10%	6%	0%
Senior, tenured men	42	28	0
All	2	4	0
Chairman	12	38	63
Chairman and senior, tenured men	24	14	0
No response	10	10	37
TOTAL	100%	100%	100%
	(59)	(50)	(30)

ferentiated schools, on the other hand, power and influence are much more diffused, with the department—at least the senior men—acting as the most important operative collectivity.

The interviews were coded for any locus identification of the key promotional decision. We were able to code only 95 interviews in this manner; the findings are presented in Table 27. Although only a small number gave answers to this question, it is clear from the findings that our remarks on the importance of collegial influence in the structure of decision-making is crucial, even in light of the power to make binding decisions.

Faculty control centering in the department increases with higher levels of differentiation. Looking simultaneously at Tables 26 and 27, we see that whereas the department is the operative collectivity both in the assessment

TABLE 27
LOCUS OF KEY PROMOTIONAL DECISION BY SID

	Level of Differentiation		
	High	*Medium*	*Low*
Department	61%	29%	11%
Standing committee	14	37	0
President	11	7	44
Administration (other than the president)	14	27	45
TOTAL	(36)	(41)	(18)

and decision about promotion at high- and medium-differentiated institutions, the situation is radically different at low-differentiated schools. Here, the president and administration are viewed as the major operative units. To the extent that the department chairman participates, respondents tend to view him as a representative of the administration rather than as a colleague. We feel this is reflected in the basis of his appointment: when asked about the selection of department chairmen at their colleges, 77 percent at low-differentiated institutions said it was by administrative fiat. The overview of replies to this question may be seen in Table 28. Again, the

TABLE 28
SELECTION OF DEPARTMENT CHAIRMAN BY SID

| | Level of Differentiation | | |
	High	Medium	Low
Administrative decision	14%	30%	77%
Admin. selects, dept. advises	49	17	5
Dept. selects, admin. advises	14	13	9
Department decision	9	30	0
Misc. responses	14	10	9
TOTAL	100%	100%	100%
	(43)	(54)	(22)

relative lack of separation between the administration and the department at low-differentiated institutions is underlined as a means of helping to explain the large percentage of respondents at these institutions who cited the administration as the key decision-making body.

ACADEMIC FREEDOM AND TENURE

A discussion of academic freedom and tenure affords a useful way of rounding out our analysis of power and influence in academia. Academic freedom and tenure constitute two crucial components of structure protecting the exchange of commitments for influence and power. The two are, of course, different types of structural components. Academic freedom is a generalized normative *orientation* with primary reference to the cultural system. Tenure, on the other hand, is a normative *structure* backed up with organizational sanctions and having primary reference to the social system levels of analysis.

The main functional considerations for these two structural components are focused around the "outputs" of the academic endeavor. The academic environment is nonutilitarian; that is, it is generally impossible to make short-run assessments of the practical use of academic outputs. Over the long run, of course, achievement does enter the picture through what is generally referred to as the "reputation" of an academic system or of an institution, etc. But with reference to the immediate context, there can be few direct pay-offs. Social level assessments thus concentrate on implementation. It is assumed that by drawing the best minds into the academic profession by periodic efforts to upgrade curricula, Ph.D. programs, etc., the cultural and social values of academia will be implemented.

In this context, academic freedom and tenure insulate and protect the academic endeavor and its functionaries from internal and external pressures, influences, and the impingement of power and money in the implementation and achievement of academic values. From another viewpoint, they constitute structural conditions providing a degree of autonomy in decision-making to the unit of action. Finally, academic freedom and tenure constitute recognition of high levels of personal commitment to academic values, and act to assure the conditions requisite to their implementation and achievement.

Consequently, in light of the difficulty in assessing the nonutilitarian context of academia, structural safeguards have been instituted to give a relatively autonomous sphere of power to academic units and to protect them from external impingement. Such conditions underlie the importance of personal commitments and their exchange for influence, power, and even money. As we have seen, the sphere of power is more restricted with increasing differentiation.[13] Although our data are rather spotty, they indicate that academic freedom and tenure are more effectively institutionalized at higher levels of differentiation.

ROLE CONTEXTS OF ACADEMIC FREEDOM

In this section we shall concentrate on the relationship between academic freedom and teaching. Teaching, which straddles the cultural and social aspects of the academic system, is the meeting place for the implementation of academic freedom and tenure. In general, the greater the stress on cognitive transference, the more the emphasis will be on academic freedom in contrast to tenure. The point is that the "exchange of ideas," the transmission of cognitive rationality, etc., which involve the transmission of higher level and more inclusive values, must be afforded a broadly-based and more inclusive form of protection than in those cases where more social values are involved, e.g., teaching, service, practical application of knowledge or vocational training. In the latter contexts, the dimension of protection focuses on full institutional citizenship (tenure) in the transmission process.

The question of course content is central to academic freedom and tenure. The findings show that academic men do indeed have a good deal of control over the contents of the courses they teach. Nevertheless, the extent of this control was found to be directly related to increasing differentiation, as can be seen in Tables 29–31.

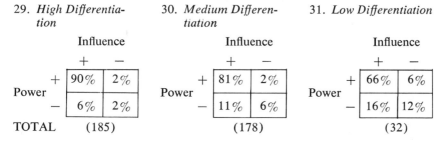

TABLES 29–31
POWER AND INFLUENCE OF RESPONDENT IN SHAPING COURSE
CONTENT BY SID

29. *High Differentia-tion*   30. *Medium Differen-tiation*   31. *Low Differentiation*

	Influence +	Influence −
Power +	90%	2%
Power −	6%	2%

TOTAL (185)

	Influence +	Influence −
Power +	81%	2%
Power −	11%	6%

(178)

	Influence +	Influence −
Power +	66%	6%
Power −	16%	12%

(32)

From Tables 29–31, we can infer that academic freedom and tenure protect the teaching function most effectively at higher differentiated institutions. Tables 32–34 show the increasing power and influence of department chairmen over course content with decreasing level of differentiation.

TABLES 32–34
POWER AND INFLUENCE OF DEPARTMENT CHAIRMEN
ON COURSE CONTENT BY SID

32. High Differentia-   *33. Medium Differen-*   *34. Low Differentiation*
tion   *tiation*

	Influence				Influence				Influence	
	+	−			+	−			+	−
Power +	1%	1%		Power +	3%	3%		Power +	13%	7%
Power −	3%	95%		Power −	12%	82%		Power −	30%	50%
TOTAL	(173)				(169)				(30)	

While 95 percent of the respondents at high-differentiated schools reported that the department chairmen have neither power nor influence (in our technical sense) over course content, only 50 percent did so at low.

ACADEMIC FREEDOM AND INSTITUTIONAL DIFFERENTIATION

Academic freedom and tenure offer both protection and responsibility to academic men. Basic to the effectiveness of academic freedom and tenure is their ability to provide to faculties and departments relative autonomy in decision-making matters. In systems with a low level of differentiation between departments, faculties, and administration, academic freedom and tenure are likely to be less effective in providing this autonomy. Such conditions often imply a tendency to bureaucratize the faculty and to make academic men far more susceptible to administrative power.

The data presented herein have shown this clearly. It has been demonstrated that the administration and board of trustees generally play a greater role in low-differentiated systems. This was clearly seen in such issues as hiring policy. The individual at low-differentiated institutions also has less control over the content of his course. Data showing influences on the respondent concerning the issue of controversial speakers also suggests greater administrative control with decreasing differentiation. (We have not reported these findings yet. This trend is manifest in the pilot and national study data.) Finally, in our examination of influence exchange between the department chairman and the respondent, we found a greater use of power at low-differentiated institutions.

Aside from the level of differentiation, other dimensions which can impinge on the domains of autonomy and protection offered by academic freedom and tenure include student rule, institutional paternalism, religious, business or governmental impingement (including secret research and prohibitions on the publication of findings), etc. Regrettably, in our pilot study we were not able to examine these other potential sources of impingement.

Concluding Remarks: Power, Influence and Corporate Faculty Responsibility, The Harvard Case

We have argued that academic faculties tend to be more associational and collegial than bureaucratic, and that the principal mechanism of their operation in the service of the implementation of commitments to academic values is *influence* rather than political-type *power*. This associational or collegial primacy, and the use of the media of influence, is dependent upon a delicate balance of forces; the pattern has been clearly favored at the most highly differentiated institutions.

Certain pressures emanating from outside of faculties, however, have tended to alter this balance. A common reaction to outside pressures has been to stimulate the assumption of a greater share of power by faculties in their corporate capacity. This was the case with reference to pressures by trustees of academic institutions in matters of economic opinion which eventually led to the establishment of the American Association of University Professors and the formulation of its standards of academic freedom and tenure. Still another case was the pressure which McCarthyism exerted on academia. Recently, however, it has been the pressure of student dissent which has become particularly acute and widespread, and has extended, in fact, far beyond the American system (Parsons and Platt, 1970; Parsons, 1968a).

We have pointed out that the institutionalization of faculty members' principal functions, i.e., research and teaching, has tended to be highly decentralized. The power aspect of these functions has rested largely with the individual faculty member or with small "teams" of them. Decisions made by individuals or teams in this regard then become binding on the institutional collectivity. This is the case, for example, in relation both to the planning of curriculum for students, hiring and promoting faculty, and to the planning and administration of research. Thus, admission to a seminar course or giving a grade to a student binds the total faculty, as do decisions on the expenditure of research funds, or the decision to increase the number of junior faculty.

The most important collective bodies involved here have been departments, and more recently with increasing frequency, committees, e.g., with degree-program powers. The faculty as a whole, and the administration in complex coordination with it, has stood mainly in a permissive, facilitating, and protective role. The fundamental normative institutions of academic freedom and tenure constitute the frameworks within which individual faculty members can assume their own responsibility in making their "contributions" to research and teaching with minimal supervision even by corporate colleagues.

Such a situation has been able to exist in part by the "delegation" of a large share of power by faculties to the administration, particularly with regard to certain academic issues such as financial policy. This was clearly documented by our pilot study data, and is an interpretation which we feel is sound in spite of the reverse legal situation in which trustees are, as it were, the "proprietors" who delegate some of their powers to faculties. The rationale of our view rests, of course, on the primacy of the academic function for the university and the primacy of competence and responsibility on the part of members of the profession in the performance of this function.

As a result of this delegation of power, it is natural that the first target of student complaint should be the administration, since it is the locus of what is alleged to be the "real power." This is true especially with reference to the relations of the university to the outside society. At Harvard, this has recently been the case in terms of the Harvard Corporation with reference to the status of the Reserve Officers' Training Corps and the issue of alleged encroachment on the local community by the University, that is, the so-called "Harvardization" expansion issue. Internally, perhaps the main issue has been that of responsibility for discipline; the Harvard governing board formally gave this power to the Faculty long ago, but except for the very severe penalties of dismissal and expulsion (the former allows readmission by two-thirds vote of the Faculty, the latter not at all), disciplinary powers for Harvard College have been exercised on a *de facto* basis by the Administrative Board consisting mainly of deans and house senior tutors. With some exceptions, student protest has not attacked the performance of the traditional functions of faculty members, but has focused mainly on the above issues.

There have been, however, two faculty functions which have become salient, one external, the other internal. The former, an application of the general movement against the war in Vietnam and "imperialism," has taken the form of an attack on research funded by government agencies, especially war-connected research, though the more extreme version has been that any governmental support should be condemned. In this connection, Harvard has been in a relatively favorable position because of the decision, made shortly after World War II, not to accept contracts or grants which would involve "classification" of the findings. This was a corporate decision, however, and it did not prevent individual faculty members from engaging in classified or secret research or consultation. Given this background, both the Administration and a large majority of the Faculty have strongly defended the freedom of faculty members to accept or reject research support largely on their own terms. To our knowledge, the Faculty as a whole has never taken corporate action on this issue.

The other, internal, problem has come to a head most saliently in the case of one course offering, which happened to be located in our own Department, that of Social Relations. In the summer of 1968, when the Department could not be assembled for a corporate decision, there was a petition to establish a radically-oriented course, which was entitled "Radical Perspectives on American Society." This petition was rather routinely granted by the Chairman and the Associate Chairman. The course was to be given in small sections, with no lectures. In the fall term, it attracted over 300 students. Its spring term successor grew to over 700 students. However, this course raised two sets of important issues: one concerned the place of explicit political partisanship at the formal instructional level of the Faculty. There was little doubt of the staff's position on this issue. They explicitly stated its goal to be to "gain converts to the 'radical' point of view." Further, it was understood that commitment to that position was a necessary but not sufficient prerequisite for membership on the teaching staff. The other prerequisite was expertise, frequently in the form of first-hand experience.

Neither the Department nor the Faculty committee which dealt with the issue, the Committee on Educational Policy, chose to meet that issue directly, we think largely because of the difficulty of defining the boundaries of academic freedom. Thus, proponents of the course strongly argued that every teacher has a political point of view, even though it is not usually made explicit.

The other set of issues which the course raised could be said in a broad sense to be procedural; it concerned the qualifications of members of the teaching staff and their responsibilities, e.g., for grading performance. Here, Social Relations 148–149, the radical courses, had brought in many section leaders who did not meet usual qualifications. These persons included some undergraduates and even some individuals who had no formal connection with Harvard. The issue raised here is a complex one, and we wish to be as fair as possible in describing the situation. It was known by the Department early in the fall that some staff "teaching fellows" who were to lead some sections would be undergraduates. This was considered to be experimental and was largely approved. However, it was voted by the Department of Social Relations that the undergraduate section leaders could not grade students because of the standing University policy that only a Corporation Appointee can evaluate and grade undergraduates. The term "Corporation Appointee" refers to one who has, at minimum, graduate student teaching fellow status. Following the fall term, the course received a reputation for being exciting and stimulating. The reading list was thought widely to be a good one, while at the same time, it was thought that the course was an easy one in which to get a good grade.

We do not know which factors explicitly affected the course registration in the spring, but, as noted above, it more than doubled. As a result, sections proliferated on a very wide range of topics—the course in the fall had focused on only three topics: poverty, race, and education. In the spring there was also a proliferation of sectionmen. Out of this developed concern that the course went beyond the bounds of the topical range of the Social Relations Department and that the qualifications of the new sectionmen were extremely problematic. Although a list of section instructors and their members was requested, it was never forthcoming. It was discovered that the junior faculty member responsible for the course admittedly exercised only minimal supervision over his sectionmen, and could make no decision concerning the course without first consulting with his staff.

Faced with this situation, the Department imposed, not only on this, but on all courses, a set of rules for qualifying section leaders, to be administered by the Department's Committee on Undergraduate Instruction. In addition, a committee of three Departmental faculty members, not members of the staff of Social Relations 148–49, but chosen by them, was to be established to advise the staff and report to the Department on the course. Finally, the Committee on Educational Policy invoked the long-standing rule that only those qualifying for Corporation Appointments could give instruction, even at the section level. It was announced in the student paper, the *Crimson,* that in light of these restrictions, the staff had decided not to offer the course next year.

Two particularly salient issues which have also shifted more responsibility and concern with students to the Harvard Faculty have been the acceptable limits of student participation and discipline of students. When the first action on ROTC was on the agenda of the meeting of the Faculty of Arts and Sciences, the Students for a Democratic Society (SDS) demanded the right of an indefinite number of students to attend the Faculty meeting and to participate in that discussion, though not to vote. When this demand was denied on the grounds that faculty privacy for meetings has long been traditional at Harvard, a substantial number of students occupied Paine Hall, the building where the meeting was to be held. When asked to leave, the students refused, and the meeting was cancelled.

At a special meeting then called to consider the situation, three representatives of the dissident students were invited to state their views. They were not present, however, for the ensuing decision-making discussion and vote. The Faculty at that meeting approved the imposition of "probation" on students who sat in at Paine Hall, but did not recommend "suspension" for the few students for whom this was a second offense, that is, for those who were involved in the obstruction of a Dow Chemical Company campus recruiter some months earlier. The Faculty thus repudiated the Administrative Board's recommendation, an unusual action. Later, however, the Administrative Board withdrew scholarships from some of these students, thus adding to student tension.

At nearly the same time, the Faculty discussed and accepted the "Rosovsky Report," which recommended the establishment of a program in Afro-American studies. This report recommended limited student participation in that new program, that is, three voting student members on the personnel "Search Committee" which was to make recommendations to the faculty "Standing Committee" in charge of setting up the program.

Preceding the April ninth SDS occupation of University Hall, the administrative center of the Faculty of Arts and Sciences, there were a number of developments too complex to relate here. There were, however, two aspects of the occupation which were regarded as quite serious, namely the rifling of confidential files, and the physical ejection from the building of several deans. This action was then followed by the dawn police "bust" requested by the President of the University.

The reaction to the police intervention was a broadening from what initially was a narrow base of the protest movement, followed by an effective student "strike" which lasted about a week and received wide national attention. The Faculty had not been consulted about the police action, but met in emergency session on April eleventh, the day following the bust. On this occasion, the Faculty took the exceedingly significant action of voting, by an overwhelming majority, to set up an *elected* joint faculty-student committee to perform three functions: to report on the causes of the crisis, to take responsibility for disciplining offending students, and to make recommendations regarding the restructuring of the University where necessary. This was a major step in asserting faculty prerogative, not only beyond the traditional practice, but also beyond that adopted following the "Paine Hall" sit-in.

In the University Hall case, however, the Faculty in effect took the initiative out of the hands of the Administration and assumed it itself. Though nominally a committee of the Faculty of Arts and Sciences, it was to be comprised of nine Faculty of Arts and Sciences members, five students, and was to include a Professor of Law. All faculty members—seven with tenure, and two without—were elected by the Faculty; the students were elected by the student body, and the Law Professor was elected by his Law School colleagues. It is not unprecedented to constitute a faculty committee by election, but it is a rare practice, and in recent times unheard of at Harvard. The committee came to be known as the "Committee of Fifteen."

Two subsequent events confirm our interpretation of the firmness of the faculty decision to "take charge" in a limited area. The Committee of Fifteen worked out and announced a procedure for handling disciplinary cases which was detailed and quasi-judicial in nature. The SDS, however, denied the legitimacy of the Committee, and demanded total amnesty for the protesters. It announced, in fact, that it intended to be uncooperative, and would perhaps disrupt the proceedings of the Committee. At the next Faculty meeting, a resolution was introduced by the Committee which stated that since the Committee *was* an organ of the faculty, any attack on it would be regarded as an attack on the Faculty itself. This resolution was passed *unanimously*.

On June ninth, the Committee reported its disciplinary decisions to the Faculty. By a long-standing rule, a penalty as severe as dismissal could be imposed only by two-thirds vote of the members of the Faculty present and voting. The dismissal of three students was recommended, all of whom had been prominently involved in the physical manhandling of the deans on April ninth. In accordance with the SDS boycott, none so accused appeared in person or sent representatives to the disciplinary hearings which took place earlier. The recommendations of dismissal were approved by the Faculty in an approximate ratio of seven to one. This, in turn, legitimized the authority of the Committee to impose lesser penalties without formal action by the Faculty. Fifteen or so others were given various levels of "suspension" and the rest of the 136 students involved in the University Hall occupation were given much milder penalties.

The other significant action in this area at the June ninth Faculty meeting was on a set of "guidelines" for the definition of unacceptable student behavior tentatively set forth by the Committee of Fifteen. These guidelines referred to the use of force against faculty and administrative personnel, the deliberate disruption of instructional processes, the denial of freedom of speech, and so on; they were approved by the Faculty by a slightly higher ratio of votes than were the dismissals.

An open "convocation" was then held by the Committee of Fifteen the evening following the faculty vote on June ninth. It turned into a melee, during which the members of the Committee were shouted down and denied the opportunity to explain their actions. Subsequently, the SDS threatened to disrupt the coming University Commencement by forcibly seizing the microphone so that an SDS speaker could state the organization's point of view. This confrontation was avoided by the President of the University who acceded to the request of the Senior Class Marshalls to permit a brief speech by an individual representing the SDS. The SDS speaker rambled on beyond the time allotted to him, and after several promptings, was ushered off the platform by the same Senior Class Marshalls who had previously interceded upon behalf of the SDS. The speaker did not, however, physically resist his removal.

One other development in the spring Harvard crisis should be reviewed here. In the course of the general unsettlement at that time, the previous arrangements for developing an "Afro" program, which are outlined above, became "unstuck." A more militant set of demands was put forward by the Afro-American Student Society, the association of black students on campus. A somewhat moderated, but still extreme set of demands formulated by that group then came before the Faculty and, to the surprise of many, were passed by about a 60 to 40 majority. There was a shift from a "program of concentration" to a full Department for Afro-American studies, but the most radical move was the inclusion of six student members with full voting status, as well as the six faculty members and faculty chairman who were to make up a "Standing Committee" charged with setting up the new Department. This was the first time in Harvard history that students had been given full equality with faculty members in the appointment process, including that of tenured members of the Faculty. It was argued that this was a very special case not to be generalized in the future, but how far this limitation will hold still remains to be seen.[14]

The primary concern of this highly schematic discussion of the Harvard case has not been to evaluate the process of coping, or failing to cope, with the University's involvement in the present wave of student unrest. At this time, it is too early to judge what the longer run outcomes will be. Our concern, rather, was to illustrate that under the kind of stress which has recently been operating, there is a strong tendency for faculties to assume a substantially enhanced share of collective responsibility—the hypothesis we offered previously.

This tendency can be seen in the first instance in the greatly enhanced assumption of responsibility by faculties for student discipline in matters involving participation in the academic community on levels not primarily concerned with the private lives of students, as were such regulations as parietal hours, dress regulation in the dining halls, and so on. The tendency also extends to a variety of problems of faculty procedures, including the very important problem of the range and limitations of student participation in academic decision-making. The action on the "Afro" issue, however dubious it has seemed to many members of the Harvard Faculty, was a case of the Faculty taking corporate action on a line which was surely not congenial to most members of the Administration. However, even larger questions of the constitution of the Faculty and its relations to the Administration as well as to students, have come into flux, with the Faculty in its corporate capacity playing a substantially enhanced role.

It is true that these trends have appeared "under pressure" and even under threats, but it seems quite clear that the main trend is not, as some observers tend to hold, simply a "capitulation" to these pressures and threats. Perhaps the clearest evidence of this lies in the disciplinary actions of the Committee of Fifteen and their overwhelming endorsement by the Faculty as a whole.

Our general interpretation is that it is the faculty guardianship of the values of the academic system which principally explains this reaction to stress. The faculty stands, in Shils's sense, at the "centre" of the academic system and is charged with the implementation of its values, a function which no administration, for all its customarily greater "power," can ordinarily perform. This is true especially in the higher differentiated institutions (Shils, 1961), as the evidence above clearly demonstrates. When these values are seriously threatened, the elements most fully committed to them can be expected to rally to their defense, as has been true in earlier situations as well as those pressing on academia today.

In this connection, two particular points should be stressed. First, the importance of faculty responsibility for discipline may be interpreted in terms of Durkheim's second "law of punishment." (See Durkheim, 1960, 1938, 1899–1900.) This is to say that in addition to functions either of expiation or of deterrence, punishment can, if "properly" administered, serve as an affirmation of the collective commitment to the normative structure. The violation of this structure cannot be treated with impunity without the risk of undermining the commitment to the values thought to be crucial. We do not mean to imply that we consider the magnitude of discipline meted out to be perfectly articulated to the offense, or even that it was just and fair, nor do we condone the one violence (the police bust) over the other (the University Hall take-over). We are simply noting that those committed to a particular value system must take the responsibility for its maintenance and also its change; violation and attack upon those values must invariably lead to countermeasures for their preservation.

The second point is focused at broadly procedural levels. The academic community is one particularly concerned with freedoms, and is hence especially sensitive to infringement of such freedoms in the name of any "orthodoxy." As noted, this seems to be the main reason for the Department's reluctance, in the case of Social Relations 148–49, to act against the political goals of the course—though certainly the failure to do so may be problematical in other ways. An academic community cannot function without the maintenance of procedural "civilities," the most elementary of which is perhaps the prevention of physical coercion and disruption within the academic community itself. It is for this reason that the Committee of Fifteen reserved its most severe punishment for those students who ejected persons from University Hall by physical force.

The pattern of academic freedom, however, goes beyond this to require not only freedom of opinion, but also of discussion, so that disruption by "shouting down," by the use of insults, obscenities, and other forms of abuse, must be treated as impermissible. Even the observance of time limitations so that others can have their turn is essential, as was the case with the SDS speaker at the Harvard Commencement—though in this case, the discipline of removal was administered by his peers and not by the Faculty.

Finally, certain features of the structure of the academic community have been brought into flux by recent events which have affected the internal constitution of the faculty itself and its relations not only to students, but to the administration and to the outside society. It would seem to be essential that the occupants of the value "center" of that community, for whom the implementation of academic values is a part of their "job," should take a special share of responsibility with reference to institutional restructuring as it may occur (Parsons and Platt, 1970). To do otherwise would be to deny the claim that commitment to academic values is the core commitment not only of faculty members and of the faculty as a collectivity, but essentially of the academic system, most particularly at its "Arts and Sciences" core.

Thus we argue that under conditions of special stress, it is both to be expected and, in terms of academic values, it is "right and proper" for faculties, especially at the collective, corporate level, to assume substantially greater "power" in the analytic sense which we have described. In the long run, however, we do *not* think that the exercise of "faculty power," in the sense of a near monopoly of the power component of the governance of the university is an acceptable or a wise program. Rather, we have argued in the earlier part of this paper on the basis of evidence from our research that the primary mechanism of "control," not only of faculty behavior, but of the academic community as a whole, has come to be *influence,* not power, and that this is in accord with the primary academic values of cognitive rationality. Indeed, we suggest that too much faculty power, consolidated for too long, would lead in the direction of the bureaucratization of faculties and would severely inhibit their primary functions, which do *not* reside primarily in corporate decision-making. Hence the importance of procedural institutions, which we have stressed for the current situation, is of wider import because procedural emphasis is characteristic of the collegial and associational type of structure which we have described, including the relation of actual government to a relatively independent legal system. We suggest, in fact, that the slogan of "student power" may prove to be of dubious value for long-run student interests, however seductively appealing it may appear at the moment.

Indeed, we can say that a collegial, influence-oriented social system, under stress, tends to *regress* to the level of greatly enhanced emphasis on power relations. This regression may be necessary and constructive for the purposes of defense and reorganization. Its constructive outcome, however, will depend mainly on the effectiveness with which it can provide a more effective base in "power relationships," i.e., formal allocation of rights and obligations in decision-making for the various constituent subgroups of the academic community. If this base is both relatively "secure" and the allocations are appropriate to the value system and to realistic exigencies of function, it should then be possible to erect on this base a substantially more ramified, extensive and adequate complex of influence-relations than existed before and thereby better integrate the total community.

It seems to us to be no accident that the "confrontation" between SDS and the adult sectors of the academic community has come to a head in the question of discipline which, as we have noted at Harvard and elsewhere, has tended to move on the adult side from administration to faculty responsibility (Lipset and Altbach, 1967; Lipset, 1968). It is well known that confrontations tend to escalate, and that in such power relations more and more severe negative sanctions tend to be used. For SDS the ultimate has been their version of the use of physical force, while on the other side, apart from the use of police, the ultimate internal sanction is dismissal, i.e., extrusion from the academic community. From our point of view, the SDS demand for "total amnesty," no matter what the infractions of the procedural system, is a direct challenge to the existence of an academic community at any operative level. As we have stated, willingness to punish for validated infractions of academic values and norms in appropriate ways and appropriate degrees is an essential factor in asserting the integrity of the academic community itself, and hence of building the base on which restoration and further extension of the influence system can take place.

We have, throughout this paper, maintained a focus on faculty involvement in university governance. This is the case not because we are unaware of the contribution of other collectivities in this process, but because of our own special theoretical and empirical interests in the role of the faculty. Further, it is our belief that given the functions and values institutionalized in the university system, faculties play a primary role in these matters.

Should the present circumstances of stress terminate, even with structural changes in the university, the primary obligations of faculties will still be those of teaching and research. Issues such as "relevance," "involvement," and "emotionality," which have been advocated by students, are not on the same level as the two primary academic functions. To some degree, teaching and research can become more relevant and more involved with contemporary problems and issues, but the performance of these functions cannot afford to surrender the more general standards of quality and of scholarship as these have been established over the years, nor can all scholarship be immediately relevant if for no other reason than that not all faculty may wish to engage in immediate and contemporary problems in the performance of their teaching and research. More important, it is necessary to maintain the normative conditions of academic freedom, thereby permitting faculty a degree of autonomy in order to "go their own way" in implementing academic values, that is, in the development of knowledge and in instruction of students.

It is impossible to develop here all the ramifications involved, but faculty and even student autonomy would have to be sacrificed to a serious degree, particularly at higher level differentiated institutions, if the governance of the university were constantly to remain in the hands of either or both of these groups. Autonomy, in a practical way, is often achieved by the delegation of power to other units, for example, in some instances, the administration. Thus, in spite of the recent regression to faculty "power" and the struggles between administration, trustees, faculty, and students and in spite of the frequent cry for faculty senates at lower differentiated institutions, there will still be a necessity to delegate realms of authority to the administration, as well as to faculty, to student committees, and so on. As our data indicate, there should be and there will be different areas, issues, and domains of power and influence for the various sub-segments of the university community. For example, at Harvard it would be an enormous waste of time and intellectual acumen to have the entire Faculty constantly involved in student discipline. This function will have to be returned to an administrative board even if in the future this body includes student members. So, too, issues such as undergraduate recruitment, screening, and even community relations, including the problem of Harvard's physical growth, are matters that are more readily discharged by the administration than they are by the students or the faculty.

We should make clear, however, that such a line of thought does not suggest or recommend the "abdication of responsibility" upon the part of the faculty. Rather, we are suggesting that in the "normal" operation of higher educational institutions, the problem lies in the inclusion of *all* segments in a collective arrangement where each of the major subunits, such as the faculty, students, and administration, will have the basis and capacity appropriately to influence each other and thereby to arrive at policy decisions integrating the various interests of the subgroups. The academic value system cannot be served at its highest level whenever and wherever there is an organizational over-emphasis, whether it is constituted by administrative bureaucratization, exclusive faculty power, or student domination.

NOTES

1. This report was entitled *The American Academic Profession: A Pilot Study* by Talcott Parsons and Gerald M. Platt, Cambridge, Mass.: (multilith) March 1968. It is subsequently referred to as the "pilot report" or "pilot study." The study was supported by the National Science Foundation, Grant GS 513. We would once again like to acknowledge and thank the National Science Foundation for this support. We regret that copies of this report are no longer available for distribution.

2. For sampling purposes, institutional size was characterized by total graduate and undergraduate enrollment following previous literature using this method. Schools with 2,500 students or less were considered small size; 2,501 to 7,499, medium size; 7,500 and more, large size. Quality is, of course, an extremely difficult variable to quantify. We selected and combined four char-

acteristics from Astin's factor analysis of 33 variables. These were (1) general and educational monies per student, (2) scholarship funds per student, (3) number of library volumes per student, and (4) teacher-student ratio. The data were obtained from Cartter, 1964. Also, in connection with the development of the sampling matrix, see, Astin, 1962.

3. A technical "Note on Pilot Sample Bias" can be found in Appendix C of the pilot report. The research orientation of an institution figured heavily in our analysis. Its importance will be made explicit later in the text.

4. This scale was constructed by combining a measurement of faculty size with an assessment of orientation to research and an institutional quality index. Research orientation was measured by (1) the proportion of graduate students among all arts and sciences students, (2) amount of grant funds per faculty member, (3) number of periodicals taken by the university library per faculty member. Quality was measured by (1) general and educational monies per student, (2) percentage of staff members holding Ph.D.'s, (3) the student-teacher ratio. Size was defined by the number of full-time faculty and their equivalent part-time faculty, and not by student size as employed in the sampling matrix. All three indices, size, quality, and research, were combined to form our scale of institutional differentiation (SID).

5. Our SID has a correlation of .285 (p < .05) with degree of religious secularization, and .827 (p < .01) with number of academic departments, to mention a few of the more theoretically relevant correlates of "external" and "internal" differentiations. A full description of the scale is given in Chapter IV of the pilot report.

6. For further discussions of cognitive rationality, see the pilot report, Chapter I, "Theoretical Considerations"; Parsons and Platt, 1968b; and Parsons, 1968a.

7. The institutionalization of academic freedom and tenure as the bases for the freedom required for teaching and research is documented in Hofstadter and Metzger, 1955; see also MacIver, 1955.

8. The discipline and personal control of students has also been an administrative province, but recent events at Berkeley, Columbia, and Harvard make this function and its relation to the administration, to say the least, a problematic one. We examine this topic in the concluding section of the text.

9. On the issue of generalized media of exchange at the social system level, see Parsons, 1963a, 1963b, 1968c; for a discussion of media on the general action level see Parsons, forthcoming.

10. The two indices were constructed from the following items in the questionnaire as indicated.

Prestige of Respondent:

A.   1. "How many articles have you authored or coauthored?"
       Six point scale, weighted for prestige of journal or publication.
     2. "How many of your articles have appeared in what would be considered high prestige journals in your field?"
       Four point scale from "most" to "none" ("most" scored high).
B.   "How many books have you authored or coauthored?"
       Multiplied by a conversion factor of five. (Product recoded to a single digit scale.)
C.   Number of publications partially weighted for prestige of publication, formed by summing A and B. (Recoded to a single digit scale.)
D.   "Compared with your contemporaries (i.e., those who entered your discipline at about the same time as you did), how would you rate

your own career advancement (in terms of salary, rank, honors, etc.)?"
Seven point scale from "about the top ten percent" to "bottom ten percent." ("Top ten percent" scored high.)

E.   Professional association offices. (Weighted score for the highest office
          in a professional disciplinary association.)

          Prestige of Respondent index formed by the addition of C, D, and E.

Campus Influential Scale

Scale based on the frequency of respondent's discussion of departmental, faculty, college, and other educational affairs with the college
president, academic dean, and department chairman. In constructing
the influential scale, we deliberately chose contact with campus roles
associated with positions of power. If faculty attempt to influence those
in power while they themselves are not in positions of power, we have
assumed they will also attempt to influence their colleagues in less
formal positions. We believe the reverse could not as readily be assumed. However, for analytic purposes in the influence process, there
is no difference whether ego or alter is in a position of power. We have
assumed only that those academic men most frequently willing to
attempt to influence persons such as deans and chairmen will be "influentials" on campus.

11. *Eta* is a correlation ratio used to measure the closeness of the relationship between two variables when the regression is non-linear. It can be used as
a measure of the extent of the predictive value of one variable on another, although it does give the direction of prediction. See Guilford, 1950: 316–323.

12. When speaking of the question of the relationship between power and
influence, we must again deal with the deficiencies of our data on power. Since
the respondents were allowed to check only one of nine possible decision-
makers, the statistical probability of any one individual or collectivity being
checked was only one in nine. In contrast, influence ratings were performed
separately for each agent. Therefore, in comparing power and influence, it
was decided to count only perceptions of an agent as having "strong" influence
as positive responses. It was for this reason that we operationalized positive
influence ($+$) by respondents checking a "great deal" and "considerable"
categories in Table 6, and this procedure has been continued. Negative influence ($-$) in this context is calculated by the addition of the other three categories, "moderate," "some," and "little." Similarly, negative power ($-$) means
that another group was chosen as the decision-maker.

13. It is fair to say that academic freedom—by delegating a relatively autonomous sphere of power and influence to the faculty and department *vis a vis*
the administration—serves to shift the locus of social-level assessment to cultural types of collectivities, e.g., disciplinary. Although academic men may
make decisions within social collectivities, for example the faculty or department, probably most academic decisions (assessment of individual scholarship,
appointment, etc.) are viewed in terms of membership and standards derived
from more cultural collectivities.

14. Talcott Parsons has been acting as Chairman of the "Search Committee"
under the prior arrangement, and hence *ex-officio* as a member of the Standing
Committee. He opposed and voted against the new action, but decided to remain on the new Committee to try to help to "make it work." Two of the seven
members of the old Committee, including Professor Rosovsky, have resigned.

REFERENCES

Astin, Alexander W. (1962) "An empirical characterization of higher educational institutions." *Journal of Educational Psychology* 53 No. 5: 224–232.

Cartter, Allan, Ed. (1964) *American Universities and Colleges.* Washington, D.C.: American Council on Education.

Demerath, Nicholas J., Richard W. Stephens, and R. Robb Taylor (1967) *Power, Presidents and Professors.* New York: Basic Books.

Durkheim, Emile (1899–1900) "Deux lois de l'évolution penale." *L'Année Sociologique* IV: 65–96.

—— (1938) *The Rules of the Sociological Method.* Sarah A. Solovay and John H. Mueller (trans.), E. G. Catlin (ed.). Chicago: University of Chicago Press.

—— (1960) *The Division of Labor in Society,* George Simpson (trans.). New York: The Free Press.

Earnest, E. (1953) *Academic Procession: An Informal History of the American College, 1663–1953.* Indianapolis: Bobbs-Merrill.

Freidson, Eliot, and Buford Rhea (1963) "Processes of control in a company of equals." *Social Problems* 11, No. 2 (Fall): 119–131.

Goss, Mary E. W. (1961) "Influence and authority among physicians in an outpatient clinic." *American Sociological Review* 26: 39–50.

Guilford, J. P. (1950) *Fundamental Statistics in Psychology and Education.* New York: McGraw-Hill.

Hofstadter, Richard, and Walter P. Metzger (1955) *The Development of Academic Freedom in the United States.* New York: Columbia University Press.

Lazarsfeld, P., and W. Thielens (1958) *The Academic Mind.* New York: The Free Press.

Lipset, Seymour M. (1968) "Student politics in comparative perspective." *Daedalus* 97 (Winter): 1–20.

Lipset, Seymour M., and Philip G. Altbach (1967) "Student politics and higher education in the United States." Pp. 199–252 in S. M. Lipset (ed.) *Student Politics.* New York: Basic Books.

MacIver, Robert (1955) *Academic Freedom in Our Time.* Staten Island, New York: Gardian.

Parsons, Talcott (1960) "Durkheim's contribution to the theory of integration of social systems." In Kurt Wolff (ed.) *Emile Durkheim 1858–1917: A Collection of Essays with Translations and a Bibliography.* Columbus: Ohio State Univ. Press; reprinted (1967) in T. Parsons *Sociological Theory and Modern Society.* New York: The Free Press.

—— (1963a) "On the concept of influence." *Public Opinion Quarterly* 27: 37–62.

—— (1963b) "On the concept of political power." *Proceedings of the American Philosophical Society* 107: 3.

—— (1968a) "The academic system: a sociologist's view." *The Public Interest* 13: 173–197.

—— (1968b) "Professions." Pp. 536–547 in David L. Sills (ed.) *International Encyclopedia of the Social Sciences,* Vol. 12. New York: Macmillan and The Free Press.

—— (1968c) "On the concept of value-commitments." *Sociological Inquiry* 39, No. 2 (Spring).

—— (forthcoming) "Some problems of general theory in sociology." In John C. McKinney and Edward A. Tiryakian (eds.) *Theoretical Sociology: Perspectives and Developments.* New York: Appleton-Century-Crofts.

PARSONS, TALCOTT, and GERALD M. PLATT (1968a) *The American Academic Profession: A Pilot Study.* Cambridge, Mass. (multilith).

—— (1968b) "Considerations on the American academic system." *Minerva* 6, No. 4 (Summer): 497–523.

—— (1970) "Social structure and socialization in higher education." *Sociology of Education* (Winter), forthcoming. An expanded version will appear in Matilda White Riley, Marilyn E. Johnson, Anne Foner, et al. (eds.), *A Sociology of Age Stratification,* Vol. 3 of the series *Aging and Society.* New York: Russell Sage Foundation.

PARSONS, TALCOTT, and NEIL J. SMELSER (1956) *Economy and Society.* London: Routledge and Kegan Paul.

PARSONS, TALCOTT, and WINSTON WHITE (1961) "The link between character and society." In S. M. Lipset and L. Lowenthal (eds.) *Culture and Social Character.* New York: The Free Press; reprinted (1967) in T. Parsons (ed.) *Sociological Theory and Modern Society,* New York: The Free Press.

SHILS, EDWARD (1961) "Centre and periphery." Pp. 117–131 in *The Logic of Personal Knowledge: Essays Presented to Michael Polanyi.* London: Routledge and Kegan Paul.

STINCHCOMBE, ARTHUR L. (1965) "Social structure and organizations." Pp. 142–193 in James G. March (ed.) *Handbook of Organizations.* Chicago: Rand McNally.

WEBER, MAX (1946) "Science as a vocation." In H. H. Gerth and C. W. Mills (eds.) *Max Weber: Essays in Sociology.* New York: Oxford University Press.

CHAPTER 8

STUDENT VOICE—FACULTY RESPONSE

Robert C. Wilson and Jerry G. Gaff

Campus confrontations over Black Studies programs, ROTC, and military research have attracted national attention this year. At the same time, in less dramatic and public ways, students have been applying continuing pressure for greater involvement in the governing processes of their campuses. Students have been asking not only for less restrictive rules governing their personal and social lives, but for a greater say in the formation of those rules. They have been asking not only for changes in the curriculum, but for a greater voice in planning the curriculum.

The attitudes of American college students about these matters have been well-explored in research studies. There have been few studies of faculty members, however. This is not to say that much has not been written about them. College faculties are freely accused of being the real enemies of progress, of being indifferent to students, or of being the fomenters of student discontent. But while much has been written about professors and their attitudes, little has been based on data obtained from faculty members themselves.

The purpose of this chapter is to present evidence about the attitudes of faculty members toward student participation in campus governance. As will be shown by the data, faculty are generally favorable toward student participation in the formulation of social regulations, but are generally reluctant to grant students a similar role in academic policy-making. The range of individual faculty opinions on both of these issues is great, however, and these opinions are related to other factors, including educational philosophy, teaching practices, type of contact with students, and general political orientation.

The data are drawn from a larger study of Faculty Characteristics and Faculty Influence on Students being conducted at the Center. Questionnaires covering a wide variety of faculty attitudes, values, and behaviors

EDITORS' NOTE: This chapter is based on an article of the same title previously published in *The Research Reporter* (1969) 4: 1–4, with the permission of the authors and The Center for Research and Development in Higher Education, University of California, Berkeley.

were sent to over 1,500 faculty members at six diverse colleges and universities located in three states; usable returns were received from 70 percent, or 1,069 persons. The institutions included a large public university, a large state college, a medium-sized private university, a medium-sized public junior college, a small private university, and a small private liberal arts college. While the questionnaire covered a wide spectrum of issues, it is those questions concerned with faculty attitudes toward the role of students in institutional policy-making that are of particular relevance here.

Student Participation in Policy-Making

Two-thirds of the faculty respondents were in favor of students having formal responsibility for formulating social rules and regulations. As Figure 1 indicates, 45 percent would give students an equal vote on committees, and another 21 percent would give students sole responsibility for their own social regulations. These results may reflect faculty disinclination to be directly involved in matters of dormitory regulation, student discipline, and student government; since they are primarily responsible for the intellectual life of students, faculty typically hold a laissez-faire attitude toward student activities outside the classroom. Moreover, in recent years, professionally trained personnel have assumed many of the faculty's former duties in regulating student activities outside the classroom.

Indeed, from the faculty point of view, the concept of *in loco parentis* is a dead issue. The majority reported opposition to dress regulations, curfews in women's dormitories, restrictions on the use of alcohol, and strong college rules against marijuana. Additionally, 65 percent of the respondents thought the college should not prohibit an unmarried student couple from sharing the same apartment.

Faculty response to student participation in setting academic policies is quite another matter. Although only 4 percent of the faculty said students should play no role in "formulating academic policies, such as graduation requirements, curriculum design, and related issues," it is apparent from Figure 1 that professors are reluctant to share their academic power. Sixty percent said students should have some voice, either through being consulted informally or being permitted to sit as nonvoting members on "relevant committees to discuss the issues." A sizable minority of 36 percent would accord students a formal role by allowing them a vote on academic policy matters; only 9 percent, however, were willing to grant students "an equal vote with the faculty."

Faculty resistance to student involvement in academic affairs is also understandable. Demands for student participation in academic governance challenge faculty members in their areas of professional competence. One view is, for instance, that only a physicist knows what a physics curriculum should include. Further, faculties have fought hard to gain and retain power over these areas. Just as they have striven, historically, to preserve their prerogatives from intrusions by college administrators, boards of trus-

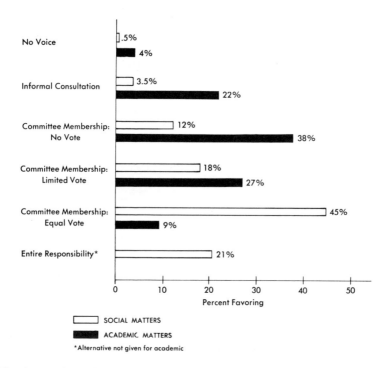

Fig. 1. Faculty attitudes about student participation in decisions regarding
social and academic policies.

tees, and state governments, so do they evidently wish to resist encroachment from students.

In the present climate of pressure for greater student power, and with
the likelihood that this pressure will continue, it is of interest to understand
the thinking of both those faculty who are supportive of student demands
for participation in academic policy-making and those who oppose such demands. What is each group like? How do they differ from each other? Perhaps these differences can best be illustrated by focusing on some of the
characteristics of the two "extreme" groups—those 95 professors in the
sample who thought students should have an equal vote with the faculty
and those 41 faculty members who believed students should have no role.
On all the characteristics considered, faculty with more moderate views fell
between these extremes.

Educational Philosophy

First, the two groups of faculty differ in their beliefs about the nature
and goals of a college education. Faculty who would share their power with
students believe college primarily should serve the expressive and self-de-

velopmental needs of students (Table 1). When asked about the most important goal of a college education they most commonly responded that the goal was to help students attain "self-knowledge and personal identity"; very few favored such utilitarian or future-oriented goals as "knowledge and skills directly applicable to their careers," or "an understanding and mastery of some specialized body of knowledge." On the other hand, very few of the *No voice* faculty chose self-knowledge, preferring instead the career and specialized knowledge alternatives.

The *Equal vote* group also expressed a more positive view of students' academic motivation and capacity for taking responsibility for their own actions: 81 percent agreed that "class attendance should be optional," and 73 percent disagreed that "without tests and grades to prod them most stu-

TABLE 1

MOST IMPORTANT GOAL OF UNDERGRADUATE EDUCATION, AS SELECTED BY TWO DISPARATE FACULTY GROUPS, IN PERCENTAGES

	Faculty groups	
	Equal Vote	No Voice
An undergraduate education should help students acquire:		
Knowledge and skills directly applicable to their careers	7	32
An understanding and mastery of some specialized body of knowledge	4	22
Preparation for further formal education	1	7
Self-knowledge and a personal identity	42	7
A broad general education	35	29
Knowledge of and interest in community and world problems	11	3

dents would learn little." In contrast, the *No voice* group held a more negative attitude on both counts; only 49 percent and 24 percent respectively gave those answers. On other questions a much larger proportion of the *Equal vote* group felt that colleges should afford their students the freedoms of adults, and that students would use these freedoms responsibly.

Those who favored student participation in academic policy-making held more flexible views of classroom teaching and reported they involved students more in their teaching. Specifically, they were more likely to endorse the notions that class assignments should be tailored to the needs of individual students and that students should be encouraged to pursue their own intellectual interests in courses. Also, many more of them said that they invite students to help make class plans and policy, that they solicit student criticism of their ideas, and that they ask for student evaluation of their courses.

More of the *Equal vote* group supported academic innovation in their college. Most of these faculty members thought that emphasis on grades should be decreased and that there should be an increase in the proportion of courses directed at contemporary social problems, the proportion of interdisciplinary courses, and the use of independent study. On the other hand, those who thought students should have no voice preferred the status quo; their most common response to each of these questions was that the situation should be unchanged.

Although all faculty were markedly permissive about regulations pertaining to students' personal lives, those who believe students should have an equal vote were the most permissive. They were opposed to dress regulations, dormitory curfews for women, restrictions on the use of alcohol, and strong college rules regarding marijuana to a vastly greater degree than their *No voice* colleagues. For example, 85 percent of the *Equal vote* group agreed that dress regulations have no place on a college campus, compared with 32 percent of the *No voice* group.

The above paragraphs summarize several dimensions of the educational ideology and teaching practices of faculty who are most and least hospitable to student participation in academic policy-making. Close examination of the several aspects of this ideology suggest a second level generalization: Faculty members who would share their power with students share an essentially positive view of the nature of students. That is, when the *Equal vote* group said that they had a positive view of student academic motivation, valued a flexible style of teaching, involved students in their classes, and favored many social freedoms, they seemed to be declaring faith in the ability of students to control and direct their own lives and to be expressing confidence that students can participate constructively in determining the nature of their own education. On the other hand, faculty members who were most opposed to student participation seemed to be turning the familiar slogan around and saying, "Don't trust anyone *under* 30." Their beliefs tended to stress that external control, motivation, and direction were needed in order for students to profit maximally from their education.

Related Faculty Characteristics

Faculty responses to student participation are not only related to their educational philosophies and their conceptions of students, but to other factors as well. Some clues to these are provided by other information gathered from the questionnaire. Among other things, the groups differed in amount of extra-academic contact with students. That is, 71 percent of the *Equal vote* group said that during the two weeks preceding their questionnaire responses they had helped a student resolve a disturbing personal problem, 76 percent indicated they had discussed a campus issue or problem with a student, and 87 percent reported they had socialized informally with a student. The comparable percentages of the *No voice* group were 47 percent, 46 percent, and 59 percent.

A further observation is that faculty who favor equal student participation are disproportionately represented in the social sciences; only 17 percent of the total sample, but 30 percent of the *Equal vote* group are in these departments. Faculty in applied fields (a combined group including agriculture, business administration, engineering, education, physical education, and vocational training areas) were overrepresented in the *No voice* group. Other recent research studies (Astin, 1965; Gamson, 1967; Spaulding and Turner, 1968) have also found that faculty in different fields of study differ in their attitudes and personal characteristics.

Political orientation is also related to faculty attitudes toward student participation. Seventy-eight percent of the *Equal vote* group checked the terms "liberal," "very liberal," or "radical" to describe their political position, 15 percent choosing the latter designation. Only 12 percent of the *No voice* group chose any of these three terms, but 78 percent said they were either politically "moderate" or "conservative." From these data, it would appear that faculty who subscribe to a "liberal" educational policy (i.e., involving students in academic policy making) take that stance as a specific expression of their more general view of society and life.

Additional evidence indicates that the *Equal vote* group is more politically active. A fair minority of them said that the major sources of satisfaction in their lives included "participation as a citizen" in community affairs and "participation in activities directed toward national or international betterment." They appear to be even more involved in college politics; 76 percent of the *Equal vote* group said they had "discussed a campus issue or problem" with at least one student—21 percent had discussed such matters with five or more students—during the previous two weeks. These responses were significantly greater than for the *No voice* group. Collectively, the evidence suggests that the minority of faculty actively committed to coequal faculty-student determination of academic policies is also concerned with campus reform, in keeping with their educational and political philosophies.

To counter any impression that the two groups of teachers are entirely dissimilar, several similarities between the *Equal vote* and *No voice* groups should be mentioned. First, both groups appear to be equally committed to teaching. About nine out of ten in both groups said teaching was one of the "major sources of satisfaction" in their lives, and the majority of each group thought effectiveness as a teacher should be "very important" in "decisions pertaining to promotion and salary matters." Second, the professors appear to adhere to what are commonly accepted as responsible teaching practices. Specifically, most of both groups reported that their classroom behavior included the following: "Describe objectives at the beginning of class;" "Relate the course work to other fields of study"; "Discuss points of view other than my own"; and "Mention reading references for points I make." Third, they do not differ with respect to advising students. Nearly all faculty members said they usually keep office hours, and the majority of each group reported that within the previous two weeks they had seen students outside of class to discuss their academic programs and to discuss their future careers. None of these comparisons yielded statistically significant differences. In sum, both groups are composed mainly of committed and responsible teachers; as teachers, they simply differ in some of their conceptions of what effective teaching involves.

The Future

There is some evidence that the attention of the student activists is turning away from administrators and toward the faculty, away from social regulations and toward academic practices. Recent disorders already have touched upon academic matters, an area which traditionally has been regarded as the province of the faculty. These skirmishes typically have been won by students; faculties across the country have voted to end secret military research, remove ROTC courses from the curriculum, and sanction new Third World colleges or departments. Some observers believe that students, encouraged by these early successes, will increasingly question practices closer to the core of faculty concerns. It is likely that students increasingly will demand changes in course requirements, grading practices, and teaching methods. In short, where the confrontations of the past have pitted students against administrators over issues of all-university significance (e.g., support of the war, "racism," and student rules) now student activists are increasingly confronting the faculty over academic issues.

Concerning these future developments, Donald Bowles (1968), academic dean at the American University in Washington, D.C., has ventured, "As academic questions go, it seems unusually clear that greater student participation, as well as faculty participation, in the academic governance of a college or university should be regarded . . . as inevitable" (Bowles, 1968: 261). This projection is supported by evidence from Richard Peterson's (1968) national survey, which revealed an increase in the incidence of organized student protest over academic issues in the past three years, especially at large public universities, and from Ann Heiss's contention (1969) that today's reform-minded graduate students will be tomorrow's new professors.

Support for a greater student voice in academic policy-making will come from certain kinds of faculty members, currently in the minority in this sample of institutions. Such faculty members tend to believe a college education should aid students in self-development, to have more faith in students' academic motivation and their ability to take responsibility, to involve students in the conduct of their courses, to advocate change and innovation in their colleges, and to hold relatively permissive views about the personal life of students. They are likely to have much contact with students outside of class, to teach in the social sciences, and to be both liberal and relatively active in politics, both on- and off-campus.

Faculty who oppose greater student participation tend to believe a college education should lead primarily to mastery of a particular body of knowledge or to preparation for a career, to feel students need considerable direction and supervision in their studies, and to be generally satisfied with their colleges' current academic practices. Such faculty members report relatively little nonacademic contact with students outside of class, and tend to be politically moderate and inactive.

Unless student pressure abates, or unless a larger number of faculty members become willing to share their academic authority with students, conflicts over academic policies seem destined to increase. In such an event, it is the two types of faculty members sketched in this essay who will undoubtedly help to shape the course of these conflicts and thereby determine the eventual role of students in the governing of the nation's colleges and universities.

REFERENCES

ASTIN, ALEXANDER W. (1965) "Classroom environment in different fields of study." *Journal of Educational Psychology* 56: 275–282.

BOWLES, W. DONALD (1968) "Student participation in academic governance." *Educational Record* 49: 257–262.

GAMSON, ZELDA F. (1967) "Performance and personalism in student-faculty relations." *Sociology of Education* 40: 279–301.

HEISS, ANN M. (1969) "Today's graduate student—tomorrow's faculty member." In *The Research Reporter*. Berkeley: University of California, Center for Research and Development in Higher Education.

PETERSON, RICHARD E. (1968) *The Scope of Organized Student Protest in 1967–1968*. Princeton: Educational Testing Service.

SPAULDING, CHARLES B., and HENRY A. TURNER (1968) "Political orientation and field of specialization among college professors." *Sociology of Education* 41: 247–262.

PART IV

STUDENTS

CHAPTER 9

STUDENT INTERESTS, STUDENT POWER, AND THE SWEDISH EXPERIENCE

Troy Duster

The Berkeley Free Speech Movement crystallized two views about the proper role of students at American universities. One view is sometimes summarized in the phrase "the right of students is the right to learn." [1] The other asserts the right of students to participate in university governance.[2] Many who take the latter view feel that such participation should not be limited to extracurricular matters. They demand student involvement in the formulation of educational policy and student participation in decisions on the nature and direction of the university itself.

Much of the debate on this issue appears to me to be premature. This is not because the debate categorically rejects or affirms student rights, but because another issue must be raised and resolved before meaningful discussion can proceed. Whether or not students should be directly represented in the governing councils of the university can be answered only after discussion of whether there are important differences of interests between students and those who now govern. If the answer to this is positive, we can then turn to the question of whether those "student interests" should have representation.

In the United States both faculty and administrators have typically denied or minimized the presence of separate and conflicting student interests. Faculty members have taken it for granted that what is good for them is good for students. And administrators, with a professional proclivity for accommodation, have been as much committed to an ideology of harmony of interests as the faculty. In rhetoric, the university is either a "voluntary scholarly community" or a "rational bureaucracy," but rarely a conflict model (See Lunsford, 1968).

AUTHOR'S NOTE: Material in the segment on Swedish student government was collected under an Office of Education, Department of Health, Education, and Welfare Contract No. OE-6-10-106, Cooperative Research Project No. C-07. I have benefited from critical commentary from Harland Bloland, Terry Lunsford, and David Makofsky.

This chapter is reprinted (in slightly revised form) from *The American Behavioral Scientist*, May–June, 1968 (Volume XI, Number 5).

In this chapter, I will try to look more closely at these matters. To do so, I shall examine the problem of "interests" at the university in the first section. Then, in the concluding segment, I shall briefly discuss the student role in the governance of Swedish universities. These stand in sharp contrast to the Latin American universities, which are often trotted out to make the case that a politicized version of the university is untenable because students "get control." The Swedish experience, on the contrary, provides a viable model of the accommodation of differing interests.

System Rewards and the Interests of Faculty and Administration

To speak of the "interest of the faculty" does not necessarily imply a simple homogeneous group. There is great diversity, with clear differences, for example, both within and between the engineering, law, and medical faculties and the humanities and social science faculties about the role of teaching, relations between faculty and students, and other matters. However, the major drift of rewards that accrue to the faculty has been in one direction, and this drift affects the professors of art, music, drama, classical languages, and medieval English no less than it affects the professors of physics, engineering, and microbiology. Every commentator on the scene agrees that the *system* rewards go to the specialist and researcher, not to the generalist and teacher. This is to be contrasted with the notion of *personal* rewards, since a professor can surely obtain a great deal of personal satisfaction from having his teaching well-received by bright and enthusiastic students. Indeed, he may get personal satisfaction from doing an excellent bit of research and having it published in a major journal in his field. But the point is that those who are part of a social system tend to be most responsive to success as it is defined in that system. Thus I will argue that it is legitimate to refer to the "interests of the faculty" to the degree that we can identify one major system of rewards.

Now, occasional mavericks aside, the faculty at most large American universities share very definite career concerns. These have to do with such prosaic matters as promotion, success in one's field, and tenure on the job, three matters that revolve around the single and simple measure of one's publication record. There is nothing new in the characterization of the major modern university as possessed and distressed by the publication devil, impatient with those elements of life which get in the way of publishing—students and teaching. It has reached the point, however, where a faculty recruiter can openly try to lure a prospective colleague to his campus with the inviting wink around the remark that "he hadn't seen an undergraduate in two years." [3] There is nothing new either in the public rhetoric which deplores this condition or in the public practice of rewarding it with the Nobel prize (or its moral equivalent in other disciplines), while for scores of reasons, no such parallel is imaginable on the teaching side of the ledger.

Of course, in the abstract, good research and good teaching are not incompatible, and there is a widely shared belief that in some fields, one cannot be a good teacher unless he is a good researcher. The argument can be misleading, however, for some take it to mean that because there is no necessary incompatibility, there is no problem. If incentives and rewards for research and teaching were more equal, the balance in the emphasis and efforts of the faculty would be more even. But since all of the system rewards are on the research side, heterogeneity among the faculty is less important for determining the direction in which the faculty in general has been and will be moving.

What of the administration? Can we speak of its "interests"? The administration is, in one sense, more homogeneous than the faculty and, in another, more heterogeneous. It is more homogeneous in that all administrators are engaged in a bureaucratic work situation that has as its central task the management of the affairs of others in the university. There is little room for the eccentric, and little reward for innovation. The organization man is a more likely figure in administration than any place else in the university. At the same time, the administration is more heterogeneous than the faculty because of the clearly different "classes" of persons in the bureaucracy. Even the most junior faculty member is regarded as a colleague by the most senior member, and the junior member may engage the senior as an intellectual equal (indeed, inferior) in the discourse of his own field —or in politics, the arts, life. That is not so in administration. There status and communication lines carry more clearly with the office. Lower echelon administrators act as if they were a different social breed from the clerical workers, and neither lunches with such persons as the divisional heads, the deans, the assistant deans, or the special assistants to the chancellors and presidents.

Still, it serves an analytic purpose to talk of "the administration and its interests" as a general phenomenon capable of being identified and isolated from the students and the faculty along very important lines. Just as the organization of rewards for the faculty produces for them a dominant interest in publishing, so there is a dominant reference point of rewards for administration. In a bureaucracy, the most certain path to promotion and organizational success is compliance with the orders of one's line superior. The rewards go to that right combination of the ability to follow orders and to work efficiently, and to do both in the proper attitude. The structure of authority makes the administrator responsible to those at the top who make decisions. Those decisions reflect the view that the university ought to be run in an efficient, productive, low-cost, well-organized, and moral manner (Beck, 1947).[4]

Given the direction in which the two are now moving, I see no fundamental or *systematic* interest conflict between faculty and administration. The two groups operate in different spheres that intersect occasionally, but the reward system for one is not the obverse side of the reward system of the other. They have, for the most part, very significantly different interests, though they may occasionally conflict over matters of resource allocation, priority, and the like.

However, to the degree that the faculty moves further and further along the road to increasing careerism, professionalism, and specialization, to that extent conflicts will be fewer and fewer. For example, the administrator is *accountable* to his superiors in the line organization of his bureaucracy. This preoccupation with accountability orients him to the faculty and to students in such a way that he is concerned with clear products, such as the number of Woodrow Wilson Fellows, the proportion who enter graduate school, the number of journal articles, etc. If the faculty has the same "interest" in seeing this proportion high (as would a faculty of careerists), then conflict in this whole area is mitigated. Of course, some faculty have a primary view of education as a broadening, humanizing experience. In such cases it is difficult to *account* for success in clear, empirical, and precise terms. For example, an important reformist document by a student-faculty committee at Berkeley (Study Commission on University Governance, 1968: 7–8) has this to say about that subject:

> The inertia of our institutions and our lack of a rooted tradition of educational innovation have had a paradoxical result: they have led to a brave and unwarranted complacency, as though the campus truly believed its official rhetoric that this is a 'great university,' the peer of any institution of higher learning in the world. We are skeptical, however, that a count of Nobel prize winners, the high national rating of graduate departments, or the presence of a distinguished faculty provide conclusive measures of a university's greatness. These attributes do not in themselves represent a university's ultimate goals, but rather means toward achieving them. In our view, the most important single goal of a university, and therefore the best measure of its excellence, is the intellectual growth of its students: their initiation into the life of the mind, their commitment to the use of reason in the resolution of problems, their development of both technical competence and intellectual integrity.

Such a view of the importance of the university experience involves a greater interest conflict than where the faculty itself is concerned with the publicly accountable character of their own product.

In this chapter, there is a purposeful deemphasis of the differences and conflicts between faculty and administration. That is taken up elsewhere in this book and bears less directly upon the emergence of the concerns for student interests. Whereas the faculty and the administration confront each other only incidentally and occasionally, the faculty confronts the students systematically. I will return to that point momentarily.

The Interests of Students

The question has already been raised: is what is good for the faculty good for the students? The question can just as easily be posed: is what is good for administrators good for students? Answers are not forthcoming until we examine what it is that can be identified as "student interests."

Of the three bodies, students are overwhelmingly the largest and certainly the most heterogeneous. Their heterogeneity is greater along almost every dimension. On the surface of a social profile, they are more mixed than either faculty or administrators with respect to social class, sex, ethnicity, and, probably, political proclivity. (The one exception is that students are relatively homogeneous with regard to age, which, of course, has important consequences for their "interests.") Both the faculty and the administration are far more exclusively white males with a middle-class life style, if not ideology. But, perhaps the most real and significant difference in the heterogeneity of students lies in the wide variance of interests and visions of what is possible in their own lives. The students, *relatively* speaking, are an uncommitted lot. Both the faculty and the administration are many times over more committed to the university as an established institution. It is for them much more of an end and a way of life. For the student, it is more of a means, a way-station, a delaying or stalling time, or a time for the construction and resolution of possibilities and decisions about the future. Most students believe that they will leave the university after a few years.

The faculty recognize this. Their predominantly "professional" orientation leads them to regard teaching as a time for recruiting young committed physicists or chemists or psychologists into the profession. Accordingly, for example, the faculty tends to deprecate general survey courses. The lowest or newest or most unfortunate colleague is saddled with teaching those students whose level of specialized commitment to the field of inquiry is problematic. This, I propose, reflects not an incidental but a systematic interest difference. It is systematic in the sense that it is a perpetual and integral part of the way in which the professor conceives of the relationship between himself and the student and will become more so with greater professionalism.

Now, because the level of commitment for students is far less than for faculty and administration, it makes far less sense to identify student interests by identifying the formal system of rewards. Of course, we might choose to view student interests in terms of the formal criteria of academic success, high grades, and the achievement of the degree. If we make that choice, we will see little cause for differences or conflict. But the student revolt of the 1960s has been based at least partially on the *disjunction* between the formal social organization of rewards in the university and something which I will leave momentarily undefined as their "interests." Neither the faculty nor the administration has expressed as much disagreement or impatience with their reward system. There is, of course, the annual rhetoric of the college president and the commencement speaker about the importance of teaching and character building and independence. But few seriously attempt to shift rewards away from publishing toward teaching, or to mitigate *in loco parentis* in favor of greater student independence and control. And those who do are not currently in the vanguard of the great universities.

To put it another way, the most respected elements among faculty and administrators are not mounting anything like a revolt against the present structure of the university. Quite the opposite, they act to bring the university further along the segmentalized, compartmentalized, and professionalized path it has been traveling.

In contrast, the clear tendency is for student leaders to question and challenge the existing structure of control as, most charitably put, increasingly neglectful of the student voice. This is true not only of the militant, vociferous New Left on the campus, but also of student body presidents in major universities, who were once unashamedly the handmaidens of the deans of students (Robertson, 1967; Brann, 1967). It is true not only for those who can claim to be leaders on the grounds of their political persuasiveness or charisma, but also for those student leaders with formal positions of leadership.

Where it was possible to identify and to speak generally of the interests of both the faculty and the administration, the greater heterogeneity of the students compounds the difficulty of even the grossest characterization of "student interests" in the same sense. Many females see their primary "interest" in the undergraduate years as getting a husband. Or, dividing students into the four subcultures that Clark and Trow (1963) have suggested, it is easy to see how wide the divergence is between and among students. The "intellectual interests" of the bohemian student and activists are not served by the same development as that of the fraternity-sorority crowd.

My tactic in identifying the interests of the faculty and administrators was to point to the social organization of rewards available to each. I shall not, however, attempt the impossible task of identifying a similar one-dimensional reward system for students. Rather, I shall attempt to abstract something called "student interests" by identifying the quest of students for "citizenship," or *the right to present their interests whatever they may be.* In suggesting that the relationship between faculty and administration is increasingly accommodative, I tried to illustrate how the rewards accruing to one did not detract from the rewards accruing to the other. In fact, one might posit a positive complementarity between the two in that the more the faculty "put out" in a factory-like way, the better the administration is able to account to its superiors, be they a board of governors, legislators, the general public, or alumni. The situation is quite different, however, between faculty and students, and the notion of complementarity gives way to something akin to a "zero-sum" game. This would be a situation where more for one side means less for the other.

An example of this has already been given in the discussion concerning how the faculty as professionals invest themselves far more in the teaching and recruiting of "departmental majors," who constitute a professional pay-off. Contrast this with the situation that exists between faculty and administration. It is not true that "success" for the faculty systematically, or even usually, diminishes "success" for the administration. It is not true that promotions in the administrative ranks get in the way of the faculty members' publishing and promotion. With students, however, whether they want more time for "play" or "guided work," or whether more freedom in which to fill that time, they are in systematic conflict with the two groups who respectively have almost everything to say about these matters.

The Quest for "Citizenship"

In this section I shall attempt to explain (a) why students have begun to identify their interests as separate from those of the faculty and the administration, and will do more so in the future, and (b) why they will increasingly aspire to representation of that interest. Conceptual tools drawn from studies of political communities are very pertinent.

In de Tocqueville's analysis of the great transformation in the social and political structure of western Europe from feudalism to capitalism, he attempted to explain how and why the servant classes rebelled. Bendix' (1964: 54) summary is succinct:

> Tocqueville does not attempt to predict the final outcome of the tendencies he discerns or to explain away ideas by reference to some ultimate determinant like the organization of production. He seeks to account for the frame of mind in which servants reject the 'rules of the game' on which the established society is founded. To do this he formulates a theory of crisis in the relations of master and servants: (1) in an earlier condition the socially inferior person possesses a recognized status . . . ; (2) in the crisis of transition the masters retain their privileges but no longer perform their functions, while the servants retain their obligation but perceive new opportunities; (3) in consequence the servants consider that the traditional claims of their status have been abrogated unilaterally and/or that they are now entitled to an equality of rights with all other social ranks, since in his capacity as a citizen every man is the equal of every other.
>
> Tocqueville's theory of crisis in 'domestic government' refers to the master's evasion of 'his obligation to protect and to remunerate,' but then gives special attention to the ideas of equality which elicit and shape the lower-class protest that initiates the 'age of democratic revolution.'

In such an analysis, heterogeneity within the mass is specifically neglected for the purpose of speaking to the matter that made the lower and servant classes commonly share a given station—their disenfranchisement and their social and political vulnerability to the whim and caprice of the aristocracy or the landed classes. To be drawn into an examination of the myriad of differences of subsidiary groups, subcultures, or nations is to derail the analysis from an overview of the common interest in the achievement of a political power to wield in whatever manner they may later define. After all, the substantive interests of groups may change over time, but the ascension to a political position for the purpose of carrying out those interests is less subject to variance.

I, too, am concerned with explicating the general form of a relationship. And though I realize that all analogies, including that between a civic community and a university must be qualified, with proper caution a "political" model can serve a useful and analytic purpose. In these terms, the faculty and the administration have "citizenship" in the university community, while students do not. The analogy suggests the reason for shifting the identification of student interests to the quest for citizenship.

In analyzing the development of the emergence of universal citizenship in the political community, de Tocqueville spells out the earliest relationship between the subordinate and the superordinate as one in which the former had a view of the traditional obligations being met by the latter. In the university, this might parallel the traditional view of the learning experience: the tutorial session, the seminar, the discussion session with the professor, or any other *exchange* with the "master" *which the master honored* as his obligation. The professor's commitments were to the local scene and to tutelage of students in the local university community. Then, ". . . in the crisis of transition, the masters retain their privileges but no longer perform their functions, while the servants retain their obligations but perceive new opportunities" (Bendix, 1964: 54). In the university situation, one version of this would be the professor's retaining the privileges without performing that function which the students had come traditionally to expect. In the Berkeley Free Speech Movement, a recurrent theme in both the student rhetoric and the expressions of some of the faculty guilt was that the faculty had abandoned the students to pursue "faculty interests" (Lipset and Wolin, 1965: 303–366).

After all, many faculty believe that there is no virtue in, or commitment to, the democratic process within the halls of academia. The university is not a polity, they argue, and students are there to acquire skills and learn. Others maintain that, while the greater society is a democracy, this in no sense requires that the political structure of the university itself should be democratic. Democracies have armies, but that does not mean that the political structure of authority of the army must be democratic. But this construction merely begs the question with which the students increasingly confront the administration: who does have the right to make the rules in the university?

Haunted by a Latin American image of student participation in university governance, administrators and some faculty express the following fears of the probable consequences of student power: (a) students will not know when to stop, will be excessive in their demands, (b) students will try to institute "democracy" in the classroom and in the dormitories, and (c) because of their greater numbers, students will win all the battles. I shall return below to the question of administrators' models of student participation. But, first, the appropriateness of the "citizenship" analogy should be demonstrated by applying it to the relationship between students and policy-making administrators.

Very recently at Berkeley, a dispute arose between the student government and the administration over the control of the student budget. Simultaneously, there was a conflict over whether graduate students were eligible to vote in student elections. In November, 1967, the student government held an election and permitted graduate students to vote. (Radical left students won office, a remark which I will let remain parenthetical, even though it may have something more than parenthetical force, for the student government allocated funds to supply bail money to students arrested in demonstrations against the selective service system.) The chancellor not only voided the elections and ruled that new elections would have to be held, but he also removed the funds of the student government from their control. He moved to set up a new board to handle the student funds and also suggested that membership in the student union might be made voluntary.

Student leaders responded defiantly. They seated elected students who had been suspended from the university by the chancellor, and they carried on student government as if the elections had not been voided. Further, they retained an attorney to challenge the administration's removal of control of student funds to a new board, where students would have only minority representation.

In this case, the conflict of interests between students and administrators can be couched in terms of an aspiration to "citizenship." The chancellor ruled that he could void the elections because he was acting in his authoritative capacity, and that the students had violated the university-wide rules which prohibited graduate students from voting in elections. The students countered in a way that can only be interpreted as a challenge to the very authority upon which the chancellor based his actions, namely, "Who is it who has the right to set the rules at the university?" Once that question is posed by a body which has traditionally complied with the rules, it makes explicit a skepticism about the legitimacy to govern that is at the foundation of the social order. It means that the students do see an abrogation of their rights and move to insure that they have some voice in constructing the rules of the university community. In discussing Weber's concept of authority, Bendix (1964: 16–17) has pointed out the necessity to

> . . . distinguish between social relations (such as the supply-and-demand relation on the market) that are maintained by the reciprocity of expectations, and others that are maintained through orientation toward an exercise of authority. The latter orientation typically involves a belief in the existence of a legitimate order. Identifiable persons maintain that order through the exercise of authority.
>
> This order endures as long as the conception of its legitimacy is shared by those who exercise authority and those who are subject to it. In addition, a legitimate order depends upon an organizational structure maintained by the persons who exercise authority and claim legitimacy for this exercise.
>
> The shared conception of a legitimate order and the persons in formal organizations who help to maintain that order through the exercise of authority constitute a network of social relations which differs qualitatively from the social relationships arising out of a 'coalescence of interests.' In this way actions may arise from the 'legitimate order' and effect the pursuit of interests in the society, just as the latter has multiple effects upon the exercise of authority. Throughout his work Weber insists that this interdependence of all social conditions must be recognized, but that at the same time the scholar must make distinctions such as that between a 'co-

alescence of interests' and a 'legitimate order' of authority, arbitrary as such distinctions inevitably are.

Thus, when students begin to question the legitimacy of the social order of the university, they shift to a view that the university should be a coalescence of interests. Such an organization would mean that the students want their own representation in the control of that order.

At the outset, I said that whether student interests should have representation was dependent upon the identification of those interests and the determination of whether or not they were different from, or perhaps even in conflict with, the interests of the faculty and the administration. Without even considering the content of the interests of the students, the very assertion of the students' right to enter into decision-making and policy matters constitutes a quest for citizenship. In a historical perspective I have implied that a significant source of the burgeoning student quest for citizenship, or for an authoritative voice in the construction of policy of the university, lies in a reaction to increasing professionalism of faculty and administration.

The Swedish Experience with Student "Interests" and "Power"

American educators intent on minimizing the authority of students in education policy often refer to the example of the Latin American universities. They argue that to make explicit the polarization of the university into conflicting parties with openly conflicting interests is to invite the kind of "anarchistic" educational system that appears in certain Latin American universities. This viewpoint assumes that student participation in high level decisions about university policy will undermine the *necessary* authority of the faculty on curriculum matters. While it is true that highly politicized universities in Latin America may, for example, witness student strikes when a professor interprets material in a way unacceptable to the students, this is not an inevitable outcome of "student power." Indeed, "student power," like "black power," has become a shibboleth in the United States. While "Latinization" is one outcome of "student power," it is by no means the only possible one.

The remainder of the chapter explores an alternative model of viable student participation in university governance.

In Sweden the seat of student power is the formally organized union of students at each of the five universities and the national federation of these five unions, *Sveriges Förenade Studentkårer* (SFS). Membership and fees are compulsory, so there is a base of about 75,000 students. The union is independent of faculty or government control; students collect the fees and administer the funds collected. The interests of the typical student in the affairs of the union is not very great, despite the fact that the local and national unions make policy which touches upon all facets of student life. A small core of the interested and committed dedicate themselves to performing the organizational tasks, while the vast majority simply pay their dues and neither know nor care about the union's activities or structure.

Until recently, the SFS leadership was made up of politically moderate or conservative students who would be known in the United States as "activity majors." Though the tasks and powers of the Swedish student officials far exceeded that of their counterparts in American student governing boards and student unions, they bore a remarkable resemblance to each other as social and political animals. In recent years, however, a double insurgency has affected the leadership in some of the local unions, and this has also been reflected in the national congresses. On the one hand, leftist students have made a stronger bid for organizational office and have met with some success. While there is still a strong conservative bias among Swedish university students, owing to their predominantly upper- and middle-class origins, the disinterest and inactivity of the majority permitted the activists on the left to make themselves a very potent force. A second factor has been the rapidly increased enrollment which created new organizational and administrative problems for the student unions that have shaken the traditional structure. The rapid growth has brought with it a demand for the rethinking and reshaping of old policy positions.

The local student unions actually operate and control all university student housing, the mechanisms of the registration of students, student buildings and recreational facilities, and food services. The functions performed in American universities by deans of students, deans of admission, and registrars are carried out in Sweden by the students through their union. There is no separate body of "administration," as American students could identify it. This raises an interesting question for a comparative analysis of social order, namely, what are the consequences of a given function, like housing, when different "structures" fulfill them? It may be that the function is altered so dramatically that it can no longer be considered the *same* function. In any case, when the faculty, the "administration," and the students define their interests in different ways, it matters mightily which one of them controls, say, the housing of students, faculty salaries, or promotion of administrators.

Student influence on educational policy is felt at every level, from the individual departments or institutes to the ministry of education. At the department level, two student representatives are elected by the local association of students to sit on a board consisting of the professor and the teaching staff. The dominance of the professor is so great that only if he decides to listen need he be affected by the student (or other faculty) advice. Nonetheless, the mechanism and the opportunity for such contact and communication is established. The professors are divided into broad groupings, such as the "law faculty" and the "humanities faculty," and each of these sections of the university has an educational committee whose membership consists of the chairman of that faculty (chosen from among the professors in the general area), three representatives of the teaching staff, three students representing local student unions, and a representative of the graduate assistants:

> The Educational Committee in each faculty has important duties such as the preparation of study plans and determination of the content of each subject taught at the faculty. It observes the procedure of examinations and checks on student progress in the different subjects [Sveriges Förenade Studentkårer].

The proposals and recommendations of the educational committee are subject to the approval of both the general faculty affected and also the chancellor. This is more than simply an advisory function, however, for these committees may frame the questions and set the discourse which gives substance and direction to educational policy.

In the last few years, the student organization has cautiously tried to influence policy in realms that have previously been reserved to the professors. So far, this has not resulted in any significant open antagonism, but as the students find that their suggestions are met with either success or failure, this is a predictable development. Success will feed the notion of the ability to effect change, and thus act as a spur to bolder innovation, while failure on these minor "reasonable demands" will help to identify the professors as the real enemies of reform, and draw the battle lines more clearly for the next thrust.

Two recent cases of the encroachment of the students into matters previously reserved only for the faculty may serve as illustrations. In the past, positions for graduate teaching fellows and "temporary" lectureships were filled through appointments made by the professors.[5] While the professor possessed full formal powers to make such appointments, he normally consulted with the existing faculty of the department in question. As a matter of official policy, the SFS is presently demanding that such vacant posts be publicly announced, so that a wider range of qualified applicants might compete for the position. This is a cautious demand that will not really antagonize the professors, for it does not violate their right to hire and fire persons to these posts. Though no basic shift of rights is involved, the students are attempting to influence hiring practices. If successful, they will be encouraged to press for more significant reforms, and they say as much.

A second problem area where the student unions have decided to lobby and influence educational policy on issues previously reserved to the faculty has been curriculum organization and, more specifically, interdisciplinary teaching and research. This involves something of a student reaction against what the faculty has taken for granted, namely, specialization at the university. Students in Sweden have, for the most part, accepted the notion of university studies as specialized occupational training, but there is every indication that the new activists see interdisciplinary teaching efforts as a positive development which they should support. The immediate source of this concern was an isolated initiative in 1966 from a wing of the medical faculty at one of the universities, which presented a report to the government pointing out the advantages of an interdisciplinary teaching program in their institute. The national student union picked up the theme of the report and asked that the question be held up for a time so that a thorough *general* investigation could be made to determine the feasibility of more generic reforms for interdisciplinary teaching. A review of the situation is now taking place, and though there will be resistance from some of the faculties, it seems likely that many institutes will make changes that range from a token integrated course to more thoroughgoing curriculum revisions.

This is simply one of many examples in Swedish higher education where (a) the ideology surrounding student participation in educational policy has resulted in the structuring of institutions that make possible such student participation and (b) the existence of such institutional student structures serves as its own implementation of such power. As long as Americans take seriously theses such as "the only right of students is the right to learn," the presumption is not so much that the students do not know enough, but that they have *no right* to influence the nature of the learning experience, namely, how, when, and what things should be taught. Indeed, the Swedish experience sheds some light on that subject, because SFS has made an attempt to influence *what is taught* at the universities. Once structures are established for the furtherance of some interests, there will be demands, pressures, and problems in line with that purpose. For example, the SFS has an International Secretariat, and from this group there has come the suggestion that the Swedish universities develop greater contacts with technologically underdeveloped countries by creating new positions in social anthropology. These new teaching and research positions would be designed specifically to increase the amount of substantive knowledge available and offered in Sweden on such countries.

Within SFS, there is a group of students who are pressing for a greater student voice in the determination of the curriculum. The vision of these students is idealistic, but they translate the request for a program into the moderate demand that the university be a place for the training of individuals for certain occupational roles. Thus, concern for increased contact between, and aid to, technologically underdeveloped countries is translated into the more acceptable academic position of a demand for more non-European languages at the university, a demand for new courses that inform Swedish students of the political, economic, and cultural situations in these countries, and so forth. In fact, one of the primary themes of the student reformists concerns the exhortation that all education should be either occupationally or "goal" directed. Under this banner, they can bring all manner of claims about the various changes they would like to see in the organization and pursuit of education, and justify it in terms of its goal-related or occupational-related character.

The basic issue should be rephrased. It is whether or not the student proposals for change are to be treated as a legitimate voice in a two- or three-party accommodation of interests. We need not even raise the question here about the "reasonable content" of the students' suggestion, for it is to change the issue if we say: students have the right to participate in educational policy decisions *if and when they are reasonable*. That is an equivocal "concession," for it then becomes a matter for negotiation to determine when students are being reasonable—and when it is decided they are not, their suggestions can be dismissed out of hand. This is to give the students no more than advisory status in the decision-making, and while this is preferable to no role at all, it does not address the problem of the rights of participating elements in a new light.

It is in the area of student housing, where things are so concrete and clear (buildings and their operation), that the comparative technique yields some answers about different interests, different functions, and different actors. As previously stated, a functional analysis, by positing that the function (of student housing) would be fulfilled (whether the fulfilling agent is the government, the faculty, the "administration," or the students themselves), leads one away from concerns with how, and what difference it makes. In the analysis of a single society or culture, the best one can do is posit functional alternatives for speculative purposes. However, when we look at two different cultures where the "same" tasks are performed by different agents, empirical differences compel us to raise the question of whether it is legitimate to label that development as the same function.

In Sweden, the function of providing student housing is in the hands of students. At each of the five universities, student unions determine everything from architectural design and floor space to coeducational corridor policy. The housing is supported by government funds, but the students retain decision-making authority at the highest level of what Americans would term "administration." Swedish students make the rules which relate to the kind of personal and communal associations possible in the living units. As a policy matter, the student unions assign one student to one room, and he shares a kitchen and bath along a corridor with from three to nine other students.[6] There being no dean of students to act as the keeper of morality after classes, the unions have at their discretion (and sometimes use it) the assignment of corridors on a coeducational basis. If career administrators were performing the function of assigning students, one could easily see that their interests in acting in such a way that they appease the community (*even in Sweden*) would lead them to a different structuring of the housing situation. In the United States, one common view of administrators is that students learn to live together. Thus, they assign, as common practice, two students to a single bedroom. Perhaps if American students obtained such control, they would decide upon more to a room, or fewer, but, in any case, I doubt that their rationale for doing so would have anything to do with "learning to be good citizens." That is rhetoric reflecting the interest of an administrator, and it is of importance to note that the "function" may be performed qualitatively different, depending upon what interest group performs the task.

In summary, the Swedish experience with student participation in governance of both student affairs and larger educational policy suggests that (a) there is little basis for the fear that the explicit conception of different interests for students (with the organization of their institutional authority) leads inevitably to anarchy and perpetual conflict, (b) student "encroachment" upon the territory of administrators and faculty brings with it no necessary domino-effect or a stampede of student power, and (c) the choice of which of the three parties controls an institution or segment of life on the campus makes a significant difference in the way in which the institution performs or functions. Unless we are willing to attribute the Swedish variation described entirely to style, the last statement compels us to take seriously the proposition that a separate set of "student interests" does exist.

There are some obvious problems with using the Swedish experience of student participation in university governance to illuminate the situation in the United States. For example, Sweden is a small, homogeneous country with a long tradition of student autonomy at the university. But Latin America, too, differs greatly from the United States in its traditions and university structure, yet some seem to have less difficulty envisioning parallels of likely development.

The fact that countries are not perfect replicas of each other does not mean that what works in one necessarily fails (or succeeds) in another. What is needed now is a careful analysis of the relevance of the various models of university governance to the American situation. We can, at the least, begin a serious examination of causes where students possess "citizenship" to see what similarities and differences apply to the meaning of "student acquisition of citizenship" in the United States, attempting to extrapolate the kinds of structural implementation most suited to the American context.

NOTES

1. Sidney Hook published an article in the *New York Times Magazine* with a title that suggested this phrase, and the content of the article carried the argument. Later, in the *Partisan Review,* Spring, 1967, Hook said that the title was not of his choosing. Nevertheless, the position often associated with him probably represents a large enough segment of opinion to be called a representative rallying cry of those who oppose "student power."

2. See the article by Nan Robertson (1967). See also the article by James Brann (1967). Also see Study Commission on University Governance (1968).

3. When I had just finished my graduate training, I was interviewed by a recruiter from a major university, who explicitly used this as a definite lure from one professional to another.

4. Also see T. Duster (1967) for an updated version of the Beck study on boards of governors.

5. *Högre utbildning och forskning,* Universitetskanslerämbetets petita för budgetåret, 1967–1968. "Temporary lektors" are based solely upon the number of students enrolled and thus may fluctuate from year to year by institute.

6. Sometimes the number to a corridor may be as high as eighteen, but this is very unusual except in some Stockholm dormitories.

REFERENCES

BECK, H. P. (1947) *Men Who Control Our Universities.* New York: King's Crown Press.

BENDIX, R. (1964) *Nation Building and Citizenship.* New York: John Wiley.
BRANN, J. (1967) "National rally for student power." *The Nation* (December 18): 658–660.
CLARK, B. R. and M. TROW (1963) *Determinants of College Student Subcultures.* Berkeley: Center for Research and Development in Higher Education.
Daily Californian (1968) Berkeley: University of California (January 11): 1.
—— (1968) Berkeley: University of California (January 10): 1.
DUSTER, T. (1967) "The aims of higher learning and the control of the universities." Berkeley: Center for Research and Development in Higher Education.
HOOK, S. (1965) *New York Times Magazine* (January 3): 8–9, 16, 18.
LIPSET, S. M. and S. WOLIN, Eds. (1965) *The Berkeley Student Revolt, Facts and Interpretations.* New York: Anchor Books.
LUNSFORD, T. (1968) "Authority and ideology in the administered university." *American Behavioral Scientist* 11, No. 5 (May–June): 5–14.
ROBERTSON, N. (1967) "The student scene: militant anger." *New York Times* (November 20).
Study Commission on University Governance (1968) "The culture of the university: governance and education." Pp. 31–56 in Report of the Study Commission on University Governance. Berkeley: University of California (January 15).
Sveriges Förenade Studentkärer, Stockholm (1965) Introducing SFS, The Swedish National Union of Students. Stockholm: Sveriges Förenade Studentkårer.

CHAPTER 10

RULING OUT PATERNALISM
Students and Administrators
at Berkeley

C. Michael Otten

The present well-publicized crisis of campus authority has been attributed to the civil rights movement, the Vietnam war, a small band of militant agitators, the generation gap, and even to television. The following pages offer another interpretation, one which may go further in explaining the past and clarifying the present. I shall suggest that the earlier basis of authority in the university, that which produced consent and legitimated administrative action, was the loyalty of students to the institution—fond affection for the campus community, devotion to its traditions, and self-sacrificing commitment to its welfare. This basis for authority, which has been declining since the 1920s, has now largely disappeared. The sources of decline are several, and some will be mentioned. Of particular interest, however, will be one source, administrative responses to the decline itself. These, I shall assert, have hastened the decline of loyalty. More important, they have contributed to the establishment of a new basis for authority, though one that remains ambiguous in its implications for freedom and stability in the university.

The chapter begins with a brief discussion of the phenomenon of loyalty and then turns to an examination of student loyalty to the university, and administrative responses to its decline in particular. Materials are drawn largely from the history of the University of California although I have little doubt that the forces discussed also are found elsewhere.

AUTHOR'S NOTE: Many people have contributed to the general ideas and the historical content of the dissertation from which this chapter is derived. Professors Philip Selznick and Philippe Nonet have aided me in the general research for order in the often chaotic history of the university, while Sheldon L. Messinger has been especially helpful. Also, the work would not have been possible without financial support from the Russell Sage Foundation, administered by the Center for the Study of Law and Society, University of California, Berkeley.

This chapter is reprinted (in slightly revised form) from *The American Behavioral Scientist,* May–June, 1968 (Volume XI, Number 5).

I

"Loyalty" is a personal commitment that binds a person to something outside of himself. This commitment can have powerful consequences for action, for it may transcend, and even contradict, narrow self-interest. Loyalty is also an effective, subtle, and powerful form of control. As John Schaar (1957: 6) has noted:

> Loyalty is felt to impose obligations which must be fulfilled if one is to please others and be judged in their eyes. There are few explicit and formal sanctions against a breach of loyalty; the controls . . . are worked into the very fabric of the group life . . . . [Loyalty is a] cement that binds men together in an harmonious union. Through shared commitments individuals break the shell isolating them from other persons.

Loyalty to the university, then, is a commitment to the good of the institution over and above other interests, a source of control and a "cement that binds." It binds not only equals to equals but also subordinates to superordinates. Where there is loyalty, alienation is minimized, order prevails, and compliance is nearly automatic.[1] This is the ideal, and under Benjamin Ide Wheeler's presidency (1899–1919) the University of California approximated that ideal.

Nowhere are the bonds of loyalty more fully realized than in the family, and it is especially significant that Wheeler stressed family imagery when talking about the university. His first official speech to students (1926: 23–29, emphasis added) contained the following exhortation, which remained a dominant theme during his twenty-year reign: "This University shall be the family's *Glorious Old Mother*. . . . *Love her.*" [2] Referring to the university as "the family's Glorious Old Mother" proved to be more than a rhetorical device. Wheeler, himself, acted like a father to the students and even addressed them as "my children." The infusion of familial imagery into the structures of authority was exemplified by the President's Report to the Governor, in which he called the powerful student judicial body the "household tribunal."

Loyalty was not just an emotional byproduct of a gathered group of undergraduates; it was consciously defined, carefully nurtured, and deliberately sustained by Wheeler himself.[3] From about 1900 to World War I, honor societies, student self-government, and classroom honor systems swept through higher education, bringing with them institutional allegiances which remain strong even today.[4] Within the university, the honor societies, composed of outstanding young men, embodied the highest aspirations of the community. President Wheeler encouraged and used the societies; indeed, his whole system of "student self-government" rested upon the prominent senior men who belonged to the "Royal Order of the Golden Bear." The "Golden Bear" contained within itself the leaders of nearly all the "command posts" of student life—major fraternities, student newspaper, judicial committee, team athletics, etc. Wheeler also attended most of the important rallies and student meetings; he went to the football practice sessions and led the collegians in the bimonthly "senior singings." His presence and availability [5] personified the university, and affectionate identification with the President was easily transferred to the institution.

Student leaders seem to have shared Wheeler's intense institutional commitment. For example, the editor of the student newspaper urged everyone to attend the freshman rally, declaring:

> . . . for at this first rally of the year the freshman realizes that there are some things bigger than books. The last doubt is wiped out, it is no longer a question of California or somewhere else. *It is California or nothing . . . a torrent of unselfish devotion and love. . . . Allegiance* sworn at the freshman rally is not a great mistake [*The Daily Californian,* 1912a, emphasis added].

At the same rally, the president of the student body spoke of the event as a great "religious festival." Indeed, it was a religious happening, in Durkheim's sense of a community rite intensifying loyal devotion to the group.

Loyalty did not terminate with graduation. The alumni attended the rallies, made generous contributions, occasionally attended honor society meetings, and gave advice to students. In a letter to the student newspaper, one alumnus expressed his own hierarchy of commitments, a hierarchy that a beleaguered modern administrator might well envy. Hearing that students were involved in politics, the alumnus raised a "serious complaint" against student members of the California League of Republicans (Progressives). He urged every student ". . . who places allegiance to his alma mater *above* his political aspirations to unite in putting an end to . . . political exploitation," i.e., club meetings in the fraternities (*Daily Californian,* 1912b, emphasis added). Thus, even political loyalty was subordinated to the "family's Glorious Old Mother."

Loyalty had its uses for university authorities, as well as for students basking in communal fellowship. First, devotion to the university operated as a self-imposed check against those activities which might harm the institution. It is no accident that most disciplinary cases involved freshmen. By the time the student reached the exalted and responsible heights of the upper classes, he knew of, and was committed to, the conduct standards of this homogeneous community.

Secondly, and this was quite conscious, students could be trusted with authority because they were "responsible." Students, administrators, and prominent faculty worked side by side, sharing the same goals, the same standards, and the same loyalties. A college man who contributed to the myriad of collegiate activities, student offices, and the honor societies, developed close relations with the permanent members of the community, and he shared their devotion to "Cal."

During this golden age of collegiate loyalty, a philosophy of student government emerged that was to last for nearly half a century. Little was formalized; student government was, to quote President Robert Gordon Sproul,[6] a "gift" that was based upon friendly cooperation between members of the "university family."

Third, and in sharp contrast to the present-day situation, devotion to the "family's Glorious Old Mother" legitimized authorities submitting to outside pressures. No loyal son of California wanted to see the reputation of his revered institution dragged through the mud of public disgrace. Even before Wheeler's time, students had expressed concern for the university's reputation:

> Its [the university's] life is a public one. It lives only upon the esteem in which it is held and can increase only by extending that esteem. . . . It is this consideration that ought to be constantly in the minds of all students and govern them in all their actions [*Occident,* 1886].[7]

The difficulties of the modern university administrator, caught between student activists and outside pressure, were unknown in the more tranquil days when submission to "the better classes" was a justified principle of governance. Discipline was uncomplicated by elaborate procedures designed to protect student rights standing above loyalty to the alma mater.

Loyalty further made for tranquility, because the system of authority based upon diffuse devotion was profoundly apolitical. Conflicting interests and potential power struggles were submerged in cooperative devotion to the over-all good of the community. Cooperation, not conflict; unity, not diversity; shared goals, not competing group interests—these were the ideals and, to a large extent, the actuality.

II

In the recurring campaigns to raise "school spirit," loyalty remained a popular undergraduate theme; but as academic standards were improved, and as students became more cosmopolitan and politicized, the old ties weakened. The decline cannot be attributed to any single cause, but rather was the outcome of numerous interacting events. Wheeler's two immediate successors, General David Barrows (1919–1923) and William Campbell (1923–1930) did not have the same personal appeal, the leisure, nor the inclination to befriend the students. And although Sproul apparently had appeal (if less time than Wheeler), by the time he took over in 1930, the depression had radically changed the entire situation. But the causes of change lie deeper than presidential personalities.

In 1920, the faculty "revolted" and gained significant powers over promotion, academic standards, and administration; with this came greater emphasis on scholarship. A new era of intellectual seriousness was unequivocally announced in the 1922–1923 Report of the President to the Governor of the State:

> Much of the mediocre scholarship of our undergraduate student body is due to the actual conditions permeating the institution. The *excessive attention given to undergraduate activities and social affairs* among student organizations, and the *relegation of scholarship to a secondary place* by many students, are the chief causes of the conditions (of mediocre scholarship) to which I refer [Putnam, 1922–1923: 28].[8]

Raising educational standards allowed less time for fun; it also implied less prestige for the extracurricular activities which supported student government. Without the blessing of a popular university president, being a student leader had far less appeal.

At the same time, it appears that students themselves became more intellectually serious. A small, sophisticated group, centering around the literary journals, were downright cynical about the old way of life. They were at least as committed to literary standards as they were to the institution. As an editor of one student journal put it, "The dark days of rah-rah are over . . . many of the [students] drink, neck, and steal fire axes. But all of them think a little. College administrators are beginning to get worried" (*Occident,* 1926). Dissent was literary, not political, inspired by Mencken, not Marx; but it was real dissent, nevertheless. And although the number of dissenters was small, their voice was loud and public. The transfer of loyalty from the community to literary standards induced problems of control. A powerful segment of the public, ranging from mothers and ministers to the governor of California, was outraged by the "filth" pouring from student pens. But students refused to compromise their "art" to please the philistines and to protect the university's reputation, and despite the support of a few younger faculty members, they were either expelled or their publications banned.

At the same time, World War I dramatically demonstrated that the university was part of the larger world. The Army mobilized the campus, planted tents on the playing fields, and led the boys off to war; returning veterans did not think Cal's winning football team was the most important thing in life. In response to, and also promoting, the growing concern with the larger world, the *Daily Californian* hooked into the national news services. The student newspaper carried front page headlines about major events and included editorials, letters, and articles on important news items.

Size was another factor breaking down the old ties. From 1910 to 1920 the student population grew from 3,700 to over 10,000. During Wheeler's early days, probably every student personally knew at least one student leader. Overlapping networks of friendship helped to transmit traditions, insure knowledge of standards, and serve as a source of social control. Later presidents had less time to spend with students; and they established intermediaries between themselves and the student body. The institution had become impersonal and less easy to identify with. Furthermore, the dominance of the undergraduate was receding as the proportion of graduate students rose from 11 percent in 1920 to 22 percent in 1930.

All the above-mentioned trends—emphasis on scholarship, de-emphasis on extracurricular activities, growing student sophistication, decreasing isolation, and increasing impersonality—began in the 1920s and carried through to the modern university. In 1932, another extremely important element was added to the decline of loyalty. That was radical politics, and its coming spelled the end of an era in American education.

Young, well-educated, articulate Norman Thomas had special appeal to the "college men" when he ran against Roosevelt and Hoover. He was the first socialist to make a dent at conservative "Cal." Socialism, and later communism, provided an alternative focus for student commitment. Eventually the new political commitment gave rise to the accusation that the "family's Glorious Old Mother" had taken up a new female role, catering to the desires of big business. The "militant minority," as politically active students were sometimes called, developed political skills, which they put to use off and on the campus. Their activities upset the conservative powers which controlled the state of California. These powers, in turn, expressed disapproval of student political activities. The administration could not legally prevent individual students from political involvement and expression, but it could ban political activities from campus. This the administration proceeded to do. As a consequence of administrative actions, activist students increasingly came to view the administration as an agent of suppression for reactionaries. In brief, the response of university administrators to students active in politics furthered the decline of loyalty; student activists, in particular, found it increasingly difficult to feel affection for their "alma mater" or for the officials who ruled her.

III

The administration could not fall back upon ties of sentiment to control dissident students. They turned, instead, to elaboration of formal rules.

From the administration's point of view, the most extreme dissidents were "disloyal." They were not concerned with the "welfare of the entire university" but sought to "exploit their university connections." In view of the former uses of devotion to the "family's Glorious Old Mother," the situation had far-reaching consequences. Self-control and subtle social pressure to protect the university's reputation were rendered ineffective. Radicals had developed a social system of their own, and they shunned the old ideals and norms of behavior embedded in collegiate culture. Furthermore, it was no longer legitimate for the administration to submit to outside pressures, for these pressure groups were the "enemy" of the radicals.

Finally, the radicals gained control of student government and it became "irresponsible."[9] Yet the whole system of student government was founded upon "responsibility," trust, and friendly cooperation. It did not rest upon power and rights but upon cooperation and privilege. Sproul never hesitated to pronounce that his idea of student government was a direct descendant of Wheeler's, that the structure was ". . . subject always to the approval of the President as head of the *University family"* and that ". . . such a relationship can be maintained only upon the basis of *mutual goodwill and cooperation* between *all members of the family,* with the interests of the university as a whole always in mind" (Pettitt, 1966: 102, emphasis added).[10] The activists, on the other hand, rejected the family imagery, and they sharply dissented from the administration's definition of the "good of the whole." They argued that student government was a "right," not a "privilege"; that the good of the whole was not furthered by banning political activity from the campus, but only the good of the conservatives.

As goodwill, trust, and "responsibility" ebbed, administrative control moved in to fill the void. The less personal pattern of authority clearly started in the 1930s, when the administration established formal regulations which were to govern student activists. Little if any consultation with students preceded the promulgation of these rules. The general policy was to keep the university ". . . entirely independent of all political and sectarian influence" by banning all partisan activity from the campus.[11] Written regulations specified the policy, and they also unequivocally placed the administration in charge of interpreting and implementing the regulations.[12]

Other instances of formalization during this period may be listed: In the early 1930s, students officially lost control of discipline; in 1936, university regulations explicitly gave the President final decision-making power over the use of student facilities; in 1938, the ban on political events was extended to "spontaneous rallies"; in 1941, the American Student Union, which had gained control of the student government, lost its campus privileges; in the early 1950s, student government lost control of athletics and its own finances. However, as long as amiable and persuasive President Sproul reigned, there were limits to the reliance on rules. President Sproul thoroughly enjoyed, and made time for, face-to-face meetings with all kinds of student leaders, whether they were radicals, reactionaries, or moderates. With his famous booming voice, incredible memory for names, and easy laugh, he was uniquely capable of personalizing the hard edge of bureaucratic rules.

The movement toward governance by rules accelerated with the appointment of Clark Kerr as president in 1958. Although President Sproul had elaborated rules aimed at controlling student activities, particularly activities with political repercussions, he was able to temper the rules with personal appeals, persuasive arguments, and "man-to-man" talks. Further, Sproul, operating under less politicized conditions, had taken a "hard line," as his fellow administrators called it, against all political activity on the campus. And the "hard line," whatever else might be said of it, had the virtues of simplicity and clarity and, therefore, defensibility against charges that the administration was being inconsistent with its own proclaimed policies. President Kerr, on the other hand, because of temperament and circumstances, did not temper the rules with personal appeals. Even more important, he liberalized the rules to permit more political discussion on the campus itself. But in the activist 1960s [13] the lines between permitted discussion and banned advocacy, between action and partisanship, became extremely complicated. To protect the political non-alignment of the university, rules had to be elaborated and procedures spelled out. Ironically, if understandably, it was the elaboration of rules—"bureaucratization"—not liberalization, that became the focus of attention for the activist students. A myth developed about the "whittling away" of student "rights" when, in reality, they had never existed.

IV

Long before the Free Speech Movement (FSM) of 1964, the emergent pattern of rule-based authority was attacked by a growing number of student activists and concerned faculty. Criticism began with attacks on specific rules; but, as the conflict revealed the inner workings of the administrative process, the issues became more general. Eventually, the very basis of consent eroded to the point where the entire pattern of authority seemed illegitimate to sectors of the student body.[14] These criticisms are worth examining because they highlight the inherent strains in the style of authority adopted by the university administration, and they suggest possible future trends.

First, the policy of "neutrality" came to be regarded as unduly restrictive in that it banned all political activity from campus. Such anomalous incidents as Presidential candidate Adlai E. Stevenson having to speak in the city streets bordering the campus raised questions about the right of university authorities to deny students permission to engage in activities which were open to other citizens. Second, it was argued that administrative application of the policy was biased, favoring the "power structure." Critics pointed to such decisions as allowing Episcopal Bishop Pike to speak on the campus but denying Malcolm X the same privilege two days later because he was a "religious leader." Third, with an increase in student political activity, administrative interpretation and implementation of the rules appeared increasingly "bureaucratic," in the pejorative sense of that term. A plethora of detailed rules were created to specify general regulations. At the same time, there often seemed to be no rules to guide difficult decisions. A maze of administrators with unclear and overlapping jurisdictions developed, creating confusion. A decision could, and sometimes did, go to the secretaries in the dean's office, to a vice-chancellor, to the chancellor, to the president, and even to the regents. Confronted with vague rules and undefined channels of authority, rumors would spread about "behind-the scenes maneuvering" and "submission to outside pressures." Finally, in cases of rule violation, disciplinary proceedings centered around the office of the dean of students. Students argued that the administration was acting as legislature, prosecutor, judge, and jury, and that the whole sysem lacked the most minimum standards of due process.

Over the years, attacks on the restrictiveness of the policy of neutrality, administrative bias, inconsistency, and the lack of due process added up to a full-scale challenge to the legitimacy of university authority. The only elements missing were a demand for formal participation of students in the formulation and implementation of the rules, and the mobilization of students to press that demand. These came in 1964.

Thus, in the area of student political activities, an area which came to have central importance, the administration moved from reliance on personal appeals and persuasions to a constitutionally justified principle of neutrality. This led to a necessity for written rules in order to specify the general principle; and, as these rules were challenged, even more elaboration was required.

Retrospectively we may interpret these events to mean that a pattern of "legal-rational" authority has come to characterize the university, to replace the "traditional" and "paternalistic" pattern that existed earlier. Such a pattern, abstractly considered, is legitimated by an appeal to rules and to the principles such rules are purported to express, rather than to sentiments of loyalty or devotion. Legal-rational authority, it has been said,

assumes the existence of a formally established body of social norms designed to organize conduct for the rational pursuit of specified goals. In

such a system obedience is owed not to a person—but to a set of impersonal principles [Blau and Scott, 1962: 31].[15]

Now the criticisms enumerated above suggest that it was less the general pattern of legal-rational authority that came under attack than the specific style in which this authority was exercised. In fact, despite occasional
grumblings about impersonality, criticism largely called for an increasing,
not a lessening, of the legal-rational pattern. But it also calls for a new
style of control, one more along the lines of what may be called "private
government" rather than "managerialism." Such a style of legal-rational authority would be more deeply concerned with the consent and the rights of
the governed; concretely, the governed would participate in the formulation
of general principles and policies, as well as in the writing of the rules
which define the exercise and limits of authoritative power. Further, the
structure of internal government would be viewed as a *private legal system,*
and thus attention would be directed to incorporation of standards of due
process.[16]

The difference between the "managerial" and the "private government"
models of legal-rational authority can be further clarified by a brief comparison. "Governance" explicitly deals with ultimate community values, the
purposes of the institution; in theory, though not necessarily in fact, "management," or administration, accepts the general values as given (Michels,
1949; Selznick, 1949).[17] Governance promotes open debate and open decisions based upon community participation; management decides on the
basis of expertise and legal responsibilities. Governing decisions are guided
by standards of freedom, justice, and participation; management decisions
are judged by standards of efficiency and technical results. To put the matter another way, "managerialism" is rule by the administration, whose authority rests upon their legally charged and defined responsibilities combined with their special skills. In "private government," authority would
also rest upon legal delegation and specialized skills; however, it would be
further conditioned by careful acknowledgment of the consent and the
rights of the governed.

Although the legal-rational pattern has been distinctly "managerial," elements of the "private government" pattern have weakly begun to manifest
themselves. Considerable analysis of, and agitation for, a system which increases participation and insures due process has already been made
(Study Commission on University Governance, 1968).[18] Such a system of
control would have far-reaching consequences. Participation in the formulation of policies and rules implies debate and open decisions. Such publicly
exposed actions could go a long way toward guaranteeing decisions which
are defensible in light of the general policies, student "rights," and mutually acceptable rules. Without participation, the administration leaves itself open to the charge of submitting to outside pressures which operate behind the scenes. Probably no other accusation has been more detrimental
to establishing relationships of trust.

Another implication of conceiving administration as a form of private
government is that the exercise of authority is then expected to restrain itself: to honor due process standards providing clear rules and fair trial pro-

cedures. Due process has particular salience in the modern situation because the issues raised by the activist students are considerably more complicated than those of their panty-raiding predecessors. Why should an essentially constitutional question, such as the advocacy of civil disobedience, be handled in the same manner and by the same office that previously dealt with the old collegiate-type problems? Education has become too important to the individual, the issues have become too complicated, and students are too mature for either the old informal style of the friendly dean or the recent "managerial" manner.[19]

V

Yet neither criticism of the "managerial" style nor the weak trends toward "private government" mean that radical change is forthcoming. The history of the institution makes one fact manifestly clear: Universities and colleges are not free from public pressures. For nearly one hundred years, public relations with its myriad manifestations has been a guiding, if not the guiding, force determining the pattern of authority. Only in some idealized sense can the University be considered a "self-contained cosmos." In reality, the institution is dependent upon forces over which it has no control, and frequently those forces are hostile to the conditions allowing for, and the consequences flowing from, our notion of private government. Thus, despite all the logical and practical arguments for private government, as we defined the term, it is not likely to become a reality in the near future.

Student participation in shaping policy and a self-contained legal system free from outside interference are the essence of private government. Private government requires genuine participation and power in all levels of decision-making; and justice can only prevail if it is freed from public pressure, political expediency, and organizational needs. To participate without genuine authority is to be impotent and useless. Such has been the nature of student government.[20] But to have participation and a formal legal system requires radical decentralization and vastly increased institutional autonomy. Neither condition exists at the present, nor is either likely to emerge in the near future.

Even within the University itself there is suggestive evidence that the faculty is not anxious for such a structural revolution. Data is not available for the Berkeley campus as such, but on similar campuses around the nation the faculty and the administration ranked student participation in university governance number forty-seventh on a priority list of goals. Top ranking went to protecting the "faculty's right to academic freedom." Next was increasing the "prestige of the University." We have seen how these goals may actually conflict with student participation (Gross, 1968).

Nor is it likely that the majority of the Board of Regents would approve meaningful student participation in governance. After all, the faculty, with its Nobel Prize winners and world-famous scholars does not even have formal representation on the Board. In the past and in the present, the Board has consistently acted in a managerial manner. They have been reluctant to recognize the legitimacy and the reality of "political" problems revolving around the definition of University purposes. Karl Mannheim (1968: 118, brackets added) has cast light on the managerial mentality that seems to predominate on the Board:

> Bureaucratic conservatism may be explained . . . by the fact that the sphere of activity of the official exists only within the limits of laws already formulated. . . . He takes it for granted that the specific order prescribed by the concrete law is equivalent to order in general. . . . When faced with the play of hitherto unharnessed forces, as for example, the eruption of collective energies in a revolution, [the administrator] conceives of them only as momentary disturbances. . . . Bureaucratic thought does not deny the possibility of the science of politics, but regards it as identical with the science of administration. Thus, irrational factors [meaning nonroutine forces outside of the administrator's organized and rationalized system] are overlooked, and when these nevertheless force themselves to the fore, they are treated as 'routine matters of state'.[21]

Actually, we can go a step further than Mannheim. Deeply divisive issues, such as disputes over the very uses of the University, are frequently treated as problems of "law and order" and not primarily as problems involving legitimate disputes over organizational goals and functions.

"Bureaucratic conservatism" is not only rooted in the Regent's managerial role in the educational system but probably reflects their own private occupations as well. Extremely few Regents have a background in education; most often they are businessmen governing huge corporations and financial institutions. A recent nationwide study shows 57 percent of the trustees of public universities had incomes exceeding $40,000 a year; 40 percent were either manufacturing, bank, or insurance executives. The same study revealed that they are even reluctant to allow faculty participation on the boards of control, not to mention students. Only 16 percent of the trustees think there "should be more professional educators on the boards of trustees." Less than one-third think the faculty should be represented. More relevant to student participation, 39 percent felt that "only trustees and administrators" should have "majority authority" in making decisions on the "determination of institutional policy regarding organized student protests." (Hartnett, 1969: 57–70)

The present governor of California, like most of his predecessors and counterparts around the nation, manifests a paternalistic attitude that reflects public opinion and, thus, his political self-interests and probably his personal views as well. For example, ". . . while Robert Kennedy was fighting for his life . . ." Governor Ronald Reagan (1968) wrote the following letter to the Regents:

> I suggest that it is time for them to reassess their own goals, their pattern of only reacting to crises meeting by meeting, and the degree to which they have delegated away responsibility and abandoned principle. A sick campus community in California in many ways is responsible for a sick community around those campuses. . . . Let these campuses then be models for what is good for society.

Notice a cause for the "sickness"—a sickness so profound and heinous that it was suggestively connected with Kennedy's murder—was the "delegating away of responsibility." Within such a political framework, further delegation is unlikely, and grows less and less likely, as the Board comes under the domination of the present Governor's appointees.

The Governor does not stand alone in his hostility toward the campus unrest nor in his desire to rid the institution of troublemakers. As the 1960s drew to a close, there was probably no other issue which provoked such widespread support from the California public as control of students. On the basis of a random sample, the California Poll showed that 83 percent of the public agreed with the following statement, "Students who challenge or defy University and college authority should be kicked out to make room for those willing to obey the rules." On the question of student participation in governing the campuses, the public showed little enthusiasm (*San Francisco Chronicle,* 1969).

"Students should be given more voice in deciding
campus rules and regulations"

Strongly agree	14 percent
Agree somewhat	25
No opinion	4
Disagree somewhat	21
Disagree strongly	36

Few politicians seem sympathetic to the students, and only the bravest or most secure of those could afford to take up a cause that is so unpopular. More practically, those who might be either personally outraged, or just plain opportunistic, can find plenty of political gain by taking a hard line against students. Indeed, in the spring of 1969 there were many bills, with strong legislative support, that would sharply limit campus autonomy and further centralize control in the Board of Regents.

In short, decentralization in the present political climate seems most unlikely. In the past, as this study has shown, student participation has been inversely proportional to the amount of conflict between students, administrators, and the public. At no time in the entire history of the University has conflict been more intense. Thus, one must conclude, tentatively, that decentralized authority allowing students to participate in policy-making is a remote possibility at best.

And it must be added that even if private government could be established, it would probably soon undermine the central institutional goal of academic freedom. Academic freedom is the very soul of the modern university, yet that freedom has never been complete and is constantly threatened. The existing freedoms have centered around faculty self-interest in teaching and research. It is not in their professional interests, as that is now defined, to take time from their teaching and research in order to serve on time-consuming committees dealing with policy questions raised by students or with inefficient complications of "due process." But there are more subtle problems.

Colleges and universities have traditionally served the powerful classes, the prevailing economic interests, and the established definitions of national defense. Berkeley, and the California campuses in general, despite their tuition-free services, have catered to the better-off classes and to the white majority. Although the California population in the mid-sixties was composed of 9 percent Mexican Americans and 5.6 percent Negroes, these groups made up only a tiny fraction of the student population. Furthermore, the emergence of specific departments of study and the allocation of money reflects the productive needs of the state, whether these be agriculture or space science; and Berkeley's contribution to national defense, especially in the field of atomic energy, is well known. The point needs further documentation, but it is more than reasonable to assume that these contributions to the state, the powerful classes, and national defense have paradoxically supported traditional academic freedom. With the universities contributing so much, it was possible to tolerate the opprobrious behavior of so few. Those "few" have now become many, if not the majority. When more students profess admiration for Che Guevara than for Richard Nixon, when 26 percent of the Berkeley students think that "American society is basically unjust," when 63 percent think the University is "too closely tied to the establishment," then granting power to the students is likely to undermine traditional freedoms protecting the "educational functions" (*Fortune*, 1969; Somers, 1968).

To fully comprehend this point, one must see the present tensions in historical perspective. The intensive conflicts of the late 1960s are the culmination of a trend that began in the 1930s. That trend is the growing amalgamation of serious political activity and higher education. So long as students remained concerned with local campus issues or else only took part in "respectable" politics that did not fundamentally challenge the system, they could be tolerated. But students have changed. They have become a major force in movements of dissent and are anxious to transform the universities, which are now the sparkplugs of the technological society, into levers of social change. So long as deep social conflict and gross injustices exist in the larger society—as far as students are concerned those problems are deeper now than any time since the Civil War—and so long as students maintain a serious interest in those problems, the campuses will be arenas of conflict. Furthermore, students are likely to remain left and "radical" by general public standards. In a sense, students are "fanatics" who frequently attach themselves with single-minded dedication to a particular cause. In Max Weber's terms, students are prone to the ethic of "ultimate ends" rather than to the ethic of "responsibility." An ethic passionately focused on a single moral value is scornful of compromise and impatient with slow-moving institutions. (Universities are nothing if not slow moving.) Student passion for reform is not motivated by a sense of responsibility and a role directed toward maintaining the system. Students are likely to follow through despite the institutional cost.

Thus, to grant students more power and to institute an elaborate system of rules that assures due process and full citizenship rights would alter the existing system toward serving new groups, ignoring some and challenging others. In all likelihood, such a radical change would further upset the very tenuous institutional autonomy. Ultimately, the problem is that the University is not private. "Its life is a public one. It lives only upon the es-

teem in which it is held and can only increase by extending that esteem
. . ." (*Occident,* 1886). That statement was written in 1886, but it is still
valid.

It now seems as though the people of California are unwilling to tolerate, not to mention support, an institutional center of radical critique and
dissenting action. To those relatively satisfied with the status quo or else
afraid to change, campus unrest can only be explained by such things as
conspiracy, neurosis, child rearing practices, and administrative cowardice.
In this climate, the objective validity of the demands have little relevance.
The issues raised by the dissenters are reduced to matters of control and
law and order. Hence the next phase of University control may well be
"policed managerialism," not "private government." Indeed, in the Spring
of 1969, as demonstrators were shot in the streets and as a helicopter
sprayed gas over Sproul Hall Plaza, it seemed as if the University of California had already entered the era of policed managerialism.

NOTES

1. Of course, there is another side of the loyalty syndrome. In the university marked by students loyal in this sense, conformity to the simple ideals of
the collegiate culture was mandatory. Dissenters were hardly tolerated. The
faculty was frequently appalled by the stress on loyalty at the expense of
scholarship, and social criticism was nearly nonexistent.

2. The quote is from a speech delivered October 30, 1899.

3. Strong emphasis on loyalty fitted into the contemporary philosophy of
education. Colleges still had their obligation to develop the full character of
the student. They no longer demanded chapel, nor did they uphold the "Chris-
tian gentleman" ideal; but educators still adhered to a secularized version of
education being a moral, as well as an intellectual, endeavor. Furthermore, the
object of training good citizens was an important part of the Progressive Republican philosophy that Wheeler, and many other college presidents, adhered to. (See Rudolph, 1965: 355–373.)

4. Incidentally, the movement was closely allied to the Progressive Republican Party that emphasized the salutary political role of the good, honest, well-
educated college graduate.

5. President Wheeler's daily rides around campus on his white horse are
legendary today.

6. Sproul, President of the University of California from 1930 to 1958, was
involved in the Progressive Republican movement during his undergraduate
days (1909–1913). He introduced the basic regulations which governed the
university until 1964.

7. Although beyond the scope of this paper, it is highly interesting that major
reference groups were the rich and respectable. Labor unions were practically
nonexistent, and, until about 1910, the state was dominated by the Southern
Pacific railroad, commonly known as the "Octopus."

8. Putnam was Dean of the Undergraduate Division at Berkeley.

9. In the late 1930s, the left formed a coalition through the American Student Union (ASU) and won important elections. At various times, the left controlled the student newspaper, the literary magazine, and the student humor
publication. Perhaps the most telling indicator of fundamental change took

place when the humor magazine turned from obscenity to political satire, thus ending a half-century tradition.

10. Sproul to editors of the "Daily Bruin," quoted in George Pettitt.

11. The quoted phrase is taken from Section 9, Article 9, of the California State Constitution. A policy of "neutrality," which was claimed to be a specification of the State Constitution, became university "law" on February 15, 1935. Nearly all controversy raised by students has flowed from this policy. It aimed to keep the university, as an institution, politically non-aligned by banning all political activity from the campus. Logically, *this* goal could have been accomplished by allowing, not banning, all such activity from the campuses. It seems obvious that other, unstated, goals were also being implemented through this interpretation of the policy of "neutrality," but this is a topic that cannot be developed here.

12. Only once were the students carefully consulted on rule modifications, and that consultation was initiated by the students. In 1957 a group of established student leaders led a major effort to revise the twenty-year-old Regulation 17, which governed the use of facilities. With the support of Chancellor Kerr, the policy was liberalized to allow political candidates to appear on campus and to allow "off-campus" student groups to meet on the campus. Permission had to be obtained from the administration, however, and their approval was not automatic. Since about 1959, when a major revision occurred, rule-making has received increased attention from the highest formal source of university authority, namely, the board of regents. From time to time, the regents discussed proposed revisions, and even implementations, of the regulations. After 1964 they were deeply and publically involved in student affairs.

13. There is little doubt that students were increasingly politicized in the late 1950s and 1960s. Everything points to this fact—the number of student political groups, the number of political speakers, demonstrations, pickets, newspaper commentaries, and personal recollections of students, faculty, and administration. The same kind of evidence overwhelmingly suggests that the 1960s were also more politically active than the 1930s.

14. Judging from the student support of the Free Speech Movement (FSM), criticisms of the administration had fairly wide appeal. At least one study has suggested that support for the FSM was positively related to academic achievement, as measured by the grade-point average. (See Kathleen Gales, 1966.)

15. Blau and Scott are, of course, paraphrasing Max Weber.

16. Many of these general notions about "private government" have been derived from Philip Selznick. His forthcoming book, *Law, Society and Industrial Justice,* will develop these ideas at length. Also see Arthur Miller (1959).

17. Both authors give examples of management goal-setting. At the University of California, it was actually the president, with the local campus administrators, who outlined the original policies governing the use of facilities and, in effect, the uses of the university. The evidence further suggests that the regents did not establish earlier policies.

18. By far, this report is the most significant effort along these lines. It was prepared by an eminently qualified staff, jointly sponsored by the academic senate and the student government. To my knowledge, it is the most thorough study yet to appear on the contemporary problems of governance in large state universities.

19. William Van Alstyne (1965) has spoken of the importance of education as a reason for changing court attitudes toward the student.

20. Students have never had autonomous powers of governance, but rather "student government" has been a device used to coordinate leisure time ac-

tivities. Efforts to move beyond this arena were blocked mainly because they affected the "welfare of the entire University," which any real governance does.

21. Working, as he was, with an image of the military in the back of his mind, Mannheim may have overstated the case, but he has illuminated a fundamental tendency in the administrative perspective toward defining the "eruption of collective energies."

REFERENCES

BLAU, P. R. and R. SCOTT (1962) *Formal Organizations: A Comparative Approach.* San Francisco: Chandler Publishing.

Daily Californian (1912) September 5.

—— (1912b) August 30.

Fortune (1969) "What they believe." (January): 70.

GROSS, E. (1968) "Universities as organizations: a research approach." *American Sociological Review* 33, No. 4 (August): 518–543.

GALES, K. (1966) "A campus revolution." *British Journal of Sociology* 17, No. 1 (March): 1–19.

HARTNETT, R. T. (1969) *College and University Trustees: Their Backgrounds, Roles, and Educational Attitudes.* Princeton: Educational Testing Service.

MICHELS, R. (1949) *Political Parties.* New York: The Free Press.

MILLER, A. (1959) *Private Governments and the Constitution. An Occasional Paper on the Role of the Corporation in the Free Society.* Santa Barbara: Center for the Study of Democratic Institutions (mimeo.).

MANNHEIM, K. (1936) *Ideology and Utopia.* New York: Harcourt, Brace & World.

Occident (1926) Editorial. September.

—— (1886) Editorial. May 28.

PETTITT, G. (1966) *Twenty-Eight Years in the Life of a University President.* Berkeley: University of California Press.

PUTNAM, T. (1922–1923) Presidential Reports to the Governor.

REAGAN, R. (1968) *Daily Californian.* Letter from Governor Reagan to the Board of Regents and the trustees. June 14.

RUDOLPH, F. (1965) *The American College and University.* New York: Vintage Books.

San Francisco Chronicle (1969) California Poll (March 4): 6.

SCHAAR, J. (1957) *Loyalty in America.* Berkeley: University of California Press.

SELZNICK, P. (1949) *TVA and the Grass Roots.* Berkeley: University of California Press.

SOMERS, R. (1968) "The Berkeley campus in the twilight of the Free Speech Movement—hope or futility?" Berkeley: University of California, Department of Sociology (mimeo.), August.

Study Commission on University Governance (1968) "The culture of the university: governance and education." Report of the Study Commission on University Governance. Berkeley: University of California, January 15.

VAN ALSTYNE, W. (1965) "Student academic freedom and rule-making powers of public universities: some constitutional considerations." *Law and Society in Transition* 2 (Winter): 7.

WHEELER, B. I. (1926) *Abundant Life.* Berkeley: University of California Press.

PART V

EMERGENT GROUPINGS

CHAPTER 11

THE VICISSITUDES OF THE *PRIVATDOZENT*
Breakdown and Adaptation in the Recruitment of the German University Teacher

Alexander Busch

I

The German universities, like their modern British counterparts, grew up at a time in which, owing to their small size, the major share of teaching was done by professors who also more or less monopolized the internal administrative power of the university. In Germany, the corps of professors was supplemented by a class of teachers who were not on the payroll of the university and who had no part in the government of the university. These were the *Privatdozenten*. They were remunerated only on a capitation basis from the fees paid by students who attended their lectures. They drew no regular salary from the university; they were, moreover, expected to conduct such research as they wished without aid from the universities.

As the student body increased in size in the German universities, the number of Privatdozenten increased with them, while the number of full professors lagged behind. Thus, between 1886 and 1911, the student body increased by 94 percent, while that of full professors increased by only 23 percent (Busch, 1959: 77). From 1864 to 1953, the proportion of full professors in the university teaching staff fell from 49 percent to 26 percent (Busch, 1959: 76). A disproportionate burden was being carried by the Privatdozenten. Their burdens were further increased as research changed in scale and costliness, so that the Privatdozent of very limited means—as the typical Privatdozent came increasingly to be—was prevented from fulfilling his obligation and desire to do research.

The situation could not continue as it was. The old German university had been rendered out of date by the growth in the size of its student body

EDITORS' NOTE: This chapter is reprinted (in slightly revised form), with permission, from *Minerva*, Volume I, Number 3, Spring 1963, pp. 319–341.

and by the changed importance and character of scientific research. In the following essay, the evolution of the Privatdozent, that essential institution of the nineteenth-century German university, is examined in order to illustrate the process of adaptation which the contemporary German university is now undergoing in response to the democratization of university education and the recent development of science.

II

The rather wide variety of teaching and research personnel at the German universities may be classified as follows: (1) Full professors, the university teachers in the proper sense of the word; (2) Privatdozenten (who, after a certain number of years, may officially be appointed to "professorships"); (3) appointed university lecturers (Lehrbeauftagte), employed for supplementary teaching; and (4) assistants, who generally are young persons assisting the full professors in their research, teaching, and administration.

In 1960 all German universities employed a total academic staff of 17,000 persons, of whom 2,906 were full professors, 3,673 were Privatdozenten, 3,583 were appointed university lecturers,[1] and 7,238 were assistants.

In this chapter, we are concerned primarily with the Privatdozenten. In 1945, Eugen Rosenstock-Huessey called them "the secret of the universities"; in 1878, an American author called them the "life-blood" of the universities; and even as long ago as 1832, V. Cousin in his report *de l'Instruction Publique dans Quelques Pays de l'Allemagne* (Cousin, 1832–1833) characterized them as "the power and life of the university." It is remarkable that this unique institution has retained its importance over such a long period, when so many changes have occurred in the structure of German society and of the German university system.

Before going further, I must point out that I am using the term "university" to comprise all institutions offering an education on the university level. Special attention must be paid to the fact that the German universities have always included all branches of knowledge, i.e., theology, law and medicine as well as agriculture and forestry, to say nothing of classics, history, natural science, etc. There are special technical colleges (*Technische Hochschulen*), which are also "universities" in the sense here used. The training of teachers for primary and lower grade secondary schools, which was recently, in some cases, made part of university teaching, but which generally is given at special training colleges for teachers (*Padagogische Hochschulen*), will not be included. I should also point out that I am here using the term "science" (*Wissenschaft*) to refer to any systematic body of knowledge, i.e., to any intellectual discipline conducted by orderly methods. In this definition, the physical, the biological and the social sciences, as well as the humanistic disciplines, will be covered by the term "science." I will use the term "natural science" when I have in mind sciences like physics, biology, etc.

To explain why the Privatdozent is such an important element in the German university, one should first examine the conditions under which the institution of the Privatdozent originated. An historical analysis, even of earlier history of the institution of the Privatdozent, is of more than antiquarian interest. The period of its origin was also the period of origin of systematically conducted scientific work, and the conditions of its origin are, therefore, not entirely alien to the present situation. Furthermore, much of what is problematic in the Privatdozent system can be adequately understood only when its earlier history is taken into account.

III

The status of the Privatdozent is a product of the eighteenth century, when, with a few exceptions, the German universities were in a state of decline. Eighteenth-century science in Germany did not originate in the universities. Only some of the great scholars of the eighteenth century were university teachers. Many had positions outside the universities in various professions, often at the courts of the numerous absolutist princes. The universities were a kind of secondary school which trained civil servants for the administration of services of the state, for the judiciary, for the teaching profession, and for the church. Whereas today the unity of teaching and research is a characteristic feature of the German university, in the eighteenth century, teaching was the exclusive concern of the university.

There are various reasons why there was no scientific activity in the universities: the constricted financial condition of the universities made it necessary for professors to earn their living through an auxiliary occupation. This was one of the main reasons why the atmosphere of the eighteenth-century university was poisoned by intrigue, spitefulness, jealousy, and envy. The intellectual standard was not exacting. The professors, from year to year, gave the same lectures, sometimes inherited from their fathers. The social prestige of the professors had reached its lowest point, so that the people could say:

> The over-industrious scholars have so little contact with other men that, from the point of view of social life, they will forever remain something like half-savages who have not been properly tamed. . . . If the great of the earth in former times came to see a scholar of high reputation, or if they invited him, they usually intended to take delight in the skills of the learned monsters [Meiners, 1802: 20].

The students' situation was no better. The life of the eighteenth-century German university student was a degenerate affair. The students, thanks to their share in academic freedom, had their own privileges: they were, as a result, only too often engaged in duels, rows, drinking bouts, physical assaults on the citizenry, etc.

At the same time, the constantly increasing demand for qualified civil servants, growing out of the development of the modern state, even as early as the eighteenth century, helped to bring about reforms in the rather somber situation of the German university. But it was not only the state that precipitated the reforms. If it had been just a matter of the initiative of the state, the German universities never would have become the great institutions into which they developed in the nineteenth century. Governmental initiative was important because there were no other bodies or authorities which could supply the universities with the financial and material necessities which could meet their needs. The new bourgeoisie, not yet having attained its nineteenth-century prosperity, was not in a position to do so, and the nobility had no sympathy or interest in the universities. Government initiative was, however, expressed largely in the readiness to found and maintain academies, institutes narrowly specialized for immediate practical purposes,[2] and to support individual scholars at the princely courts. The increasing interest of the state in the production of administrators, judges, lawyers, and clergymen, however, also had its more fruitful aspects. It led to a greater concern with the universities and the supply of professors. The remuneration of the full professors was increased. Government departments responsible for universities had noticed how difficult it was to find qualified incumbents for vacant chairs.

The interests of the states were adversely affected by the situation of their universities in two ways. The state had an interest in the training of urgently needed civil servants. It also had an economic interest in the distinction of the universities in its territory. Universities with capable and famous professors attracted students, above all foreign students, from the numerous petty states. They were, thus, a source of income for the state. This was the age of mercantilism, and the administration of the state tried to take advantage of the universities as a source of financial strength. For these reasons, the state began to be concerned about the supply of university teachers. Governments, which could not find any *professorabiles* within their own boundaries, sent a recruiting agent (*Universitatsbereiser*) to foreign territories to look for sound scholars, whom they wanted for their own universities.

About the same time, however, an intellectual movement started, which exerted a powerful influence on the status and attainments of the university. Originating not in the natural sciences but in classical philology, archaeology, and classical languages, and closely bound up with the new philosophical idealism of Kant, Fichte, Hegel and Schelling, a new and more "scientific" view of the university, entailing stringent technical and substantive standards, made its way. It was no longer sufficient to learn the traditional stock of knowledge and to pass it on to others. A critical and creative disposition was required now. A quite novel stress was laid on systematic, scientific research. Philology was the first field in which the scientific methods were applied; in the beginning, scientific accuracy was coterminous with philological rigor. At the same time, there came forth from the study of classical antiquity a new conception of man which played an important part in the development of the outlook of the middle class in Germany.

The great social impulse towards university reform at the beginning of the nineteenth century was associated with the efforts of the middle class persons to emancipate themselves from the legal and social constraints of the *ancien regime*. Freedom for research and teaching was part of a more general program of public liberties; the universities were viewed as parts of a free "republic of the mind." The universities were middle-class institutions in the sense that their reformed constitution was part of the larger program espoused by the middle classes for the reconstruction of German society.

Thus the scholar and the professor were idealized and, as a result, association with the universities conferred prestige on those who taught and did research under their auspices. It is also characteristic of the nascent nationalism of the age that science in the universities became a national concern.

This is the background of the regulations which governed and partly still govern the status of the Privatdozent. They were first fixed in 1816 for the University of Berlin, which had been founded in 1810. Later, they were adopted by the other universities. These regulations merely fixed the qualifications of a university teacher. They made no reference to working conditions or remuneration.

Up to the Reform, the right to give lectures at the university was acquired together with the doctor's degree. The graduate obtained the *venia legendi* automatically. This was his license as a university teacher. It entitled him to nothing else, however; he had neither a seat nor a vote in the academic bodies, nor did he receive a salary. As a university teacher, he was merely entitled to the small lecture fees which his students had to pay for every lecture hour, but which he often did not receive.

The students used to pay their auditor's fees directly to the Dozenten whose lectures they attended, and it was only in the nineteenth century that the university took over the function of collecting the money and distributing it to the Privatdozenten. It happened, unfortunately too frequently, that the students did not turn up on the day when they were to make their payments, or else they just let their fee-debts accumulate and then disappeared, nevermore to be seen. The collection of fees was a difficult affair for the Privatdozenten. To make the students pay in advance was, however, also difficult because there was a danger that the students would be frightened off, and with them would go the possible income which they could provide.

It was the poor quality of the work done for the degree which had led to the decline of the universities. It is therefore understandable that the Reform should have begun at this point.[3] In addition to raising the qualifications for the doctoral degree, the Reform introduced the habilitation as a condition for granting the *venia legendi*. The procedure of habilitation required the aspirant to an academic post, who already possessed his doctorate, to present a scientific or scholarly work, to participate in a colloquium with the full professors of his faculty, and to give a trial lecture. If he was successful, he was given the *venia legendi,* except that, in contrast with older regulations, it was only for individual subjects and not for the whole field covered by his faculty.[4] It was important that at first, above all in Berlin where the habilitation was first introduced, persons who held high public office observed the new regulations and underwent the habilitation. In the personnel registers of the universities, they were not listed as "Privy Councillor" or whatever their titles might have been, but as Privatdozent and *Doktor*. When, for example, the name of the *Staatsrat* Niebuhr, a well-known and much-respected personality, appeared in the university catalogue as "Privatdozent Dr. Niebuhr," this was an "event" which was much discussed and which was interpreted as evidence that "the class of scholars and teachers could scarcely be more respected than it is" (Stoll, 1929: 54). Academic titles gained in prestige from their association with public dignitaries; the universities which had had a rather marginal position socially and in public opinion and which, it might be said, had enjoyed a certain measure of "fool's freedom," thereby acquired a higher social standing.

The economic position of the *doctor legens,* who had undergone two examinations remained as it was before: he remained a private teacher, licensed by the university but not paid by it. He "did not exist," as was said of him early in the nineteenth century, as far as the university budget was concerned. The financial side of the university was part of the administrative structure of the state and only full professors were acknowledged. The fact that the university reform of 1810 did not deal with the financial side of the Privatdozent's role was not due to a desire of the reformers to exploit this class of teacher. They did not regard the question of remuneration as an important one. The modest economic aspirations of the ambitious universities, and of association with them, enabled them to leave the economic aspects of the Privatdozent's position as they were previously. But as a result of this, they perpetuated the older system in which the teaching staff of the university was divided into two classes, that of the full professors with a full panoply of rights within the university and an income guaranteed by the state, and that of the Privatdozent without any fixed income and with only the right to give lectures.

The status of a full professor became the ardently sought goal of the Privatdozenten, especially of those who were impecunious—and many were. Competition, as a result of this situation, brought advantages to science and scholarship. Not all Privatdozenten could survive under this system; some had to give up. The system had an inherent tendency towards social injustice. He who had a private income and did not have to worry about his subsistence, had a much better chance to do scientific work than the starveling who had to earn his living by regular employment. The poverty of the Privatdozenten became an almost unquestioned tradition. It gave rise to an ideology which was of no advantage to science or to the university and which still exists. It is the idea that poverty is the sine qua non of scientific work. From the very beginning, however, there were renowned scholars who vigorously criticized the academic, moral and political harmfulness of the poverty of so many university teachers.

It was of the utmost importance for the development of the German university that admission to the profession of university teaching was made subject to the habilitation. Previously, only the mastery of the existing state of knowledge in a subject and proof of one's knowledge of this subject in the doctoral examinations had been required. As a result of the Reform, much more and something quite different was required: the discovery of new truths now became an obligation of the university teacher. The institution of the obligation to do research, to do productive work as a scientist, and its combination with teaching, contributed to the establishment of the

principle of the unity of research and teaching. The constant danger of os-
sification of the universities was thereby averted. Research became the
basis for an academic "career." The achievement in research was what led
to appointment to full professorship. The personal union of research and
teaching, embodied in the role of the Privatdozent, sustained the dynamic,
productive activity, through which the German universities acquired their
worldwide reputation.

IV

The nineteenth-century university, which was helped into existence by
the Reform of 1810–1816, has, in the meantime, changed considerably
and has become a large-scale enterprise. The intertwinement of social and
scientific developments has become richer. The greatly enhanced significance of science in economic and social life and the vastly broadened demand for university education are two features of this development, which
has called for marked changes in the contemporary university (Plessner,
1924).

The contemporary university is a large-scale enterprise, whereas the
nineteenth-century university was a small organization with an intimate atmosphere. This does not only refer to the number of students and university teachers which, to a large extent, made it possible to get personally
acquainted with one another. It also refers to the buildings and equipment
of the universities, to the seminars and institutes with their "equipment."
Books and manuscripts, even libraries, which were the main scientific instruments of the scholar, could be found in private homes, where there was
also room for collections of natural history specimens, and the modest apparatus of the physicist and the chemist. In the early nineteenth century
and as late as 1860, we even find lectures being delivered in the private
homes of some scholars. There were no scientific institutes with their scientific equipment and laboratories. There were no large libraries with their
lending arrangements and reading rooms. For many generations, there has
been an intimate relationship between the scholar-scientist and his place
of work. The developments in science which came at the end of the nineteenth century have changed all this.

One result of the Reform was the qualification of many more Privatdozenten than could ultimately become professors. This, of course, contributed to the improvement of the quality of those appointed to professorships. The faculties in which only the full professors had a seat, and which
were responsible for filling vacancies in their ranks, did not have to make
their choice from a narrow field of candidates. They could select from a
rich supply. They could, therefore, afford to be very fastidious.

There are many witnesses of the post-Reform period who saw the situation of the Privatdozenten at that time in the same perspective in which we
are viewing it here. In 1850, Wilhelm Heinrich Riehl called the Privatdozenten the "intellectual proletariat." The position of the Privatdozenten did,
in fact, have certain proletarian features: they were more or less without
rights, but they were under great pressure to do good work as scientists
and as teachers. The Privatdozenten were, in a sense, the "proletarian re-

serve army" serving the "ruling class" of full professors. And it is interesting that in the class struggle, which really occurred between Privatdozenten and full professors, the struggle for financial concessions was second to that of rights, status, and working conditions. The Privatdozenten had no scarcity value. They were very numerous relative to the demand for their services—which meant that, in this respect too, they were "proletarians."

v

It was especially the creation of scientific institutes which changed the working conditions of the Privatdozenten and reduced their status. In the nineteenth-century university, the scientist had been able, more or less, to work on his own account. The new development, in which the natural sciences with their combination of clinical hospital and laboratory took the lead, resulted in big, well-equipped and expensive research institutes on which the individual investigator became dependent. Books and laboratory equipment had previously been personal tools and were kept—as in the craftsman's workshop—under the roof of the scholar's or scientist's residence. The concentration of the means of intellectual production in the university institutes reduced the individual scholar's independence because it rendered him subject to the administrative body of the institute which was constituted by full professors. He who controlled the institutes, the means of production in the field of research, controlled therewith the research workers, their opportunities and their prospects. The director of the institute was, on his side, becoming more dependent on his collaborators, but —as in other fields of activity—he was not as dependent on them as they were on him. Thus, the liberty which the Privatdozenten had enjoyed as teachers was being lost in their scientific activities as they came increasingly to depend on the institutes.

The institutes, which were established by the state and directed by a full professor, transformed a system which was once a more or less egalitarian republic of learning into a hierarchical relation of master and subordinate.

Max Weber described this situation as follows:

> The great medical and natural scientific research institutes are 'state capitalist' enterprises. They cannot be administered without considerable resources. And as a result there emerge the same circumstances which everywhere characterize the capitalist enterprise—the separation of the worker from the means of production. The workman, in this instance the assistant, uses the tools which are placed at his disposal by the state. He is, in this way, as dependent on the director of the institute as an employee in a factory—since the institute director imagines in all good conscience that the institute is 'his' institute and acts accordingly. The position of the assistant is, therefore, as precarious as that of anyone in a more or less proletarian situation [M. Weber, 1951: 570].

This transformation was fostered by the creation of the role of the assistant, directly employed by the institute as an aide of the director. The assistants were appointed by the government, on the basis of the recommendations of the institute director—just as they are today. They appeared for the first time in 1830 in the faculties of natural science and medicine. In 1874, there were 24 assistants in all at the University of Gottingen; in 1960 there were 338. The assistantships, which were made available by the state, constituted only a small fraction of what was necessary. Wilhelm Ostwald, for example, once said "I am able to manage personally by employing, in addition to the assistants who are officially provided for me, at least two . . . to whom I pay an identical salary from my own pocket. In this way, in recent years, I have spent more than 50,000 marks in connection with my teaching activities" (Ostwald, 1927: 231).

The completion of one's studies was, from the beginning, more or less the precondition for appointment as an assistant. There were, of course, exceptions. Today the assistants are officials appointed not, however, with permanent tenure, but for a specified time period, and their remuneration corresponds to that of the unhabilitated official in the scientific service. It is somewhere between DM. 900 and DM. 1,300 monthly; those who have habilitated get between DM. 900 and DM. 1,400 (See Felgentraeger, 1961).

In 1908, almost half of the Privatdozenten, including the older ones (so called *Extraordinarius*), in the medical faculties and almost a third in the natural science faculties, were assistants (Eulenburg, 1908). In 1960, about a third of the Privatdozenten were assistants (See Busch, 1962).

Strictly speaking, the assistant's position was not institutionalized until the 1920s, but in actual practice it existed much earlier. The assistantship was an inevitable outgrowth of the increased scale of research projects. As a rule, the assistants were young people, who had recently taken the doctorate. They were intimately connected with the director of the institute, sometimes to such an extent that the assistant lived in the director's home, ate his meals with him, and wore his cast-off clothing. Salaries differed greatly and were often settled rather arbitrarily. But in principle, and in contrast to the Privatdozent, the assistant received a salary. The great advantage of the assistant's position was the close collaboration with the director of the institute, the personal contact that could be decisive for his future academic advancement. Difficulties arose when the assistant's own scientific work competed with the work of the director, especially if the latter was of an authoritarian character. The director of the institute had it within his power to determine whether research results should be published, under whose name they should appear, and also whether publication should be postponed. In extreme cases, this served the interest of the institute director and operated to the disadvantage of his collaborator especially if he was a candidate for a regular post or a professorship. If the assistant sought habilitation—and there were hardly any who did not—he confronted the full professor not only as a member of the faculty which passed judgment on his inaugural dissertation, but also as his official superior in the institute. Wherever there was no institute, the Privatdozent was entirely dependent on the opinion of the full professor.

In consequence, the free competition of ideas in science was confined and constrained by the power of the professor over his juniors. The hierarchical structure could easily influence the pattern of intellectual interest. "Science as a calling" began to yield to "science as a professional job," as

Max Weber declared in his relentless criticism of German practice (Weber, 1919). The Privatdozent's increased dependence on the institute and its chief was further intensified by the fact that the former often had to become an assistant to eke out his livelihood so that, even after his habilitation, he depended on the institute for the means of his research as well as for his income. This dependence became all the more oppressive with the lengthening of the period during which the Privatdozent had to wait for an appointment to a full professorship and the increasing severity of the competition among the Privatdozenten. The situation was aggravated as the Privatdozenten and even the assistants became indispensable to university teaching, for which, officially, the full professor alone was responsible.[5] They could not very well refuse to assume these tasks. Their situation did not improve by having to do the donkey-work of the full professors in order to preserve the possibility of being appointed full professors. Bitterness was a frequent result. Such was the situation from about 1880 until the First World War.

VI

Until about the 1840s, the institution of the Privatdozent "functioned" more or less to the advantage of the university. The liberal idealism of the middle class, the internal freedom of the university, and the general belief that science would lead to a "new humanity" assured the universities an ample supply of persons of outstanding quality. The level of aspiration of the "educated" middle class of these generations was influenced by the traditionally low incomes of the civil service. When, for example, in the revolutionary years of 1848–1849, there were several conferences of university teachers, at which the Privatdozenten attacked the privileged status of the full professors, the question of income was mentioned only incidentally. The main concern of the Privatdozenten was a fuller participation in the life of the university, not only through teaching but with respect to rights, status, and influence. They wanted, for instance, to be considered more favorably when lecture rooms were assigned, when degrees were conferred, when academic offices were vacant. Despite the modesty of their economic aspirations, the position of the Privatdozenten remained unchanged, and in the ensuing decades a scarcity of Privatdozenten began to be noticed. The financial factor, in which the reformers of the beginning of the century and the critics of the middle of the century had not been interested, was making itself felt. In 1868, a member of the Royal Commission on universities in Great Britain attributed the cause of the considerable defects of the German universities to a lack of funds (Dr. Walter Perry, quoted in von Sybel, 1868: 28). For some time, the moral idealism, scientific *elan,* the favorable conjuncture of a particular historical situation were able, somehow, to offset the lack of funds. They succeeded in doing so in the period of industrialization when other professions, which required academic qualifications, were beginning to offer new and more remunerative vocational opportunities. The university had to compete with the other professions which were attracting educated persons. The increasing dependence of scientific work on the institutes and its expansion depleted the reservoir of academically trained persons that had existed in former times and from which, in the past, the university could draw its Privatdozenten and professors. In 1875, in order to counteract the shortage, the Prussian Minister of Education created a fund "for stipends for Privatdozenten and other young scholars who are probably qualified for a university career." Other German states followed suit. But the fund was "chronically exhausted," even though it was renewed from time to time in the following decades. It can hardly be said that the treasury, the government departments, or the lower and upper houses of the legislatures had a particular interest in science. Science was condescendingly encouraged by some sovereigns who conferred their patronage on progressive officials, scholars, and industrial entrepreneurs. The scale of university operations was increasing, but they were hampered in their adaptation to their new situation by insufficient funds and by their archaic system of recruitment. They were just able to cope with their problems, thanks to the initiative of certain excellent administrative officials, particularly Althoff, the Prussian Minister of Culture, and to what Alfred Weber called the *Rentenintellektuellentum,* i.e., scholars with private financial resources.

The *Rentenintellektuellen* were the products of the social changes in Germany which took place after the middle of the nineteenth century, and especially after the Franco-Prussian War. Large middle-class groups had succeeded in accumulating capital, in obtaining a certain measure of prosperity and even considerable fortunes. Their wealth might not have been great enough to enable them to dispense entirely with work and earned income, but made it possible for them to survive the long period of unpaid preparation and waiting for an appointment to an intellectual post which did provide an income. Later on, the income from property supplemented their salary and at the same time served as a basis for a certain degree of freedom from social and institutional pressures (A. Weber, 1923: 13).

In other words, the German universities were able to retain, and even benefit from, the antiquated methods of recruitment of their staff, only because the German economy was productive enough to produce a new leisured class who wished to devote themselves to academic pursuits. Among the full professors, who underwent habilitation between 1890 and 1919, i.e., became Privatdozenten, the proportion of those whose fathers were factory owners and merchants doubled (about 25 percent compared with the earlier 12 percent). The growth of capitalism was solving the problem of supply of academic personnel for the universities. The prestige of the universities was sufficiently great for the new bourgeoisie to disregard their economic disadvantages. The state was avoiding the responsibility for the expense of the long periods of training and preparation by transferring it to private households. This was one of the reasons why the teaching body of the universities appeared to such a great extent to be a "bourgeois institution" (von Ferber, 1956: 176).

Still, many problems remained unsolved. The *"rentier* intellectuals" helped to overcome severe shortages in the supply of qualified personnel. Their readiness to work without official status and without a regular salary made it possible to increase greatly the number of Privatdozenten. The traditional standard of the scientific work of the Privatdozenten was not impaired by their recruitment from families with sound financial backgrounds.[6] But the social and economic strain on those Privatdozenten who came from less favored backgrounds was intensified.

From 1886 to 1910, the number of full professors increased by 23 percent, whereas the number of students rose by 97 percent. Within the same period, the number of Privatdozenten increased by 94 percent. The figures show that the rapidly growing demand for lecturers and teachers was not met by a corresponding increase in the number of full professorships. It fell to the Privatdozenten to meet this increased demand for university education. New tensions and occasionally acrid disputes between full professors and Privatdozenten arose. One of the causes of the tension was the regulation, which still exists, that the "major lectures" which the student must attend for his examination remained the exclusive property of the full professors. The latter also had the exclusive right to set examinations and to be appointed to deanships and rectorates. As a rule, these offices conferred a considerable additional income, which was thus denied to the Privatdozenten. Nowadays, major lecture courses and academic administrative posts no longer play this role since, on the one hand, the establishment of posts of middle rank has opened up new sources of income, and on the other, the income from major lecture courses and academic administrative posts has been reduced and is no longer so attractive. The professorial chair was the object of all aspirations and deference in the university world, just as much for those with private incomes as for those who had none. ("For a professorship I would crawl on my knees through the whole of Germany"; quoted by R. Willstatter in Stoll, 1949: 62.) At the same time, the distance between Privatdozenten and full professor was increasing. Only the full professor was a "genuine" professor, and he alone could fully enjoy the glory of the academic position.

There was a certain embarrassment about this situation and particularly about the financial inequity; it was, therefore, a taboo subject. It was not "good manners" to discuss it in public. Memoirs show, however, that people were not unaware of the anomalies of the situation. The Privatdozenten themselves responded by the formation of a union; emergency measures were taken to aid the Privatdozenten by arranging paid lectures, scholarships and grants, which, as a rule, were rather scarce. There were, however, no real remedies. Nothing could hide the fact that the infrastructure of the teaching staff was being neglected. It was not only the avalanche of students that necessitated the services of the Privatdozenten. Research, and the management and administration of the institutes, as well as the increasing teaching responsibilities were exceeding the capacities of the full professors. None of these things could have been done without the help of the Privatdozenten. Their services were freely used, but they were given little consideration. As the number of Privatdozenten increased, competition for the relatively scarcer professorships increased, and the chances of any particular Privatdozent to become a professor diminished. The faculties which appointed the full professors were often placed in a quandary. The appointing body had to choose between the excellent work of the recently habilitated and the fairly old gentlemen who could present a substantial number of excellent works, and who had, furthermore, an amount of teaching experience impossible for the beginner. Appointment practice tended to favor the older Privatdozenten. As a result, the waiting period increased and the criterion of efficiency was sometimes supplanted by the criterion of age and experience.[7] What happened to the Privatdozenten who could not see the end of their long period of waiting—which in a slogan of those days was called the "hunger and suffering period"? The old Privatdozent who somehow managed to keep his head above water by such activities as keeping boarding houses for foreign students, by giving private tuition, or aiding in the revision of lectures was a failure in his academic career, simply by virtue of not being appointed to a professorship. Such men became typical figures in the universities. Their lives were miserable. Many of them were married and had families for whom they could not provide an appropriate standard of living.

The tendency towards greater occupational and institutional specialization outside the university, whereby each occupation had its own definite examinations and waiting period, established barriers between careers and made a shift from one occupation to another more difficult. If, for instance, somebody wanted to be a *Gymnasium* or secondary school teacher, he did not need a doctorate but he had to have passed a so-called *Staatsexamen.* Thus, the Privatdozent who had taken the doctorate and who had also habilitated but who, as a rule, had taken no *Staatsexamen,* could not qualify to teach in such schools.

Where, moreover, such shifts could be made, they were a public confession of failure. To be deemed a failure was a nightmare. The chances for employment outside the university differed from subject to subject. For the medical man it was, and it still is, easy, since being attached to the clinical staff of a university hospital increased his chances in the profession considerably. On the whole, however, the chances of transfer were poor, and the university became a closed world which few could leave. This is why advancement within the university became more and more critical.

The continuing attractiveness of scientific research and the university is an indication of their incomparable and increasing prestige. At the beginning of the nineteenth century the humanistic disciplines created this prestige, whereas at the end of the century and even more so in the present century, it was the medical and natural sciences which took a central position in the image of the university. The increasing preponderance of the laboratory, institute and clinical hospital, with their increasingly expensive apparatus, with their new claim for exactitude, went hand in hand with the displacement of the scholar of the old university by the scientist who was a staff member of a research institute. The Privatdozent was forced to yield and to become the research worker who wanted the "honor and reward of a full time occupation."

These shifts in the internal balance of the universities were accompanied in subsequent decades by changes in position of the universities, in the total system of intellectual institutions. In 1910–11 the *Kaiser-Wilhelm-Gesellschaft* was founded. (It was replaced after 1945 by the *Max Planck Ge-*

sellschaft zur Forderung der Wissenschaften.) The institutes which it founded were highly specialized research organizations with permanent salaried staffs. As they also had ample financial resources, they generally offered more favorable working conditions than the universities. The institutes of the *Kaiser-Wilhelm-Gesellschaft* did not replace the institutes attached to the universities, but through their existence, the universities lost their monopoly.

VII

The 1920s did not add any essentially new problems to those that had already existed on the eve of the First World War. They only saw these problems become more difficult and more pressing as a result of the economic and political crises of the post-war period.

The inflation at the beginning of the twenties, as well as the world depression of 1929 and the following years, badly damaged those middle class circles which had been the greatest suppliers of university teachers. As capital reserves were diminished, dependence on earned income increased and the "free" Privatdozent was made impossible.

The considerable endowments which some of the universities had possessed were also being dissipated by the inflation. In spite of these conditions or under their pressure, important measures were taken on behalf of the assistants. These measures adumbrated future development: assistants were assigned a formal position and their salaries were laid down in precise form. (In Prussia and Bavaria, the two largest states, the remuneration was fixed by law.) It was becoming evident that the assistant was regarded as a prospective Privatdozent and since then the assistant's position became the legitimate stage preceding that of the Privatdozent. Assistant—Privatdozent —Professor became the main stages of the academic career, the only exception being engineering where, to this day, there has been a much greater movement between university and nonacademic fields of activity.

The consolidation of the assistant's position meant that for the first time a real concern was being shown for personnel below the level of the professor. It is true that in principle as well as in fact the assistants remained aides of the full professors, but the reforms, however limited, had important implications. The legal position of the Privatdozent, however, was left untouched. His function as a full time teacher was increasingly being taken for granted. What was previously a sort of probationary period had been turned in practice into fulltime employment with a certain income. This did not take the form of a fixed salary but was reflected in the regularity with which the Privatdozent received other forms of financial compensation. In fact, however, they were, as before, nothing more than temporary teaching assignments, research grants for particular projects, or supplementary living allowances sometimes tied to some editorial tasks on a journal. Legally, however, the change did not entail any financial security for the Privatdozent.

In the 1920s a crisis in the supply of academic personnel had not yet arisen. Not only were the sciences advancing and enhancing the prestige of the universities, but the social revolution through Germany at the end of the First World War destroyed the reality and the prestige of many of the institutions with which the universities had previously to share their eminence. As a result the relative position of the universities was improved in the post-war period and the anomalies in the internal structure of the universities did not come to outweigh the attractiveness of the academic career. The university became a haven and refuge when so many other once honored institutions of German society were in ruins. Able young men, therefore, still sought to make their careers there.

The years of national socialist rule were a catastrophe for the German universities and inflicted upon them a substantial loss (Boekelmann, 1962: 57). This loss has not been made good, even up to the present. We need not go into details about what nazism meant to the university and to science. By 1934 the faculties lost their right to appoint members of their teaching staff, this power being taken into the jurisdiction of the Ministry of Education in Berlin. The expulsion of Jewish scholars was the greatest loss suffered by the German universities. The contributions which German science and scholarship owes to Jewish scholars since the emancipation of the Jews at the beginning of the nineteenth century are immeasurable. They were an integral part of the German universities and to try to eliminate them, as the nazis did, meant the destruction of the whole.

The devastations as a result of the persecution of the Jews and political opponents were followed by the physical devastation of the war, the territorial losses and the stream of refugees at the end of the war. When after the war the universities again started their work, they made every effort to take up where development had stopped in 1933.

VIII

The method of selection for teaching posts in the German universities involved both examination and probation. The candidate's scientific abilities were revealed through the research which he submitted for habilitation; his abilities as a teacher and his development as a research worker were put to the test in subsequent years. It was not just a matter of demonstrating one's ability as a teacher and research worker, once and for all, but over a longer period under the eyes of the full professors. Success as a teacher, even if in a somewhat roundabout way, was assessable by the attendance at the Privatdozent's lectures and by the students' achievements in their written and oral examinations. The Privatdozent's publications increasingly became the criterion of success in research. Thus, the examination which he took and the habilitation were less important than his performance during the period of probation and this in fact determined his appointment to a full professorship.

Once appointed, the Privatdozent was no one's responsibility, nor was he responsible to anyone. This freedom, which was the counterpart of his having no official part in the corporate life of the university, also meant that he had time for his own work. The factors which determined the term of recruitment and the allocation of responsibilities were approximately the following: (1) the prestige of the academic teacher and of the university in German society; (2) the size of the student body; (3) the situation in the intellectual labor market; (4) the financial situation of the university teacher; and finally, (5) the conditions of work at the universities as scientific institutions.

If any one of these factors is prejudicial to the working of the old system, there must be some compensatory functioning of the others. Otherwise the system of the Privatdozenten will not work. If there is no compensatory functioning, then other institutional arrangements will be necessary to replace the system of the Privatdozent.

In the days when the prestige of the university was high, when the student body not so large in relation to the number of professors, when there were few alternative employments for persons with university education, and when finally there was a class of persons with some private income who could defray the costs of their research, the institution of the Privatdozent was a useful and practicable arrangement.

But can the system work in the present situation of the German university?

The disproportionate burden carried by the Privatdozenten is shown by the following table (from Busch, 1962):

UNIVERSITY PERSONNEL IN THE FEDERAL REPUBLIC, INCLUDING WEST BERLIN

	1949	1960
Full professors	1,693	2,906
Privatdozenten	1,578	3,673
Number of older ones with professorial designations among these	671	1,651
Total number of students	105,300	213,500
Number of foreign students among these	2,800	20,400

It is obvious that this means a strain on the individual teacher. In addition to the strain of teaching larger groups of students whom he cannot know individually, he needs more time for consultations on examinations, financial assistance and scholarships and for the setting and assessment of examinations. As a result of this, the time available for proper scientific work and research is being steadily reduced.

Wilhelm von Humboldt, one of the patriarchs of the old university, had demanded "solitude and liberty" for the scholar. These requirements were met by the principle of freedom for the Privatdozent from any official control and from any sort of distracting duties. There is, however, scarcely anything like "solitude and liberty" in Humboldt's sense to be found in the contemporary German university.

The problems are: how to do justice to the different functions of teaching, administration and research, which are constantly increasing in magnitude; how to delegate certain of these functions effectively, and how to maintain the unity of research and teaching. Academic persons now have more connections with public bodies and business enterprises as expert consultants; they are active as popularizers and as adult educators. Teaching within the university includes new tasks, such as routine survey lecture courses. All these activities mean that the university can no longer consist of a core of full professors surrounded by a larger circle of Privatdozenten, who have no legal or financial claims on the university and to whom the university has no corresponding obligations.

The universities need larger teaching and research staffs and the system of the Privatdozent which served Germany so long and so fruitfully will not suffice for the recruitment of persons of sufficiently high quality. The universities no longer monopolize the opportunities for scientific work, to say nothing of the best opportunities. Industry has, in many fields, created its own research units, which are often able to offer more favorable conditions than the universities. With full employment in the intellectual labor market, the universities are no longer free to choose and reject as they will. They have to compete for the choice of the best persons. On top of all this is the fact that, since 1933, German science has sunk to a "provincial" level, as far as the world intellectual community is concerned. The setback administered to the German universities by national socialism has not yet been undone and German science has not yet been able to regain its earlier position in the international world of science. One of the results of this decline has been a further aggravation of the relative shortage of German scientific personnel, through the emigration of specially qualified scientists.

The Recommendations of the Science Council which appeared in 1960 (see *Minerva,* 1962: 64) are an attempt to improve the situation by the development of existing institutions and by various innovations. The Recommendations take as their point of departure the proposition that the ordinary professorship should not be "the inevitable final stage of a bureaucratic career. . . . It should be filled by the most qualified of all those who are engaged in scientific research and teaching." The decisive point is that the prospective elite of the universities should not and cannot invariably be formed by the automatic promotion of those who are in subordinate positions in teaching and research. Privatdozenten should have a period of some years in which they are free from heavy burdens connected with research directed by others, or teaching, so that they can devote themselves to their own scientific development by working on problems which they themselves have chosen (*Empfehlungen des Wissenschaftsrates,* 1960: 63 et seq.).

The following positions should be open to the Privatdozenten:

(1) Heads of sections: these are the chiefs of the larger permanent sections in the big institutes and clinics. The incumbents are officials with permanent tenure. They have a budget of their own and they have available to them such personnel as are necessary in order to carry out independent research.

(2) Scientific councillors: these are officials with permanent tenure who have particular obligations assigned to them as individuals. They should be guaranteed the possibility of independent scientific work.

(3) Custodians: these are officials with permanent tenure who have certain permanent obligations which arise in connection with the work of a

faculty or an institute (for example, the management and surveillance of particularly complicated and expensive instruments, the care of collections or archives or the exercise of similar activities in a university clinic).

(4) *Diatendozenten:* these are official posts with tenure for life or specified periods. These are intended to be posts exclusively for the prospective intellectual elite but, partly because of the shortage of other posts, their incumbents have been diverted to other uses and have been employed for routine tasks.

(3) and (4) are already older types of appointments which the Science Council intends, with its Recommendations, to restore to their original purposes. Apart from these posts, Privatdozenten have open to them senior assistantships, posts of senior physicians and senior engineers, which are directly connected with particular institutes or clinics.

The current basic monthly salaries of these four groups are approximately: heads of sections from DM. 960 to DM. 1,600, other positions from DM. 900 to DM. 1,400. The level of remuneration and the regulations governing it, as well as supplements, etc., vary from *Land* to *Land* in the Federal Republic.

Thus the old German university teaching staff, which was dominated by the full professors, has changed greatly. The "intermediate grades" which were created to cope with the problems arising from an ill-provided class of Privatdozenten, have helped to adapt the system to the new situation of the German university. He who has reached the "intermediate grade" has some measure of security. The "intermediate grade," which was mainly instituted for the Privatdozenten, has made the word *Privat* in the term Privatdozent largely a reminder of its historical origin in private risk. Though habilitation and *venia legendi,* which admit a person to the status of a Privatdozent, do not guarantee a position in the intermediate grade; nontheless, the Privatdozent does, in fact, very frequently find an appointment there.

Even though the Recommendations of the Science Council had not yet been fulfilled, in 1960 already 53 percent of the "older" Privatdozenten, who had been nominated to unofficial professorships, and 73 percent of all Privatdozenten, found their livelihood through some job within the university. Those who gained their livelihood outside the university were, for the most part, physicians who often occupied leading positions in hospitals.

The rights and obligations of Privatdozenten, in so far as they are not laid down in their conditions of service in an institute or similar body, rest on the law of the university as a corporation. The Privatdozent may claim a lecture room and he receives full protection of his academic freedom in the face of the state and the university authorities. His lecture announcements are only subject to the Dean's inspection to ensure that he remains within the realm of the subject in which he is authorized to teach. He may, under certain conditions, also deliver so-called major lecture courses. His lectures are recognized in admission to governmental and academic examinations. He has the right to suggest research for diplomas and for doctoral dissertations and to supervise as well as to participate in doctoral examinations, although a professor must also participate. Privatdozenten are only indirectly involved in academic self-administration through their representatives in the so-called "inner circle of the faculty" and in the senate. In matters which concern them immediately, they have the right to be heard by the inner circle of the faculty. They also have a right to use research apparatus, although the scope of this right may be limited by the regulations of the directorate of the institute (Thieme, 1956: 281 et seq.).

When we look back, we see that the institution of the Privatdozent, which was established more than 150 years ago, still retains one major feature: the aspiration towards scientific and scholarly achievement to be realized and demonstrated in the greatest possible freedom. It has come to be realized that this aspiration can only be attained under certain conditions and that these were not available to the Privatdozent in recent decades. Gradually, however, alongside the idealistic conception of the Privatdozent, which flourished in earlier times and which disregarded, and could to a large extent disregard, the facts of life, there has grown up a more realistic and more sober understanding of the situation. Now the universities, through the establishment and the development of an infrastructure of middle rank appointments, are trying to create that greater flexibility which is necessary if they are to survive and succeed in the world as it is today.

NOTES

1. These 3,583 include the following:

(a) 668 honorary professors. They were originally scholars who, for the most part, had habilitated, but for whom no chair was available and who were, therefore, granted special distinction by this title. Nowadays honorary professors are usually persons of some prominence, for example, high executives in the chemical or electrical industries, high ranking judges, chief physicians of important hospitals, etc. They receive no salaries for their lectures, only attendance fees from their audience. The honorary professorship is intended to be an honor for the person appointed and for the appointing university.

(b) 781 officials and employees of the scientific services, who have not habilitated. They have been appointed for regular tasks, such as the care of collections, apparatus, etc., without any question of associating a teaching post with their appointment. They have completed their university studies but have not, or have not yet, habilitated. They are a part of the infrastructure (*Mittelbau*). Their monthly basic salary begins about DM. 900 and may rise to DM. 1,400. As officials they have permanent tenure.

(c) 60 visiting professors and teachers from other universities, or from abroad, for whom a special contract is made for their period of service.

(d) 1,806 authorized teachers who, as a rule, are pursuing an academic career and who do both routine teaching and supplementary teaching, in very specialized fields, and who usually have not habilitated. In the main they receive an honorarium (*Vergutung*) for the number of semester hours they teach; their travel expenses are also paid for. Insofar as they devote all their time to this, their honoraria can amount to DM. 600 per semester hour; insofar as they do it as an auxiliary occupation they might get as much as DM. 250 per semester hour.

(e) Others, particularly *Lektoren,* who are appointed either on a full time basis or on a part time basis, mainly in language instruction. Some of them are still students and others have finished their studies and perform their duties on a full time basis. In that case, they are officials paid like other unhabilitated officials.

All of these are distinguished from the Privatdozent in the sense that, as a rule, they are not regarded as prospective incumbents of regular teaching posts, nor, for the most part, have they "habilitated."

2. *Cf.* the establishment of the following institutions in Berlin: 1770 The Academy of Mines; 1790 School of Veterinary Medicine; 1795 Academy of Military Medicine (*Pepiniere*): 1796 Academy of Arts: 1799 Academy of Architecture and Building Construction (*Bauakademie*); 1806 Mogelin Institute of Agriculture.

3. Various efforts had already been made in the course of the eighteenth century in order to cope with these difficulties. In Halle, for example, a special seminar was established to prepare qualified young people as university teachers; in Frankfurt an der Oder an attempt was made to appoint *doctores legentes* on a salaried basis in order to attach them to a university, but resources failed. In Berlin the Privatdozent appears in the statutes for the first time, being recognized as the reservoir from which future appointments to professorial chairs would be made. They were institutionalized and confirmed as an integral component of the teaching corps of the university.

4. The *jus ubique docendi* was originally involved in the granting of a doctor's degree. The *doctor legens* could claim the right to teach at any university and in any subject, and these possibilities were indeed utilized. The practice was to announce lectures in those subjects which promised the largest number of students, and, accordingly, the largest possible income. So it happened that there were scholars who taught in more that fifty different fields from medicine and biology through mineralogy, economics, mathematics to logic and aesthetics, the monetary system of the ancients, as well as glass-making and astronomy. (See von Heister, 1860: 64.)

5. Assistants are not, as such, entitled to deliver lectures but may, in particular circumstances, be authorized to do so. The teaching activity of the assistants is limited to exercises, the supervision of laboratory and similar work, the conduct of seminars, clinical work and the practical examination of the sick, etc. The teaching rights of a Privatdozent are not affected by his concurrent status as an assistant.

6. Those who had the means could travel abroad and utilize foreign archives and sources. They could then improve their scholarly reputation by writing. They could avoid becoming schoolteachers in the mere struggle for existence and could use their time for scholarly and scientific work and making the results available for publication. The number and bulk of publications of a scholar were, and still are, the criterion of scientific and scholarly achievement.

7. In the middle of the nineteenth century the average age for taking the doctorate for those who later became professors was 23, while their professorial appointment came at 35. One hundred years later (1950) the average age at which the doctorate was taken was 26–8, while the professorial appointment came at 44–5 years of age. The waiting period had been extended by seven years (Busch, 1959: 46).

REFERENCES

BOEKELMANN, P. (1962) *Aufgaben und Aussichten der Hochschulreform.* Gottingen: Vandenhoeck u. Ruprecht.

BUSCH, A. (1959) *Die Geschichte des Privatdozenten.* Stuttgart: F. Enke.

—— (1962) "Hochschullehrer und sonstiges wissenschaftliches Personal an den wissenschaftliches Hochschulen 1960." P. 403 in *Wirtschaft und Statistik,* Heft 7 (July).

COUSIN, V. (1832–1833) *De l'Instruction Publique dans Quelques Pays de l'Allemagne.* Altona-Hammerich: J. C. Kroger.

Empfehlungen des Wissenschaftsrates zum Ausbau der wissenschaftlichen Einrichtungen, Teil 1 (1960). Bonn: Bundesdruckerei.

EULENBURG, F. (1908) *Der "akademische Nachwuchs": Eine Untersuchung ueber die Lage und die Aufgaben der Extraordinarien und Privatdozenten.* Berlin and Leipzig: B. G. Tuebner.

FELGENTRAEGER, W. (1961) "Zum gegenwartigen Besoldungsrecht der Hochschullehrer," p. 152 in *Mitteilungen des Hochschulverbandes,* Bd. 9.

MEINERS, C. (1802) *Ueber die Verfassung und Verwaltung deutscher Universitaten.* Gottingen: Rower.

Minerva (1962) I (Autumn) 1.

OSTWALD, W. (1927) *Lebenslinien, Zweiter Teil (1887–1905).* Berlin: Klasing.

PLESSNER, H. (1924) "Zur Soziologie der modernen Forschung und ihrer Organisation in der deutschen Universitat." In Max Scheler (ed.) *Versuche zu einer Soziologie des Wissens,* Munich and Leipzig: Duncker und Humbolt; reprinted (1956) at p. 27 in H. Plessner (ed.) *Untersuchungen zur Lage der deutschen Hochschullehrer,* Bd. 1 Gottingen: Vandenhoeck und Ruprecht.

STOLL, A. (1929) *Friedrich Karl von Savigny: Professorenjahre in Berlin, 1810–1842.* Berlin: C. Heymann.

——, Ed. (1949) *Aus meinem Leben.* Basel: Verlag Chemie.

THIEME, W. (1956) *Deutsches Hochschulrecht.* Berlin-Cologne: Carl Heymann.

von FERBER, C. (1956) *Die Entwicklung des Lehrkorpers der deutschen Universitaten und Hochschulen 1864–1954.* Gottingen: Vandenhoeck und Ruprecht.

von HEISTER, C. (1860) *Nachrichten ueber Gottfried Christoph Beireis.* Berlin: Nicolaische Verlagshandlung.

von SYBEL, H. (1868) *Die deutschen und die auswartigen Universitaten.* Bonn: Cohen und Sohn.

WEBER, ALFRED (1923) *Die Not der geistigen Arbeiter.* Munich and Leipzig: Duncker und Humbolt.

WEBER, MAX (1919) *Wissenschaft als Beruf.* Munich: J. C. B. Mohr (Paul Siebeck).

—— (1951) "Wissenschaft als beruf." In *Gesammelte Aufsatze zur Wissenschaftslehre,* Tubingen: J. C. B. Mohr (Paul Siebeck): pp. 524–555 in 2nd Edition; trans. into English (1947) at p. 48, H. H. Gerth and C. W. Mills (trans. and eds.) *From Max Weber: Essays in Sociology,* London: Kegan Paul, Trench, Trubner and Co.

CHAPTER 12

UNEQUAL PEERS
The Situation of Researchers
at Berkeley

Carlos E. Kruytbosch and Sheldon L. Messinger

The national commitment to basic research has drastically shifted the distribution of effort in large American universities. One of the lesser-known responses to this shift has been the differentiation of a new class of university personnel—the researchers.[1] This paper explores the situation and some of the characteristics of a group of researchers at Berkeley. It seems likely that the group has its counterpart on the campuses of most similar institutions.[2]

Method

The March, 1966, Berkeley payroll was scanned for individuals receiving payments as researchers. In April, 1966, after eliminating the names of those also receiving payments as regular faculty members, questions were

AUTHORS' NOTE: This chapter draws on materials collected in studies of the role of organized research and the development of rules in university and other settings. Carlos E. Kruytbosch's studies were partially supported by the National Aeronautics and Space Administration under Grant #NSG 243 to the University of California, a grant administered by the Social Sciences Project of the Space Science Laboratory, University of California, Berkeley; Sheldon L. Messinger's studies were partially supported by the Russell Sage Foundation under a grant administered by the Center for the Study of Law and Society, University of California, Berkeley. The authors also received valuable assistance from the Office of the Chancellor, University of California, Berkeley; from members of the Executive Council, Academic Research and Professional Association (Berkeley); and from the many respondents and informants who participated in the studies.

The authors take full, joint, and equal responsibility for all alleged facts and value judgments expressed; those who supported or participated in the studies should in no way be held responsible.

This chapter is reprinted (in slightly revised form) from *The American Behavioral Scientist*, May–June, 1968 (Volume XI, Number 5).

sent by campus mail to 1,142 persons. An accompanying letter indicated that the survey was sponsored by the Research Committee of the Academic Research and Professional Association (ARAPA).[3] ARAPA was formed in the winter of 1964–1965 to give research and professional staff members a voice in university affairs. The purpose of the survey was described as an effort to provide a profile of these persons at Berkeley, to clarify the position and role of the group in the university structure, and to give expression to some of the current concerns of people appointed to these positions. Finally, anonymity was guaranteed.

In addition to the survey, structured and unstructured interviews were conducted at Berkeley with researchers, members of the regular faculty, and campus administrators. Some interviews were also conducted with such persons on other campuses of the University of California and at other universities. Administrative documents bearing on policy toward researchers were examined, as well as such studies of researchers at Berkeley or elsewhere as could be found. Finally, but not least, as researchers at Berkeley we have tried to be observant participants.

This paper focuses on one group of researchers covered in the study, persons appointed to the "professional research" title.[4] Among the several research titles at Berkeley, this is the most prestigious. Questionnaires were sent to 333 persons with appointments to this title, none of whom had regular faculty appointments. Usable returns were received from 212 persons, a response rate of 64 percent. Responses were received from 74 percent of the full, 68 percent of the associate, and 58 percent of the assistant researchers. The more frequent response of those in higher ranks reflects both degree of interest and differentially permanent mailing address.

Formal Status

Prior to 1952 there were two salaried research appointments at Berkeley.[5] Researchers of lesser accomplishment were appointed as "research fellows," those of greater accomplishment as "research associates." Salary schedules existed for these positions, but they were flexibly used. A 1953 letter from a Berkeley dean pinpointed the personnel problem that accompanied the easy availability of research funds after the war:

> In 1948 the President had been concerned about complaints that research projects (usually supported by 'extra-mural' funds) were draining some of our important [departmental] laboratories of needed staff, as well as making it hard for them to recruit new people. This seemed to happen because the directors of most such projects were not restricted, except by their total funds, as to the salaries they might offer. In some cases they 'kidnapped' instructors and assistant professors by offering nearly double their academic stipends, and there was no uniformity whatever in pay levels for non-faculty professional research personnel.[6]

In these circumstances, the president appointed a committee to look into the matter. A presidential directive (Sproul, 1952) established a

new system for handling research appointments. A "professional research" title was created, with ranks paralleling regular faculty ranks (assistant, associate, and full, e.g., associate research entomologist). Candidates for this title were required to have research qualifications equivalent
to those specified for appointments to the parallel "professorial" title; they
were also to receive salaries equivalent to professors of parallel rank, with
appointments for similar terms. In context, these changes were intended to
reduce the attractive power of research positions. An additional rule was to
help insure this: professors were to receive a professional research title for
fractional and summer research appointments.

More important for our purposes here, these changes formalized a kind
of rough equivalence between appointees to professorial and research positions. As the presidential directive itself made clear, the professional research series created a "range of promotion and salaries"—in short, a career line—for researchers not available before.

However, a number of critical rights and perquisites associated with
regular faculty status were not accorded to researchers. Researchers were
not admitted to membership in the academic senate, and no provision was
made for their formal inclusion in any other administrative or policy-making bodies. They were not given the right to generate their own research
funding, i.e., to be "principal investigators" on extra-murally supported
grants or contracts. No provision was made for their security of employment, nor were paid leaves of absence included among their privileges. Administrative documents made clear that the denial of these perquisites was
largely a matter of course. It was also suggested that the absence of these
perquisites would reduce the attractiveness of research appointments, further facilitating recruitment for regular faculty positions.

The situation of researchers in 1966 remained essentially the same as
described above.[7] In sum, although in some respects regarded as professional peers of the professors, the researchers were otherwise treated as
something less.

Other Organizational Characteristics

We shall now turn to some survey data.

Over 80 percent of the researchers reported full-time appointments at
the university, and, as one might expect, the largest proportion of these appointments (68 percent) were in research units organized outside departments and schools. However, significant numbers listed affiliations with departments (36 percent), schools or colleges (15 percent), and other
university administrative units (2 percent). (The percentages add to more
than 100 due to multiple appointments.)

Within the sample, 25 percent of researchers were full researchers, 21
percent were associate, and 54 percent were assistant level researchers.
Most departmental affiliations of the full researchers represented lectureships, though a few were engaged in full-time research in departmental re-

search enclaves. On the other hand, although 15 percent of the assistant researchers held lectureships, most of their departmental appointments
represented full-time research work within research enclaves.

ACADEMIC SPECIALTY

The distribution of researchers among academic specialties—as measured by the field of their highest degree—is one key to understanding the
role of this group on the campus. It is especially instructive to compare this
parameter with the proportions of professors in various fields at Berkeley
(as measured by their departmental affiliations). (See Table 1.)

TABLE 1
PROFESSIONAL RESEARCHERS AND PROFESSORS, AND ACADEMIC FIELDS
AT BERKELEY (IN PERCENT)

	Researchers (questionnaire responses)	Professors (listed in 1964/65 catalogue)
Life sciences	40	17
Physical sciences and engineering	25	31
Social sciences	33	32
Humanities and arts	2	20
	100%	100%
(Number)	(212)	(1415)

It is clear, as we shall show below, that the appointment of researchers has
been a way of augmenting the graduate faculty; the data in Table 1 suggests that this augmentation has taken place disproportionately in the life
sciences and that the humanities have not benefited at all. The real number
of physical science researchers is, of course, very much larger than shown
in this table because we have not included those at the Lawrence Radiation
Laboratory.[8]

FINANCIAL SUPPORT

The principal financial fact of life with regard to the researchers is the
predominance of extra-mural funding—primarily grants and contracts. The
survey data showed that 84 percent of the respondents received all or some
part of their salaries from extra-mural funds. On the other hand, only 64
percent of the sample were totally supported from extra-mural sources. Of
32 percent at least partially supported intramurally, 12 percent indicated
total support from university sources and 20 percent partial university support, mostly through lectureships. (Four percent were not sure about the
origin of their support.)

This intertwining of sources of support for large numbers of research
personnel is of interest in view of the fact that a major assumption informing the university's administrative posture toward its researchers has been

that grant and contract funds are time-limited. This assumption conditions policy statements like the following:

> As a general rule organized research units, with the exception of non-departmental laboratories, shall not have a permanent or quasi-permanent staff except for necessary administrative assistance and technical and clerical staff. . . . This rule shall not preclude the employment of . . . non-faculty research appointments for the duration of specific research projects [University of California, 1961 and 1963: 4].

Though it remains true that the bulk of researcher time is supported on so-called "soft" extra-mural funds, the data suggest a good deal of sharing of the salaries of individual researchers between intramural and extra-mural sources.

"PERMANENCE"

Other survey data indicate that notwithstanding the university's posture in the matter, "a permanent or semi-permanent staff" of researchers has in fact developed. Many researchers have been at Berkeley for long periods, many expect to stay for long periods, and a substantial number feel that their appointments will continue, barring some catastrophe.

Although about two-fifths (38 percent) had been at Berkeley for less than three years, one-fifth (16 percent) reported three to five years' employment, and about one-fifth each fell into groups checking five to nine years (23 percent) and more than ten years (23 percent). A rather similar overall picture emerges when we look at future stay estimates. While 22 percent of the researchers estimated they would leave within a year, 28 percent expected to remain for a year or two, 18 percent estimated three to four years, and 32 percent felt they would stay on at Berkeley for more than five years.

If the two measures are combined, the researchers fall into three roughly equal groupings. At the extremes, a "short-stay" group (with past employment of less than five years and future employment expectations of less than three years) made up 34 percent of the respondents; and a "long-stay" group (with more than five years past employment and more than three years future expectation) totaled 30 percent of the sample. An intermediate grouping of people with short past and long future, and long past and short future, employment made up the remaining 36 percent of the respondents.

The survey further indicated that about half (48 percent) of the respondents rejected the official view of their employment as specifically tied to the duration of individual grants or contracts. They felt that barring drastic fund cuts they would continue to be kept on as long as they produced good work. One quarter (27 percent) of the respondents, on the other hand, felt their appointment to be circumscribed by the limits of a specific project. Some 24 percent of the researchers were not sure whether their appointment would end when their current project finished.

Backgrounds and Orientations [9]

EDUCATION

Almost all—87 percent—of the researchers held the Ph.D. degree. Seven researchers held a bachelor's degree, nineteen a master's, and one held a law degree. Presumably, these persons in some sense had a doctoral "equivalent" as required by university rules. (See University of California, 1962b.)

It is worth noting that a sizeable proportion of the researchers, 42 percent, received their highest degrees from Berkeley, and an additional five percent received some other, but not their highest, degree from Berkeley. The meaning of this proportion deserves further exploration than is possible here. Two hypotheses, both of which may be true, come to mind. First, for a number of reasons, persons close at hand seek and are sought for research appointments; those at a distance are less likely to seek or be sought for them.

A second hypothesis is in some ways more interesting. Although the proportion of Berkeley professors having Berkeley degrees is not known, it seems likely that it is a lesser proportion. [10] Organizations primarily devoted to the dissemination of knowledge, like departments and schools, often put a premium on the breadth of their offerings, and their personnel tend to develop notions about the dangers of "in-breeding." Such notions seem less prevalent with reference to organizations primarily devoted to the development and implementation of programs of advanced research; rather than seeking breadth as such, research organizations appear to place a premium on colleagues interested in the same "problems." This kind of interest probably requires a considerable period of association, especially in fields where "problems" are not clearly defined or widely shared—and many organized research units and enclaves (or parts of them) are committed to the articulation of just such fields. Under these conditions, it might be expected that, for example, many former students would be appointed to research positions to continue, as colleagues, work begun with their professors. In this connection, it may be significant that one-quarter of the researchers indicate having studied with their formal superiors; one-third of those at the assistant rank have done so. [11]

EXPERIENCE

Researchers have had a variety of work experiences relevant to their positions. Over half (54 percent) have taught or done research at a college or university before coming to Berkeley. Many have done research in other organizational settings. Thus 23 percent have done research in government agencies, 13 percent in non-profit organizations, 17 percent have done research in industry, and a fifth (22 percent) have done "other professional work" before coming to Berkeley. (The percentages add to more than 100 percent, because respondents could check or write in more than one alternative.) Only among researchers at the assistant rank do we find any significant number—26 percent—for whom the Berkeley research appointment was the first academic or academic-relevant work experience.

ORIENTATION

The survey data provide a number of indicators that researchers have been and are heavily invested in scholarly careers.

Scholarly Investment. About one in five (19 percent) of the researchers indicated having authored or co-authored one or more published books.[12] Exactly a third of those at the full rank and a quarter of those at the associate rank have done so. Still others have edited books. The vast majority of the group—87 percent—have authored or co-authored one or more published scholarly articles.

Other survey data indicate that substantially all researchers (94 percent) belonged to scholarly societies and read one or more scholarly journals each month. A third (34 percent) of those in the two senior ranks were or had been editors of journals in their field.

Aspirations. Researchers were asked to indicate which of a number of alternative positions they would find "attractive" if available five years hence; they could check more than one alternative and could add choices not listed. The alternatives were these: a professorship at "Berkeley," at a "major university," at "another university," at a "California state college," or at a "good liberal arts college"; a research position at "Berkeley," at a "major university," in "industry," or in a "government or nonprofit" organization.

Of the 205 researchers indicating some choice, 68 percent said they would find a Berkeley professorship attractive; a slightly smaller proportion —65 percent—said that a professorship at some other major university would be attractive. In addition, 37 percent indicated that a position at (just) another university would be attractive, 21 percent would find a liberal arts college attractive, and 16 percent said a position at a California state college would be attractive.

Nor are professorships the only kinds of positions in academic settings that would be attractive to researchers five years from now. Over half the group (54 percent) would find a Berkeley senior research position attractive; and about four in ten (37 percent) indicated interest in a senior research position at another major university.[13]

It is worth emphasizing the fact that research positions in university settings, especially Berkeley, are considered attractive by the group. Thus, as noted, 54 percent of the researchers said they would find a Berkeley senior research position attractive five years hence; this is not many fewer than the 68 percent who indicated interest in a Berkeley professorship. Further, another 10 percent would also find a senior research position at some other

major university attractive, making some 64 percent in all who were attracted by prospect of research positions at major universities.

In sum, it is apparent that Berkeley researchers as a group look toward
work in academic settings and that a substantial majority consider a research position in such a setting an attractive possibility.[14]

SOME ASPECTS OF RESEARCH POSITIONS

Major universities like Berkeley are increasingly being chosen as sites
for post-doctoral work by both junior and senior scholars (See NAS,
1963: 15–17). Further, the Berkeley evidence strongly suggests that successful operation of university research organizations requires "permanent
or semi-permanent" academic staffs.[15] Thus the university clearly has a
stake in the attractiveness of its research positions.

TABLE 2

HOW WOULD YOU RATE YOUR PRESENT POSITION IN TERMS OF THE
FOLLOWING FACTORS? (IN PERCENT)

	Ratings			
	Excellent	Good	Average	Poor
Geographical location	66	26	6	2
Opportunities for self-selected work	44	37	12	7
Stimulating work environment	39	34	17	10
Opportunities for career advancement	22	36	22	20
Financial rewards	14	42	34	10
Job security	12	22	26	40

(N = 201-208)

What makes a research position at Berkeley atttractive, and what keeps
it attractive? Table 2 shows how the researchers rated six aspects of their
current positions. Almost all (92 percent) rated the geographic location
"excellent" or "good." Six percent said it was "average," and 2 percent
(perhaps from southern California or Florida) rated it "poor."

Other ratings may be read in the same way. Thus, 81 percent of the researchers were apparently pleased with their opportunities to do self-
selected work. Seventy-three percent of the researchers gave high ratings to
the stimulus provided by their current positions. Over half the group (58
percent) gave a high rating to their opportunities for career advancement.
And 56 percent of the researchers considered the financial reward of their
position "excellent" or "good."

Of the factors explored, only one, job security, was rated "average" or
"poor" by the majority of respondents. Clearly, the absence of any guarantees of security of employment disturbs the researchers. Only among those
senior researchers who had been at the university more than two years and
expected to stay five or more did more than half (56 percent) rate job security "excellent" or "good." As is shown below, such a rating is not necessarily to be interpreted as approval of the university's policy in this matter.

University Functions

The survey materials indicate that researchers are involved in far more than purely research functions. One-third (32 percent) of the respondents reported spending less than half their working time on research, and only one-fifth (20 percent) said they spent all their working time on research. The higher the rank of the researcher, the more time reported spent on functions other than research; further, both researchers who had been at Berkeley longer and those expecting to stay longer reported more time spent on other functions.

TEACHING ACTIVITIES

Almost all (88 percent) of the survey respondents reported they felt qualified to teach formal courses at the university level—as their possession of Ph.D. degrees would suggest they might. Six in ten (64 percent) reported formal classroom teaching experience at the college or university level. Further, four in ten reported being involved in classroom teaching in the last year: nineteen percent at Berkeley only, 13 percent only at some other institution, and 8 percent at both. In addition to formal course work, the researchers reported widespread participation at Berkeley in forms of classroom teaching not explicitly recognized in the degree credit system; for example, giving a lecture or series of lectures by invitation within the framework of a formal course conducted by a professor.

But by far the most significant form of "teaching" conducted by the researchers was their involvement with graduate students in research projects, research seminars, and thesis work at Berkeley. Very little of this is reflected in any formal degree credit accounting. The basic datum in this connection is that 82 percent of the respondents reported having working contacts with graduate students during an average week.[16]

As mentors and guides in the research process, 46 percent of the researchers reported formal (i.e., service on thesis committees) or intimate involvement in graduate theses during the previous two years. Such involvement was more frequent among persons in the two senior ranks, 60 percent reporting it, while one-third of the assistant researchers indicated formal or intimate involvement with graduate theses in the previous two years. An additional quarter of the respondents reported "casual" involvement, which may be taken to mean an occasional consultative relation. Twenty-nine percent did not report any involvement in graduate thesis work.

About four in ten (44 percent) of the professional researchers reported currently having graduate students working under their direction. Interestingly, although the senior personnel were considerably more involved than the assistant researchers in the educational role of thesis adviser, there was relatively little difference between the ranks in the exercise of the supervisory role.

Whichever role is assumed, mentor or supervisor—and clearly in the concrete social situation they are closely intertwined—the data strongly suggest that researchers are functioning in significant degree as an extramurally funded graduate faculty.

ADMINISTRATIVE ACTIVITIES

The researcher's role as administrative superior to graduate students has already been discussed. However, the survey materials and other evidence suggest a much deeper involvement on the part of many Berkeley researchers in the administration and direction of research units. Half a dozen researchers known to the writers occupy publicly recognized administrative positions in research units with such titles as associate, assistant, or acting director, vice chairman, and group leader. Each of these exercises wide responsibilities in the operation of these units—both in day-to-day matters and in policy formation. Others, also known to the writers, play similar roles without public recognition.[17]

Among the survey respondents some 39 percent reported spending time on general administration, and 58 percent said they spent some portion of their time supervising the research or professional activities of others. Further, close to half the researchers reported that their work normally included involvement in budgeting and purchase of equipment. Finally, about a third of the researchers reported frequent or occasional dealings with the campus research office, suggesting involvement in the details of research grant and contract administration. As might be expected, somewhat greater proportions of senior researchers, as well as those who have been at Berkeley longer or expect to stay longer, are involved in administration.

RESEARCH ACTIVITIES

The survey did not explore the nature of the research conducted by respondents. Instead, various indications of researcher autonomy in their work were sought. This is an important issue not only for researchers but for universities, as the latter seek to control the volume and character of their research programs.

The survey suggests that researchers are relatively autonomous with respect to their research work. (Presumably they are autonomous *within* broad policy set by the directorships of the units within which they work, directorships of which they may be a part.) Some 81 percent of the respondents reported being personally involved in research design, and 76 percent in data analysis, two central aspects of the research process. Research design, in particular, implies a significant degree of decision-making autonomy and freedom of choice of research problems and methods.

More compelling, a large majority of the respondents claimed to have no formal superior (8 percent) or described their relation to their formal superior (usually a faculty principal investigator) as one of nominal supervision (56 percent) or a collegial relationship (18 percent). Thus 82 percent of the researchers appear to be relatively independent of their formal superiors. Sixteen percent of the researchers said they received general supervision, and only 5 percent reported detailed direction.

Further, a similar large proportion (81 percent) reported that their choice of research problems and methods took place independently or within a loose framework of consultation. Very few reported their choices to be limited to strictly defined problem areas (15 percent) or merely assigned (4 percent), and these were preponderantly in the assistant ranks. Finally, the majority of researchers (64 percent) reported they were working on their own individual projects by themselves or with others under their direction. Some 22 percent were involved in group projects where decisions were made by consensus, and a small percentage (14 percent) were involved in projects directed by others.

TABLE 3

DEGREE OF AUTONOMY AND SATISFACTION WITH DEGREE OF INDEPENDENCE (IN PERCENT)

Satisfaction with Independence	Degree of Autonomy (type of relation with formal superior)			
	Independent	Consultation	Defined Areas or Assigned	Total
Satisfied	93	82	40	79
Want little more independence	4	14	38	15
Want lot more independence	3	4	22	6
	100%	100%	100%	100%
(Number)	(89)	(77)	(40)	(206) *

* Six persons failed to answer one or both questions.

The survey suggests that even in the area of funding, researchers have considerable autonomy. Researchers with some extra-mural fund support fell into three roughly equal-sized groups with regard to their relation to their source of financial support. One-third (36 percent) said they had written their own proposals for the funding of their current work (in fact if not in name), one-third (33 percent) were working in the framework of projects proposed by their superior, and one-third (27 percent) were doing research within the framework of some comprehensive grant or contract funding. Almost half (47 percent) of the two senior ranks, however, reported having written their own proposals. It might also be mentioned that about two-thirds (69 percent) of the researchers were confident of their ability to obtain grant or contract funding for their research proposals in their own name should they move to another institution.

The picture reflected in the survey material, then, is one of a great deal of researcher autonomy. Indeed, about 80 percent of the sample reported they felt satisfied with the degree of independence they enjoyed in this area. Of course, a normal reluctance of academics to admit any degree of outside control over their activities might account for the high degree of autonomy reported. We checked this possibility by cross-tabulating autonomy in decision-making with satisfaction with degree of independence. This showed that almost all of those who saw their work situation as in fact autonomous were satisfied with their degree of independence, while a majority of those who felt themselves in fact to be working on assigned problems or within a strictly defined area indicated a desire for a greater degree of independence. (See Table 3.)

Formal Status Revisited

The formal status of researchers at Berkeley has been described. Here we consider researchers' attitudes toward this status. Researchers were asked to indicate whether persons in their particular position and rank should or should not be accorded a variety of rights and privileges traditionally associated with academic status.[18] The list of prerogatives was se-

TABLE 4

DO YOU THINK THAT A PERSON IN YOUR PARTICULAR POSITION AND RANK
SHOULD BE ACCORDED THESE RIGHTS AND PRIVILEGES? (IN PERCENT) *

| | | | Position | |
| | | | Don't | Not |
Issues	Yes	No	Know	Applicable
Parking, library, etc., privileges equal to regular faculty	86	2	5	7
Right to be a principal investigator	81	5	5	9
Some formal guarantee of job security	74	10	8	8
Right to serve on university and/or departmental committees	70	14	11	5
Right to have sabbatical leave	69	13	9	9
Right to participate in appointment and promotion of professional people	67	15	12	6
Recognition of current teaching function	65	3	8	24

* Those not responding were excluded. N's vary from 193 to 202.

lected as representative of those accorded to professors at Berkeley but denied to researchers or extended in qualified form. The list included not only rights and privileges generally held "important" by professors but others seemingly "trivial" that researchers mentioned frequently during interviews. Table 4 shows the list and the results.

"ETC." PRIVILEGES

Almost nine in ten researchers felt that "parking, library, etc., privileges" should be equalized, as Table 4 shows, a greater proportion than on any other issue. There are several reasons for this being the most popular issue. First, almost all researchers are affected by the parking and library situations, and they are affected frequently. Further, parking arrangements are a widespread subject of complaint among Berkeley professors as well as researchers.[19] To have lesser parking privileges than professors only complicates an already difficult situation.

Third, the query was phrased in a way that probably rendered it a stimulus for a response of general discontent with what many researchers call their "second-class status." The "etc." doubtless contributed to this effect. This is not to imply that the troubles associated with this status are not quite specific, but rather that there are many such troubles, and that, collectively, these troubles constitute assaults on researchers' sense of themselves as full-fledged members of the academic community.

Thus the parking permits issued to researchers (for $72 a year currently, the same fee paid by professors) confine them to parking lots on the periphery of the campus, wherever their offices, and to a very few parking lots to boot. Researchers have not been permitted to have their student assistants check out books for them from the library, nor are library privileges extended to their wives; professors routinely have both privileges. Researchers' wives are subject to fees should they want to attend the university, while these fees are waived for professors' wives—and out-of-state fees, in particular, may put a major dent in a researcher's budget. Researchers have not had access to campus travel funds to attend scholarly meetings, except under the most special circumstances; even a recently announced more liberal policy pointedly distinguishes between the privileges of professors and researchers with respect to such funds.[20]

Even more generally, researchers find that they are not notified of or asked to participate in matters deemed important to "members of the university community." Apparently through neglect rather than design, researchers are excluded from the administrative channels of information provided routinely to professors; and, not being members, they are of course denied communications from or with the academic senate. They are even left out of speeches addressed to the university community, a community composed for speechmakers of "faculty, students, and administration." And should researchers, nonetheless, act on the assumption that they, too, are part of this community, they typically find they have no place to sit.[21] All of these matters, and more, help account for the widespread positive response on this issue from researchers.

PRINCIPAL INVESTIGATOR STATUS

Researchers at Berkeley are not formally permitted to initiate grant requests to extra-mural agencies or, thus, to be named as the person responsible for execution of a research project.[22] Researchers were asked whether persons in their position and rank should or should not be accorded the right to be a principal investigator. Eight in ten members of the group felt the right should be extended to them, as Table 4 indicates. To the extent that rules about principal investigators restrict the opportunities of researchers to decide the character of their work, it seems obvious that they would feel discontent.

On the other hand, it has already been shown that most researchers, by their own account, have much independence in this matter. It is worth noting again, too, that over 80 percent reported satisfaction with their independence in these areas. And, when researchers were asked to rate their opportunities for doing self-selected work, 81 percent rated them "excellent" or "good," while only 7 percent rated them "poor."

All these items together suggest that researcher responses on the principal investigator prerogative may not be, by and large, an expression of discontent with working conditions inside research units. Researchers do not appear to be asking mainly for an increase in their already considerable independence or control over their work. Perhaps the most compelling finding to this effect is the fact that roughly the same proportions of researchers who rate their opportunities for self-selected work "excellent" through "poor" felt they should have the right to be a principal investigator, as shown in Table 5. ˙

TABLE 5

POSITION ON WHETHER RESEARCHERS SHOULD HAVE THE RIGHT
TO BE A PRINCIPAL INVESTIGATOR, AND RATING OF OPPORTUNITIES
FOR SELF-SELECTED WORK (IN PERCENT) *

	Rating of Opportunities			
Position	Excellent	Good	Average	Poor
Yes	76	74	79	73
No	4	9	4	—
No position	20	17	17	27
	100%	100%	100%	100%
(Number)	(92)	(76)	(24)	(15)

* We have combined "don't know," "not applicable," and "no response" on the principal investigator issue. Five persons did not rate opportunities for self-selected work.

What does seem to engender these responses (as well as responses on other issues) is the researcher's feeling that although he has considerable independence and responsibility at work, university rules, like those about principal investigators, *formally* do not recognize this fact. He finds this inconsistent with both his situation at work and with his position as a full-fledged member of his scholarly discipline.

It is to be noted, finally, that this was one of the two issues about which a considerable proportion of researchers felt "strongly." (The other issue was job security.) About two in ten (21 percent) indicated such sentiment.[23] (This may be contrasted with one in ten [11 percent] who felt "strongly" about parking, library, and other privileges.) In interviews, the researchers said that they felt the existing policy required sham, was undignifying, and facilitated exploitation; it was not difficult to detect that many researchers felt their competence and integrity were implicitly questioned by this policy. Further, as participants in a game where a byline is the apparent, and often the only, road to career advancement, researchers felt cheated. Moreover, they felt cheated unnecessarily, given the fact that controls over the quantity and quality of research would appear to be about the same whether or not researchers were permitted to be principal investigators.[24]

JOB SECURITY

As matters now stand (early 1968), researchers have neither tenure nor any other guarantee of job security (e.g., a right to notice). This is true no matter what the rank of the researcher, his actual position, or his length of service. And, as Table 4 shows, three-quarters of the researchers felt something should be done about the matter. Further analysis shows that this feeling is especially widespread among the senior researchers who have been at Berkeley five years or more, or who expect to stay for three or more years; indeed, 97 percent of those in this group who considered the query applicable said a formal guarantee of job security should be extended to persons like them.

Interviews suggested that several considerations underlie these responses. First, under current conditions researchers are vulnerable to discharge for any reason at all; at the time of the survey there were no grievance procedures of any sort formally available for researchers, nor any clear statements as to proper grounds for dismissal.[25] Although communication among researchers is demonstrably poor, each seems to have heard some tale of discharge or termination that strikes him as unfair in the circumstances. Second, for many there appears to be a lack of clarity about the terms of their employment. Researchers are uncertain just how long they may expect to stay or what conditions, specifically, might affect continuance. The most permanent group appears to have an additional concern: they believe that after long service the university should undertake to formally guarantee their permanent tenure.

One final matter. Those who rated the security of their current positions differently were checked to see if they took varying positions on this issue. They did not: between 86 and 90 percent of those who rated the security of their present positions "excellent" through "poor" held that a formal guarantee of job security should be extended to persons in their position and rank. This suggests, again, that it is not conditions within research units that are primarily at issue.

COMMITTEE PARTICIPATION

Researchers were asked whether persons in their position and rank should have the "right to serve on university and/or departmental committees." Table 4 shows that 70 percent believed they should.

Several matters should be kept in mind in assessing these results. First, although we failed to explore the matter sufficiently in the survey, we know from interviews that there is wide variation in the degree to which research-

ers already participate in organized research unit or departmental committees. It is not entirely clear, then, whether a researcher who responded
"yes" was opining that he and others like him should have greater opportunities to participate at the unit level, the campus level, or both. Second, it
is not altogether clear that researchers, any more than other academic men,
consider that participation on committees is best described as a "right"; for
some, we suspect, it is a "duty" they would just as soon avoid. We believe
that this accounts for the more substantial "no" response to this issue.

Over-all, however, what is probably worth notice is that a majority of
researchers are willing to serve on committees. Given their qualifications as
academic men, they appear to be an available resource that is currently little used. And the fact that an important segment of operating personnel are
left out of the formal decision-making cannot contribute to effective policy-making.

SABBATICALS

Researchers are not eligible for sabbatical leave under current regulations. Seven in ten indicated a belief that persons in their position and rank
should have this right, as Table 4 shows. This issue would appear to
require no particular comment, except to say that the idea that sabbaticals
are for "doing research," an idea sometimes heard when researcher leaves
are discussed (thus "what do they need them for?"), seems rather quaint
in the context of the modern university. Presumably, in this context, sabbaticals are to be used for professional development, whatever this turns
out concretely to mean. As the data show, many professional researchers,
like professors, are enmeshed in a network of administrative-teaching-
counseling-research activities. This is especially true of the more permanent researchers in the senior ranks. They, too, may find that they need
"time out." At least most think so.

APPOINTMENTS AND PROMOTIONS

Do researchers feel that persons in their position and rank should have
the right to participate in appointment and promotion of research people?
Table 4 shows that most of the group felt this right should be extended to
them. On the other hand, some 15 percent, the highest proportion of
"no's" on any issue, felt differently. Further analysis shows that those who
expect to stay at Berkeley a shorter time are less certain they should participate in appointment and promotion matters. Further, it is clear that it is
assistant researchers, above all, who are uncertain that it is appropriate for
them to participate in appointment and promotion matters.

CURRENT TEACHING FUNCTION

Table 4 shows researchers' responses to the question of whether there
should be "recognition of [your] current teaching function"; 65 percent
said there should be. We knew that many did have such a function, partic-

ularly if supervision of research by graduate students and post-doctoral fellows is conceived as "teaching." It is notable, nonetheless, that almost one out of four researchers said that the query was inapplicable to his situation. Interviews, as well as further analysis of the survey material, suggest some interpretations.

First of all, some researchers find that their current teaching function within organized research units and enclaves *is* recognized. Their contacts with students as supervisors, mentors, and guides are counted among the regular tasks they perform, and the way they perform them is taken into account by unit directors and perhaps deans and others in assessing their performance. Some of these persons may have answered that a right to recognition of their teaching function was inapplicable; they already have such a "right," if informally.

For many researchers, however, probably including many who said "inapplicable," this is not the case. Another factor of importance is that, given the terms of many federal grants and contracts, some researchers cannot "teach." Such grants and contracts require that those paid for "research" do "research" during those hours for which they are paid. Persons working under these terms are, in part for this reason, unlikely to construe supervision of students as "teaching." They, too, may have said "inapplicable." [26]

The terms of federal grants and contracts are not the only factors leading to a rather rigid distinction between "research" and "teaching," a distinction that may be particularly inappropriate in the setting of the modern university. At Berkeley, such a distinction is built into the structure of the university, into the formal division between "organized research units" and "departments of instruction and research," for example, and into the university's budget and accounting systems. It is, moreover, a part of an older academic lexicon still current in some circles, and one shared by many researchers. For these researchers, "teaching" can only mean formal classroom teaching. They, too, may have said "inapplicable." Although harbingers of a new style of instruction, they, like many of their peers in professorial positions, continue to use an older language.[27]

Conclusion

Our survey of researchers at Berkeley shows they are academic people in terms of background, qualifications, scholarly accomplishments, and aspirations. A substantial number have been at Berkeley for years, and many more plan to stay. They are heavily involved in the full range of university activities. Besides participating in programs of advanced research, many are or have been lecturers, offering undergraduate courses. Most act as mentors and guides to graduate students in the research process. Many help administer research organizations. In their latter capacity, many are *de facto* policy-makers, helping give direction to the university's research programs, hiring graduate and other personnel, and developing funding sources.

In their capacity as researchers most feel they possess the requisite autonomy and freedom of scientific decision-making. At the same time, they deeply resent the absence of formal protections. Thus, although a large proportion of researchers feel that their appointments at Berkeley will continue, barring catastrophic cuts in funding, the informal nature of the university's commitment causes them considerable ambivalence and sometimes acute embarrassment. Though they may be encouraged to develop independent research proposals to enrich a unit's program, and apparently have little difficulty in finding faculty members to "sponsor" such proposals as "principal investigators," researchers resent the subterfuge and lack of explicit recognition of the role they play. In the cases of both security of employment and principal investigatorship, researchers, however trusting they may be, feel vulnerable to the whims of others and demeaned by such dependence.

As members of the university community, too, researchers feel slighted. On the one hand, they feel they contribute to accomplishment of important university goals. On the other hand, they feel excluded from the councils where these goals are formulated. Further, nagging daily reminders of their low formal status in the university reside in the discrepancies, often trivial, between privileges accorded to them and to the regular faculty. Slights turn into shock, however, when some important event involves the campus or university as a whole, such as a crisis in governance, and researchers discover that they have no formal place, no voice, that they are "invisible."

One is led to wonder what, if anything, should be done about the situation of researchers. This is not the place for specific policy recommendations, and none will be made. This can be said, however. If in the past the primary role of the university, like the liberal arts college, was the transmission of knowledge, now the creation of knowledge vies for recognition as an equivalent function. If once undergraduate education held stage center, now graduate and post-doctoral education have moved out of the wings. Sustained programs of research are of obvious, if yet but partially realized, relevance to both ends. With such programs has come the need for well-trained academic persons whose primary commitment, within the university, is to their operation and perfection. There is also a need to consider the proper position of such persons in the university.

Now one may approach a position by asking who is available to fill it, and then shape the rights and responsibilities assigned to the person in this position to his presumed or proven competence. There is, of course, another approach. One may ask what rights and responsibilities should be assigned to a position to maximize the chance that someone in it will be able to perform needed functions successfully and with dignity. Then one searches for persons competent to exercise such rights and to assume such responsibilities. As a matter of organizational policy, the second approach seems clearly superior, although one will expect that in individual instances policy will have to be tempered with the practical wisdom implicit in the first approach.

We assume that the root issue for the university is revealed by the second approach. The primary question is this: what rights and responsibilities are needed to maximize the chances that researchers will be able to perform needed functions successfully and with dignity? We have shown that the functions performed by researchers are not so few or so narrow as is sometimes believed. And we have shown that most researchers feel full dignity is denied them. We have not attempted to discuss in any detail whether or not researchers are able to fulfill their functions successfully. There is little reason to suppose that this is not the case—at least for those researchers who are retained and promoted. But there is good reason to suppose that researchers might better fulfill needed functions were certain changes made in their rights and responsibilities. Changes that will help accomplish both this end and the not unrelated end of increasing the dignity of the research position seem clearly needed.

As a result of two and a half decades of boom and solution of problems by expansion, many changes have taken place in major universities— but universities are only beginning to explore the possibilities of a more rational management of research and graduate education. Many problems stem from this fact. The university continues to attempt to fit greatly expanded research and graduate education functions into administrative and organizational forms designed for an undergraduate teaching institution. The situation has forced definitional contortions and semi-legitimate practices upon researchers and research administrators, among others, thus contributing to cynicism about university governance. Open discussion of the problems has been inhibited, partly by the danger of exposing the inconsistencies and semi-legitimacies and the risk of endangering funding, and partly because of a lack of systematic information about the nature of the research enterprise and its intimate involvement in graduate education. The organizational limbo in which the Berkeley professional researcher moves is but one of the vexing phenomena generated by this confusion of means and goals.

NOTES

1. Data from various sources indicate that research personnel make up from 20 to 33 percent of the academic staffs of graduate degree granting institutions, with the proportions rising to over 50 percent in a few major universities. These figures and the ones cited below exclude graduate students employed less than full time. (See U.S. Office of Education, 1966: esp. 9, 10, 20; NSF, 1965: esp. 55; see also the April issues of *Industrial Research* from 1963 through 1967.)

This has been a recent and rapid development. At Berkeley in 1940, already a major research institution, researchers made up some 7 percent of the academic staff. By 1960 their proportion had risen to 31 percent, and in 1964 it was 33 percent. Comparable national figures are not available for 1940, but the Office of Education data cited above show that in 1960 researchers made up 21 percent of the academic staffs of the nation's universities. By 1964 this figure had risen to 29 percent.

2. As far as could be determined, no previous studies of the characteristics of researchers exist. However, several discussions of the "problem" of research

personnel are available which suggest indirectly that the problems of Berkeley's researchers are mirrored elsewhere. The best of these discussions is in Bowen, 1962, Ch. 8. Other treatments of the topic include Orlans, 1962, esp. Ch. 5; Kidd, 1959, esp. 152–154; McMillen, 1958; Rossi, 1964; University of California, 1962a.

Further data assembled by the writers on the policies of seventeen major institutions toward their research staffs indicate remarkably uniform organizational responses to the new class of personnel. By and large, the universities impose academic standards upon their research personnel without formally conferring upon them the customary academic benefits and prerogatives. Although one or two institutions have virtually integrated researchers into their regular faculties and some few have recognized research personnel as members of the "faculty" with certain restrictions, most have chosen to keep their researchers unequivocally separate from the faculty. The University of California's Berkeley campus has adopted the majority position in this matter.

3. At the time of the survey, Kruytbosch was chairman of ARAPA's Research Committee, and he signed the letter in that capacity. Messinger was president of ARAPA.

4. It should be noted that although we confine analysis to survey and other materials on appointees to the "professional research" title and although we shall use the term "researcher" to refer to persons appointed to this title, the large number of persons at Berkeley appointed to other titles have more or less similar qualifications, perform more or less similar functions, and are accorded a more or less similar status. Our search of the March, 1966, Berkeley payroll located some 800 such persons, besides those with professional research appointments (also excluding about 850 students with appointments as research assistants). Still others, an estimated 200 to 300, supported by various extramural funds not administered by the university, may have no titles at all, and cannot be found through a search of the payroll. Also excluded from our study are the approximately 300 researchers of the Lawrence Radiation Laboratory at Berkeley; a brief discussion of this group is in footnote 9.

For comparison, it might be noted that in March, 1966, there were about 1,400 persons at Berkeley with regular faculty appointments, from instructors through full professors. In addition, there were perhaps 2,000 persons with irregular teaching appointments, including lecturers and student teaching assistants. This part of what Clark Kerr has wittily dubbed the "un-faculty" is perhaps more widely known than the research part. (See Kerr, 1964: 67.)

5. Astronomers and researchers in the Agricultural Experiment Station were partial exceptions to the following generalizations. The former enjoyed full academic status, while the agriculturalists had most academic perquisites with the notable exception of membership in the academic senate. The number of astronomers and agriculturalists on campus was very small.

6. This was not a problem peculiar to the University of California. See ACE, 1954, esp. 37, 83–84. This pioneering work predicted many of the problems of research management currently being faced by major universities. It is worth noting that, although the report applauded the creative social role played by university research, the general tenor of the conclusions was one of warning of the hazards to education of sponsored research programs. The report spoke of "domesticating" large-scale sponsored research primarily in terms of placing checks and limitations upon participation in it.

7. One change was that, in 1962, the academic senate committee on budget and interdepartmental relations, which oversees professorial appointments and promotions, began to take part in the appointment and promotion of the two

senior professional research ranks. Previously, these matters required only administrative approval. The apparent intent was to subject senior researcher appointments to greater faculty scrutiny, presumably to assure greater equivalence between professors and researchers in qualifications and competence.

8. One of the more extreme inconsistencies at Berkeley is that the Lawrence Radiation Laboratory leads an autonomous administrative existence. This is in spite of the fact that from one-third to one-half of the various segments of the physics and chemistry departments, nearly 10 percent of the regular faculty, have a continuing relationship with the laboratory; some 350 graduate students are employed there on research projects; and, in 1963, nearly 15 percent of *all* Ph.D. degrees granted at Berkeley were based on research performed there. Notwithstanding this heavy "educational" involvement, the Lawrence Radiation Laboratory remains outside the realm of campus information-gathering and campus-wide educational policy. If the "cost" of running a Bevatron experiment for a doctoral dissertation is $100,000, this is not reflected in any campus cost-benefit calculations of the expense of graduate study.

It should also be noted that there are about 300 Ph.D.-level physicists, chemists, materials scientists, biophysicists, etc., currently at work in the Radiation Laboratory at Berkeley who do not have regular faculty appointments. The problems of this group are in many ways similar to those of the campus professional researchers we studied, but there are also real differences. The Radiation Laboratory personnel were not included in the survey partly due to difficulty of access and partly because their different concrete situation would have required a new questionnaire instrument.

9. A few demographic characteristics of the sample may be of interest. Twenty percent of the researchers were female. Eighty-five percent were married. Logically enough, while 41 percent of the married women were employed full time, this was true of 80 percent of the single women. Among men, marital status was unrelated to time employed. Finally, the modal age groups of the several ranks were: full, 40–54 years; associate, 40–44 years; and assistant, 30–34 years.

10. A study made in the framework of the State Master Plan showed that 18.9 percent of the new regular ladder faculty appointed at the University of California between 1954 and 1958 had received their doctorates from the university. See California State Master Plan, 1961: 89.

11. Thomas Kuhn (1962) has written on the general problem of the functions of association and consensus among scientists. A useful reference on the question of the extent, causes, and consequences of academic "in-breeding" is McGee, 1960: 483–488.

12. As one might expect, there was a difference between members of different disciplines in the propensity to write books. Book-writing was least likely among life scientists—10 percent had published one or more books; 17 percent of the physical scientists and engineers had done so; and 31 percent of the social scientists.

13. Some 33 percent would find a government or non-profit research position attractive; 16 percent indicated an interest in government research; 8 percent listed a variety of other choices.

14. The last point bears indirectly on the following argument: professorships, given their prerogatives, are more attractive than research positions; therefore, better-qualified persons can be recruited for professorships; thus, professors must be of higher caliber than researchers.

Although the survey data do not permit the inference that Berkeley research positions are more attractive than Berkeley professorships (or, for that matter, vice versa), they do show that a large proportion of persons in the professional research series find such research positions an attractive prospect. Indeed, thirty-three persons—16 percent of the persons making a choice—said a Berkeley research position would be attractive but *not* a Berkeley professorship.

It should be noted that we have not marshaled the data necessary to examine directly the assumption that researchers are "less competent" than their faculty colleagues. Such an assumption underlies much discussion of the proper status of researchers at the university. We know that most Berkeley researchers possess the basic qualification for their positions required by administrative statute—the Ph.D. degree. Whether their "research qualifications" are "equivalent" to those of parallel rank professors, as is also required, we cannot be certain, although the survey respondents list respectable publication achievements. Further, the survey indicated that most researchers feel themselves of equivalent caliber to their faculty counterparts. Seventy-three percent of the respondents were of this opinion, while 11 percent adjudged researchers to be of generally higher caliber than faculty at equivalent rank levels, and 16 percent felt that faculty at equivalent levels generally have superior research accomplishments.

It may be, however, that the relevant question in this context is *not* the comparative one. If the recent growth of researcher ranks at major universities represents the emergence of a new academic role, then requisite qualities and levels of competence can only be assessed in the light of the requirements of this new role. We shall return to this issue in the conclusion.

15. Assuming only that those responsible for developing programs of advanced research at Berkeley have not been willfully irresponsible or subject to moral blackmail from professional researchers, the presence on campus of large numbers of researchers with long past and long future expectations of employment suggests that such people are necessary.

Obviously not everyone is ready to grant these assumptions. The notion of "empire-building" is premised on an assumption of willful irresponsibility; the charge is sometimes heard. Thus, Lewis Feuer, former Berkeley professor of philosophy and social science, has said on this matter: ". . . [T]he managerial professor receives grants, overt and covert, for needless travel, books, magazines, research assistants who write his books, flunkeys who unpack his books and flatter his ego. The project-partitioning professor makes the pork-barrel politician and the fee-splitting physician look like petty operators." (See Feuer, 1964.)

As for moral blackmail, consider the following statement in a recent report on researchers at Berkeley: "Some members of the PR [professional research] staff believe that some of the current projects actually represent *de facto* projects of a PR employee with only nominal sponsorship by a faculty member. This situation almost certainly exists, but in my opinion, it should be discouraged and does not constitute a ground for changing the policy [that researchers cannot be principal investigators]. I suspect that this arrangement is most often entered into for the convenience of the PR staff." (See Garbarino, 1966: 33.)

16. The segregation of graduate and undergraduate education at Berkeley is emphasized by the finding that only one-third of the researchers reported such contacts with undergraduates—mainly those researchers currently engaged in classroom teaching through appointments as lecturers.

17. The results of interviewing and participant observation are more impressive with respect to the administrative and policy-making activities of researchers than the results of the survey. This was a major area insufficiently explored in our questionnaire instrument.

18. The possible responses were "yes, strongly," "yes," "no," "no, strongly," "don't know," "not applicable," and, of course, "no response." For most purposes, we have collapsed the "strong" responses with their matching simple forms.

19. Clark Kerr notes that he sometimes thought of the university "as a series of individual faculty entrepreneurs held together by a common grievance over parking." (See Kerr, 1964: 20.)

20. A university directive, dated November 23, 1966, states that such travel grants "shall be . . . restricted to faculty members . . . *except that* . . . grants may be made" to researchers and others "when such a person has been designated by the proper administrative officer to represent his academic department, or organized research unit." (Emphasis added.) Also, faculty members can apply for grants for foreign travel, but not researchers.

21. One of the authors remembers vividly entering the Greek Theater for a convocation of "all members of the university community" during the height of Berkeley's 1964 "free speech crisis." Plainly marked was a section for faculty seating and another for student seating; the administration, not then at the height of its popularity, had a section reserved but not marked. There was no place for researchers. (The problem was solved by sitting in the faculty section—with misgivings.)

22. Berkeley policy appears to be more restrictive than that required by statewide University of California requirements. Compare Berkeley's *Contracts and Grants Research Policy Manual* (July, 1962) with *Interim Revised Statewide Research Manual* (November, 1964). The latter specifically mentions appointees to the professional research title as among those who can become principal investigators.

23. This is the proportion of the total group answering "yes, strongly"; 81 percent answered "yes" or "yes, strongly."

24. University policy calls for approval of research projects by unit chairmen or directors, the relevant dean, and others before such projects are forwarded to possible grantors, whoever is the principal investigator. Similar controls are formally exerted over appointment of personnel to research projects.

25. The latter remains true at the time of writing (1968), although "interim" grievance procedures have been promulgated.

26. Some 18 percent of the researchers with graduate students under their supervision said that the right to recognition of current teaching was inapplicable to their situation. About 27 percent who were not supervising graduate students said "inapplicable." In both cases, of course, some may have considered that they already had the "right."

27. We have found in many discussions with researchers that some are surprised to think that helping students design and implement research projects, criticizing the papers they produce, advising students on appropriate bibliography, conducting informal seminars for small groups of students, etc., is "teaching." Molière has of course described this phenomenon in another context.

REFERENCES

ACE [American Council on Education] (1954) Committee on Institutional Research, *Sponsored Research Policy of Colleges and Universities*. Washington, D.C.: American Council on Education.

BOWEN, WILLIAM G. (1962) *The Federal Government and Princeton University*. Princeton, New Jersey: Princeton University Press.

California State Master Plan (1961) *Institutional Capacities and Area Needs of California Public Education, 1960–1975*. Master Plan Survey Team Study made for the Liaison Committee of the Regents of the University of California and the State Board of Education. Berkeley and Sacramento: University of California, Office of the President.

FEUER, LEWIS (1964) "Rebellion at Berkeley." *The New Leader* (December 14): 4.

GARBARINO, JOSEPH W. (1966) *Professional Research Personnel at Berkeley: Problems and Policies*. Berkeley, California: Institute of Business and Economic Research (mimeo.).

KERR, CLARK (1964) *The Uses of the University*. Cambridge: Harvard University Press.

KIDD, CHARLES V. (1959) *American Universities and Federal Research*. Cambridge: Harvard University Press.

KUHN, THOMAS (1962) *The Structure of Scientific Revolutions*. Chicago: University of Chicago Press.

McGEE, REECE (1960) "The Function of Institutional Inbreeding." *American Journal of Sociology* 45 (March): 483–488.

McMILLEN, J. H. (1958) "Our universities' research associate positions in physics." *Physics Today* 11 (August): 14–15.

NAS [National Academy of Sciences] (1963) *Profiles of Ph.D.'s in the Sciences*, Publication 1293. Washington, D.C.: National Academy of Sciences, National Research Council.

NSF [National Science Foundation] (1965) *Scientists and Engineers in Colleges and Universities*, NSF 65-8. Washington, D.C.: U.S. Government Printing Office.

ORLANS, HAROLD (1962) *The Effects of Federal Programs on Higher Education*. Washington, D.C.: Brookings Institution.

ROSSI, PETER H. (1964) "Researchers, scholars, and policy makers: the politics of large-scale research." *Daedalus* 93 (Fall): 1142–1161.

SPROUL, ROBERT G. (1952) *Subject: personnel rules, qualifications and salary scales governing the appointment of non-faculty professional research personnel*, memorandum from the President to the Chairmen of Departments and Administrative Officers of the University of California at Berkeley, January 19.

U.S. Office of Education (1966) *Faculty and Other Professional Staff in Institutions of Higher Education, Fall Term 1963–1964*, Circular 794. Washington, D.C.: U.S. Government Printing Office.

University of California (1961 and 1963) *Policy of University of California on Organized Research Units*, December 15, 1961; revised October 22, 1963. Berkeley: University of California.

University of California (1962a) "The future academic status of non-faculty professional research personnel." In *Proceedings of the 17th All-University Faculty Conference*. Berkeley: University of California.

University of California (1962b) *Administrative Manual*, Section 54, revised September 1. Berkeley: University of California.

CHAPTER 13

THE ASSISTANT: ACADEMIC SUBALTERN

Robert Dubin and Fredric Beisse

College student ferment and revolt in the mid-1960s appeared to have two sources. Some analysts claimed that students felt mature and politically sophisticated, and were demanding recognition of that maturity by college faculties and administrators.[1] Other analysts claimed that faculties appeared to be increasingly disinterested in teaching undergraduates (Select Committee on Education, 1966).[2]

It is the thesis of this chapter that student activism against professors and college administrators had its principal source in the position and function of the graduate assistants in American higher education, which have made the career of graduate students anomalous and have changed the undergraduate student teaching function. Student revolt was rooted in the graduate student body, among assistants, who have teaching responsibilities without corresponding legitimation of their authority and perquisites to carry them out. Undergraduates experienced their graduate assistant teachers as illegitimate performers of the teaching function and were shocked, dismayed, and alienated.

A sociological analysis is presented of some basic structural changes that have occurred in American higher education, which focus on the position of the graduate teaching assistant. The facts marshaled include national trend data and a detailed description of the Berkeley situation, the most highly publicized example of consequences resulting from the structural changes.

We conclude that teaching assistants in the public universities of the United States view themselves as performing highly professional services—teaching—without being accorded professional legitimacy in the teaching office. The teaching assistant is treated by his departmental professors as a student even when substituting for these professors as an instructor and is,

EDITORS' NOTE: This chapter is the result of research sponsored by the Center for the Advanced Study of Educational Administration, University of Oregon. It is reprinted (in slightly revised form), with permission, from *Administrative Science Quarterly* 11, No. 4, March, 1967: 521–547.

TABLE 1
ENROLLMENTS, TEACHING STAFF, AND STUDENT-FACULTY RATIOS
FOR PUBLIC AND PRIVATE UNIVERSITIES, 1953–1954 TO 1963–1964

						Undergraduate Student-faculty Ratio	
			Teaching staff [d]			Regular Faculty and Regular Teaching	
	Enrollment [a]			Teaching			
Academic Year	Under-graduate [b]	Grad-uate [c]	Regular [e]	Assis-tants [f]	Total	Faculty Only	Assis-tants
PUBLIC UNIVERSITIES							
1953–54	493,817	74,630	46,545	11,352	57,897	10.61	8.53
1955–56	628,580	84,141	55,421	13,470	68,891	11.34	9.12
1957–58	691,527	97,392	64,159	16,787	80,946	10.78	8.54
1959–60	722,281	120,144	65,457	19,932	85,389	11.03	8.46
1961–62	839,754	146,438	70,905	25,653	96,558	11.84	8.70
1963–64	1,005,173	182,706	85,805	31,083	116,888	11.71	8.61
PRIVATE UNIVERSITIES							
1953–54	357,077	90,177	40,690	8,855	49,545	8.78	7.21
1955–56	398,263	93,663	44,525	9,958	54,483	8.94	7.31
1957–58	408,017	101,059	47,435	11,409	58,844	8.60	6.93
1959–60	412,119	114,844	51,029	11,958	62,997	8.08	6.54
1961–62	430,922	125,813	55,189	13,872	69,061	7.81	6.24
1963–64	419,066	139,301	58,422	13,513	71,935	7.17	5.83

SOURCE: Enrollment figures are from: *Biennial Survey of Education in the United States* 1952–1954 (Washington, D.C.: U.S. Department of Health, Education, and Welfare, and Office of Education), Chapter 4, Section I, Statistics of Higher Education: Faculty, Students, and Degrees 1953–1954; Table 2, p. 80; *1956–1958* edition of same title, Table 21, p. 42. Figures on resident college enrollment in four-year degree credit institutions for the first term of 1959 from Neva A. Carlson, U.S. Department of Health, Education, and Welfare, Office of Education, National Center for Educational Statistics (private correspondence); also *Resident and Extension Enrollment in Institutions of Higher Education Fall 1963* (OE 54000-63 Circular No. 776 U.S. Department of Health, Education, and Welfare, Office of Education [Washington, D.C., 1963]), Table 3, pp. 8–18.

Faculty figures are from *Biennial Survey of Education in the United States,* 1952–1954 edition, Table 2, pp. 80–81; 1956–1958 edition, Table 11, pp. 24–27; also *Faculty and Other Professional Staff in Institutions of Higher Education* (Washington, D.C.: U.S. Department of Health, Education, and Welfare; Office of Education), 1959–1960 edition, Table 11, p. 12 (OE 53000-60 Circular No. 714); *1961–1962* edition, Table 8, pp. 11–12 (OE 53000-62 Circular No. 747); 1963–1964 edition, Table 6, p. 9 (OE 53000-64 Circular No. 794).

a. Students are those registered for "resident degree credit," which means that the students are enrolled in the main or branch campus either in the day or evening (not extension, mail, radio, TV, short courses, or by individual professors only) whose current program can be credited toward a bachelor's or higher degree.

therefore, viewed as a nonlegitimate performer of a central academic function.

It is scarcely surprising that the teaching assistants revolted against the disjunction between their legitimate functions and their lack of rights, privileges, and payoffs. It is also to be expected that the clients of teaching assistants, the undergraduate students, would readily perceive this disjunction and conclude that they were getting inadequate teaching with a resultant alienation from its legitimate source, the faculty and university.

National Trends

The national trends of enrollment in American universities reveal two broad patterns.[3] The first is a differential growth in total enrollments. Public universities have grown much more rapidly than private universities, both absolutely and proportionately. The second national trend has been the parallel growth in the number of graduate students as the total enrollment increased.

Data on national trends show that the need for more instructors to teach the increased population of undergraduate students was readily satisfied by dipping into the increased pool of graduate students for teaching assistants. The "warm body problem" of putting an instructor in front of every undergraduate class was readily solved by using the teaching assistant. There has never been and is not now an actual teacher shortage in American higher education. The podium is occupied in every university undergraduate classroom, but increasingly by graduate teaching assistants.

Table 1 displays the data on trends. The enrollment trends for public and private universities are plotted in Chart 1, for graduate and undergraduate groups.[4] For the ten-year period, the number of undergraduates in public universities doubled to one million; undergraduates in private universities increased from 357,000 to 419,000, with the enrollment actually

b. Undergraduate students working for a bachelor's degree plus students working for a first professional degree, the first degree signifying completion of the academic requirements for practice of a profession; thus, the LL.B., B.S. in Engineering, B.D. (Bachelor of Divinity), M.D., D.D.S., D.V.M., M.L.S. (Master of Library Science), and M.S.W.

c. Graduate students in liberal arts and sciences studying for an advanced degree and students beyond the first professional degree.

d. Teaching staff figures are those listed as "faculty for resident instruction in degree-credit courses." Faculty are listed in this category if they teach a degree credit course.

e. Instructor and above: all persons who teach resident degree-credit courses if they hold the rank of instructor or above, even though they hold other professional positions.

f. Junior instructional staff: persons below the rank of instructor or equivalent, whose functions include instruction of students, such as assistant instructors, teaching fellows, teaching assistants and laboratory assistants. ROTC enlisted personnel who are drill instructors or who teach courses, but do not have faculty rank are included. Nonteaching assistants to the instructional staff are excluded.

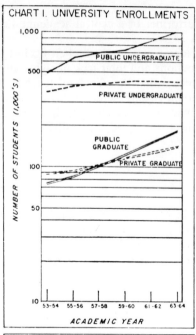

CHART I. UNIVERSITY ENROLLMENTS

NUMBER OF STUDENTS (1,000'S)

PUBLIC UNDERGRADUATE

PRIVATE UNDERGRADUATE

PUBLIC GRADUATE

PRIVATE GRADUATE

ACADEMIC YEAR

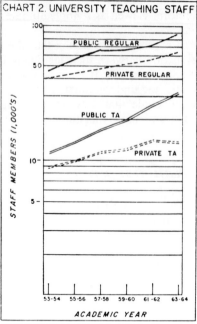

CHART 2. UNIVERSITY TEACHING STAFF

STAFF MEMBERS (1,000'S)

PUBLIC REGULAR

PRIVATE REGULAR

PUBLIC TA

PRIVATE TA

ACADEMIC YEAR

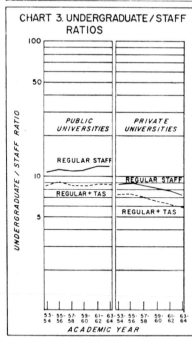

CHART 3. UNDERGRADUATE/STAFF RATIOS

UNDERGRADUATE / STAFF RATIO

PUBLIC UNIVERSITIES

PRIVATE UNIVERSITIES

REGULAR STAFF

REGULAR STAFF

REGULAR + TAS

REGULAR + TAS

ACADEMIC YEAR

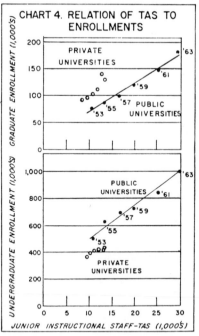

CHART 4. RELATION OF TAS TO ENROLLMENTS

GRADUATE ENROLLMENT (1,000S)

PRIVATE UNIVERSITIES

PUBLIC UNIVERSITIES

'63
'61
'59
'57
'55
'53

UNDERGRADUATE ENROLLMENT (1,000S)

PUBLIC UNIVERSITIES

PRIVATE UNIVERSITIES

'63
'61
'59
'57
'55
'53

JUNIOR INSTRUCTIONAL STAFF-TAS (1,000S)

274

declining in the last two-year period. The major pressure was obviously in public universities, where both the rate of growth of undergraduate enrollments and the absolute growth in numbers was greater than in private universities; therefore, the need to provide more teachers to meet more students in classes was felt most strongly among public universities.

At the same time that public universities were feeling the pressure of an increased enrollment of undergraduates, they were experiencing an even greater rate of increase among graduate students; the slope of the curve for graduates being steeper than for undergraduates. Graduate students added a second pressure on faculty time, since the instruction of graduate students is usually more time-consuming than the instruction of undergraduates.[5] Also, the total graduate student population in public universities exceeded that in private ones by 1959, and the disparity widened because of the greater rate of growth in the public universities.

Chart 2, which plots the trend data on faculties, shows that the rate of growth of regular faculty of instructor rank and above was no greater in public universities than in private ones. As we have already seen, the student bodies grew more rapidly in the public than in the private universities. Hence, that gap between the demand for teachers and their supply is clearly focused on the public universities.

Where was this supply secured? From the junior instructional staff, the teaching assistant, as Chart 2 indicates. In the public universities the teaching assistants increased from a little over 11,000 to 31,000 during the ten-year period; in the private universities, they increased from almost 9,000 to 13,500. The slopes of the curves make clear that the public universities almost tripled while the private universities did not double their use of teaching assistants. Indeed, of all the growth curves for the instructional staff, the curve representing the growth in number in teaching assistants in public universities has the steepest slope.

Chart 3 sets forth the data on student-faculty ratios. For the regular instructional staff (consisting of instructors and professors), the ratio of undergraduate students to this staff group rises from about 10.5 to almost 12 in the public universities, and decreases from almost 9 to almost 7 in the private universities. Thus, if only undergraduate students were taught, the student-teacher ratio has been and remains more favorable for the student in the private university than in the public one. Furthermore, the situation had worsened over the ten-year period in the public university at the same time that it had improved in private universities.

Since teaching assistants teach undergraduates exclusively, they can be added to the regular instructional staff, and an undergraduate-faculty ratio computed. The results show that the ratio has remained constant for the public universities, at about 8.5, but decreased in private universities from a little over 7 to less than 6. Again the student-faculty ratio is more favorable in the private universities. It is significant that the student-faculty ratio had remained constant in public universities when teaching assistants were included among the faculty. This may well suggest that the "warm body problem" of placing teachers in charge of classes was not as pressing as has been alleged.[6] Furthermore, undergraduate student-teacher ratios had neither fluctuated widely, nor worsened, during the ten-year period when appropriate weight was given to the TA as a teacher of undergraduates.

A clear way of summarizing the role that the graduate student has played as substitute professor is revealed in Chart 4. Here the relation between the number of teaching assistants is examined with respect to undergraduate enrollment on the one hand and graduate enrollment on the other hand. The relationship is very high for public universities, and suggests that the need for added teachers moved public universities to employ teaching assistants from the ranks of graduate students. At the same time, the increase in the number of graduate students was great enough that the demand for teaching assistants could readily be filled.

It has been assumed that the regular teaching staff had retreated from its undergraduate teaching responsibilities, either to concentrate on the education of graduate students, or to do research, or both. To fill the teaching needs for undergraduates, whose number had vastly increased, we are arguing that the teaching assistant was employed. What is the evidence from individual universities for this conclusion?

Two major universities provide some revealing answers. In a survey at the University of California (Berkeley) of the graduating class of 1965, 31 percent of the number of all undergraduate classes taken during the four years of undergraduate work were regularly taught by teaching assistants, or were laboratory sessions supervised by assistants. The proportion of the number of all classes taught by teaching assistants was even greater (41 percent) for lower-division courses taken by the 1965 graduating class. The traditional picture of the professor reserving to himself the opportunity to meet with smaller groups of students in seminar-like sessions is also inaccurate. In the undergraduate classes of fifteen or fewer students, fully 65 percent were instructed by assistants at Berkeley (Select Committee on Education, 1966: 175).

At the University of Michigan, another outstanding graduate school that takes special pride in its emphasis on undergraduate instruction, a similar picture emerged. In the fall of 1965, approximately 33 percent of the credit hours earned by undergraduates in Arts and Sciences were in courses taught by assistants. Again, this figure was larger (45 percent) in lower-division courses (Center for Research on Learning and Teaching, 1965).

From the data for the University of California (Berkeley) and the University of Michigan, the following conclusions may be drawn:

(1) Every time an undergraduate student registers for a course (or discussion section), the chances are one in three that he will get a teaching assistant for an instructor.

(2) In his first two years, the undergraduate has even less chance of seeing a professor in charge of any class taken (two chances in five it will be a teaching assistant).

(3) If the undergraduate student is looking for a small class with its intimate contact with a professor, there is only one chance in three that the teacher will be of professorial rank in the small classes available.

If these two universities are typical of other universities, it is clear significant proportions of undergraduates are met by teachers who are not fully qualified. This practice of shifting teaching duties to assistants on a large scale may raise important questions about the quality of the education being given undergraduates. The recent growth in the number of student-sponsored publications that evaluate faculty and course content may be symptomatic of an awareness by undergraduate students of deficiencies in the instruction they receive. The broad trend of response to enrollment pressures in American public universities seems clear. The gap between professionally certified teachers and the total demand for teachers has been readily filled by the teaching assistant. This conclusion is supported by the gross statistics for higher education as a whole, and individual analyses of two major universities, where the percentage of undergraduate classes taught by teaching assistants was measured.

Nonlegitimacy

A brief excursion is necessary to provide a framework for analyzing the reactions of teaching assistants to their position. The teaching assistant almost invariably is an officer of instruction in the very department in which he is a student studying for an advanced degree. These are incompatible if not irreconcilable positions.

As an officer of instruction, the teaching assistant warrants treatment comparable to the regular teaching faculty, including consulting him regarding the courses he is assigned to teach, when classes meet, the outline and content of instruction, the text and supplementary material used, and tests and other evaluation methods employed. In addition, facilitating expectations must be considered—factors like desk or office space to meet students, typing services for examinations, and telephone service for student appointments and other business. Whether these and related features of the professional teaching position, and the perquisites of office are actually accorded the teaching assistant may be questionable. Indeed, our analysis will show that one concern of graduate assistants has been to claim professional recognition as college teachers by securing a voice about, and even control over, professional activities necessary to perform teaching functions. Thus, the teaching assistant is protesting not being accorded professional treatment, when he is under obligation to perform a professional function.

Academic administrations and faculties have failed to recognize this striving for professional prerogatives, because their image of the teaching assistant is that of an apprentice learning his profession, under the guidance of a certified professor. The teaching assistant, as a substitute for the professor, is concerned about professional prerogatives necessary to fill the professors' teaching position. The professor, in turn, views teaching assistants as apprentices whose lack of full qualifications disqualifies them from a right to these prerogatives. The real operating position of the teaching assistant does not correspond with the image of his position held by his supervisors, college administrators, and professors.

This disjunction between real and ascribed positions cannot lead to open revolt on the part of teaching assistants, because of their role as graduate students. The long-term professional fate of all graduate students depends upon securing their advanced degrees as prerequisites for certification as professionals. This means that each graduate student is solely dependent upon his professors and the department's executive for evaluation of his performance as a graduate student and for granting his degree. The graduate student as an individual has marshaled against him the awesome power of his faculty to say "Yea" or "Nay" to his professional certification. There is absolutely no appeal from the departmental decision regarding the graduate student's career. It is not surprising, therefore, that individual graduate students might accept the difficulties of their teaching assistantship without public protest.

The relationship is materially altered if teaching assistants act in concert. The power of collective action by graduate students rests on two factors: (a) Collective action to refuse to perform the teaching function can immediately create chaos in the undergraduate instruction program. If some teachers fail to meet undergraduate classes, the routine of a university is disrupted. (b) Collective action, and the solidarity among graduate students that this implies, threatens the entire graduate program and, ultimately, the profesisonal image of a department in its respective discipline. If graduate students leave a department in large numbers before receiving their degrees, this may subsequently seriously impair the ability of that department to attract new students. Furthermore, with the generous availability of assistantships throughout the academic labor market, the threat of leaving the graduate program of a single department is a serious one.[7]

We might, therefore, expect that the solution to the structural problem of teaching without being accorded the prerogatives of teachers, will be resolved, if at all, only through collective action by the teaching assistants. The one case examined in detail, the Berkeley case, supports this conclusion.

The Berkeley Case

GENERAL BACKGROUND

Although the student unrest at Berkeley did not receive national attention until the Free Speech Movement (FSM) in the fall of 1964, there had been a continuous debate between the students and the University administration since 1960. The important features of this debate are outlined by H. May (1965: 456–457):

> Since 1960, the student movement has carried on guerrilla war with the Kerr administration over a set of presidential directives which then attempted, plausibly but unrealistically, to define the rights and duties of several distinct and complicated categories of undergraduate organizations. Since then, important concessions have been made and student victories won. By this fall (1964), it was nonsense to talk about a "climate of op-

pression" in Berkeley. Students, by observing certain forms and rules, could *say* (although in theory they could not *do*) what they wanted. The climate was rather one of bureaucracy. It is particularly hard to explain to our students why a given kind of organization can have open meetings but not membership meetings on campus, why Communism or free love may be advocated here but not there, as long as one has an associate or full professor—but not an assistant professor—as chairman. All these rules had their historical *raisons d'etre,* but this kind of history is not a favorite subject here. . . . Last year, the movement's center of attention shifted with new intensity to the compelling cause of civil rights. Berkeley contributed a few students to Mississippi and many to militant demonstrations in the Bay region. And finally at the beginning of the fall term of 1964, before administration errors revived the question of campus political action, a publication of the student organization called Slate seems to suggest another major shift of emphasis, this time to the alleged outrages of the academic system itself. A Slate pamphlet called for "AN OPEN, FIERCE, AND THOROUGHGOING REBELLION ON THIS CAMPUS," demanding that grades be eliminated in the social sciences and humanities, rules be abolished in university housing units, and negotiations undertaken about the question of examinations. Ways suggested to achieve these dazzling goals included civil disobedience at university public ceremonies and maybe "a mass student strike . . . something which seems unthinkable at present [May, 1965: 456–457]."

This quotation indicates that the machinery for a free speech movement had existed at Berkeley before the events of late 1964, and that when student dissatisfaction led to direct action, the free speech issue was emphasized because it was "at hand," and had been since 1960.

The Free Speech Movement of 1964–1965 metamorphosed into a filthy speech movement, and then disappeared from public view. An enduring consequence of the FSM was the permanent organization of the teaching assistants into a labor union and their subsequent "collective bargaining" with the University administration. This suggests that the FSM and its sequel, the filthy speech movement (fsm) were symptoms and not causes of the Berkeley turmoil.

The collective action in the Free Speech Movement proved to the Berkeley students that, through collective action, they could generate responses from the University administration. Furthermore, many administrative responses reacted affirmatively to the students' grievances. Thus, the free speech turmoil was the proving ground for establishing the effectiveness of direct collective action by the students.

ORGANIZATION OF ASSISTANTS' UNION

In October, 1964, graduate students organized the Graduate Coordinating Council (GCC) to support the general aims of the FSM. The issues raised by the GCC received little publicity during the events of the free speech movement and extended far beyond the immediate free speech issue.

The following excerpt is from a GCC-sponsored pamphlet "Are You All Right, Jack?" issued in November, 1964.

> We are concerned with TA, RA, Reader and Proctor salaries, medical benefits, tax exemptions, unemployment compensation and social security, fellowships and grants, bookstore discounts, and housing and parking facilities. Academic concerns include fair hiring practices for both faculty and students, library improvement and privileges, the revision of courses under the quarter system, the transition from tutorial to automated instruction, the improvement of education generally, and long-range educational aims and policy.[8]

The pamphlet urged the formation of a union of University-employed graduate students. It was emphasized that "disunited we remain without a voice, individuals alone, completely impotent in our situation, whereas unity will provide us with an organization which will express and effectuate both our individual and common interests and protect us from an arbitrary administration" (Draper, 1965: 197).

The activities of the FSM (and its graduate wing, the GCC) culminated in the strike of teaching assistants. At the height of the free speech movement, there was a one-week strike (December 3–7, 1964) by the teaching assistants during which they refused to meet their assigned classes. Out of this strike there arose the organization of a chapter of the American Federation of Teachers, which was composed almost exclusively of teaching assistants and which subsequently negotiated and bargained for them with departmental and University executives.

The teaching assistants were concerned about the possibility of reprisal on the part of the administration for their participation in the strike. In one social science department, the faculty assured the assistants that no disciplinary action would be taken against individuals who struck; and, in fact, that individual faculty members would take it upon themselves to cancel classes in support of the teaching assistants. In a physical science department, the departmental administration took the position that any assistants who participated in the strike by cancelling classes would be dismissed; despite this, many teaching assistants did cancel their classes.

Although the immediate issue of the strike was free speech, one outcome was that the graduate assistants realized the power they commanded through collective action.[9] The union of teaching assistants was chartered in February, 1965, as a local of the American Federation of Teachers, AFL-CIO. In its formative stages, the Union was confronted with a serious policy struggle, the consequences of which are still evident. One faction of the Union pressed for an organization that would take stands on political and social issues.[10] The opposing faction argued that the Union should define its objectives as being centrally concerned with the professional and personal problems of University assistants. It is significant that the latter group, pressing for a largely professional orientation, won the initial election of Union officers and still controls the Union local.[11]

This outcome supports the contention that the real concerns of the graduate assistants were with major aspects of their roles as assistants, and not with free speech and political advocacy. For assistants, the illegitimacy of their status, and their lack of the professional amenities, were apparently seen as more worthy of their collective efforts than political and social issues.

Almost at its inception, the Union shared a common concern with the University administration. In the aftermath of the 1964 free speech movement and teaching assistant strike, a proposed budgetary cut in the funds allocated for teaching assistants originated in the California State Legislature in May, 1965. Union action was directed at influencing legislators to restore the funds which were cut, with newspaper ads run by the Union outlining their demands for a restoration of funds, in order that there not be "a sharp decline in the quality of undergraduate education" (*Daily Californian,* 1965: 11).[12] The Union also sent representatives to the legislature to argue against the cut. The legislature did not restore the funds for hiring teaching assistants, but the University used other funds to hire assistants in the fall of 1965, many of whom would not otherwise have been hired. The teaching assistants cutback was the only university-wide Union issue.[13]

SPECIFIC ISSUES

Union action on specific issues in individual academic departments depended on the strength and character of the Union in each department. The Union is, at present, a more or less loose federation of departmental unions. The issues that attracted Union attention included: (a) those related to the functions of assistants as teachers and as researchers, (b) selection and reappointment policies, (c) salaries and other monetary concerns, (d) working conditions and other nonfinancial perquisites of employment, and (e) the relationship of assistants to faculty and administrative committees, and University functionaries.[14]

In some departments, the Union directed attention to the procedures for the selection of teaching assistants. Departmental policies varied from a formal statement of qualifications and guidelines, to a completely unstructured and informal system. In one humanities department, the Union pressed for a rationalization of the selection process to include the following procedures:

(1) Adoption of grade point average as the sole criterion for qualification.
(2) Including a Union representative on the selection committee.
(3) Guaranteeing an assistantship (or fellowship) to all Ph.D. candidates who had passed their qualifying exams.
(4) Adoption of a date in the spring on which announcements of assistantships would be made for the following year.
(5) Publication of a list of alternates (graduate students who would receive assistantships turned down by other students).

The attitude of the faculty in this department had been largely anti-union, and, therefore, practically no concessions have been made over any of these points, except that the department "agrees in principle" with item 3.

In the reappointment of teaching assistants, the Union took up the cases of eight assistants who were not rehired, because the department (a social science department) made changes in its hiring practices "arbitrarily and without warning," according to a Union representative. Union action took the form of an informational picket line in front of the departmental office. Soon after these events, the University-wide teaching assistant cutback helped to take some of the pressure off department officials. The outcome, however, was that all of those not rehired were eventually given some type of support.

In another social science department, the Union approached the administration about the number of hours of classroom teaching required of assistants. Although six hours was the norm in that department, four hours was the maximum in-class time in other departments. The department administration promptly reduced the load of the assistants in line with their request.

In a physical science department, the Union met with the administration to discuss the following grievances:

(1) Class size in discussion sections should be limited to twenty-four students, the number to exceed twenty-four only with Union approval.
(2) Teaching assistants in good standing in the department (academically) should be automatically reappointed for the duration of their graduate study.
(3) Workload of teaching assistants should be standardized to four hours per week in-class as a maximum.
(4) Telephones should be installed in the offices of teaching assistants.

These concessions were agreed to in principle, although no formal agreement was signed. The department also agreed to notify the Union of any actions taken which would affect the members of the Union or nonmember assistants.

These are examples of the kinds of issues that have attracted the attention of the Assistants' Union at Berkeley. Other issues range from union representation on the selection committee for teaching assistants to the installation of a clock in an office.

It is clear from this summary that Union activity was focused on the fate and conditions of assistants, not on the surrounding social and political milieu. The assistants were demanding that their position in the academic community be formally recognized. They sought to legitimize their role by seeking those prerogatives and prerequisites that would accord their position a measure of status.

Undergraduate Reaction

The satisfaction or dissatisfaction of members with their organization is difficult to isolate. One important reason for this is the attention focus. The classic Western Electric studies showed that focusing attention on behavior is a necessary prelude to generating reaction to the behavior (Rothlisberger and Dickson, 1938).[15] The attention factor also underlies Merton's distinction between manifest and latent functions. From the standpoint of participants, a behavior has a manifest function that can be identified by the visibility of the behavior and the participants' attention to it, but may also have latent functions, which escape the attention of participants. Other behaviors may be wholly latent because they are entirely beyond the attention of the participants (Merton, 1957: Ch. I).

If it is usual for undergraduate students to be taught by graduate assistants, then we would not expect them to react negatively, because their attention would not be focused on this special teaching situation. We might, therefore, argue that manifest displeasure with teaching assistants as substitutes for professors would not be revealed unless the substitution was called to the attention of the undergraduate students.

At the Miami University, Ohio, a study (Experimental Study in Instructional Procedures, 1960: 36) was made of small sections of between twenty-five and thirty-five students. These sections were taught either by teaching assistants or regular faculty members. Twenty-four questions were used to elicit responses on the teaching effectiveness. The results showed that students "quite uniformly favored instruction by regular faculty over instruction by graduate assistants." Here, the contrast between teaching assistants and regular faculty was made the focus of student attention. We might even suggest that there could be a corresponding student *dislike* for being taught by assistants, although the questions were designed to elicit positive rather than negative evaluations.

Two interpretations have been offered of the bases for undergraduate student attitudes and behavior at Berkeley. One interpretation, proposed by professional educators and educational administrators, is that the students' protest was basically the result of a bureaucratization of education, featuring an educational process that was impersonal, mechanistic, and irrelevant to the needs of students.[16] An important part of this bureaucratization was the shifting of teaching functions at the undergraduate level to assistants.[17] These analysts concluded that the inadequacies of the student's educational experiences were finally made manifest and resulted in the Free Speech Movement as one method of combatting administrative indifference (and possibly contempt) toward undergraduate education, and toward working conditions of teaching assistants.

A second interpretation was that the students at Berkeley had a free-floating alienation from the world as a whole and could perceive no connection between their disaffections and any particular source.[18] This diffuse alienation without a manifest source would, therefore, reveal itself in collective action against any convenient target. In 1964, the Civil Rights Movement, the war in Viet Nam, political action, and freedom of speech, and even the right to filthy speech all provided visible and affectively significant targets for student attention. From this second viewpoint, the general alienation of students could focus protest action in any convenient field. It thus came as no surprise that social protest, or narcissistic behavior like the use of LSD, pot, and the Free Sex Movement (again FSM) emerged as avenues for expressing free-floating alienation. This second position, of course, assumes that the disaffecting features of the student's social environment have latent functions in supporting and sustaining his alienation. The students' reaction to the bureaucratization of education and his alienation from society as a whole lead to random protest behaviors. Available data do not clearly support either of the two interpretations of how undergraduate students came to engage in their protest behaviors. The only survey which attempted to sample a cross-section of student opinion and attitudes during the free speech movement was the Somers' survey (Somers, 1965: 530–577). Attacking directly the issue of whether the students were specifically opposed to their educational experiences, the Somers' survey asked students how well-satisfied they were with "courses, examinations, professors, etc." at the University. One-fifth of the students replied very satisfied, and another three-fifths were satisfied. A second question asked whether the students felt that the administration treated them "as mature and responsible adults" and three-fourths of the students agreed.

The Somers' survey and analysis led to the conclusion that the students were positively committed to Civil Rights activities, a defense of students' freedom of speech and political action, and the students' rights as citizens to protest national policy in Viet Nam. Thus, Somers concluded that the students were not alienated from the University as much as they were idealistically attracted to the larger issues of their society.

The evidence of the survey is less than convincing as a basis for choosing between the views of the source of the student revolt. First, Somers' sample of 285 students included 32 percent who were in their first semester at Berkeley, hardly in proportion to entering freshmen in the University. Since the poll was taken in early November, these students had been attending the University only about five weeks. It seems scarcely credible that this one-third of the sample, totally inexperienced with the University, could have any meaningful knowledge or opinions about "courses, examinations, professors, etc." Their answers obviously biased the results.[19] Second, the questions employed to measure dissatisfaction with the educational processes were so general as to be inadequate and incomplete tests of specific sentiments and attitudes. Finally, when an opinion survey is made during a period of heightened social agitation, it seems fair to suggest that the focus of agitation will attract the highest attention level of those who respond to questions about the sources of unrest. Perhaps the immediate events of the free speech controversy overshadowed dissatisfaction with the educational bureaucracy, and served to direct the attention of Somers' respondents away from this issue. In short, the agitated situation had a "halo effect" on the respondents.

Other studies of undergraduate reaction have produced contradictory results. A survey in April, 1965, found that about 90 percent of a sample of 439 students agreed with the statement, "taking everything into account, Cal is a good place to go to school" (Gales, 1966). Conversely, Freedman and Nichols, in a survey made about 9 months after the Free Speech Movement demonstrations and including 2203 undergraduate student respondents out of 2576 in their initial sample (prepared especially for the Muscatine Committee), revealed that one-third of the students said that classes were too large to learn very much in them; 47 percent thought the grading system inadequate to measure knowledge and understanding of course content; 46 percent mentioned that student-faculty contact was unsatisfactory; 42 percent mentioned that most professors were more interested in research than in teaching; and one-half suggested that undergraduates should have a greater voice in the formulation of educational policies. Furthermore, almost 80 percent said that the University operated as a factory (Freedman and Nichols, 1965). The Freedman and Nichols survey suffers from a liability similar to that of Somers' (for example, seniors who were graduated in June, 1965, were not part of the sample). Apart from these studies, the data in support of the competing analytical models of undergraduate reaction are largely incidental reports of observers.[20] (See Experimental Study Program, 1960; *Berkeley Daily Gazette,* 1964.)

Additional evidence for the dissatisfaction with education point of view is that, subsequent to the climax activities of the Free Speech Movement, University administrators directed much of their attention to proposals for improving undergraduate instruction. This at least suggests that the academic administrators believe enough in their own analysis to make it the basis for University policy.[21] Also, it should be noted that the subsequent collective behavior by students continued to be a mixture of genuine social protest and narcissistic preoccupations. This lends support to the idea that a genuine alienation from some aspect of social experience, including educational experiences, could be the dominant theme of narcissistic behavior, although it does not argue that there was not, at the same time, positive attachment to affirmative goals of social action.

The evidence is not conclusive in favor of either explanation of the source of undergraduate student protest. However, the weight of evidence points to the conclusion that among undergraduate students, one source of their disaffection was their educational experiences.

Conclusions

The teaching assistant in American higher education has been an academic subaltern without any professional status to certify his position. Graduate students have supplied the needed additional undergraduate teachers. The widespread use of teaching assistants has changed the function of this position from that of an apprenticeship in teaching, to that of teaching subaltern, with all the requirements of professional performance expected of a teacher. For the graduate assistant, this shift in function gave rise to the expectation that professional perquisites would be accorded in line with the professional expectations. Since the assistant was not accorded these perquisites, he had a nonprofessional image, while at the same time performing legitimate professional tasks.

Although the assistant occupied a position competitive with his own teachers, the discrepancy between legitimacy of task and nonlegitimacy of status placed the teaching assistant in American public universities in a structural bind. The assistant could see, and experience, in performing his teaching task, the need for decision-making opportunities and perquisites to make his teaching effective. This need could not be realized as long as the assistant was viewed as an apprentice learning his future profession.

The contemporary plight of the teaching assistant is illustrative of a much more general phenomenon. Whenever there is pressure on an established occupation or profession to provide more services, and the demand cannot be met through normal expansion of the supply of certified experts, then portions of the skill will be shifted, by a division of labor, to lower skilled and lower status work colleagues. This history has been evidenced in many professions especially, including medicine (from doctor to registered nurse to practical nurse to aide, or from doctor to technician), engineering (from registered engineer to computer technologist most recently, and earlier from registered engineer to draftsman to detailer), and even primary and secondary school teaching (from teacher to teacher aide).

What makes the teaching assistant position special is that the incumbent of this office is viewed as occupying his position only *temporarily* and is expected to move up to the full professional position when certified. This is not, of course, true of the lesser-skilled groups in other professional and occupational areas, whose tasks are determined by a process of "job breakdown" of the original task complex, and whose members have *permanent* status in their lower-skilled positions.

College administrators and professors have been very slow to recognize the nature of this problem and the means for its solution. Teaching assistants have, therefore, been forced to demand solutions; but because of their student status, they have been able to do so only through collective action.

The collective action of the sort employed by the assistants at Berkeley, while effective, is the antithesis of professional behavior. The long-term effects may be to produce a generation of professors whose notions of professional behavior and decorum differ sharply from those of the present generation.

The most likely administrative responses to pressure from assistants will be to grant to teaching assistants such status-conferring marks as assigned parking spaces, usable office space, increases in salary, specified working hours, and the like. This is the coin with which administrators have traditionally dealt. Academic administrators may be hard pressed to understand the teaching assistants' demands for the professionalization of *their* teaching functions. Furthermore, administrators probably will not secure good advice from professors because of their failure to understand this problem.[22]

The clients of the educational organization, its undergraduate students, are not unaffected by the plight of the teaching assistants instructing them. The weight of evidence suggests that the undergraduates are concerned about the quality of instruction received, and are aware that this is caused by the withdrawal of the professor from the undergraduate classroom. Thus, one outcome has been dissatisfaction with the university and the learning experiences it affords. Undergraduate dissatisfaction and active protest may have positive outcomes in forcing correction of the conditions which produce it. Evidence already exists that academic administrators are moving to improve the educational experiences of undergraduates by enticing professors back into the classroom and otherwise improving student-professor contacts.

An alternative interpretation of student response is the alienation hypothesis in two distinctive forms. The view that there is alienation with anomic results suggests that the student is alienated from all aspects of his society. His response is randomly to strike out against the society through any protest movements currently in vogue or to withdraw to a narcissistic preoccupation by undertaking self-isolating activities like the use of narcotics or psychedelic drugs. The second form of the hypothesis, that of alienation with ameliorative results, points to the idealistic urges to recreate the society. This kind of student responds to his negative view of his society by seeking to reconstruct it through constructive action programs.

There is no doubt that the behavior exhibited by the students at Berkeley conforms to the predictions of both general models. The thrust of the evidence indicates that many more students were reacting to imperfections in their educational experiences than were alienated in either of the two senses suggested. The American college student still apparently sees his education as a stepping-stone to a rewarded place in American society and evaluates the quality of this education in pragmatic terms—how effectively does it move him toward his adult rewards.

The difficult position of the teaching assistant plus the reaction of undergraduate students against being taught by assistants generated a crisis which may be the engine of significant change in the multiversity. At least the pressure from students is something new on the American academic scene. In the past, the academic community has been pressured by regents and trustees, by academic administrators, by publics, and by governmental contracting agencies. All of these pressures could be resisted by the professors, wrapped securely in their cloak of academic freedom. But an aroused student body may be different—academic freedom *not* to teach, or to refuse others adequate means for teaching, seem hardly defensible positions!

NOTES

1. These analysts have focused on two aspects of the "new generation" of students. Henry May (1965), chairman of the History Department at the University of California (Berkeley), writes that, "The most striking fact about the present generation, to me, is that large groups are both more idealistic and more alienated than any but a handful in the radical thirties." He suggests that the idealism of the students is not unlike that of a Whitman, a Thoreau, or a Gandhi (May, 1965). The idealism of the current generation of students is translated into social and political action. For example, Hal Draper (1965: 157) points out that "the civil-rights issue is, of course, made-to-order for the release of such radical energies." At the University of California (Berkeley) in 1964, student action took the form of a challenge to the University's authority to regulate on-campus political activities of students. It was argued that such regulations and the sanctions for noncompliance were not within the purview of the Uni-

versity administration. "They do not want to evade the law; they want only to avoid 'double jeopardy.' They were 'willing' to be subject to the jurisdiction of the courts, they say, but not to incur the additional punishment *as students* for off-campus activities" [italics added]. Compare with William Peterson (1965).

2. This report, better known as the Muscatine Report, presents this point of view. Most of the recommendations of the report are directed toward improving undergraduate instruction, and fifteen items which focus attention on the lack of interest in the teaching function of professors can be found on p. 40 in "Education at Berkeley" (Select Committee on Education, 1966).

3. Our attention is limited to universities. The public and private *colleges* have a totally different problem in manning teaching posts. The universities have been the academic units which have felt the brunt of the expansion of college enrollments and have met the teaching task by employing graduate assistants.

4. In this and Charts 2 and 3, a logarithmic scale is employed. Such a scale shows the rate of change rather than the absolute amount of change. The steeper the slope of the line, the greater is the rate of change.

5. It should be pointed out that faculty members usually prefer teaching graduate students to undergraduates. This suggests another reason why faculty members withdraw from undergraduate teaching.

6. We are fully aware that the usual manner for handling the addition of teaching assistants to regular staff is to do it in terms of "full-time equivalent" positions, with assistants usually being considered as one-third to one-half full-time equivalent positions. We have chosen not to do this, precisely because the teaching assistant is used exclusively to teach undergraduates, and a significant portion of regular faculty teaching time is devoted to teaching graduate students, or is spent on research with equivalent relief from teaching duties. Staff members who spend a considerable amount of time on research are counted in the total of regular faculty members, as are part-time staff. We do not believe that the full-time equivalent measure is any more accurate than our "warm body" method of counting total staff, for purposes of understanding what has happened to undergraduate teaching in our public universities.

7. The proportion of graduate students who hold an assistantship is increasing rapidly. In a 1954 National Science Foundation survey, about 20 percent of all graduate students held assistantships; compare with Government Printing Office (1957: 35). By 1960, the proportion who held assistantships was 40 percent, and the greatest increase was in the proportion of teaching assistants; compare with James Davis (1962: 59). Bernard Berelson (1960: 148) concludes that most graduate students who progress to the Ph.D. level have had some type of support (assistantship or fellowship) at one time or another during their academic careers; Elbridge Sibley (1963: 109) makes a similar point with regard to graduate students in sociology. The relatively small proportion who held assistantships in the mid-1950s suggests one reason why the revolution among assistants did not occur earlier. With as few as 20 percent of a department's graduate students holding assistantships, the threat of a mass exodus was not as great as when 40 percent or more are assistants. Collective action is possible only when the percentage of assistants represents a significant proportion of the graduate students.

8. The full text of this leaflet can be found reprinted in Draper (1965: 196–199).

9. Accounts of the actual effectiveness of the strike vary, but apparently about 60 percent of the University classes were cancelled, and many others had less than normal attendance (Draper, 1965: 116).

10. The political and social action wing of the Union, for example, thought that a stand should be taken on Viet Nam, and went so far as to suggest that Union members participate in antiwar demonstrations *as Union members,* according to informants knowledgeable about the organization of the Union.

11. Although the Union voted to devote itself primarily to the immediate day-to-day concerns of its membership, there remains a clear division between the two factions. As one member put it, "we have learned to get along with each other." The different points of view expressed by the opposing factions is still a source of Union instability. The professionally oriented faction within the Union is in control primarily by virtue of their threat to withdraw if the Union takes a public stand on social and political issues. (1966 interviews with individuals who have participant knowledge of the Union.)

12. It is, of course, interesting that the graduate assistants, in protecting their own jobs, appealed for support on grounds of the dire consequences for undergraduate education.

13. For the 1966–1967 academic year, the Union again lobbied for the Legislature to appropriate more money for teaching assistants. It is difficult to assess the actual effectiveness of the Union in the resolution of this issue, because the University administration sided with the Union in opposition to the cutback. Nevertheless, it is clear that this issue was seen as a threat to assistants by the Union membership, it did attract University-wide support by various departmentally organized Union groups, and the Union took direct action to influence the outcome.

14. Following is a catalog of issues dealt with by various groups within the Union. (a) Issues related to the functions of assistants as teachers and as researchers include: some teaching assistants would like instruction in how to teach, others would not; there is some confusion over job descriptions (Readers have been asked in some cases to do work that teaching assistants would normally do); some departmental Unions have argued that the position of "Reader" should be abolished, and these jobs should be expanded to teaching assistant positions; teaching assistants should be allowed to offer seminars in areas of special interest to them; assistants should have a direct voice in planning course content, in choosing books, and in other matters directly related to their teaching functions; research assistants should have rights to the data they have collected, including the right to joint authorship of materials published from this data. (b) Issues related to the selection and reappointment policies include: appointments are made too late for an individual to find other employment if he is not hired; the selection process in some departments is unfair because there is no formal procedure. (c) Issues related to salaries and other monetary concerns: the payment system in the switch-over from semesters to quarters needs revision; waiver of the nonresident tuition fee for assistants; more research assistant jobs should be created to provide more employment; there is no standard, University-wide policy for (the payment of) research assistants; pay for some classifications of employees is too low (this is especially true for readers); the Union has asked the administration for a check-off for union dues which would deduct the dues from paychecks; the inclusion of the assistants in the University's health plan, also extending coverage to the dependents of assistants; there should be no one-fourth time assistants, all should be appointed for one-half time; assistantships should be tax-free, and assistants with dependents should be compensated accordingly. (d) Issues related to working conditions and other nonfinancial perquisites of employment include: assistants have worked for departmental libraries, newspapers, and journals; teaching assistants should be provided desk copies of books for courses which they help teach; bulletin boards

should be installed for Union and assistants' use in their offices; restroom facilities in some of the buildings should be improved; more parking spaces should be provided for faculty and graduate assistants. (e) Issues related to the relationship of assistants to faculty and administrative committees and University functionaries include: some teaching assistants feel that they are not getting proper supervision, and in some cases, no supervision at all; graduate assistants should be represented in academic bodies which make decisions that affect assistants or graduate students in general; research assistants should be assigned to professors in line with the academic interests of each.

15. The early lighting experiments are the data supporting this generalization.

16. A number of articles in Lipset and Wolin (1965) suggest this interpretation. See especially, S. M. Lipset and Paul Seabury (1965); Sheldon S. Wolin and John Schaar (1965). The Muscatine report, *Education at Berkeley* (Select Committee on Education, 1966: 40) also summarizes this point of view.

17. A writer in the Berkeley paper underscored this aspect: "Part of the unrest expressed by the FSM could be a sense of frustration over the lack of contact (undergraduate) students have with professors." Compare with *Berkeley Daily Gazette* (1964: 10).

18. Among the writers who support this interpretation are: Jerome Byrne (1965), Nathan Glazer (1965), and Robert Somers (1965: 530–557).

19. Somers did not repeat this breakdown on his sample, but another study by Glen Lyonns of the activists in the Free Speech Movement used Somers' sample to check the representativeness of his own sample and reported the 32 percent. See Glen Lyonns (1965).

20. See also Experimental Study in Institutional Procedures (1960: 36) and source cited in note 17; also the 15 items listed in *Education at Berkeley* (Select Committee on Education, 1966: 40) which are largely impressionistic accounts and editorial interpretations of the events at Berkeley. The Byrne Report, commissioned by the Regents of the University of California, was never published. This report was apparently based upon empirical studies, including surveys of student opinion.

21. Following is a partial list of recommendations of the Muscatine Report (Select Committee on Education, 1966: 44) that dealt specifically with teaching functions: (1) Evidence of teaching performance should be considered in hiring and promoting instructors. (2) Alternatives to lecturing should be sought. (3) Students should be allowed to undertake supervised independent study. (4) The proportion of lecture courses should be decreased in favor of discussion sections, small classes, seminars, and tutorials. (5) Senior faculty members should participate more in teaching lower-division courses. (6) The faculty should experiment with the use of student ratings to evaluate courses. (7) The faculty and administration should consult with students to determine their views on educational policy, and lines of communication should be established to that end. (8) More pass-not pass courses should be offered. (9) Some two- and three-quarter courses should be offered such that final grades would not be determined until the completion of the sequence. (10) More undergraduate seminars should be offered, especially in the freshman and sophomore years, to encourage close faculty-student contact. (11) *Ad hoc* courses which deal with the relevant scholarly and intellectual subjects should be offered.

22. To grant a graduate student a second-order or second-level degree (like a M.Phil, as has been proposed at Yale and elsewhere), which certifies only his teaching skills, but not his full professional competence, is not a solution to the problem of a graduate student earning a degree, while substituting for a professor in the classroom.

REFERENCES

BERELSON, B. (1960) *Graduate Education in the United States.* New York: McGraw-Hill.

Berkeley Daily Gazette (1964) December 13.

BYRNE, J. (1965) "Report to the Regents of the University of California." Pp. 230–237 in Draper (ed.) *Berkeley: The New Student Revolt.* New York: Grove Press.

Center for Research on Learning and Teaching (1965) "Memo to the faculty." Memo 13. University of Michigan, September.

Daily Californian (1965) September 16.

DAVIS, J. (1962) *Stipends and Spouses.* National Opinion Research Center study. Chicago: University of Chicago.

DRAPER, H. (1965) *Berkeley: The New Student Revolt.* New York: Grove Press.

Experimental Study in Instructional Procedures. Oxford, Ohio: Miami University, 1960.

FREEDMAN, M. and W. NICHOLS II (1966) "Select Committee survey." P. 12 in *Education at Berkeley.* Berkeley: University of California Printing Dept., March (mimeo.).

GALES, K. (1966) "Berkeley student opinion, April, 1965." P. 11 in *Education at Berkeley.* Berkeley: University of California Printing Dept., March (mimeo.).

GLAZER, N. (1965) "What happened at Berkeley." Pp. 294–295 in S. M. Lipset and S. Wolin (eds.) *The Berkeley Student Revolt.* New York: Anchor Books.

Government Printing Office (1957) "Graduate student enrollment and support in American colleges and universities." Washington, D.C.

LIPSET, S. M. and P. SEABURY (1965) "The lesson of Berkeley." Pp. 343–344 in S. M. Lipset and S. Wolin (eds.) *The Berkeley Student Revolt.* New York: Anchor Books.

LIPSET, S. M. and S. WOLIN, Eds. (1965) *The Berkeley Student Revolt.* New York: Anchor Books.

LYONNS, G. (1965) "The police car demonstration: a survey of participants." P. 521 in S. M. Lipset and S. Wolin (eds.) *The Berkeley Student Revolt.* New York: Anchor Books.

MAY, H. (1965) "The student movement at Berkeley: some impressions." Pp. 456–462 in S. M. Lipset and S. Wolin (eds.) *The Berkeley Student Revolt.* New York: Anchor Books.

MERTON, R. (1957) *Social Theory and Social Structure.* New York: The Free Press.

PETERSON, W. (1965) "What is left at Berkeley." P. 374 in S. M. Lipset and S. Wolin (eds.) *The Berkeley Student Revolt.* New York: Anchor Books.

ROTHLISBERGER, F. J. and W. J. DICKSON (1938) *Management and Worker.* Cambridge: Harvard University Press.

Select Committee on Education (1966) *Education at Berkeley.* Report of the Select Committee on Education, Academic Senate. Berkeley: University of California Printing Dept., March.

SIBLEY, E. (1963) *The Education of Sociologists in the United States.* New York: The Russell Sage Foundation.

SOMERS, R. (1965) "The mainsprings of the rebellion: a survey of Berkeley students in November, 1964." Pp. 530–557 in S. M. Lipset and S. Wolin (eds.) *The Berkeley Student Revolt.* New York: Anchor Books.

WOLIN, S. S. and J. SCHAAR (1965) "The abuses of the multiversity." Pp. 352–361 in S. M. Lipset and S. Wolin (eds.) *The Berkeley Student Revolt.* New York: Anchor Books.

PART VI

RESEARCH
AND THE RELEVANCE
OF PROPOSALS FOR
REFORM

CHAPTER 14

BELL, BOOK AND BERKELEY

Martin Trow

If nothing else, most academic men will agree that undergraduate education in large American universities is in need of reform. Changes in secondary education, the role of academic men, the scope of knowledge encompassed by the academic disciplines, the character of students, the impact of post-graduate education, together have created, if not a crisis, then at least widespread dissatisfaction with the organization and content of undergraduate education.

Two important recent responses to these developments are the reports by Daniel Bell (1966) and by a faculty committee, chaired by Charles Muscatine (Select Committee on Education, 1966), to the faculty and administrative officers of Columbia University and the University of California at Berkeley, respectively. Bell's report, *The Reforming of General Education,* and *Education at Berkeley,* generally known as The Muscatine Report, are each instructive individually; taken together, the sharp contrast between them sheds light on the differences between the two institutions, as well as on the conceptions of education, and indeed of the university, held by their respective authors. The differences may also illuminate educational constraints and opportunities that take similar or slightly different forms in other universities.

I

Daniel Bell's admirable book was written as a report to the Dean of Columbia College on the program in general education at Columbia University. It is, in fact, much more than that: it includes a broad-ranging discussion of trends in American society and their relevance for education; of the character of American universities and of undergraduate education; of the possibilities of a "common learning" in an age of specialization and in the face of an explosive growth of knowledge; of the rise and decline of general education at Harvard and Chicago, as well as at Columbia. Interpolated are thoughtful essays on cultural styles in "post-industrial society," the impact of computers on modern thought; the problems and possibilities

EDITORS' NOTE: This chapter is reprinted (in slightly revised form) from *The American Behavioral Scientist*, May–June, 1968 (Volume XI, Number 5).

inherent in, what he calls, "the new intellectual technology"—game theory, decision theory, simulation, linear programming, cybernetics, and operations research; and the impact of large-scale research on the role of the professor and the functions of the university. And, as the advertisement says, much, much more.

A friend asked me what I had learned from Bell's book. I learned something about the history of general education in this country, something also about currents of thought in (to me) unfamiliar disciplines. More important, I learned a good deal about how to think about an undergraduate curriculum. I doubt whether even in the same circumstances my proposals would be the same as Bell's—indeed, much of the strength of this book lies in its individual (though not idiosyncratic) flavor. But the book is a model of educational planning, taking into account and weaving together basic values and hard facts, conceptions of man and the actual state of "advanced placement," the common learning and the ambitious professor. And, best of all, he avoids inexpensive moralizing which condemns institutional realities in the name of high principle and results in irrelevant prescriptions to imaginary universities with real names.

Bell begins with a sketch of the origins and development of general education at the three universities whose names are most closely associated with the idea. In its broadest terms, as Dean David Truman reminds us in his foreword, general education

> has never referred to a single set of courses offered uniformly by all colleges subscribing to the idea. Rather it has indicated acceptance of the policy of providing a common, if not always uniform, intellectual experience for all students for at least a portion of their undergraduate years, that experience not being bound by the conventional limits of particular disciplines. General education programs, whatever their individual forms and content, have in consequence indicated acceptance by the colleges of a responsibility for setting priorities among types of knowledge. They have also implied a responsibility for exploring at least some of the persistent and changing relations among modes of human thinking, a responsibility whose effective discharge alone warrants the label "liberal" education [Bell, 1966: x–xi].

The differences in the sources, conceptions, and fates of general education at Harvard, Chicago, and Columbia are considerable, and Bell makes clear the interplay of their different traditions, student constituencies, and institutional structures as these gave form and content to the courses of general education at those institutions. What they shared in common is evident throughout Bell's book: a concern for the possibilities and the character of a "common learning," in the face of powerful divisive and fragmenting forces in society, in education, and in science and scholarship themselves. At a number of places, he assays the ends of education: for him, this is pre-eminently liberal education, of which general education is not merely one variety but the form that liberal education takes when it is integrated, coherent, the outcome of planning rather than of *laissez faire* and indifference. For Bell, the ends of education are many:

to instill an awareness of the diversity of human societies and desires; to be responsive to great philosophers and imaginative writers who have given thought to the predicaments that have tried and tested men; to acquaint a student with the limits of ambition and the reaches of humility; to realize that no general principles or moral absolute, however strongly rooted in a philosophical tradition, can give an infallible answer to any particular dilemma [Bell, 1966: 289].

What saves these and similar statements of intellectual purpose and educational principle from the emptiness of similar high-flown rhetoric expressed on ritual academic occasions is that, for Bell, they inform a closely reasoned effort to specify, in the broad and in detail, an undergraduate curriculum. They are, thus, not platitudes but grounds for deciding on the subjects, books, traditions of thought and work that would be included in his curriculum. Equally important, these statements of principle and goal are set against a tough-minded and empirically grounded analysis of the actual conditions and forces at work in American society and education. To neglect these institutional forces when making educational choices, Bell argues, is to risk being irrelevant to the world in which higher education is enmeshed. In a characteristic passage he observes that:

It is much easier, and more the academic habit, to deal with ideological questions than with the organizational difficulties, and many of the problems of the general education courses, which are actually rooted in institutional dilemmas, have been masked by arguments about intellectual content [Bell, 1966: 66].

He then proceeds to discuss the problem of staffing general education courses, a problem, in all three universities, greater than those arising out of differences within the faculty about intellectual content or educational philosophy.

In Chapter Three, "The Tableau of Social Change," Bell analyzes forces in the society and within universities which affect both the kinds of education that men need and the kinds of institutions and ideas that exist to serve those needs. A central dilemma is that the growth of research and the pre-eminence of the graduate schools has produced great numbers of specialists; at the same time, both the rate of change of knowledge and the requirements of social life call for an education transcending the narrow limits of a specialty, one that acquaints students with the nature of conceptual inquiry, "the conduct and strategy of inquiry itself," and also gives them a share in the common learning of educated men.

If there is a single dominant theme in his discussion of the curriculum, it is Bell's repeated emphasis on the notion of the central role of "conceptual inquiry" in general education.

In this emphasis on the centrality of method, there is, as I have argued before, a positive new role for the college as an institution standing between the secondary school and graduate research work. One of its fundamental purposes must be to deal with the modes of conceptualization, the principles of explanation, and the nature of verification. The world is always double-storied: the factual order, and the logical order imposed on it. The emphasis in the college must be less on what one knows and more on the self-conscious ground of knowledge; how one knows what one knows, and the principle of the relevant selection of facts [Bell, 1966: 164–165].

Bell does not confine this principle to the teaching of science, but retains it as the central theme for his whole curriculum. But it should not be imagined that he envisions a series of courses on the philosophy of science and the modes of inquiry. On the contrary, he is very much concerned with the content and quality of the books and ideas actually confronted, as well as how they are treated. And far from neglecting the factual order, he puts history (more accurately, the social historical perspective) at the core of his reformed contemporary civilization and humanities sequences.

To summarize his specific suggestions for Columbia, Bell would require students to take a three-semester contemporary civilization sequence, a three-semester humanities sequence, and a two-year math-physics or math-biology sequence. A fourth semester following the contemporary civilization sequence would be a linked departmental course; following the humanities sequence, there would be a term in visual arts and a term in music (or, in some cases, a year of one or the other). In the senior year, together with seminar work, a series of "third-tier" courses would be offered in the sciences, social sciences, and humanities. These, to which Bell attaches considerable importance, would "give a student a sense of how his major subject can be applied to a problem area, or will demonstrate the broad conceptual foundations he has acquired." The majors would also be somewhat modified to build on the required general education sequences of the first two years and would be capped by the seminars and third-tier courses of the senior year.

II

About the value of curriculum planning, Bell has no doubt. He believes that the forms and content of undergraduate education deserve the kind of intelligence that we give to our academic subjects, and that the curriculum should be shaped primarily by intellectual rather than administrative or logistical considerations. Moreover—and this is crucial—he believes that there are better and poorer kinds and sequences of courses, and that his suggestions are better than alternatives. Bell nowhere argues the virtues of academic planning on a college-wide basis: the argument is the book itself. But many academic men do not share his belief in the virtues of a "coherent" educational plan for undergraduates. They argue, as often by acquiescence in administrative arrangements as in words, that the curriculum to which young men or women are exposed in college is among the least important influences on their minds and characters—that most of what they are and come to be is a product of their life experience outside college in their homes, among their friends, on their jobs. The specific books and courses that make up an undergraduate curriculum, so this argument goes, are the most marginal of influences on students and simply not worth the thought and attention Bell gives them. By contrast, if we speak of technical skills or professional competence, rather than the qualities of mind of the

liberally educated man, the course work a student takes in college is rather
more consequential: a really solid grounding in math or physics or economics may make a real difference to what a student can do in his life.
Moreover, this argument continues, a man's character will be more substantially affected by his ability to accept responsibility, or contribute to
knowledge, or shape social policy, because that competence will directly affect the kind of life he will lead as an adult. Thus, the argument goes, the
ultimate qualities of mind and character that Bell is concerned about are
shaped more by the competence we can give a student for liberating and
challenging adult social roles than by the direct effort to cultivate these
qualities in college. Moreover, there is evidence which suggests that what
able young men and women take from higher education is much more a
function of the qualities they bring with them than of what happens to
them in college.[1] All this makes it easier for people who have little interest
in teaching undergraduates to justify giving it little attention.

But Bell's book, by ignoring the research on the impact of higher education, carries the conviction that some things do not have to be justified
by research into their consequences: they are good in themselves. Among
these are intelligence and discrimination in education; and to argue the
conflicting claims of Carlyle and Camus for the limited time of the undergraduate course itself involves the kind of judgment and choice that liberal
education is concerned with. And whatever studies say about the "effects"
of higher education (and the studies are as yet neither impressive nor persuasive), it is right to talk of the forms and content of liberal education,
and right also to consider how that might best be furthered through a college curriculum. That is what Bell does.

What relevance does Bell's book have for Berkeley? Berkeley, as an institution, has no conception of the educated man, nor any plan for liberal
education. This is not to say that there is no liberal education at Berkeley:
in the hundreds of courses offered by the forty-odd departments of Berkeley's College of Letters and Science, many students lose their provincialism
and gain an understanding of the role of values in inquiry, of the social
source of ideas, of the nature of conceptual innovation. Yet, admittedly, it
happens haphazardly; there is no common learning, and no one knows how
many students pass through the university without any substantial experience of liberal education. From another perspective, there are at Berkeley
few collective decisions about the undergraduate curriculum that have real
consequences for the several departments. Instead, there are breadth and
depth requirements, whose merits are assumed to be so obvious they do not
require much discussion. Chief among the merits of the breadth and depth
requirements is precisely that they do not require much discussion; in any
event, the College of Letters and Science would be hard put to enforce on
its constituent departments any decision which went much further toward a
coherent curriculum.

It may appear, at least to people outside Berkeley, oddly perverse to
claim that Berkeley does not debate education, in view of the debate over
the Muscatine proposals. But the Muscatine Report did not initiate any
substantial debate about education at Berkeley; the only recommendations

that gave rise to any real controversy had to do with certain administrative arrangements which would allow individuals who wanted to develop innovative courses to circumvent existing course review machinery, thus making it somewhat easier for them to do what they wished. (The conflict, thus, was between "spontaneity" and academic standards, rather than between different conceptions of the university or of liberal education.)

The Muscatine Report offers an instructive contrast to the Bell report. The charge to the Muscatine committee was somewhat broader than Bell's: "To find ways in which the traditions of humane learning and scientific inquiry can be best advanced under the challenging conditions of size and scale that confront our university community." But the difference in the charge cannot explain the enormous disparity in the attention the two reports give to the undergraduate curriculum. That, essentially, is at the center of the whole of Bell's book; even when he is discussing esoteric developments in information theory, he is asking what place it or other new conceptual tools should have in the undergraduate curriculum. By contrast, *Education at Berkeley* gives no more than ten or twelve pages to the undergraduate curriculum, and even that brief discussion is perfunctory and casual.[2] Aside from an introductory section on the students, the bulk of the Report is a series of recommendations *designed to free individual instructors from the constraints of faculty committees* (or, less successfully, of their departments). By contrast, a plan for general education imposes additional restraints on the freedom of faculty members and departments affected by it. Nowhere in the Report is the idea suggested that one general curriculum might be better than another; educational wisdom resides not in the college and its reasoned decisions (to which the committee might have contributed), but in the individual instructor chafing under the constraints of the committee on courses and his departmental major requirements.

Bell sees the central task of general education as the reconciliation of the conflicting demands of a common learning and specialism; and this involves strengthening the college and its conception of liberal education, in relation to the departments and their conceptions of specialized studies. Where faculty are heavily involved in graduate instruction, at Columbia as at Berkeley, individual departments inexorably press for more and earlier specialized studies, faculty careers are made through publication, and research is both well supported and excitingly successful. At Columbia College, as Bell well knows, *laissez faire* would lead to autonomous departments (and their specialized course sequences); at Berkeley, the autonomous departments make for *laissez faire*. *Education at Berkeley* is a further triumph of the spirit of voluntarism, shifted from the department to the individual instructor. And if the departments cannot come together around a core curriculum, it is far less likely that a coherent plan for liberal education can arise out of the uncoordinated experiments of individual teachers. (Which is something like trying to achieve socialism by setting up a dozen socialists in private business.)

Education at Berkeley has the one (for Berkeley surely the highest) virtue of not affecting anybody who does not want to be affected by it. If the Report is notable for the lack of dispute it has occasioned, it is largely because virtually all of its many recommendations can be ignored by those who are simply not interested. They do not really even affect the life of the departments; the best evidence for that is how few departments have debated any of its recommendations in their own meetings. The Report leaves people alone to get on with their work. That is what the Berkeley faculty wants of an undergraduate program—that it not interfere too much with the real business of academic men. What the Report adds to this philosophy of education is that if a faculty member should really want to do something new or unusual with an undergraduate course, he should be able to do so and, hopefully, not be penalized for it in a promotion committee.

As the institutional response to the dilemmas of undergraduate education at Berkeley, *Education at Berkeley* is as instructive in its (very different) way as Bell's is about Columbia. Since it is so lightly encumbered by educational philosophy (behind its cheerful optimism and faith in educational experimentation and pluralism lies *laissez faire* with romantic overtones), it has little reason or basis for establishing educational priorities. A "theory," among other things, is a statement regarding relevance; it points to what is important in a world of events. Thus, it tells us what to observe, and leads to specificity and detail in a critical discussion. By contrast, the rather vague and general tone of much of the Muscatine Report is a direct outcome of its eschewing debate over educational philosophies. For example, the Report observes at one point that "For many students—both undergraduate and graduate—there has not been an adequate connection between their education and what they feel to be their primary concerns as human beings and as citizens. We need to make the connection more clear, and to replace those of our offerings that may have through obsolescence lost their contact with vital human concerns" (Select Committee on Education, 1966: 4–5). But the Report does not risk suggesting *what* offerings suffer "obsolescence" in relation to *what* "vital human concerns." And the reader can comfortably associate himself with "vital human needs" as against "obsolescent" offerings, without its, in any way, affecting anything he or anyone else does.

A theory of education may be no more (or no less) than a statement of the grounds for setting educational priorities, expressing preferences, making decisions. But the statement of preferences and priorities forces one to an analysis of real possibilities in real situations. In its absence, we have a relaxed acceptance of everything, in which exhortation replaces analysis:

> Our ideal for the student is that he be provided with rich opportunities, generous guidance, and plenty of room for experiment, and that he be enabled to make for himself as many of the important decisions about his own education as possible. . . . Greater pluralism and increased individual attention to students means a greater call on the administrative, teaching, and advisory power of the campus. . . . But nowhere do we suggest a diminution of the research activities of the faculty [Select Committee on Education, 1966: 4–5].

Pluralism, which at Berkeley is another name for *laissez faire,* whether of the autonomous department or of liberated innovators, must ultimately be justified by minimizing the importance of the nature of the curriculum as compared with the character of the faculty. Here is the Report's answer to efforts to work out a general education that is concerned with a common learning:

> The close interpenetration of teaching and research should not only give a special character to the campus; it should give an ultimate unity and coherence to our pluralistic curricula and a clear definition of role to our faculty. We have been able to find very few categorical imperatives for Berkeley education. There are very few subjects that we can agree on that *every* student should know. But we have not been unmindful of the question "what about the values?" Beneath the great variety of possible educational experiences that a pluralistic system offers, what is the common denominator? What will our students have in common? Our answer is that ideally they will have in common the exposure to a noble stance, both scientific and humane, that will be exemplified in the conduct of every one of us. It is not, then, what we teach that will give final validity to education at Berkeley, but what we are [Select Committee on Education, 1966: 6].

If the highest educational virtues lie in qualities of individual faculty members, then it is pointless to engage in long and inconclusive debates about educational principles, when what is needed is for us to assume (and exemplify in our conduct) noble stances. The corollary is that institutional constraints, whether of colleges or faculty committees or perhaps even of departments, only hinder and obscure the personal individual qualities of the faculty "which give final validity to education at Berkeley."

The difficulty is that academic men, as a group, are no more noble than anyone else. We surely include among us men of noble spirit, who exemplify their qualities in their personal and professional lives. Such men have much to teach us, and their students, beyond their professional competence. And it is certainly true that one of the consequences of the remoteness of most regular faculty from undergraduates, and especially from lower division students, is to deprive them of the experience of close association with men who can manifest these personal virtues in their learning and scholarship. The various efforts at Berkeley to "bring faculty and students more closely together" outside the curriculum fail both because the association thus engendered is superficial and because it divorces the man's personal qualities from his demonstration of them in his scholarly life.

But to struggle against the worst effects of mass higher education is not necessarily to justify our educational efforts by reference to qualities to which most of us only aspire. The fact is that we have all learned much from men of quite ordinary personal qualities, and even, on occasion, from men who were not especially admirable human beings. Max Weber, in his great essay on "Science as a Vocation" (Gerth and Mills, 1946: 129–156) reminds us that few academic men are "leaders," by which he meant possessed of those extraordinary personal qualities for which students in his time yearned, as they do in ours. Moreover, as he observed, there is no necessary relation between having those qualities of leadership and having the more mundane qualities of a scholar and a teacher. Our plain task, as he might have said, is to recognize and honor those extraordinary qualities where they appear, but also to get on with our own tasks of educating ourselves and our students. And the final validity of that effort rests as much on what we teach as on what we are.

IV

If there is little to say about the philosophy of education at Berkeley, it may be somewhat more fruitful to turn to the institutional conditions that help explain both the absence of an educational philosophy (beyond *laissez faire*) and the lack of interest in having one at Berkeley. Among these conditions are the preeminence of the departments and the weakness of the college; the character of the faculty; the resources devoted to undergraduate education; the heterogeneity of the student body.

A required curriculum imposes constraints on the freedom of departments to organize and staff their own courses of instruction. The more "coherent," the more planned interweaving of material and collaborative teaching, as in general education courses, the more the constraint on the departments. At Berkeley, the unwritten treaty governing the university (in its internal relations as well as in its foreign affairs) prescribes that the departments will provide undergraduate instruction at low cost but of high professional standard, but only if they are allowed to do it in their own way, with a minimum of interference from other agencies. The distribution requirements provide the minimum prescriptive coordination necessary for some measure of year to year "planning" and staffing by the departments (which are the units both for educational planning and staffing). One could hardly imagine an arrangement that would provide the absolutely necessary continuity and predictability of the undergraduate program yet interfere less with departmental discretion. Whether or not the distribution requirements were intended to maximize departmental autonomy (as the "treaty" metaphor implies), they have that consequence, which is surely not irrelevant either to their survival or to the absence of any significant criticism of them among the faculty.

Looked at from another perspective, the autonomy of the departments would almost insure that it would be extremely difficult to staff a general education program of any scope at Berkeley. This is so for a number of reasons. First, very few members of the regular faculty at Berkeley are, under present conditions, interested in the kind of collaborative, cross-disciplinary courses that are involved in general education. (Indeed, very few of them are interested in the curriculum reforms called for by the Muscatine Report.) Two attempts to provide cross-disciplinary general courses, the Social Science Integrated Course and the more demanding experimental college organized by Professor Joseph Tussman, have found staffing their central and continuing difficulty.[3] Out of some 1,500 members of the Academic Senate, and perhaps 1,000 in Letters and Science departments, both programs have had the greatest difficulty in getting a dozen or so men a year to teach in them.

This, of course, is partly due to the fact that the departments make their first commitment to their own undergraduate programs, and especially to their major requirements. There is almost always a problem of staffing the regular departmental offerings, and departments naturally tend not to encourage regular staff members to put precious undergraduate teaching time into outside courses. Moreover, in a rough way and over time, the permanent positions allotted to departments are tied to undergraduate enrollments in departmental courses, and this is another factor discouraging departments from investing scarce resources in extra-departmental programs for which they get little or no "credit."

But while the departmental structure at Berkeley is not hospitable to interdisciplinary programs, of greater importance is the character of the Berkeley faculty. There are, of course, many exceptions, but the basic character of the University as a world-renowned center for research and graduate work (with no comparable reputation as a center for undergraduate education) ensures that faculty members with primarily research interests dominate the Berkeley faculty, partly through self-selection, partly through the operation of the criteria regarding research promise and accomplishment that have governed appointment and promotion practices for a long time. These recruitment and retention patterns have not assembled a large body of men dedicated to undergraduate education; what interest in that direction arises is characteristically devoted to improvement in the quality of departmental offerings, or of collaboration on a quite autonomous basis between neighboring departments, as in the new introductory science courses.

We should not underestimate the amount of faculty energy and imagination which are drained out of the institution as a planning and self-governing body by the calling of research and scholarship. For many men at Berkeley, nothing in the university (or, for some, in the world) has the reality or significance of the half-finished manuscript on the desk at home or the current work in the laboratory. For such men, those concerns take clear priority over the business of running a university. Agitation over student rights, undergraduate teaching, faculty committees, the university budget, are so many distractions from that difficult passage in the manuscript, those inexplicable findings in the current study or experiment.[4] Many such men are also "good citizens" and serve conscientiously on committees, as, also, prompted by their basic scholarly values, they conscientiously prepare their undergraduate lectures. And many also have a real, though sharply limited, interest in problems of university governance and student life. Much of this interest is latent and is activated by a dramatic event, such as a student strike or the firing of a president, when it takes the form of intense short-lived "public" activity in the life of the university, for some explicitly seen as a furlough from their serious research. But, characteristically, there is, over time, increasing irritation with these distractions and a withdrawal to the perennial and enduring (and so much more interesting) work at the desk or lab.

A major effort to reform the curriculum would threaten prolonged "public" discussion, study, and committee service by large numbers, with (given the institutional impediments) very dubious outcomes. This, I think, explains the recoil from a "long and inconclusive debate" over rival educational philosophies in the first paragraph of the Muscatine Report.

Over and above departmental sovereignty and the character of the faculty is the paucity of resources available for teaching the Berkeley undergraduate. Our student-faculty ratio in the lower division is ordinarily given as 28 to 1—my own view is that it is effectively a good deal higher than that. But even that is two to three times as high as comparable figures for the three colleges Bell discusses (or for any other of the leading liberal arts colleges, inside or outside universities) and four times as high as the student-faculty ratio which obtains throughout the British university system. Moreover, this means that a very substantial part of undergraduate instruction at Berkeley is carried by graduate teaching assistants. In 1965, so we learn from *Education at Berkeley,* over 30 percent of all undergraduate courses were taught by teaching assistants; in the lower division, the figure was 41 percent. Even more striking, nearly two-thirds of all classes with fewer than thirty students were taught by assistants.[5]

General education is extremely demanding of the time of regular, and especially of senior, faculty. The kinds of broad-ranging, interdisciplinary courses Bell describes call for men who have read widely beyond their own disciplines and who have grappled with fundamental issues on the frontiers between their own and neighboring subjects. They are just not the kinds of courses that can be carried by teaching assistants whose first concern is necessarily their own specialized graduate training or thesis, and who can scarcely be expected to have the experience or scholarly resources required by Bell's curriculum, or anything comparable.

Moreover, the absence of any program of general education at Berkeley also reflects profound differences of opinion within the faculty regarding what is desirable and admirable, both in students and in their education. The distribution requirements are, in effect, a tacit agreement not to argue, not because Berkeley faculty are less argumentative than any other group of academic men, but because arguing takes time which is better spent on one's real work. And besides, it is not at all clear to many Berkeley faculty that the whole business is worth arguing about in the endless committee meetings that curriculum planning on a college scale requires. The organization of faculty government at Berkeley already burdens the hard-pressed academic man there with more committee assignments than his counterparts in most other major universities, and he is not anxious to add to the load. Anyone who doubts the reality of the added burden can observe any college in the process of curriculum design or reform: in such dissimilar institutions as MIT, the University of Sussex, and Antioch College, I have been struck by how enormously time-consuming curriculum planning is for the whole institution. None of the work can be delegated, and no decision is too trivial for discussion: taken together, it is argued, "small" questions of required readings or the sequence of work are, in fact, what make up the curriculum and are the form that any philosophy of education takes. For those doing it, it is very nearly a full-time job, and it goes on for years. Distribution requirements simply do not need much discussion; general norms of equity replace painful and disputed issues involving personal values and professional judgments.

The extraordinary heterogeneity of the Berkeley student body is another impediment to a coherent undergraduate program, with its assumptions regarding relatively high (if not common) levels of sophistication, intelligence, and motivation of the students. Among Bell's recommendations is the abolition of Columbia's composition courses, along with other courses dealing with academic deficiencies that should have been (and increasingly are) removed in high school. Berkeley still does a substantial amount of remedial teaching, both formally and informally. Moreover, the differences in the student body at Berkeley (as compared with those at Harvard, Columbia, or Chicago) are very large; one indicator of the difference is that only a little more than a third of Berkeley students who enter as freshmen graduate from Berkeley in four years, and the proportion of those who ever graduate from Berkeley is only slightly over half. Comparable figures at the leading private universities are in the neighborhood of 85 percent. With half of Berkeley's upper division students entering in the junior year, the present distribution requirements ease the administrative problems of finding some common formula for accepting majors and awarding degrees.

Columbia College has 2,700 students. Berkeley undergraduates number about 17,000, of whom over 12,000 are enrolled in its College of Letters and Science. In fairness to the Muscatine Committee, it is clear that the size and heterogeneity of this student body, the relatively small resources devoted to them, and the weakness of the College in relation to its departments, sharply limit what can be done at Berkeley; to change those parameters would take political and administrative decisions that lie beyond the power of the faculty to whom the Report was addressed. Any committee which works within those limiting conditions, as the Muscatine Committee did, can therefore only make recommendations which are peripheral to the central problems of undergraduate education at Berkeley. The Report's recommendations, which marginally increase the faculty's freedom to develop new and experimental courses, are for the most part useful and helpful, and most of them have been adopted by the faculty senate. The Report's failure lies in its presenting these marginal reforms as if they were more than that, thus obscuring the real limitations to more substantial reform of undergraduate education at Berkeley. And insofar as the Report and its recommendations give people the sense that undergraduate education at Berkeley has been reformed, it is performing a familiar conservative function.

I have heard suggested that we ought not to do at all what we do badly or absent-mindedly. Why, it is asked, cannot Berkeley be in name what it is in fact—one of the world's leading centers for research, scholarship, and graduate and professional education—and let it go at that? The notion was a bit of an academic joke a few years ago; it has ceased to be funny, and begins to look more reasonable as new campuses of the University arise without all of Berkeley's inherent bias against undergraduate education. The most recent revisions of California's Master Plan (for higher education) certainly looked toward a slow shift of student numbers at Berkeley away from the lower division.

The difficulties, and perhaps even more, the educational objections, in the way of this most radical reform of undergraduate education at Berkeley are enormous. But times of crisis hasten change; the difficulties may not seem so great in three or five years. Certainly, the transfer of our lower division to other campuses, a far less radical solution, would probably gain the support of a substantial part, and perhaps even a majority, of the faculty right now. The alternative, which includes such piecemeal efforts to strengthen the undergraduate program as the recent Berkeley Academic Senate resolution urging departments to assign to it more of their teaching staff, would probably just weaken the research faculty without substantially improving the quality of undergraduate education at Berkeley.

The most important fact about education at Berkeley is the enormous disparity in the resources—of money, energy, and imagination—that go into undergraduate education as opposed to graduate training and research. I do not think this disparity is likely to diminish much in the near future, nor would I myself want to see introduced at the expense of research and the graduate programs. But the tensions that arise from this disparity are felt by every student, teacher, and administrator at Berkeley, and these tensions reflect themselves in various kinds of troubles and discontents on that campus. It is this disparity that makes Bell's recommendations to Columbia College, for all their virtues, largely irrelevant to Berkeley, as it makes the Muscatine Report of only limited value. The disparity is embedded in the present structure of the University of California and, indeed, of most public universities in this country. But the move in this University toward greater autonomy of the several campuses, begun under President Kerr, will lead toward an increasing differentiation of character and function among them. It is in that direction, I believe, that a genuine reform of undergraduate education at Berkeley lies. But that is another, and longer, story.

NOTES

1. For example, Alexander Astin, reviewing a number of studies including his own, concludes, "Although colleges appear to differ in their effects on several aspects of the student's development, the size of these differential effects is small. In brief, the college actually attended by the student of high ability appears to make only a slight difference in his eventual career choice, academic and extra-curricular achievements during college, academic ability, persistence in college, and the eventual level of education that he obtains." (See Astin, 1965: 89.)

Astin's findings carry disturbing implications for the content and organization of higher education. Read literally, they seem to say that it does not much matter where students of high ability go to college. But there is a curious kind of determinism in the findings which presupposes that teachers and colleges continue to act *as if* their efforts really made a difference. It takes considerable effort to help students realize the potential with which they arrive at college, so that they can contribute to the figures which show little differences between colleges. Moreover, Astin's measures of the differential effects of colleges are crude and short-run. More subtle and more delayed effects may be far more substantially exerted by specific college experiences.

2. Where Bell confined his attention to the undergraduate program, the Muscatine Committee dealt with other issues as well.

3. The difficulties of staffing general education courses are everywhere bound up with changes in the nature of universities and the role of academic men. Even in their much more favorable circumstances, Bell notes: "This difficulty runs like a thread through the three colleges we are discussing" (Bell, 1966: 34).

4. Graduate teaching is not, in the same sense, a "distraction," since it is much more closely linked to a man's scholarly concerns and research interests.

5. Nevertheless, the report found "few limits to the possibilities of education at Berkeley" (Select Committee on Education, 1966: 3).

REFERENCES

ASTIN, A. W. (1965) *Who Goes Where to College.* Chicago: Science Research.

BELL, D. (1966) *The Reforming of General Education.* New York: Columbia University Press.

GERTH, H. and C. W. MILLS, Eds. (1946) *From Max Weber: Essays in Sociology.* Fairlawn, N.J.: Oxford.

Select Committee on Education (1966) *Education at Berkeley.* Report of the Select Committee on Education, Academic Senate. Berkeley: University of California Printing Dept., March.

CHAPTER 15

SOME SUGGESTED DIRECTIONS FOR RESEARCH

Terry F. Lunsford

In 1965, following the advent of the Free Speech Movement at Berkeley, I was asked by two research Centers at the Berkeley campus to gather materials on these events and to suggest issues for social and legal research raised by them. The suggestions made below are adapted with relatively few changes from the report that resulted (Lunsford, 1965). In the four years since then, many other student protests have occurred on university campuses in the United States, and if written anew today these suggestions would include somewhat different emphases—for example, the importance of the Vietnam war, issues of universities' "complicity" in the military-industrial complex, the impact of black militancy on campus and off, and the growing use of violent force by both demonstrators and police. The suggestions made here are thus somewhat dated, and are affected in their emphasis by their origins in the early days of the current student movement. However, many of the issues raised by the FSM were fundamental to the character of universities and of legal orders. For this reason these suggestions may still be of use to researchers who seek to understand the directions that these major social institutions are taking today.

Some Types of Research Issues

Many kinds of research might be suggested on the basis of recent years' student protests and the institutional responses to them. Several types are discussed briefly here: analyses of policy, study of the relevant law, "organizational" analysis, "socio-legal" inquiries, and historical-comparative studies of university governance. Issues of organizational and socio-legal research are then suggested in more detail.

EDITORS' NOTE: This chapter draws on Lunsford, T. F. (1965) and is printed with the permission of the author, the Center for Research and Development in Higher Education, and the Center for the Study of Law and Society, both of the University of California, Berkeley.

ANALYSIS OF POLICY ALTERNATIVES

Issues of "policy" need presuppose no specific, articulated theoretical perspective. They are practical questions of institutional governance which face—or may soon face—the significant participants at every U.S. university. The form in which these questions arise is normative: What should the university's goals be? What means are legitimate to pursue those goals? Who should be encouraged or permitted to participate in university government, and in what ways?

The normative context should not, however, disqualify such issues for the attention of university scholars. In the first place, the means and pre-conditions for achieving a stated goal or value often can be analyzed usefully without the analyst's subscribing to the value itself (See Kaplan, 1964: 370–387). Such analysis is important to academic life today. Current campus crises make clear again what is typically forgotten: that university scholars, administrators, and students tend to assume there is some broad consensus about the goals and means appropriate to the university—and thus neglect to discuss them. The "free speech" crisis at Berkeley, for example, revealed little consensus at any level in the University of California about either the operative goals that the University should be pursuing or the means to be encouraged in that pursuit.

Moreover, any analysis of means-ends relations leads inevitably to questions of descriptive fact and explanatory theory: What are universities' policies and practices? How internally consistent are they? What premises of value and belief are implied by each? What range of alternative actions is open? What are the effects of choosing particular goals, allowing certain groups to participate in their pursuit, or adopting certain organizational arrangements? What relevant facts beyond the immediate context should be considered before a particular policy choice is made? Thus, beyond their capacities *as participating members* of a university "community," scholars *as scholars* can illuminate the discussion of policy questions by (a) describing existing situations fully and accurately, (b) examining their internal coherence, (c) analyzing the assumptions about persons and institutions inherent in differing policy positions, (d) clarifying the range of explicit and implicit positions involved, (e) exploring the potential results of pursuing alternative policies, and (f) bringing to light new and relevant facts.

There are problems of precision, and of potential bias, in addressing policy issues—especially in the heat of predecision controversy. But every choice implies *some* assessment of the relevant facts and alternatives. Practical issues and social controversies should inspire theoretical and empirical inquiry of a fundamental kind, which continues beyond the heat of the moment. In that way better decisions and knowledge of society may both be increased.

STUDY OF THE RELEVANT LAW

One set of fact-questions to which our attention is immediately directed by policy problems concerns the applicable legal statutes and judicial precedents. The legal context in which universities operate evidently is in a state of some transition, if not disarray, and is little understood or agreed upon by competent legal scholars. What are the legal boundaries of university discretion? How are they changing, and on what bases? These are questions without good, generally available answers today, and this fact has had dramatic consequences in more than one campus crisis.

It seems particularly important to explore developing areas of the law which promise to be most significant for universities. For example, the growing law of "private governments" seems likely to bring under judicial review more areas of discretion in previously "private" or "public" but "autonomous" organizations. This trend needs much further study in relation to universities (See, among others, Miller, 1959). We need to understand more about the legal justifications for judicial scrutiny or its rejection in this area—e.g., the role in legal decisions of university functions and interests, and the current judicial substitute for such past doctrines as the university's status *in loco parentis* (See Levine, 1963; also U.S. National Student Association, n.d.; Johnston, 1962). Universities' legal powers and duties of law-enforcement on their campuses need investigation (See *California Law Review,* 1966; also *Denver Law Journal,* 1968).

Much of the research can be accomplished by the traditional methods of case-and-statute analysis, honored in legal tradition. Some will require reading these materials for more than the case-decision and its minimal basis in the court's opinion. Other types of study will also be needed, however. In a time of transition, with the circumstances of cases and the decisions of courts both shifting, forecasting the future directions of change in the law is at once the most practical, intriguing and difficult of "legal" problems. Diverse sources of information on this score might be more fully explored by interested scholars—e.g., the briefs of opposing parties in cases involving university rights and obligations. Working lawyers' contrasting statements of university functions, of the applicable precedents, and of presupposed authority-relations may be expected to mirror the interests which they seek to uphold, and should reveal much about the juridical context of university life today. More studies using questionnaires and interviews are obviously needed to clarify the attitudes of university trustees, administrators, faculty members, and students toward their respective legal rights and obligations, especially at campuses where strong controversy is now going on.

Such problems shade off imperceptibly into what may be called "socio-legal" analysis—the study of the law's relation to other social institutions and processes. That is discussed more fully below.

THEORETICAL PERSPECTIVES

We have suggested that analyses of policy issues and descriptions of past and present practices can be useful for practical ends, while informing and stimulating disinterested scholarship. But systematic study of underlying social structures and processes should not be content with such approaches. It should depart from and return to articulated theoretical perspectives, which promise explanatory interconnections going far beyond the immediate events at hand. The division between these extremes is never complete, of course. Every analysis and description implies some conceptual framework (of greater or lesser coherence), and much of social theory is still fragmentary and poorly articulated today. However, the distinction is still useful. Let us turn now to two broad analytic perspectives within modern sociology, and suggest ways in which the same events have specific theoretical relevance.

"Organizational" analysis. One perspective concentrates on the observable patterns of authority, influence, and support in a social organization (as general references, see Blau and Scott, 1962; Etzioni, 1961, 1964; Simon, 1957; Selznick, 1948). Such analysis tends to focus on the relations between the stated goals and the authority structure of an organization (for example, see Michels, 1959; Merton, 1957; Janowitz, 1959); between the "organization chart" and the informal interactions of individuals and groups (see Selznick, 1948; Roethlisberger and Dickson, 1939; Blau and Scott, 1962: 89–100, 234–237; Etzioni, 1964: 45–47); between sources of support for particular activities and the services rendered to outside "publics" (for example, see Clark, 1958; Thompson and McEwen, 1958); between the occupational roles of organization members and the social values which their actions help to fulfill (see Gouldner, 1959; Wilensky, 1956: 129–144); and so on. Concepts fitting generally within this perspective (e.g., authority) are implicit in much popular discussion of current student protests and explicit in some of it. For example, there is much disagreement about "flouting" of authority by protesting students, and alleged "abuses" of faculty members, administrators, and student representatives are matters of some concern on almost every U.S. campus. Such discussions need to be refined analytically and related more explicitly to organizational theory, as bases for further study.

"Socio-legal" inquiry. A second perspective also concerns itself with some of these same broad problems, involving concepts such as authority. However, it focuses more closely on rule-making and -enforcing processes as these relate to the spontaneous and changing patterns of social conduct and belief. Among the many interests of the developing "sociology of law" (see Selznick, 1968; Rankin, 1964; Skolnick, 1964; Grossman, et al., 1968) special attention might be given to such problems as the common characteristics of attempts to govern by rules; the relation of shared "moral" or "political" judgments to formal rules and their efficacy; the extent of reasoned justification for specific acts of authority; the applicability of traditional legal concepts and traditions to large-scale administrative organization; etc. The developing theory of "private government" seems destined to have a special relevance, both because it connects universities with the larger legal system, and because it may undergird emergent "legal" systems within universities themselves.

Other possibilities. The choice of these two theoretical perspectives is not meant to imply that others do not hold equal promise for the study of modern universities. For example, expanded study of the personal characteristics of students and others at universities of differing character is an obvious need. Such work, using personality theory as a basis, has already been extended to include student protest participants by a number of researchers (see Heist, 1965; Watts and Whittaker, 1966; Watts, et al., 1969; *Journal of Social Issues,* 1967).

Similarly, student protests have given new attention to the ways that institutional position in a formalized bureaucracy, and social roles in general, affect perceptions of what is true, right, reasonable, and relevant. The differing views stated by students and administrators often reveal widely diverging assumptions about the parts played by group interests, reason, good will, and power in social controversy. These differing views can be highly consequential for the flow of events in a crisis (see Knorr and Minter, 1965: 52, for a discussion of "The Berkeley Case").

Other examples might be given, but even these suggestions run beyond the competence of this review. They are mentioned here to encourage their exploration by those with the competence to pursue them.

COMPARATIVE STUDIES OF UNIVERSITY GOVERNANCE

Cutting across the issues suggested above is a dimension of social research that needs much fuller exploitation in this country: comparative study of differing historical, cultural, and organizational patterns.

Historical comparisons are needed in greater depth and precision on the patterns of applicable law, internal organization, "political" influence, and social functions of U.S. universities and colleges (see Rudolph, 1962; Hofstadter and Metzger, 1955; Veysey, 1965). Much more emphasis is needed on the roles of students as U.S. institutions have developed from their early collegiate forms and origins, under the impact of European models and indigenous demands. Student participation in rule-making and enforcement, and the "freedoms" and prerogatives of students as such, need special attention. Some of this attention is implied by recent efforts of the United States National Student Association, of the Association of American University Professors, and others.[1]

Cross-cultural and international comparisons are especially called for, to broaden our presently available knowledge of alternative patterns in university governance, both external and internal. Emphasis might be placed on cultures which provide key reference points for the U.S. experience. For example, we need much closer study of the German universities which have provided such important models for the research-orientation of the modern U.S. university. Also, Germany has a highly developed (and still developing) framework of statutory control over universities, within which much freedom for both faculty and students is said to exist. Closer examination of the way this system developed and operated in different historical periods is needed. Few competent works are presently available in English translation (but see Paulsen, 1895, 1906, 1908; Farmer, 1950; Ben-David and Zloczower, 1962; Flexner, 1930). Also, study of the internal government and external control of Latin American universities seems clearly indicated. The Latin American model is frequently cited as exemplary both of strong "political" involvement in administration and of students' political "sanctuary" from outside police. It is also widely criticized in this country as an example of politics at the expense of academic quality. Again, solid information is needed to replace sketchy accounts. A third obvious focus for such research is the rapidly growing universities and technical institutes of Russia. A fourth is the new nations of Africa and Asia, where establishing a university stands high on the agenda of every development-minded government (See Carr-Saunders, 1961; also Ashby, 1966). In each of these areas, the effect of the form of university governance on academic excellence, as well as on political liberties and participation, should be examined against the indigenous cultural background. The experience of visiting U.S. scholars with such diverse cultures and institutions is growing rapidly; perhaps better advantage might be taken of it.

Finally, a third set of comparisons suggests itself: contrasting the patterns of governance in universities and those in organizations with other formal goals or traditions. Since the 1964 beginnings at Berkeley, the rhetoric of controversy has been rich with organizational metaphor, and some of it has inspired new insights. The modern university has been compared variously with a happy family, a business corporation, a factory, a company town, a democratic polity, a voluntary mutual-benefit association, a custodial or correctional institution, a special-function government agency, a fourth branch of government, and so on. Comparing such organizational forms with present university patterns of authority, influence, and support might be pursued more seriously with real benefit. This is particularly true because of the tendency for courts to use such metaphors as partial bases for decisions reviewing administrative actions. But it is also suggestive of basic patterns in modern social structure.

University Forms and Functions: Organizational Issues

This section approaches recent campus controversies from a specific theoretical perspective, that of "organizational analysis." In the first part, certain general and particular problems of university authority-structures are examined. The second part concentrates on issues surrounding the interaction of universities' goals with the pressures (internal and external) of organizational life.

THE FORMS OF UNIVERSITY AUTHORITY

Much student and faculty criticism of the "multiversity" has centered on its organizational structure or form. A major focus has been the charge of impersonalized, autocratic "bureaucracy." The very word "bureaucracy" has become an epithet in the popular vocabulary of today. But the most famous analyst of bureaucracy, Max Weber, intended only to describe a particular form of organization, said to have major advantages as well as disadvantages (See Gerth and Mills, 1946: 214; Bendix, 1960: 426). Other usage takes the term as roughly coextensive with "large-scale organization," or with "administration" (compare Etzioni, 1964: 3; Crozier, 1964). These various ways of using the term, and the appeal of the general notion first delineated by Weber, have tended to dominate much of the study of formal organizations in this country (See Blau and Scott, 1962: 27).

The problem of bureaucratic organization in universities has received some attention from social scientists in recent years, but it needs much further exploration (for example, Clark, 1961, 1963; Anderson, 1963; Millett, 1962; Etzioni, 1964: 75–93; Litchfield, 1959). Even at a quite general level, questions such as these need intensified study: How bureaucratic are large modern universities? What, precisely, is meant by "bureaucracy" in this context? What specific areas of university activity tend to be bureaucratically organized? Does bureaucratic organization have distinctive value for the efficient performance of all social functions, including those of universities? What criteria of efficiency are implied? What are the inherent disadvantages of bureaucracy, and how do they affect the specific functions of universities?

Other foci, in the analysis of organizational structures have special relevance, however, for universities in particular. Some observers have emphasized the traditions of "consensual" or "collegial" authority shared by university faculty (especially those with strong "academic senate" organizations) and the tendencies of this form to break down under certain increasingly common conditions (See Clark, 1961). At the same time, there is a growing realization that still a third principle of authority operates in universities, as in other organizations which depend strongly on esoteric knowledge for their functions—the principle of certified expertise. The possession of hard-to-get knowledge carries its own "authority": no one can "validly" second-guess an "expert's" judgment except a colleague in his own narrow field of specialization. This "professional" authority, in turn, tends to carry its own "halo" effect, and to affect relationships outside the expert's special field (See Clark, 1963; Etzioni, 1964; Blau and Scott, 1962: 60–64, 208–209, 244–247).

The complex interplay of these types of authority was highlighted by the 1964–65 events at Berkeley. For example, the "collegial" decision by the Berkeley faculty on December 8, 1964 (concerning on-campus expression) clearly carried great weight with other members of the University, including its administration and Board of Regents. Yet the Board insisted on the continued formal delegation of its "ultimate authority" over student discipline to the hierarchic administrative staff headed by the President. Also, the problems of reaching consensus among large numbers of independently oriented specialists on the faculty were made doubly apparent during the Berkeley faculty's collective attempts to deal effectively with the University's crisis.

Again, even at a very general level there is a need for more clear and comprehensive analyses of such problems. What forms of organization, authority, and influence appear in the university besides the "bureaucratic"? What are the historical sources and principal functions of each type—and the inherent strains and complementarities among them? How are these diverse forms of authority reconciled in the official rhetoric of universities? How well is the rhetoric approximated in practice? What trends in university authority structures appear, and what are their probable effects on the interests of the diverse status groups within the university?

Ambiguity of formal authority. We have suggested that the *operative* authority structures of universities are complex and little understood. On examination, however, it often turns out that even the present *formal* authority structure is not clear. For example, it has been pointed out that no general, widely available codification exists of the University of California's official policies or formal structure (See Byrne, 1964, reprinted 1965). In specific areas, such as the authority of the organized faculty as distinguished from the administration, there is much ambiguity.

These facts raise a familiar, but central, issue of organizational analysis: the interplay of formal and informal social relationships in the operation of formal organizations (see Selznick, 1948; Roethlisberger and Dickson, 1939; Blau and Scott, 1962: 89–100, 234–237; Etzioni, 1964: 45–47). In the face of considerable ambiguity about who has authority to do what, how does the university actually operate? Whose *effective* authority is increased by the existence of formal ambiguities? What are the informal roles of authority, of reasoned discussion, of implicitly shared values, of the various status differences among groups in the university? What are the foci of informal authority, value-sharing, and status distinctions in today's university as compared with other formal organizations, and with the colleges and universities of the past? How do these things differ in the universities of other countries?

Further: Are university authority-relationships generally becoming more formalized and unambiguous? If so, in what ways? What forces impel this movement? Aside from the question of *whose* formal authority is increased or decreased, is increased clarity of authority an unalloyed gain? Are the "flexibility" or substantive relevance of interactions necessarily reduced when relationships become unambiguous? [2] Is formalization the only route to clarity? In the present makeup of university life, what interests are likely to emerge as dominant if formality and/or clarity of authority-relations is increased?

Mass organization of university life. Size is the trait most frequently seized upon to explain the ills of the modern university. Readers are familiar with comments on the new scale of higher learning in this country: Giant campuses serve multitudes of students. A single campus's faculty numbers more than a thousand, and assorted "professional research" staff members comprise hundreds more. Large lecture classes, large academic departments, mass record-keeping, and campus-wide "student personnel" agencies are the rule rather than the exception in today's large public universities. Thus "size" is an easily observed characteristic. It is frequently given credit for creating impersonality, unresponsiveness to individual needs, lack of student-teacher communication, and other problems with which universities are charged today. It may be time for a closer examination of the question: Which "ills" are necessarily associated with size in universities, and which are products of other factors—such as organizational forms that emphasize "economies of scale" at the expense of other values.[3]

Each form of organization has its advantages and limitations; each serves some purposes better than others. The present mass organization of the public university presumably did not arise by accident. We need to understand better its inherent advantages and disadvantages, and its evolution as U.S. college and university enrollments have burgeoned over the last half-century.

Why have single "universities" grown to enrollments of ten, twenty, thirty thousand and beyond instead of more numerous, smaller and "separate" institutions being created? Do economies of scale in the use of money, manpower, facilities, or other resources alone explain the growth of large classes, campus-wide registration procedures, or multi-campus administrative controls? What are the educational and cultural advantages of the large campus? What specific groups and interests are served by the present structure of university teaching and research? (For example, how is the present organization of large classes and teaching assistantships related to the subsidy of graduate study, or of faculty research?) To what extent are faculty or administrative pressures mobilized to maintain particular elements of the present structure? How are such pressures, if they exist, brought to bear? Answers to these and similar questions would seem basic to an understanding of organizational forms and their actual functions in the university today.

New "rules of access" on campus? Student protests against the multiversity as a "factory" have been coupled with demands for a "more human" scale of organization, breaking large-unit structures down so that repeated face-to-face interactions are possible among students, faculty members, and any others who must be involved with instruction and research. Some students point out that the "rules of access" to faculty and facilities in today's large university favor the graduate student over the undergraduate, upper division students over freshmen and sophomores, those with chosen majors over those who seek more breadth of study—and, in general, students who need the least individual attention from the university over those who need it most. Some faculty at least partially agree. For example, Burton Clark (1965) has pointed to the priority of access and convenience which a large, central campus library gives to the specialized scholar, at the expense of the undergraduate student who must use "reserve" books at times of peak demand.

Not all faculty members or administrators accept these criticisms. Some see present arrangements as properly emphasizing personal initiative, self-reliance, and competition for academic excellence among students. Access to libraries, to the scarce time of faculty members, and to individualized academic programs must be earned, they believe, by the kind of reading and writing which demonstrate students' readiness and motivation to make good use of these precious commodities. Many agree with some criticisms of the large university's impersonality, but hope to combine a more personal scale of teaching and learning with the advantages of the large urban campus (see Meyerson, 1965:5).

The many "cluster" colleges now being started, "course-less" programs such as the two-year Tussman College at Berkeley, and similar "experiments" (See Tussman, 1969) are predicated on expectations of significant changes in student-faculty relations, with assumptions that students' educational and cultural development also will be bettered. Such experiments should be systematically observed from the start by outside scholars, to determine what patterns of students and faculty relations actually occur, and how these are related to such indicators as students' perceptions of impersonality on the campus, students' scores on objective tests of academic achievement, and so on. Control of such variables as the values and personal characteristics of faculty and students would be crucial, and somewhat difficult, of course. But it seems important not to lose opportunities for comparative study of such major innovations in large-university organization from their beginnings.

In addition, case studies should be made of the decision-making processes that create or disapprove such innovations in large universities across the nation.[4] Such studies should suggest the interests and values on the large campus which lead to substructural innovations. They should reveal also the values that compete with those sought by the experimental programs—and which thus may operate to maintain the status quo, or energize trends toward still other organizational expedients.

Studies of actual use-patterns in libraries and other university facilities already are available on some campuses. These data might be systematized and compared with the needs of the different status groups in the typical university, to reveal the interests which are actually being served by these facilities at the present time.

Problems of the university "system." Student protests at Berkeley have given major impetus to still another critical development in University organization. During a long series of campus crises since 1964, the individual campuses' autonomy of regential and universitywide administrative controls have become an important issue in public discussions. In the aftermath of the FSM, the University of California began its second major "decentralization" of administrative authority to the campuses since 1958 (See Office of the President, University of California, 1965a, 1965b; Regents of the University of California, 1965). Chancellors of individual campuses were officially encouraged to decentralize administration within campuses as well. However, there is no general agreement, or even understanding, about the purposes, the effects, or even the extent of the "decentralization" that has occurred.

A second issue is closely related. Official statements of university "systems" often emphasize the blend of "unity and diversity" which is sought in the system's operations.[5] Some faculty members object that "unity" in this context means uniformity of administratively imposed regulations, across circumstances so diverse that they cannot fairly be lumped under a single rule (see Kornhauser, et al., 1965:1). It is generally conceded that there are some areas in which uniformity is desirable throughout a university. But there is no clear agreement on *what* matters should be uniform, and why.

The University of California, for example, has uniform personnel policies, salary scales, student admission policies, broad student-conduct policies, and so on. But its campuses are free (within limits) to vary their internal organizational forms, to implement broad student-conduct policies with locally tailored regulations, to exercise some discretion in admission when too many qualified students apply, etc.

In the area of substantive academic programs, the campuses are officially encouraged to develop diversity systematically, so that complementary courses, degree programs, approaches to subject matter, and faculty competences will be offered the people of the State by various parts of the University. This requirement of complementarity, itself, is seen as a burdensome restriction on occasion: campus leaders often wish to develop a program duplicated nearby because it is expected to have great demand in the future, because it seems important for a well-rounded campus offering, because of special opportunities to acquire facilities or hire distinguished faculty—or simply because the program is prestigious. Some "system" administrators therefore argue that central restraints are necessary to *discourage* uniformity, which otherwise develops "spontaneously" among the campuses serving a single state or locality.

These problems gain importance as parts of a broader pattern in today's public higher education. Recent years have seen a considerable growth in the degree of statewide "coordination" (i.e., administrative control) of budget requests, admission policies, programs, and other aspects of public colleges and universities. How much coordination should be required among institutions, how this coordination should be accomplished, and what values are served or sacrificed, are issues of immediate and practical consequence in almost every state. But decisions have proceeded on the basis of comparatively little research, and on necessarily inadequate consideration of the fundamental issues at stake (See McConnell, 1962; Glenny, 1959; Brown, 1965; Paltridge, 1968).

The evolution and blending of "single" universities and intercampus "systems" of control need fuller description in their own right. We need to go beyond descriptions to examine at a very specific level the values, activities and interests at stake in each major decision for uniformity or diversity of programs or policies. Moreover, we need careful empirical inquiries into the relation of sameness and difference to central and local determination on particular issues. Like many others in social science, these questions are important both for our basic knowledge and for practical decisions about organizational life.

UNIVERSITY AIMS AND THEIR ORGANIZATIONAL EMBODIMENT

A related but separable set of issues arises if one focuses on the institutional roles, purposes, or functions of the university, rather than its organizational forms.

Goal definition: problems and consequences. Like their authority structure, universities' goals—formal and informal—tend to lack either clear, specific referents or generally shared meaning (compare Corson, 1960: 19–22; Gross, 1968). The rhetoric of university educators generally runs to quite abstract formulations, and tends to include functions or activities not specified in legal documents. Clark Kerr (1963: 38) in his much-discussed *Uses of the University,* states the goals of universities thus:

> The ends are already given—the preservation of the eternal truths, the creation of new knowledge, the improvement of service wherever truth and knowledge of high order may serve the needs of man. The ends are there; the means must be ever improved in a competitive dynamic environment. There is no single "end" to be discovered; there are several ends and many groups to be served.

Many other formulations have been suggested. Some scholars would add "responsibility for fostering good taste and human understanding," or would emphasize "enhancement of such qualities as independence of judgment, critical thinking, creativity, freedom from irrational prejudice," and the like (See Sanford, 1962: 817, 970). At such a level of abstraction, there are obvious difficulties in determining the "fundamental purposes of a university or the relative importance of different activities in contributing to those purposes" (See Caplow and McGee, 1958: 4). In other words, the *operational* definition of these abstract ends in terms of concrete activities by persons is not easy.

The abstract character of statements about university goals produces much complex rhetoric in current campus confrontations, especially when university functions are used to legitimize specific rules of conduct or structures of governance. In a time of conflict, grand abstractions may be given whatever meanings the combatants find useful at the moment. This has led some students cynically to conclude that only power-relations count in organization life, at least where rather specific values are not shared implicitly, and that formal goals or ideals only serve to rationalize preexisting interests. Still, all sides in campus disputes often invoke ideals or goals or missions of the university in support of their own positions—usually with apparent sincerity.

As with formal and informal structures, students of social organization have wrestled for some years to clarify the relations between explicit and implicit goals, including those of the total organization, its subgroups, and its individual members. Some have declared it a central function of leadership to mobilize a working consensus about a set of institutional goals (See Selznick, 1957: 149). In the modern university, evidently, this is a job that takes some doing, and the problem deserves much further study.

A part of the problem, as the term "multiversity" implies, is that the goals of today's large institution are multiple in almost any formulation, even an abstract one. One common triad is "teaching, research, and public service." It usually is assumed that these functions complement and assist one another, or this is asserted because all depend upon specialized, esoteric knowledge. The fact that each function competes with the others for scarce resources and time would seem undeniable, but this is usually played down in official rhetoric. Again some persons argue today that performance of each function could be improved by the familiar device of a further division of labor.[6] Others emphasize that research and teaching are intimately related. Similarly, many present-day critics urge that teaching be given more reward and emphasis in universities, relative to research and expert consulting. The reply usually is made that good teaching is undefinable, that academic freedom forbids tampering with what goes on in the individual teacher's classroom, or that teaching is overemphasized (without notable excellence) in most undergraduate institutions in this country (See Clark, 1965: 301; Etzioni, 1964: 85).

These issues cannot be resolved solely by organizational analysis, obviously. Difficult questions about human learning alone pose great obstacles in any discussion of teaching. But some important organizational problems are involved: What is the actual distribution of activities, in the modern multiversity faculty, among the diverse goals that the institution espouses? What special interests of status groups inside and outside the university are served by the present intermixture and lack of concreteness in university goals? Whose special interests are slighted? Why is there no organized "profession" of advanced teaching to support that function in the university, as specialized research is supported by the associations of scholars in each academic discipline? How well do the special values shared by university intellectuals harmonize with the purposes of teaching young minds? With the demands of organized research or expert consultation, tailored to the requirements of industrial or governmental organizations? (See Kornhauser, 1962; Barber, 1962: 178ff.)

More broadly, better analysis is needed of the uses of ambiguity in organizational goals. Some educators see the broad umbrella of abstractions under which universities operate as a major safeguard of substantive relevance, creative innovation, and adaptability to changed circumstances. Within such a house, the argument runs, many mansions may rise. And the pragmatic criterion of "what works" is a better one for intellectual activities than any formally specifiable definition to which academic life might be made to conform. Some may see the modern university becoming, like the medieval Church, all things to all men. If that happens, in one view, it will be in response to "real" and legitimate needs of society—better met by creative intellectuals on university faculties than by many another, more easily "accountable," organization.

Such issues go to the heart of organizational life in the university, invoking the essential problems inherent in (a) its concern for new and fundamental knowledge, (b) its complex relation to the society which provides its resources and is affected by the results, and (c) the relation of the abstractions by which it lives to the structures of power and authority on which so much attention is focused today. Much further analysis may be necessary before useful empirical questions can be posed. But these issues should not be left by scholars solely to popular discussion and personal opinion.

A "protest industry"? Beyond such general questions about formal goals lie issues of specific—often implicit—purposes with which the institution is involved. By all odds the most troubling of these is the function of keeping alive social dissent and criticism.

It is often said that a major purpose of the university in a free society is criticism of that society for its own improvement. In the view of some educators, this means more than the provision of a "market place" for ideas. It means more than a haven for "academic" research by faculty of certified "competence." On the other hand, it does not mean indoctrination in a specific ideology, subversive or otherwise. Instead, it means the systematic education of both students and faculty in skills of intellectual analysis and criticism, which are taken as central not only to human individuality but to betterment of the common lot of mankind.

In this view every society, no matter how benign, has its injustice and corruption and misuses of power. Any university worth its keep, therefore, must create dissatisfaction with society in the very process of helping students to think independently. It does this when it makes them aware of men's aspirations throughout history, and when it sharpens their intellectual capacities to distinguish practice and principle, deeds and promises, consistency and contradiction. Wherever students progress through higher learning complacently acceptive of society as they find it, so the argument runs, just there has the university failed of its highest purpose.

A university fulfilling that purpose must necessarily be seen by much of its society as a seedbed of dissent and challenge—sometimes to that society's most cherished institutions (See Hutchins, 1956: 101–166). To tolerate that seedbed in its midst, a society must be deeply convinced of the value of its criticism, either against injustices in the present or for the sake of future generations in a rapidly changing world.[7] Thus the university compounds the social dangers inherent in free speech: it teaches intelligent youths how to make use of speech to powerful effect, by putting them in contact with the skills of logic and criticism and the materials of human history. The university produces its own dissent—and then both the society and the university must somehow live with it.

Student leaders today feel specially qualified to see the hypocrisy and contradictions in present society—and in the modern multiversity. But their challenges to university policies emphasize connections with the evils of society generally. They believe that the typical university today neglects education in understanding, analysis, and criticism, in favor of routine "requirements"—designed as preparation for over-professionalized graduate schools, which will train them as submissive "manpower" for industry and government. They believe that their education in independent thought has come largely from extracurricular sources.

Students active in recent protests have tended to emphasize the university's function of social criticism—but they see students as its only social base in the academic world. In their view, most faculty members and administrators alike have been coopted into a "system" of economic rewards and social restraints that stifles their recognition of manifest contradictions in current American society. These students see themselves and their fellows as "outside" this system. (This also is their major link with members of economic and ethnic minorities.) They are therefore peculiarly able to see and declare "the system's" pervasive and malignant effects. In other words, the students know that their conclusions from the exposure to higher learning differ from those of most of the "maturer" intellectuals in the university. But they believe the reasons do "maturity" little credit.

Many university scholars would, of course, deny the *legitimacy* of a university "function" as outlined here. For example, it is often said that universities must (and most presumably do) teach "responsible" restraint in the *expression* of social criticism, as well as skill in the use of critical intelligence. Some faculty members emphasize the affirmative "responsibility" of scholars to demand respect for fact, and careful attention to the evidence for assertions, in all the utterances of a university's members. But these are largely normative arguments, which do not deny the logic of events. Many of the persons on university campuses today would agree that student protests have involved considerable intellectual content, and that skills of analysis and criticism are abundantly employed by the movement's leaders. Few, after the past years' crises, would deny that this process has helped to create problems for universities.

It also should be clear that the view described here does not imply that dissent fostered by university education is benign for a particular society. Instead, the argument suggests that the maintenance of a "true" university would be highly destructive for some societies—especially those having most to fear from the critical use of sharpened intelligence. Prominent among them we would expect to find societies with the widest gaps between the ideals espoused and their pursuit in practice, the most damaging internal contradictions to be discovered. Such gaps, in turn, some would insist, can be the product of high aspirations and well-intentioned but modest performance, as much as of hypocrisy and conspiracy among those who hold the balance of social power.

At the moment, however, our focus is the university: the problems created for an organization when it produces its own dissent. If this effect of university education has any empirical validity today, then we would do well to examine the special imperatives it may produce. For example, an organization which tolerates or encourages unrestricted critical intelligence within it may have to meet especially high standards of consistency between principle and practice, if it is to avoid internal conflict. Alternatively, it may have to depend for its stability on low levels of moral concern among those whose intelligence has been sharpened. The much discussed political apathy of most U.S. students, even today, may be such a condition. It may need to provide its members with incentives (or other good reasons) to ignore the injustices that their intelligence tells them exist. It may have to teach them, for example, that imperfections exist everywhere, and suggest they always seem exaggerated to young people just learning to criticize. It may have to keep trainees in a special subordinate status (i.e., "student"), where criticism of society or the institution are defined as illegitimate until certified "competent." Or there may be other means to reasonable stability in such an organization.

Whatever the answers to possibilities such as these, it is suggested that analysis of this university function in modern society needs far more attention than it has received. Such analysis should lead to, and be refined by, empirical observations of university student protests.

Organizational imperatives, educational goals. Every formal organization is at once an "economy" and a group of interacting persons.[8] As an economy, it must assemble resources (usually money, material goods, and human talents); these must be allocated to specific functions and the activities of individuals and groups, along with supervisory authority and responsibility for performance. The typical problems here are adequacy of support and operating efficiency—the securing of "enough" resources, and creation of a pattern of allocation which makes "optimum" use of those resources in pursuit of the organization's stated objectives. As interacting persons, however, the organization's "members" always vie with one another and with the outside "publics" which supply its resources, for the operational definition of the goals. Thus "pursuit" of the goals takes on concrete meaning through the activities actually performed in its name.

In addition to stated goals, a formal organization usually has some formally specified sources of economic support—e.g., the dues of members or the stock-purchases of shareholders—and some formal structure of accountability to those sources for the proper performance of its functions. It may also have a more or less specific internal structure of authority, related both to goals and to support. In the organizational pattern which dominates the U.S. university scene, goals typically are quite vaguely defined; thus great freedom is left for the play of informal social and economic forces on their operational definition. As we have seen, the internal authority-structure often is ill-defined in formal terms. Now we focus on the fact that the formal accountability-relation to sources of support also is purposely blurred in the U.S. university, and in its turn is modified in ambiguous ways by traditions and other informal forces.

In the usual rhetoric of current American academic life, the lay governing board only technically wields "ultimate" authority over all internal operations. It is expected to function primarily as a "buffer" between the university and the external community.[9] "Restraint" is expected of the board on internal matters generally. Core areas such as degree requirements, content of courses, and instructional methods are supposed to be left almost solely to the assembled faculties.

In fact, this may not be the modal pattern. But it is said to prevail in the "best" universities (see Lazarsfeld and Thielens, 1958: 178–180), is given lip service in many more, and is held as an ideal in most. In this highly ambiguous situation, the opportunity for informal variations in patterns of actual influence by governing boards and outside support-sources is great. Also, certain functional areas have been progressively released from operational control by faculties and assigned to administrative specialists—e.g., admission standards, student discipline, and "student personnel services" generally (see Wilson, 1961: 3). As a result, the impact of external forces on these areas is thought by many to have increased, both through the "recommendations" of governing-board members and by means of outside "heat" brought directly on administrative officers.

Besides ambiguity of goals and accountability-relations, universities have other special characteristics. In several ways, the university is a kind of limiting case of relations between social organizations and their sources of economic support.

Arguably, the university's central goals imply special requirements: first, for freedom of internal determination. For example, the tradition of "academic freedom" has grown up to guard intellectual inquiry and discussion against the imposition of current orthodoxy from without. Even within the university, the importance of specialized expertise has necessitated leaving review of a professor's performance largely in the hands of a few colleagues, who alone are thought to have the knowledge necessary for meaningful judgments. Many faculty and students have urged the importance of an atmosphere of "openness" to all study and expression for students as well as faculty members. Second, university goals may require special qualities in the personal interactions among its participants, and a special community of values. Teaching, it would seem, has its inescapably personal dimensions, especially if it is to involve more than the transmission of bare "facts" about the conclusions of past research. A community of teachers and learners who are involved with the frontiers of knowledge and of meaning may be dependent for its internal stability upon some greater sharing of values than today's multiversity contemplates. Third, the increasing importance of formal intellectual training for effective political expression may suggest special needs for universities to maintain relatively more democratic, less hierarchically directed forms of governance than might be permitted to other organizations.

Universities' functions also are widely acknowledged to be of increasing importance to the rest of society. The tasks of manpower training for a complicated economy, and of research which undergirds technological advance, both are largely university monopolies, despite marginal efforts in government and industry. The economic growth of a society and the economic opportunities equally depend on these functions today, even in the short run. In noneconomic terms, the survival of historical perspective and traditions of free thought and criticism are also largely dependent on universities' activities. Thus the day of the university's isolation as an "ivory tower" probably is gone forever. Intensive interaction with the outside world is now inescapable.

Finally, as was suggested, earlier universities may tend inherently to produce critical dissent from the imperfections of present society. Thus universities demand special tolerance from those who must support their continuance, but who are largely satisfied with society as it is.

Such analysis suggests that our understanding both of universities and of organizations generally could profit from greater attention to universities' ways of getting support, responding to the accompanying pressures, and accommodating those pressures by internal adjustments. Even very broad, analytic comparisons of university patterns with those of business corporations, voluntary associations, government agencies, and other types of formal and informal organization should be quite revealing (See Weiss, 1965).

In addition, however, much more descriptive information is needed about the ways that universities and other groups actually do respond to their needs for outside support. For example, what are the typical modes of justifying requests for various types of support—in terms of specific services or general social functions, short-range or long-range benefits, etc.? How, in fact, do university representatives explain to donors and legislators the need for both generous support and substantial autonomy? Are there trends in the level of specificity and the substantive content of these explanations? What effects are these trends likely to have on the allocation of resources to the various university activities, such as teaching vs. research, graduate vs. undergraduate education, science vs. the humanities? How are these trends related to changes in external types of pressure, such as growing industrial demands for applied research and relevantly trained manpower, or the device of employing specialized program analysts in government fiscal agencies?

Official rhetoric tends to deny any but the most distant relation between support and internal goal-definition. Verification of this fact would itself be of considerable theoretical interest. But reexamination of this issue, by closer study of the informal processes involved, seems very much indicated today in any case.

In approaching this set of problems, much more systematic attention should be given to the roles of university administrators and trustees. Recent crises have created new interest in the "marginal" roles of administrators and governing board members in "mediating" between the values and demands of those inside and those outside the university (See Kerr, 1963: 29–41). The legal authority of the governing board and the breadth of discretion and control allowed to administrators have been openly challenged by students, and now are being subjected to new scrutiny by faculty members, government officials, and private citizens.

It has again become apparent that there is little but rough anecdotal information, and even less agreement, on how administrators and regents do, in fact, perform their functions, or what those functions are thought to be. For example, there is no agreement on the necessity for administrators to have supervisory authority; students have argued that administrators should perform only "caretaking" and facilitative roles for students and faculty members.[10] Students have repeatedly charged that Boards of Control act not as "buffers" against outside pressures, but as agents of outside pressure groups, partly by embodying their values and partly by yielding to fears of their withdrawn support (compare Veblen, 1935 and Metzger, 1961: 139–193). These charges are answered by assertions that administrative authority is functionally necessary to university goals, and that statesmanlike weighing of legitimate but competing values characterizes regents' and administrators' exercise of their broad discretion.

Research looking behind such arguments might take the following approaches:

(1) The evolution of administrative functions in universities might be traced systematically: What has led to the growth of administrative roles in academe? [11] How have differentiations of function changed administrators'

duties and authority? For example, are administrators being increasingly forced into exclusive concern with external university relations (See Clark, 1961: 297)? Are administrators gaining more control over some areas inside the university, and losing control over others? What are the backgrounds and training of persons recruited to administrative roles today, as compared with earlier decades?

(2) The strains inherent in current academic-administrative roles might be explored further: What strains are produced by the responsibility to balance needs for university "self-government" with outside demands for accountability? By responsibility for regulating the conduct of intelligent students, whose skills of analysis and criticism are being newly awakened and refined? By hierarchical authority over faculty members—who combine great skill at criticism with largely antiauthoritarian values, distaste for administrative and political problems, and primary attachments to specialized academic disciplines?

(3) Much more study might be made of the administrative subculture: How do administrators attempt to resolve their role strains by patterned beliefs and attitudes about university life? What systematic differences of viewpoint are discernible between teaching faculty and administrative officials on such questions as the meaning and relative importance of specific university goals? On the need for hierarchic authority? On the criteria for allocating resources among university activities? On the legitimacy of various pressures from outside, which seek to mold university functions? Are these differences related to other differences of basic value-orientation, between academics who are and are not recruited to administrative positions? Are such differences associated with long tenure in positions of coordinative responsibility generally (e.g., faculty committee service, departmental chairmanships, research institute directorships)? Are some positions associated with "nonfaculty" attitudes more than others—e.g., external-relations roles, or those requiring coordination among academic disciplines?

(4) Some of these questions might be adapted for members of university governing boards. Particular attention might be given here to attitudes about the legitimacy of demands for internal autonomy as against the interests and concerns of parents, taxpayers, and industrial or commercial groups. Still further extension of the inquiry, which might be of considerable interest, would sample opinions of general population groups about why a university should be given public support, and what kinds of controls should be imposed upon it.

Recent years have brought us some fascinating anecdotal accounts and preliminary analyses of administrative roles and their difficulties by present and former university presidents (See Kerr, 1963; Dodds, 1962; Stoke, 1959). These books are rich sources of insights and of questions for further study. But they are beginnings. The need and the opportunity both are great for much more analysis and systematic observation of university organization and administration.

University Governance by Rules:
Socio-legal Issues

Recent student protests have given impetus to an already growing scholarly enterprise: the study of universities as "private governments." Along with a general development of administrative law, there is today a developing body of legal and scholarly opinion that views the large, complex administrative structures of formally "autonomous" or "private" organizations (e.g., business corporations, labor unions, universities, etc.) as wielding "governmental" powers and carrying out governmental functions, which require that traditional problems of government be considered in assessing the rights and obligations within them (See, among others, Miller, 1959). Among the principal problems that arise are the scope and bases of administrative discretion, the applicability of "due process" traditions to administration, and the character and sources of administrative authority. Study of such problems requires an intermixture of legal and sociological perspectives. Issues in each of these problem areas are discussed below, along with problems concerning the effectiveness of university "legal" action and the bases of demands for freedom on the campus.

THE SCOPE AND BASES OF ADMINISTRATIVE DISCRETION

Since the Berkeley Free Speech Movement, student protesters have strenuously objected to the enforcement of specific on-campus conduct rules by their universities. They also have taken strong stands against the broad character of university rules, especially their generality and the broad discretion which they lodge in administrative officials. The FSM argued that the size and impersonality of the modern university, the apparent desire of administrators to preserve order at the expense of important freedoms, and the manifest political pressures from the outside community made University of California officials unable to use discretion fairly in student disciplinary matters. It demanded that constitutional standards of specificity and clarity be applied to University rules, and urged that jurisdiction over disciplinary cases involving political expression or activity be lodged in a committee of faculty members. On November 20, 1964, the Regents approved President Clark Kerr's recommendation:

> That rules and regulations be made more clear and specific and thus, incidentally and regrettably more detailed and legalistic; and explicit penalties, where possible, be set forth for specific violations [Lipset and Wolin, 1965: 155].

Subsequent events resulted in University-wide rules' being kept broad and general, with authority or direction to the individual Chancellors to implement them with more specific regulations. A greater range and diversity of penalties was included in the President's rules of July 1, 1965 (See University of California, 1965: 11–12).

Even at the campus level, however, it has been argued that specificity and detail in rules is inappropriate to a university.[12] Such detail destroys much of the flexibility necessary for judgmental application of rules to diverse and unforeseen circumstances, it is said. Moreover, once created, rules are troublesome and time-consuming to change. Yet the students of later years may find them wholly unsuitable to the times.

Social bases of "parental" discretion. These complaints find parallels in scholarly discussions of the social context of developing legal forms. For example, one focus of student complaint elsewhere for some years now has been the legal doctrine that university authorities stand *in loco parentis*—a piece of judicial imagery that has allowed courts to approve the broadest kinds of discretionary rulings by university and college officials in student disciplinary matters. Some modifications of this doctrine now appear in the cases, and some judges have declared the doctrine dead.[13] What theories are being substituted?

Social bases for such changes have been suggested: How important was the Southern civil rights movement in producing judicially imposed restraints which have modified the "parental" discretion of university administrators? As full-time administrative officials, rather than teaching faculty members, increasingly impose student discipline, how is the tenability of the "parental" analogy affected? What is the effect on the analogy of modern universities' great size, complexity, and impersonality? How relevant is the increased number of university students aged 21 years and over, with adult experience and responsibility for their own affairs? How relevant is the heightened importance of a university education for economic and professional opportunity, or the military obligation expected of 18-year-olds? What is the significance of long-term changes in universities' social functions—e.g., from general moral and cultural conditioning for a social and economic elite to more specific vocational and professional training for members of diverse social classes? Are judges or university officials more socially "competent" to establish the rights of students against universities' "institutional" interests in survival, economic prosperity, and general order? (See Levine, 1963: 1392–1395.) How have such social factors affected legal changes in the discretion allowed administrative officials of other organizations besides universities?

Restraints in the task-committed organization. The concerns of university administrators over "legalism" and inflexible, time-consuming procedural mechanisms also have a foundation in socio-legal literature. Like most other "private governments," the university is an organization charged with performance of a special function for society. Its main functions—the advanced education of growing sectors of the population, and the discovery and dissemination of new knowledge—are complex and demanding tasks which defy easy routinization and require flexible judgments adapted to changing circumstances. Fuller (1964: 171–175) has pointed to the difficulty with which judicial organs assess the judgments of "marginal utility" required in the management of complex enterprises.

In addition, Max Weber long ago pointed out that the growth of "legal-rational" regulation in human affairs carried with it disadvantages for the handling of particular cases. He saw that the growing "formality" of Western European law, with bureaucracy as the "pure" form of its administration, sacrificed "substantive rationality" in specific cases for the "legal certainty" which detailed and unambiguous rules make possible.

Thus basic, not illusory, dilemmas are posed by current campus disputes over administrative "arbitrariness" and student "legalism." It would appear that the modern university provides a rich social laboratory for the study of socio-legal issues in this area.

"Due process" in the university. The desire to restrain university administrators' discretion early led student protest leaders to call not only for more clear and specific rules but also for a series of procedural safeguards in disciplinary cases. These safeguards they grouped under the general rubric of "due process," as represented in the Anglo-American legal tradition.

Within that broad rubric, student leaders at various times have demanded the following guarantees: (1) a preexistent, "impartial" faculty tribunal, appointed independent of the administration, to have final authority over student discipline; (2) a deliberate and open hearing before provisional sanctions are imposed on students charged with violations; (3) prohibition of *ex parte* communications to or from the hearing committee; (4) adequate notice in writing of an alleged violation and scheduled hearing; (5) a clear statement of charges to the accused; (6) no selective or exemplary enforcement of rules (e.g., against leaders of a protest movement); (7) trial before a jury of one's peers; (8) a clear statement of the tribunal's jurisdiction (e.g., over matters concerning political expression or not); (9) charges based on preexistent rules that are specific enough to allow the accused's prior knowledge of his guilt, and are reasonably related to university purposes; (10) an opportunity to challenge the bases of rules which one is charged with violating; (11) suspension of university discipline while legal proceedings are pending on related charges, so as to avoid "double jeopardy" or "self-incrimination"; (12) no "bullying" by university counsel to admit the validity of charges; (13) the right to confront one's accusers; (14) the right to present evidence on one's behalf and to call and cross-examine witnesses; (15) counsel of one's own choosing at the hearing; (16) committee findings of fact and rulings in writing; (17) penalties reasonably related to the gravity of the offense; and (18) no subjection to "trial" on the unsupported testimony of a single administrative official.

In an immediate and practical sense, these demands are the heart of the matter: they are attempts to apply strong Anglo-American legal traditions directly to the restraint of administrative actions. At least one committee of university law professors has pointed out that, for the want of "those institutional and procedural safeguards that are available to a defendant in a criminal court of law," the U.S. Supreme Court "has denied to administrative tribunals and other nonjudicial bodies certain powers to regulate the content of expression that have been given to the courts" (Lipset and Wolin, 19: 278). However, some university attorneys have denounced student "due process" demands as "pseudo-legalism"; other officials have simply declared them unworkable and undesirably "adversary" in character for a university setting.[14] More importantly, legal scholars have pointed out that no single, universal set of procedural safeguards is required by the courts in the name of due process; instead, the procedures allowed vary widely with the nature of the case. In this connection, some faculty members have proposed simpler, "fair hearing" standards for university use in student discipline.

Thus disagreements about the proper scope of "due process" in university disciplinary proceedings remain. Research by legal scholars already has been done on this subject (See *Harvard Law Review,* 1968; Van Alstyne, 1965; Levine, 1963; *California Law Review,* 1966; *Denver Law Journal,* 1968). However, it may not be amiss to suggest some questions which deserve further study. For example:

What is the pattern of procedural restraints on administrative disciplinary action in U.S. universities? How closely does this pattern follow the requirements laid down in U.S. legal precedent (a) for courts and (b) for administrative tribunals other than those of universities? What elements of "due process" have been required of universities by courts in the past?

What are the specific purposes of each major "due process" requirement imposed in the U.S. legal tradition, and how applicable is each to the university setting? Are some procedural restraints more important than others, for students in the large university? Are some less burdensome on university officials? What specific interests and values would be sacrificed if universities' discipline were made to conform more closely to legal standards of due process?

Finally: Are there changing social conditions which alter the relevance of "due process" restraints to university procedures? How relevant are the procedures typically used in determining the dismissal of a university faculty member?

"Legality" in the university. Beyond the immediate and practical issues of specific restraints in university settings, recent student protests have raised more general questions about the nature of authority. These protests provide a shocking reminder that authority depends on consent—consent which may be withdrawn at any time, with dramatic consequences for all concerned. When this occurs on a large scale in a university, that community is faced with some of the difficult questions which have been faced by the society at large since mass "civil disobedience" gained currency as a means of social protest. The sociolegal questions involved reach close to the core of all "legal" systems.

Authority is taken to mean many things. One persuasive view sees authority as a relation between two persons which influences one of them to accept a decision of the other without "deliberation," or "critical review" of its validity. Thus the acceptance of another's authority is said to involve a "suspension of judgment" in deference to that of the other person (See Simon, 1957: 125–128). T. D. Weldon (1958: 35) has suggested this typically involves a presumption that the person exercising authority "could produce reasons, if challenged," and that these reasons would satisfy us that the decision asserted was appropriate. Thus we do *not* challenge the "authoritative" person's decision—except in the unusual case, when the tenuousness of the relation is revealed. In such a terminology, *power* (e.g., physical force) may be employed without the acquiescence of its subject, but *authority* refers to a relationship which depends primarily on characteristics which the subordinate imputes to the authority-wielder. Fear of the power he can invoke may be one of those characteristics; citizens may obey laws at times solely for fear of physical arrest and detention. But such incentives are poor substitutes for belief by the governed that those who govern them do so by "right"—by authority which is "legitimate." All reasonably stable societies, Max Weber (1961: 4) argued, depend on such beliefs.

Building on such conceptions, Selznick and others have suggested the emergence in Western society of a tradition of "legality," under which all *exercise* of authority is seen as restrained by the need of reasoned justification. Selznick (1969) argues that any system of "governance by rules" which is to be stable and effective must do more than establish its basic "legitimacy," as "right" authority *in general*. It must also develop patterns of criticism and justification for specific official *acts*. These patterns must—upon proper challenge—allow public examination of the reasons for particular rules and applications, in light of the principles which give the system and its officials their legitimacy.

Recent events indicate that study of the origins, implications, and limits of "legality" in the complex modern university holds many opportunities for productive scholarship. As before, closer analysis is the first need. For example: (1) The university has a strong tradition of consensual governance (Clark, 1961), and an inherent concern for exploring the reasons, assumptions, and principles of validation behind any assertion. These facts suggest that universities should have well-developed systems of reasoned restraint on the arbitrary use of authority. However, modern universities are also "formal" organizations, chartered by the state for the "efficient" achievement of special purposes upon the regular allocation of public funds. This fact has tended to produce a hierarchic administrative structure, and demands for central responsiveness to the public's view of those functions (see Gallagher, 1965). (2) There is growing emphasis on a "counter-principle" of authority that operates in the university, based on certified expertise. These facts have received attention primarily as illustrating one source of restraint on *bureaucratic* authority (see Blau and Scott, 1962: 35–36; Etzioni, 1964: 76). However, more attention is due the fact that the expert's authority itself is very hard to restrain "reasonably" without destroying its value altogether. (3) In the past, an open paternalism has been assumed to be necessary in the relations of both faculty members and administrators with university students. This necessity is now being subjected to strong challenges in the administrative sphere—albeit with uncertain success. Even murkier questions concerning the authority of teacher over student remain largely unexplored in today's university, and these deserve considerable attention soon. (4) Finally, the university is a complex of distinct status groups, each with its own peculiar—but ambiguous and overlapping—aspirations, values, spheres of authority, and views on the uses of "law." The effects of their interplay on the development of "legal" forms of university governance has yet to be adequately described.

Thus issues concerning "legality" in the modern university are not simple. A number of questions suggest themselves: Why has the U.S. university historically not developed more systematic, reasoned justification for its rules? Do U.S. universities differ in this regard from those of other cultures? From other "private governments"? What social conditions foster the growth of incipient "legal" systems within "non-governmental" organizations? What problems are inherent in any movement toward "legality" as an ideal of university governance? What kinds of reasons are given today by university authorities to justify official, discretionary restrictions on the conduct of university members? Are there trends in the kinds of reasons given? If so, what are their directions? What trends are observable in the bases of student challenges to university officials' actions?

Clearly, open challenges to university rules, such as have occurred at U.S. universities in the recent past, offer a prime opportunity for study of issues such as these. Parallels in other cultures and eras should not be overlooked for the important perspective they can provide on our own place and time.[15]

The legitimacy of university administration. A closely related "sociolegal" approach begins with a different focal point: the "legitimacy" ascribed to authority-relations whose continuation is accepted. Recent student protests have involved more than objections to particular university restrictions on speech and activity, and more than open refusal to obey the specific rules being contested. Protest leaders explicitly deny the basic legitimacy of universities' unqualified administrative authority over students' conduct. By words and symbolic acts of civil disobedience students have challenged *both* specific "abuses" of authority *and* the basic impropriety of a university's having rules made and enforced solely by administrators and governing boards.

For example, students may assert that specific administrators have shown "arbitrariness" by refusing to continue discussions of the reasons for disputed rules. This charge suggests only changes in behavior, or perhaps at most the unfitness of specific persons. But they may also urge that a pattern of past restrictions reveals a conscious design among administrators and board members to stifle student political expression. This charge suggests more widespread misfeasance, and possibly a conspiracy to violate a public trust. It may be argued that persons in administrative positions generally are too subject to political pressure to deal fairly with questions of political expression, and that an independent committee of faculty members should have final authority in such matters. It may be said that only students can represent students' legitimate interests adequately, so that students must have voting membership in university planning councils. It is contended by some groups that students have certain rights which no agency can legitimately grant or deny. A number of student leaders have demanded that "negotiation" or "collective bargaining" by students with university authorities replace the "advisory" consultation generally prevalent at present.

Responding to such attacks, university authorities refer to state laws, under which "ultimate authority" is vested in governing boards by "the people" of the state. Appeal is made to the advantages of a lay governing board for separation of university life from direct political intervention by government and party officials. The necessity for university authorities to enforce "law and order" against rule violators is asserted as a condition of university "self-government." The reasonableness, tolerance, decency, and good will of university officials are asserted, and called upon as evidence that their discretion is appropriate in a society where "the rule of law" protects rights amid great ideological diversity.

The principles by which authority gains legitimacy among its subordinates have been discussed by a number of social and political thinkers (Weber, 1947; Ferrero, 1942; Arendt, 1958; Lipset, 1963). Max Weber's well-known "types" of authority (traditional, charismatic, and legal-rational) are based on the principles which make each type seem "right" to the people whose consent must be engendered. Weber was interested in principles applicable not only to explicitly "political" states but to all "corporate groups." He emphasized the emergence of legal-rational legitimacy in Western society (Bendix, 1960: 291–416). In the same vein, Selznick has suggested that some principles of legitimacy are more conducive than others to the development of what he calls "legality." At a very general level, for example, a principle that treats authority as a rational means to specified ends is more conducive to reasoned justification of specific rules than one that accepts history (tradition) as its own justification (Selznick, 1968: 50–59). More specifically, if legitimacy is attached to unfettered discretion in the hands of "duly constituted" administrative officials, there is little room for reasoned dialogue over specific rules. By contrast, if structures of rules are legitimized by reference to values shared among the members of an organization, this keeps open the possibility of reasoned criticism of the rule structure and particular rules within it.

If such considerations are taken as important for universities and other "private governments," a number of significant questions arise which are relevant to the recent student protests. For example: What principles are put forward to "legitimize" the present structure of authority in U.S. universities? Are these principles well-accepted by the different status groups within the university, such as faculty, students, and professional research staffs? What are the typical grounds of challenge to administrative, regental, or faculty authority? What are the implications of specific legitimating principles for the development of stable university rule-systems? How explicit, and how widely accepted, are the principles used to justify specific university rules, or the character of a university's rule-system? How do the reasons given for particular official rules and acts affect popular acceptance of an administrative regime's legitimacy? If a specific administrative structure "loses" legitimacy with many persons in a university, what consequences are to be expected? How is administrative legitimacy reestablished, once it has been seriously questioned?

Such questions imply a thorough look at universities as "private governments." They suggest a view of the university as a complex political-legal system, whose officials and administrative arrangements depend for their effectiveness in part upon acceptance by subordinates as well as superiors. Campus events since the mid-1960s would seem to lend much urgency to such an approach.

THE EFFECTIVENESS OF UNIVERSITY "LEGAL" ACTION

The uses and limits of formal law-enforcement as a means of social control are matters of concern today in many areas of society. One complex and puzzling set of questions surrounds the increased use of mass civil disobedience as a form of social protest, and the responses to it. These problems cannot be discussed in depth here, but a number of issues especially relevant to the university context may be briefly suggested.

In the view of some scholars, some affirmative goals, such as the maintenance of "responsibility" in public speech and expression, cannot be enforced effectively by formal rules. These scholars believe that, if such goals are to be attained in a community, they must be supported by values shared widely among the community's members, and reinforced by informal respect accorded those who uphold the values in question. Attempts to create "higher" standards of expression by legislation and police action, it is said, usually result only in equating "higher" with "more restrictive."

In this view, the activity of rule-enforcement generally places a university's officials in a punitive, restrictive posture. This inevitably does violence to the development of the intellectual community which universities seek, and competes with attempts to help students evolve their own independent and coherent codes of self-directed conduct. Thus, while some rules of student conduct may always be necessary, they should be minimized as far as possible, and should be left largely to the law-enforcement agencies which are better equipped to perform them. The university should avoid assuming elaborate law-enforcement functions, particularly in regard to events which are of primary concern to the community at large rather than to the distinctive goals of academic life. Restrictive rules should be avoided especially in the area of speech and expression, this view argues—first, because of expression's close relation to the university's goals of free inquiry and discussion; second, because of the many difficult and ambiguous judgments which have plagued the courts themselves in dealing with the basic constitutional liberties involved. If the university thus "gets out of the law-enforcement business" as much as possible, it is argued, the problem of student civil disobedience also is reduced. The occasions for violation or enforcement, the distance between administrators and students, and the confrontations of principle which rally students around protest leaders all are minimized.

By contrast, some university officials and faculty members continue to feel that the university has a function and duty, along with its other purposes, to uphold affirmatively the principle of respect for "law and order" in general. They believe that the minimal order necessary for normal university functions, and for the protection of involuntary audiences from a tyrannous few, requires the university to accept responsibility for some restraints on speech and expression. These restraints may even legitimately involve matters of content, some believe, and if established they must be rigorously enforced. Finally, many feel that a university's internal order is necessary to safeguard university "self-government" from outside intervention, which in turn is a precondition to the fulfillment of university goals. Thus it is felt that overt student disobedience of university rules, no matter what its intent or origins, cannot long be tolerated.

More study seems indicated on these underlying questions: Are there inherent limits to what can be accomplished by enforcing formal rules of human conduct? (See Pound, 1917.) What is their special relevance to a community with the university's distinctive goals? Are some university goals impeded by administrative enforcement of *any* rules? Or do such problems arise primarily from special restraints on matters of speech and expression? What objective consequences might be expected from universities' minimizing rule enforcement generally on their campuses?

Further: Is student civil disobedience on the campus a cause of increased rule-enforcement activity, an effect of it, or both? What are the alternatives to formal rule enforcement, for maintaining reasonable order in a university community? Is there increasing dependence throughout American society on formal means of social control? (See Selznick, 1964; Gusfield, 1965.) If so, what are the social and economic forces which foster this trend, and how far do they affect the university? What means, if any, could be used to combat them, consistent with university goals?

The style of university rule enforcement. Behind many disputes over the "crisis of authority" on campus today lie basic differences of view as to the manner, method, or "style" of rule enforcement required to deal effectively with student protests while remaining compatible with the character of a university community. It is clear that the problem of how to treat student civil disobedience on and off the campus was and is a vexing one for university administrators. Most faculty members attempting to give advice seem to have been equally vexed by events, and a series of basic, enduring disagreements became apparent about the appropriate responses to the students' actions. These disagreements are not unrelated to convictions about who is "right" on the substantive matters at issue; however, they also involve basic questions about the character of rule enforcement in any university community.

In the view of some, a university, like any other system of order, requires firm, prompt, and impersonal enforcement of its rules by the established authorities if it is to deter its members from "anarchy," wherein each person obeys no rule with which he disagrees. An opposing view sees the university as having less need for strict orderliness than for a flexible system of personal relationships between administrators, faculty, and students, to allow taking account of the special purposes and detailed consequences of each internal "disturbance"—for example, the avowedly "moral" aims and largely non-violent character of some student demonstrations. Thus the former view takes student rule-violations as demonstrating irresponsible defiance of constituted authority, and looks to their early suppression for the sake of "the rule of law." But those with the latter view urge that students' sincerity should be assumed, and that university officials should be willing to admit early in a dispute that their rulings may be misguided. Some members of the academic community go still further, arguing that rules and authority-relations should serve affirmative, liberating functions as well as restrictive ones. Thus, they believe, university authorities should do more to encourage students' intelligent pursuit and full use of their "legitimate" on-campus freedoms, *before* being forced grudgingly to concede them under severe duress.

Similarly, some members of the university argue that unconditional "negotiations" with the student protesters are quite justified, once it is established that they have legitimate grounds for believing they have a grievance. Others maintain that the protesters' symbolic defiance of authority must be "cured" by their public acceptance of university administrative discretion, before consultation with them can be continued. One view sees amnesty for sincere protesters as humane, reasonable, and conducive to campus peace; another sees it as "surrender" to intimidation by an obstreperous few.

Student mistrust of administrators also divides the campus: some see protest leaders as irredeemably and unreasonably suspicious of all authority and of adult society in general, so that discussion with them is useless. Others called for greater efforts to meet students' mistrust on its own grounds, and to understand its bases in honest anger at the hypocrisy, administrative dissembling, and abuse of power that students believe they see in much of modern society.

Finally, the role of police on the campus has become a major subject of contention. Some persons in the university see warnings and arrests by campus officers, and the introduction of outside police squads, as orderly and proper law-enforcement against student "lawlessness." Others argue that police action all too frequently creates needless provocation of student demonstrators, and invites violence that would not otherwise occur. They urge that the discretion allowed police in regulating on-campus relations should be severely limited, and kept under the control of campus authorities. Some believe outside police should be kept completely off the campus. And some argue that arrests themselves frequently are made as unnecessary and punitive expressions of public anger, substituted for attempts to reach the root of the students' complaints.

For each of these sets of opposed views, intermediate positions and subtly differing opinions could be found. On prudential matters such as the manner of rule-enforcement in a time of crisis, each view gains much from hindsight, of course, and is highly dependent on the circumstances and assumptions of the moment. However, the oppositions described above may suggest more stable issues for socio-legal research. At a very general level, here are a few:

What is known, in an empirical way, about the deterrent or rehabilitative effects of law enforcement on its subjects? How applicable is such knowledge to the less-formalized context of university student-conduct rules? What assumptions about the goals, methods and consequences of university authority underlie most university disciplinary actions against students? What are the assumptions typically made by university authorities about students' motives, intellectual capacities, and emotional maturity? How well do these assumptions fit the students involved in recent symbolic rule-violations? What consequences on the campus might be expected if university officials treated student civil disobedience as a sincere demonstration of moral conviction rather than as reprehensible lawlessness? What reactions might be expected from the general public?

Further: What special problems does mass "civil disobedience" create in the enforcement of reasonable rules of conduct generally? Is the authority of all rules weakened or strengthened by successful use of civil disobedience as social protest? In what ways is the impact on the legal system different from mass civil disobedience, based on public rallies and political campaigns, as compared with individual "acts of conscience," involving less visible social processes? In the current student use of mass civil disobedience, what is the role of typical expectations about the severity of penalties? How are these expectations changing—e.g., do current protesters expect severer penalties or less severe? What effect, if any, has this had on university rule-enforcement activity? On university authorities' readiness to penalizing rule-violating demonstrations on campuses?

These questions are only illustrative of many that call for further study. Such questions are obviously difficult to answer in any precise way. But their import for our understanding of "legal" processes in universities is great, and the answers assumed by administrative authorities in dealing with current student protests clearly are of great practical consequence.

CIVIL LIBERTIES AND ACADEMIC FREEDOMS OF UNIVERSITY STUDENTS

The Free Speech Movement at Berkeley based its claim of student rights to on-campus political expression partly on the First and Fourteenth Amendments to the U.S. Constitution. In the words of the December 7, 1964, FSM *Position* statement:

> Civil liberties and political freedoms which are constitutionally protected off campus must be equally protected on campus for all persons [Lipset and Wolin, 1965: 201].

The Regents' actions of November 20 and December 18, 1964, recognized the argument that current constitutional cases had made some University restrictions on political expression "of doubtful legal enforceability." Thus it would seem that an appeal to constitutional liberties guaranteed by the civil courts succeeded in bringing about greater freedom of speech and action within a university. This was a surprising result for some who had long seen the university as a bastion of greater freedoms than are allowed by the general community.

For some faculty members, reliance on the U.S. Constitution to protect on-campus freedoms is not the most desirable course. The *Statement on Faculty Responsibility for the Academic Freedoms of Students,* "approved in principle" in 1965 by the Council of the American Association of University Professors, said that student "freedom to learn" involves "opportunities to exercise the rights of citizenship on and off the campus." But its declaration of faculty responsibility for student freedoms was based on the "essential attributes of a community of scholars." Thus protection of student freedoms here rests not on the constitutional rights of *citizens,* but on "rights" said to inhere in the status of *student.* The relation of the university to the outside legal system is taken largely for granted, and is discussed only to state that "institutional powers" should not be used to deprive students of "off-campus" rights of "citizenship," or "merely to duplicate the function of general laws." The emphasis is on students' freedom from restrictions *internal* to the university, and on the responsibilities of faculty members to help assure protection of "academic" freedom for students as well as for themselves. The 1965 *Statement* does not argue that the "academic freedom" of students should be identical in scope or quality to that of faculty members. It bases students' rights on the "freedom to learn" implied by their special position as learners (American Association of University Professors, 1965).

An approach similar to that of the AAUP Committee was contained in a pamphlet stating the "views" of the American Civil Liberties Union (1963) on *Academic Freedom and Civil Liberties of Students in Colleges and Universities.* This pamphlet took the position that "the function of the college or university" requires the following:

> . . . [T]he student must be viewed as an individual who is most likely to attain maturity if left free to make personal decisions and to exercise the rights, as well as shoulder the responsibilities, of citizenship on and off the campus.

> . . . Limitations on the freedom of students are not then to be seen as simple administrative decisions which adjust the school to the prevailing climate of public opinion. The college's policy vis-à-vis its students goes to the heart of the condition necessary for adequate personal growth and thus determines whether an institution of higher education turns out merely graduates or the indispensable human material for a continuing democracy.[16]

In other words, the ACLU views the encouragement of student "maturity" through the *practice* of citizenship as an inherent demand of the university's own functions. Hence it must be protected, or at least not restricted, by administrative policies and classroom activities. The freedoms and responsibilities of the student *as* student *include* those of the citizen, and these may be exercised on the campus as well as off. The ACLU by implication calls on administrators as well as faculty members to assure that such freedoms are protected.

The distinction between these bases of student freedoms can become critical in some cases. For example, political expressions of university students who are noncitizens of the U.S. might be protected by a policy based on university functions, while not on an appeal to the Constitution.[17] Persons not currently enrolled might be able to secure freedoms of political expression on a "public" university campus by reference to the U.S. Constitution, although they could not claim formal student status (see Frohnmayer, 1966). If a university's policies allowed greater freedom of expression on campus than that contemplated by state law or local ordinances, reference to special requirements inherent in the status of the student might lead a court to uphold the university policy.[18] Finally, whenever our focus is the question of how far courts are to regulate substantive conduct on the campus, the special character of the student status may come to issue.

Research in this area must soon return to analysis of the special functions or "regulatory interests" of the university, as viewed by the courts. But in addition, researchers might ask: What are the specific legal and social consequences of relying on the different bases of student freedoms mentioned above? What are the bases of student rights and duties in other nations and cultures? What is the relevance of "academic freedom" for faculty members to the situation of students in today's university? (See Metzger, 1964; Williamson, 1963.)

Such "socio-legal" questions touch upon intertwined problems of law, social status, and cultural change that have long been studied in separation, although they are often intertwined in actual events. It may be that the systematic study of such issues in their connections as well as their separateness would advance the cause of all the disciplines concerned. At present, in any event, the promise seems clearly to justify the undertaking. And few recent events have illustrated the complex interrelations of law and society as well as the disturbing and stimulating crises of governance on the campus.

NOTES

1. See American Civil Liberties Union, 1963. (With some changes of wording, much of the substance of this statement appeared in another revised edition published in 1965.) See also American Association of University Professors, Committee "S," 1965. With some changes of wording, much of the substance of this statement was embodied in the "Joint Statement on Rights and Freedoms of Students," drafted by a committee representing the Association of American Colleges, the U.S. National Student Association, and other organizations as well as the AAUP. See *AAUP Bulletin* 53, No. 4 (Winter): 365–368.

2. On the distinction between formal and substantive rationality, see Rheinstein, 1954: 224ff.; and Bendix, 1960: 398–400.

3. For an interesting perspective on the effect of large-campus facilities on student "crowd behavior," see Kaplan, 1965: 83.

4. There is much interest today in "innovations" in American universities and colleges. (See, for example, Baskin, 1965.) We need much more understanding of the relation between innovation and the processes of university governance. See Thompson, 1965; Martin, 1969.

5. See, for example, "A Proposed Academic Plan for the University of California," approved in principle by The Regents on July 21, 1961, mimeo., pp. 24–25.

6. Such suggestions tend to be stoutly resisted in today's university, however, on the ground that the creation of "two classes of faculty" can only result in one "class" being seen as inferior, with disastrous consequences for recruitment.

7. Walter Metzger (1961: 136, 232) makes the point that the "public" which academic freedom serves is no specific, present public but "an abstraction called 'posterity.' "

8. This insight has been formulated in varying ways by sociologists. See, for example, Selznick, 1948: 25–26.

9. *The Role of the Trustees of Columbia University,* report of a special committee of the trustees, adopted by the trustees November 4, 1957. Compare with Corson, 1960: 49–58, and references there cited. See also Bryant, 1964.

10. See FSM, "We Want a University," in Lipset and Wolin (1965: 210). See also *New York Times,* Monday, March 25, 1965, concerning an interuniversity student group which discussed the same idea.

11. For a recent attempt to study this question empirically, see Hawley, et al., 1965.

12. See Martin Meyerson, "Fellow Faculty and Students," *Daily Californian,* March 23, 1965: "Discretion is necessary because at a university we must operate under general rules of conduct."

13. *Buttny v. Smiley,* 281 F. Supp. 280, 286 (Denver, Colorado, 1968); *Goldberg v. Regents of Univ. of Calif.,* 248 Cal. App. 2nd 867, 57 Cal. Rptr. 463, 469 (1967). See also Van Alstyne, 1968: 591.

14. See Martin Meyerson, remarks printed in *Daily Californian,* March 19 and 23, 1965.

15. For accounts of student demands for autonomy in other cultures and earlier periods, see (e.g.) Hastings Rashdall, 1936; Friedrich Paulsen, 1906; Nicholas Hans, *Russian Educational Policy,* 1964: esp. 171; *Daedalus,* 1968; Lipset, 1967; and Emmerson, 1969.

16. See American Civil Liberties Union, 1963. (With some changes of wording, much of the substance of this statement was embodied in another revised edition published in 1965.)

17. In general, however, aliens residing in the United States are guaranteed freedom of speech. See *Bridges v. Wixon,* 326 U.S. 135, 89 L. Ed. 2103, 65 S. Cf. 1443.

18. Compare *Sweezy v. New Hampshire,* 345 U.S. 234 (1957) and *West Virginia Board of Education v. Barnette,* 319 U.S. 624 (1943).

REFERENCES

American Association of University Professors, Committee "S" (1965) "Statement on the academic freedom of students." *AAUP Bulletin* 51, No. 5 (Winter): 447–450.

American Civil Liberties Union (1963) *Academic Freedom and Civil Liberties of Students in Colleges and Universities.* New York: ACLU.

ANDERSON, G. L. (1963) "The organizational character of American colleges and universities." Pp. 1–20 in T. F. Lunsford (ed.) *The Study of Academic Administration.* Boulder, Colorado: Western Interstate Commission for Higher Education.

ARENDT, H. (1958) "What was authority?" In C. J. Friedrich (ed.) *Authority.* Cambridge: Harvard University Press.

ASHBY, E. (1966) *Universities: British, Indian, African: A Study in the Ecology of Higher Education.* Cambridge: Harvard University Press.

BARBER, B. (1962) *Science and the Social Order.* New York: Collier Books.

BASKINS, S. (1965) *Higher Education: Some Newer Developments.* New York: McGraw-Hill.

BEN-DAVID, J. and A. ZLOCZOWER (1962) "Universities and academic systems in modern societies." *European Journal of Sociology* 3: 45–85.

BENDIX, R. (1960) *Max Weber: An Intellectual Portrait.* Garden City: Anchor Books.

BLAU, P. M. and W. R. SCOTT (1962) *Formal Organizations.* San Francisco: Chandler Publishing.

BROWNE, A. D. (1965) "The institution and the system: autonomy and coordination." Pp. 39–52 in O. A. Knorr (ed.) *Long-Range Planning in Higher Education.* Boulder, Colorado: Western Interstate Commission for Higher Education.

BRYANT, V. S. (1964) "The role of the regent." *AAUP Bulletin* 50, No. 4 (December): 317–322.

BYRNE, J. C. (1964/1965) "Report of the University of California and recommendations to the special committee of the Regents of the University of California." May 7, reprinted in *Los Angeles Times,* May 12, 1965.

California Law Review (1966) "Student Rights and Campus Rules." Vol. 54, No. 1 (March).

CAPLOW, T. and R. J. McGEE (1958) *The Academic Marketplace.* New York: Basic Books.

CARR-SAUNDERS, A. (1961) *New Universities Overseas.* London: Allen & Unwin.

CLARK, B. R. (1965) "The culture of the college: its implications for the organization of learning resources." Paper prepared for the Conference on the Library and the College Climate of Learning. Syracuse University, June 20–23.

—— (1963) "Faculty organization and authority." Pp. 37–52 in T. F. Lunsford (ed.) *The Study of Academic Administration.* Boulder, Colorado: Western Interstate Commission for Higher Education.

—— (1961) "Faculty authority." *AAUP Bulletin* 47, No. 4 (Winter): 293–302.

—— (1958) *Adult Education in Transition.* Berkeley: University of California Press.

CORSON, J. (1960) *Governance of Colleges and Universities.* New York: McGraw-Hill.

CROZIER, M. (1964) *The Bureaucratic Phenomenon.* Chicago: University of Chicago Press.

Daedalus (1968) "Students and politics." *Daedalus* 97, No. 1 (Winter).

Denver Law Journal (1968) "Legal aspects of student-institutional relationships." Vol. 45, No. 4 (Special Issue): 545–557.

DODDS, H. W. (1962) *The Academic President—Educator or Caretaker?* New York: McGraw-Hill.

EMMERSON, D. K., Ed. (1969) *Students and Politics in Developing Nations.* New York: Frederick A. Praeger.

ETZIONI, A. (1964) *Modern Organization.* Englewood Cliffs: Prentice-Hall.

—— (1961) *Complex Organizations.* New York: Holt, Rinehart & Winston.

FARMER, P. (1950) "Nineteenth century ideas of the university." In M. Clapp (ed.) *The Modern University.* Ithaca: Cornell University Press.

FERRERO, G. (1942) *The Principles of Power.* New York: G. Putnam.

FLEXNER, A. (1930) *Universities: American, English, German.* New York: Oxford University Press.

FROHNMAYER, D. B. (1966) "Comment: the university and the public: the right of access by nonstudents to university property." *California Law Review* 54, No. 1 (March): 132–178.

FULLER, L. L. (1964) *The Morality of Law.* New Haven: Yale University Press.

GALLAGHER, B. G. (1965) "Who runs the institution?" Pp. 89–96 in Knorr and Minter (eds.) *Order and Freedom on the Campus.* Boulder, Colorado: Western Interstate Commission for Higher Education.

GERTH, H. and C. W. MILLS, Eds. and trans. (1946) *From Max Weber: Essays in Sociology.* New York: Oxford University Press.

GLENNY, L. (1959) *Autonomy of Public Colleges.* New York: McGraw-Hill.

GOULDNER, A. W. (1959) "Cosmopolitans and locals; toward an analysis of latent social roles." *Administrative Science Quarterly* 2: 281–306.

GROSS, E. (1968) "Universities as organizations: a research approach." *American Sociological Review* 33, No. 4 (August): 518–544.

GROSSMAN, J. B., H. JACOB and J. LADINSKY (1968) "Law and society: a selected bibliography." *Law and Society Review* 2, No. 2 (February): 291–339.

GUSFIELD, J. R. (1965) "Social sources of Levites and Samaritans." Speech given at the Conference on the Good Samaritan and the Bad, University of Chicago Law School, April 11 (excerpted in *Current* [July]: 41–44).

HANS, N. (1964) *Russian Educational Policy (1701–1917).* New York: Russell & Russell.

Harvard Law Review (1968) "Developments in the law-academic freedom." Vol. 81, No. 5 (March): 1045–1159.

HAWLEY, A. H., W. BOLAND and M. BOLAND (1965) "Population size and administration in institutions of higher education." *American Sociological Review* 30, No. 2 (April 1): 252–255.

HEIST, P. (1965) "Intellect and commitment: the faces of discontent." In O. Knorr and W. Minter (eds.) *Order and Freedom on the Campus.* Boulder, Colorado: Western Interstate Commission for Higher Education.

HOFSTADTER, R. and W. METZGER (1955) *The Development of Academic Freedom in the United States.* New York: Columbia University Press.

HUTCHINS, R. M. (1956) "The democratic dilemma," and "Education and independent thought." Pp. 101–166 in *Freedom, Education and the Fund: Essays and Address, 1946–1956.* New York: Meridan Books.

JANOWITZ, M. (1959) "Changing patterns of organizational authority." *Administrative Science Quarterly* 3: 473–493.

JOHNSTON, N. Ed. (1962) In Loco Parentis.

Journal of Social Issues (1967) "Stirrings out of apathy: student activism and the decade of protest." Vol. 23, No. 3 (July).

KAPLAN, A. (1964) *The Conduct of Inquiry.* San Francisco: Chandler Publishing.

KAPLAN, S. (1965) "The revolt of an elite: sources of the FSM victory." *The Graduate Student Journal* 4 (Spring): 26–30, 75–90.

KERR, C. (1963) *The Uses of the University.* Cambridge: Harvard University Press.

KNORR, O. A. and W. J. MINTER, Eds. (1965) *Order and Freedom on the Campus.* Boulder, Colorado: Western Interstate Commission for Higher Education.

KORNHAUSER, W. (1962) *Scientists in Industry.* Berkeley: University of California Press.

—— et al. (1965) *Campus Autonomy and the Regents: A Reply to the Meyer Report.* Berkeley: University of California (mimeo.).

LAZARSFELD, P. and W. THIELENS (1958) *The Academic Mind.* New York: The Free Press.

LEVINE, M. (1963) "Private government on the campus—judicial review of university expulsions." *Yale Law Journal* 72 (June): 1362–1410.

LIPSET, S. M. (1967) *Student Politics.* New York: Basic Books.

—— (1963) *Political Man.* Garden City: Doubleday.

—— and S. WOLIN, Eds. (1965) *The Berkeley Student Revolt.* New York: Anchor Books.

LITCHFIELD, E. H. (1959) "Organization in large American universities: the administration." *Journal of Higher Education* 30 (December): 489–504.

LUNSFORD, T. F. (1965) *The Free Speech Crises at Berkeley, 1964–65: Some Issues for Social and Legal Research.* Berkeley: Center for Research and Development in Higher Education and Center for the Study of Law and Society.

McCONNELL, T. R. (1962) *A General Pattern for American Public Higher Education.* New York: McGraw-Hill.

MARTIN, W. B. (1969) *The Institutional Character in Colleges and Universities.* Berkeley: Center for Research and Development in Higher Education.

MERTON, R. K. (1957) *Social Theory and Social Structure.* New York: The Free Press.

METZGER, W. (1964) *Academic Freedom—The Scholar's Place in Modern Society.* Dobbs Ferry, N.Y.: Oceana Publications.

—— (1961) *Academic Freedom in the Age of the University.* New York: Columbia University Press.

MEYERSON, M. (1965a) "Fellow faculty and students." *Daily Californian,* March 23.

—— (1965b) "To the educational press." Mimeo. release, January 13.

MICHELS, R. (1959) *Political Parties.* New York: Dover Press.

MILLER, A. S. (1959) Private governments and the Constitution: An Occasional Paper on the Role of the Corporation in the Free Society. Santa Barbara: Center for the Study of Democratic Institutions (includes selected bibliography).

MILLETT, J. D. (1962) *The Academic Community.* New York: McGraw-Hill.

Office of the President, University of California (1965a) "Re: a progress report on administrative changes and developments at the University of California." Memorandum of April 23.

—— (1965b) "Re: organization of the University." Memorandum of June 18.

PALTRIDGE, J. G. (1968) *Conflict and Coordination in Higher Education.* Berkeley: Center for Research and Development in Higher Education.

PAULSEN, F. (1908) *German Education: Past and Present* (T. Lorenz, trans.). London: Adelphi Terrace.

—— (1906) *The German Universities and University Study* (F. Thilly and W.W. Elwang, trans.). New York: Longmans, Green.

—— (1895) *The German Universities: Their Character and Historical Development* (E. D. Petty, trans.). New York: Macmillan.

POUND, R. (1917) "The limits of effective legal action." *International Journal of Ethics* 27: 150–167.

RANKIN, A. (1964) "A selected bibliography in the sociology of law." *Law and Society,* A Supplement to the Summer Issue of Social Problems: 54–57.

RASHDALL, H. (1936) *The Universities in Europe in the Middle Ages.* Oxford: The Clarendon Press.

Regents of the University of California (1965) Minutes of meetings of May 21, June 18, and July 16.

RHEINSTEIN, M., Ed. (1954) *Max Weber on Law in Economy and Society* (E. Shils and M. Rheinstein, trans.). Cambridge: Harvard University Press.

ROETHLISBERGER, F. J. and W. J. DICKSON (1939) *Management and the Worker.* Cambridge: Harvard University Press.

RUDOLPH, F. (1962) *The American College and University: A History.* New York: Alfred A. Knopf.

SANFORD, N., Ed. (1962) *The American College.* New York: John Wiley.

SELZNICK, P. (1968) "Sociology of law." *International Encyclopedia of the Social Sciences.* Vol. 9. New York: Macmillan and The Free Press.

—— (1969) *Law, Society, and the Industrial Justice.* New York: Russell Sage Foundation.

—— (1957) *Leadership in Administration.* New York: Row, Peterson.

—— (1948) "Foundations of the theory of organization." *American Sociological Review* 13: 25–35.

—— (1964) "Legal Institutions and Social Control." *Vanderbilt Law Review* 17: 79–90.

SIMON, H. (1957) *Administrative Behavior.* 2nd edition. New York: Macmillan.

SKOLNICK, J. H. (1964) "The sociology of law in America." *Law and Society,* A Supplement to the Summer Issue of Social Problems: 4–38.

STOKE, H. W. (1959) *The American College President.* New York: Harper.

THOMPSON, J. D. and W. J. McEWEN (1958) "Organizational goals and environment: goal setting as an interaction process." *American Sociological Review* 23 (February): 23–31.

THOMPSON, V. A. (1965) "Bureaucracy and innovation." *Administrative Science Quarterly* (June): 1–21.

TUSSMAN, J. (1969) *Experiment at Berkeley.* New York: Oxford University Press.

U.S. National Student Association (n.d.) *Academic Freedom.* Philadelphia: USNSA (mimeo.).

—— (n.d.) *Campus Justice.* Philadelphia: USNSA (mimeo.).

—— (n.d.) *Student-Faculty-Administration Relations.* Philadelphia: USNSA (mimeo.).

University of California (1965) "Appendix C: types of discipline." University of California Policies Relating to Students and Student Organizations, Use of University Facilities, and Nondiscrimination. July 1.

VAN ALSTYNE, W. W. (1968) "The student as university resident." *Denver Law Journal* 45, No. 4 (Special Issue): 591.

—— (1965) "Student academic freedom and the rule-making powers of public universities: some constitutional considerations." *Law in Transition Quarterly* (Winter): 1–34.

VEBLEN, T. (1935) *The Higher Learning in America*. New York: Viking Press.

VEYSEY, L. R. (1965) *The Emergence of the American University*. Chicago: University of Chicago Press.

WATTS, W. and D. WHITTAKER (1966) "Free speech advocates at Berkeley." *Journal of Applied Behavioral Science* 2, No. 1.

WATTS, W., S. LYNCH and D. WHITTAKER (1969) "Alienation and activism in today's college-age youth." *Journal of Counseling Psychology* 16, No. 1.

WEBER, M. (1961) "The three types of legitimate rule." (H. Gerth, trans.) Pp. 4–14 in A. Etzioni, *Complex Organizations: A Sociological Reader*. New York: Holt, Rinehart & Winston.

—— (1947) *The Theory of Social and Economic Organization* (A. M. Henderson and T. Parsons, trans.). New York: The Free Press.

WEISS, J. (1965) "The university as corporation." *New University Thought* 4, No. 2 (Summer): 31–45.

WELDON, T. D. (1958) Quoted from (1953) "The Vocabulary of Politics" in C. J. Friedrich (ed.) *Authority*. Cambridge: Harvard University Press.

WILENSKY, H. E. (1956) *Intellectuals in Labor Unions*. New York: The Free Press.

WILLIAMSON, E. G. (1963) "Students' academic freedom." *The Educational Record* 44, No. 3 (July): 214–222.

WILSON, L, (1961) "The academic man revisited." In *Studies of College Faculty*. Boulder, Colorado: Western Interstate Commission for Higher Education.

PART VII

POSTSCRIPT

CHAPTER 16

BERKELEY: THE BATTLE OF PEOPLE'S PARK

Sheldon Wolin and John Schaar

I

Shortly before 5:00 A.M., on Thursday, May 16, a motley group of about fifty hippies and "street-people" were huddled together on a lot 270 × 450 feet in Berkeley. The lot was owned by the Regents of the University of California and located a few blocks south of the Berkeley campus. Since mid-April this lot had been taken over and transformed into a "People's Park" by scores of people, most of whom had no connection with the university. Now the university was determined to reassert its legal rights of ownership. A police officer approached the group and announced that it must leave or face charges of trespassing. Except for three persons, the group left and the area was immediately occupied and surrounded by about 200 police from Berkeley, Alameda county, and the campus. The police were equipped with flak jackets, tear gas launchers, shotguns, and telescopic rifles. At 6:00 A.M. a construction crew arrived and by mid-afternoon an eight-foot steel fence encircled the lot.

At noon a rally was convened on campus and about 3,000 people gathered. The president-elect of the student body spoke. He started to suggest various courses of action that might be considered. The crowd responded to the first of these by spontaneously marching toward the lot guarded by the police. (For this speech, the speaker was charged a few days later with violating numerous campus rules, and, on the initiative of University officials, indicted for incitement to riot.) The crowd was blocked by a drawn police line. Rocks and bottles were thrown at the police, and the police loosed a tear gas barrage, scattering the crowd. Elsewhere, a car belonging to the city was burned. Meanwhile, police reinforcements poured in, soon reaching around 600. A rock was thrown from a roof-top and, without warning, police fired into a group on the roof of an adjacent building. Two persons were struck in the face by the police fire, another was

EDITORS' NOTE: Reprinted with permission from *The New York Review of Books* 12, No. 12 (June 19, 1969) pages 24–31. Copyright © 1969 *The New York Review*.

blinded, probably permanently, and a fourth, twenty-five-year-old James Rector, later died. Before the day was over, at least thirty others were wounded by police gunfire, and many more by clubs. One policeman received a minor stab wound and six more were reported as having been treated for minor cuts and bruises.

Meanwhile, action shifted to the campus itself, where police had herded a large crowd into Sproul Plaza by shooting tear gas along the bordering streets. The police then formed small detachments which continuously swept across the campus, breaking up groups of all sizes. Tear gas enfolded the main part of the campus and drifted into many of its buildings, as well as into the surrounding city. Nearby streets were littered with broken glass and rubble. At least six buckshot slugs entered the main library and three .38 calibre bullets lodged in the wall of a reference room in the same building. Before the day ended, more than ninety people had been injured by police guns and clubs.

Under a "State of Extreme Emergency" proclamation issued by Governor Reagan on February 5th in connection with the "Third World Strike" at Berkeley late last winter and never rescinded, a curfew was imposed on the city. Strict security measures were enforced on campus and in the nearby business districts, and all assemblies and rallies were prohibited. The proclamation also centralized control of the police under the command of Sheriff Frank Madigan of Alameda County.

Roger Heyns, the Chancellor of the University, saw none of this, for he had left the previous day for a meeting in Washington. His principal Vice-Chancellor had gone to the Regents' meeting in Los Angeles. The Regents took notice of the events by declaring, "It is of paramount importance that law and order be upheld." The Governor said that the lot had been seized by the street-people "as an excuse for a riot." A Berkeley councilman called the previous use of the lot a "Hippie Disneyland freak show."

The next day, May 17, 2,000 National Guardsmen appeared in full battle dress, armed with rifles, bayonets, and tear gas. They were called into action by the Governor, but apparently the initiative came from local authorities acting in consultation with University administrators. Helicopters weaved back and forth over the campus and city. Berkeley was occupied. (The next day one helicopter landed on campus and an officer came out to ask that students stop flying their kites because the strings might foul his rotors. A collection was promptly taken and the sky was soon full of brightly colored kites.)

During the next few days a pattern emerged. Each day began quietly, almost like any other day, except that people awoke to the roar of helicopters and the rumble of transports. As University classes began (they have never been officially cancelled), the Guardsmen formed a line along the south boundary of the campus. The Guard and the police would cordon off the main plaza and station smaller detachments at various points around the campus. Gradually the students crowded together, staring curiously at the Guardsmen and occasionally taunting them. The Guard stood ready with bayonets pointed directly at the crowd. This standoff would continue for an hour or two, and then the police would charge the crowd with clubs and tear gas. The crowd would scatter, the police would give chase, the students and street-people would curse and sometimes hurl rocks or return the tear gas canisters, and the police would beat or arrest some of them.

On Tuesday, May 20, the pattern and tempo changed. Previously the police had sought to break up gatherings on the campus, so now the protesters left the campus and began a peaceful march through the city. This was promptly stopped by the police. The marchers then filtered back to campus and a crowd of about 3,000 assembled. The group was pressed toward the Plaza by the police and Guardsmen and, when solidly hemmed in, was attacked by tear gas. A little later a helicopter flew low over the center of the campus and spewed gas over a wide area, even though the crowd had been thoroughly scattered. Panic broke out and people fled, weeping, choking, vomiting. Gas penetrated the University hospital, imperiling patients and interrupting hospital routines. It caused another panic at the University recreation area, nearly a mile from the center of campus, where many people, including mothers and children, were swimming. The police also threw gas into a student snack bar and into an office and classroom building.

The next day, May 21, was a turning point. More than 200 faculty members announced their refusal to teach; a local labor council condemned the police action; some church groups protested; and the newspapers and television stations began to express some criticism. Controversy arose over the ammunition which the police had used the previous Thursday. Sheriff Madigan was evasive about the size of birdshot issued, but the evidence was clear that buckshot had killed James Rector. The tear gas was first identified as the normal variety (CN) for crowd disturbances, but later it was officially acknowledged that a more dangerous gas (CS) was also used. The American army uses CS gas to flush out guerrillas in Vietnam. It can cause projectile vomiting, instant diarrhea, and skin blisters, and even death, as it has to the VC, when the victim is tubercular. The Geneva Conventions outlaw the use of CS in warfare.

On the same day the Chancellor issued his first statement. He deplored the death which had occurred, as well as "the senseless violence." He warned that attempts were being made "to polarize the community and prevent rational solutions," and he stated that a university has a responsibility to follow "civilized procedures." Heyns made no criticism of the police or National Guard tactics: that same day a Guardsman had thrown down his helmet, dropped his rifle, and reportedly shouted, "I can't stand this any more." He was handcuffed, taken away for a physical examination, and then rushed off to a psychiatric examination. He was diagnosed as suffering from "suppressed aggressions."

In Sacramento, where a deputation of Berkeley faculty members was meeting with the Governor, aggression was more open. The Governor conceded that the helicopter attack might have been a "tactical mistake," but he also insisted that "once the dogs of war are unleashed, you must expect things will happen. . . ." Meantime, the statewide commander of the Guards defended the gas attack on the grounds that his troops were threatened. He noted that the general who ordered the attack had said, "It was a Godsend that it was done at that time." The commander regretted the "discomfort and inconvenience to innocent bystanders," but added: "It is an inescapable by-product of combatting terrorists, anarchists, and hard-core militants on the streets and on the campus."

The next day, May 22, a peaceful march and flower planting procession began in downtown Berkeley. With little warning, police and Guardsmen converged on the unsuspecting participants and swept them, along with a number of shoppers, newsmen, people at lunch, and a mailman, into a parking lot, where 482 were arrested, bringing the week's total near 800. As those arrested were released on bail, disturbing stories began to circulate concerning the special treatment accorded "Berkeley types" in Santa Rita prison.

These stories, supported by numerous affidavits and news accounts submitted by journalists who had been bagged in the mass arrest, told of beatings, verbal abuse and humiliation, physical deprivations, and refusal of permission to contact counsel. Male prisoners told of being marched into the prison yard and forced to lie face down, absolutely motionless, on gravel and concrete for several hours. The slightest shift in posture, except for a head movement permitted once every half hour, was met with a blow to the kidneys or testicles. On May 24th a District Court judge issued an order restraining Sheriff Madigan's subordinates from beating and otherwise mistreating the arrestees taken to Santa Rita prison.

Despite all the arrests, the shotguns, gas, and clubs, the protesters have thus far shown remarkable restraint. Although both police and Guards have been targets of much foul language and some hard objects, nothing remotely resembling sustained violence has been employed against the police; and the Guard has been spared from all except verbal abuse. At this writing, the only damage to campus property, other than that caused by the police, has been two broken windows and one flooded floor.

After the mass arrests, the Governor lifted the curfew and the ban on assemblies, saying "a more controlled situation" existed. But he warned that no solution was likely until the trouble-making faculty and students were separated from the University. "A professional revolutionary group," he said, was behind it all. Charles Hitch, the President of the University of California, issued his first statement. (Much earlier, his own staff issued a statement protesting campus conditions of "intolerable stress" and physical danger.) The President ventured to criticize "certain tactics" of the police, but noted that these "were not the responsibility of university authorities."

In a television interview, the Chancellor agreed with the President, but added that negotiations were still possible because "we haven't stopped the rational process." A published interview (May 22) with the principal Vice-Chancellor found him saying, "Our strategy was to act with humor and sensitivity. For instance, we offered to roll up the sod in the park and return it to the people. . . . We had no reason to believe there would be trouble." Meanwhile the Governor was saying, "The police didn't kill the young man. He was killed by the first college administrator who said some time ago it was all right to break laws in the name of dissent."

The Governor also accused the President of the University, a former Assistant Secretary of Defense and RANDsman, of "trying to weasel" to the side of the street-people. Two days later the Governor refused the request of the Berkeley City Council to end the state of emergency and recall the Guard—requests, it might be added, that the University itself has not yet made. At this time the Mayor of Berkeley suggested that police tactics had been "clumsy and not efficient," to which Sheriff Madigan retorted: "If the Mayor was capable of running the city so well without problems we wouldn't be here. I advise the Mayor to take his umbrella and go to Berkeley's Munich."

On Friday, May 23, the Faculty Senate met. It listened first to a speech by the Chancellor in which he defined the occupation of the lot as an act of "unjustified aggression" against the University, and declared that the "avoidance of confrontations cannot be the absolute value." He said that the fence would remain as long as the issue was one of possession and control, and, pleading for more "elbow room," he asserted that the faculty should support or at least not oppose an administrative decision once it had been made. The faculty then defeated a motion calling for the Chancellor's removal (94 voted for, 737 against, and 99 abstained). It approved, by a vote of 737 to 94, a series of resolutions which condemned what was called "as irresponsible a police and military reaction to a civic disturbance as this country has seen in recent times."

The resolutions demanded withdrawal of "the massive police and military presence on campus"; the "cessation of all acts of belligerency and provocation by demonstrators"; an investigation by the Attorney General of California and the Department of Justice; and the prompt implementation of a plan whereby part of the lot would become "an experimental community-generated park" and the fence would be simultaneously removed. The faculty also resolved to reconvene in a few days to reassess the situation.

There is where events now stand (May 26). But pressures from all sides are increasing. A student referendum, which saw the heaviest turnout in the history of student voting, found 85 percent of the nearly 15,000 who voted favoring the use of the lot as it had been before the occupation. The students also voted to assess themselves $1.50 each quarter to help finance an ethnic studies department previously accepted by the University but now foundering. As of this writing, college students from all over the state are planning direct protests to Governor Reagan. Leaders of the protesters are preparing for a huge march against the fence on Memorial Day. The Governor remains committed to a hard line. All the issues remain unsettled.

II

What brought on this crisis? Like many of its sister institutions, the Berkeley campus has been steadily advancing its boundaries into the city. Back in 1956 it had announced its intention to purchase property in the area which includes the present disputed lot. Owing to lack of funds, very little land was actually purchased. Finally, in June, 1967, the monies were allocated and the University announced that ultimately dormitories would be built on the land, but that in the interim it would be used for recreation.

The lot itself was purchased in 1968, but no funds were then available for development. Undoubtedly the University was aware of the disastrous experience of other academic institutions which had attempted to "redevelop" surrounding areas. In fact, a short time ago the University announced, with much fanfare, its intention to mount a major attack on the problems of the cities. Despite these professions, the University's treatment of its own urban neighbors has consisted of a mixture of middle-class prejudice, aesthetic blindness, and bureaucratic callousness.

The victims in this case, however, have not been so much the Blacks as another pariah group, one whose identity is profoundly influenced by the University itself. For many years, Telegraph Avenue and "the south campus area" have constituted a major irritant to the University, the City fathers, and the business interests. It is the Berkeley demi-monde, the place where students, hippies, drop-outs, radicals, and run-aways congregate. To the respectables, it is a haven for drug addicts, sex fiends, criminals, and revolutionaries. Until the University began its expansion, it was also an architectural preserve for fine old brown shingle houses and interesting shops. It is no secret that the University has long considered the acquisition of land as a means of ridding the area not of sub-standard housing, but of its human "blight." The disputed lot was the perfect symbol of the University's way of carrying out urban regeneration: first, raze the buildings; next let the land lay idle and uncared for; then permit it to be used as an unimproved parking lot, muddy and pitted; and finally, when the local people threaten to use and enjoy the land, throw a fence around it.

Around mid-April, a movement was begun by street-people, hippies, students, radicals, and a fair sprinkling of elderly free spirits to take over the parking lot and transform it. Many possibilities were discussed: a child care clinic; a crafts fair; a baseball diamond. Soon grass and shrubs were planted, playground equipment installed, benches built, and places made for eating, lounging, and occasional speechmaking. About 200 people were involved in the beginning, but soon the Park was intensively and lovingly used by children, the young, students and street-people, and the elderly. A week after the Park began, the University announced its intention to develop a playing field by July 1, and the Park people responded by saying that the University would have to fight for it. Discussions followed, but not much else. The University said, however, that no construction would be started without proper warning and that it was willing to discuss the future design of the field.

On May 8 the Chancellor agreed to form a committee representing those who were using the lot as well as the University. But he insisted as "an essential condition" of discussions about the future of the land that all work on the People's Park cease. In addition he announced certain guidelines for his committee: University control and eventual use must be assured; the field must not produce "police and other control problems"; and no political or public meetings were to be held on the land. Suddenly, on May 13, he announced his decision to fence in the area as the first step toward developing the land for intramural recreation. "That's a hard way to make a point," he said, "but that's the way it has to be. . . . The fence will also give us time to plan and consult. Regretfully, this is the only way the entire site can be surveyed, soil tested, and planned for development . . . hence the fence."

Why did it have to be this way? Because, as the Chancellor explained, it was necessary to assert the University's title to ownership. Concerning the apparent lack of consultation with his own committee, he said that a plan could not be worked out because the Park people had not only refused to stop cultivating and improving the land, but they had "refused to organize a responsible committee" for consultative purposes. In addition, he cited problems of health, safety, and legal liability, as well as complaints from local residents.

The first response came from the faculty chairman of the Chancellor's committee. He declared that the Chancellor had allowed only two days (the weekend) for the committee to produce a plan and that the "University didn't seem interested in negotiations." On May 14 a protest rally was held and the anarchs of the Park, surprisingly, pulled themselves together and formed a negotiating committee. Although rumors of an impending fence were circulating, spokesmen for the Park people insisted that they wanted discussion, not confrontation.

On May 15, the day immediately preceding the early morning police action, the Chancellor placed an advertisement in the campus newspaper inviting students to draw up "ideas or designs" for the lot and to submit them by May 21. The ad was continued even after the military occupation. On May 18, three days after the occupation had begun, the Chancellor announced that there would be "no negotiations in regard to the land known as People's Park," although discussions might go on "while the fence is up anyway." His principal Vice-Chancellor, in an interview reported on May 22, stated that the University had not turned down a negotiating committee.

He also noted—and this was after the helicopter attack—that "the fence was necessary to permit the kind of rational discussion and planning that wasn't possible before." Once more the faculty chairman had to protest that he had not been informed of meetings between the Administration and representatives of the People's Park and that the Chancellor had consistently ignored the committee's recommendations. However, the principal Vice-Chancellor had an explanation for this lack of consultation: "I guess that's because the Chancellor didn't want him to get chewed up by this thing."

III

Why did the making of a park provoke such a desolating response? The bureaucratic nature of the multiversity and its disastrous consequences for education are by now familiar and beyond dispute. So, too, is the web of interdependence between it and the dominant military, industrial, and political institutions of our society. These explain much about the response of the University to the absurd, yet hopeful, experiment of People's Park.

What needs further comment is the increasingly ineffectual quality of the University's responses, particularly when its organizational apparatus attempts to cope with what is spontaneous, ambiguous, and disturbingly human. It is significant that the Berkeley administration repeatedly expressed irritation with the failure of the Park people to "organize" a "responsible committee" or to select "representatives" who might "negotiate." The life-styles and values of the Park people were forever escaping the categories and procedures of those who administer the academic plant.

Likewise the issue itself: the occupants of the Park wanted to use the land for a variety of projects, strange but deeply natural, which defied customary forms and expectations, whereas, at worst, the University saw the land as something to be fenced, soil-tested, processed through a score of experts and a maze of committees, and finally encased in the tight and tidy form of a rational design. At best, the most imaginative use of the land which the University could contemplate was as a "field-experiment station" where faculty and graduate students could observe their fellow beings coping with their "environment." In brief, the educational bureaucracy, like bureaucracies elsewhere, is experiencing increasing difficulty, because human life is manifesting itself in forms which are unrecognizable to the mentality of the technological age.

This suggests that part of the problem lies in the very way bureaucracies perceive the world and process information from it. It was this "bureaucratic epistemology" which largely determined how the University responded to the People's Park. Bureaucracy is both an expression of the drive for rationality and predictability, and one of the chief agencies in making the world ever more rational and predictable, for the bureaucratic mode of knowing and behaving comes to constitute the things known and done themselves.

Now this rational form of organizing human efforts employs a conception of knowledge which is also rational in specific ways (compare with Keniston, 1967: 253–272). The only legitimate instrument of knowledge is systematic cognition, and the only acceptable mode of discourse is the cognitive mode. Other paths to knowledge are suspect. Everything tainted with the personal, the subjective, and the passionate is suppressed, or dismissed as prejudice or pathology. A bureaucrat who based his decisions upon, say, intuition, dialectical reason, empathic awareness, or even common sense, would be guilty of misconduct.

The bureaucratic search for "understanding" does not begin in wonder, but in the reduction of the world to the ordinary and the manageable. In order to deal with the world in the cognitive mode, the world must first be approached as an exercise in "problem-solving." To say there is a problem is to imply there is a solution; and finding the solution largely means devising the right technique. Since most problems are "complex," they must be broken down by bureaucrats into their component parts before the right solution can be found. Reality is parsed into an ensemble of discrete though related parts, and each part is assigned to the expert specially qualified to deal with that part. Wholes can appear as nothing more than assemblages of parts, just as a whole automobile is an assemblage of parts. But in order for wholes to be broken into parts, things that are dissimilar in appearance and quality must be made similar.

This is done by abstracting from the objects dealt with those aspects as though they were the whole. Abstraction and grouping by common attributes require measuring tools that yield comparable units for analysis: favorite ones are units of money, time, space, and power; income, occupation, and party affiliation. All such measurements and comparisons subordinate qualitative dimensions, natural context, and unique and variable properties to the common, stable, external, and reproducible. This way of thinking becomes real when campus administrators define "recreation" in fixed and restrictive terms so that it may accord with the abstract demands of "lead-time." In a way Hegel might barely recognize, the Rational becomes the Real and the Real the Rational.

When men treat themselves this way, they increasingly become this way, or they desperately try to escape the "mind-forged manacles," as Blake called them, of the bureaucratic mentality and mode of conduct. In the broadest view, these two trends increasingly dominate the advanced states of our day. On the one side, we see the march toward uniformity, predictability, and the attempt to define all variety as dissent and then to force dissent into the "regular channels"—toward that state whose model citizen is Tocqueville's "industrious sheep," that state whose only greatness is its collective power.

On the other side we see an assertion of spontaneity, self-realization, and do-your-own-thing as the sum and substance of life and liberty. And this assertion, in its extreme form, does approach either madness or infantilism, for the only social institutions in which each member is really free to do his own thing are Bedlam and the nursery, where the condition may be tolerated because there is a keeper with ultimate control over the inmates. The opposing forces were not quite that pure in the confrontation over the People's Park, but the University and public officials nearly managed to make them so. That they could not do so is a comforting measure of the basic vitality of those who built the Park and who have sacrificed to preserve it.

IV

But this still does not account for the frenzy of violence which fell on Berkeley. To understand that, we must shift focus.

Clark Kerr was perceptive when he defined the multiversity as "a mechanism held together by administrative rules and powered by money." But it is important to understand that the last few years in the University have seen more and more rules and less and less money. The money is drying up because the rules are being broken. The rules are being broken because University authorities, administrators and faculty alike, have lost the respect of very many of the students. When authority leaves, power enters—first in the form of more and tougher rules, then as sheer physical force, and finally as violence, which is force unrestrained by any thought of healing and saving, force whose aim is to cleanse by devastation.

Pressed from above by politicians and from below by students, the University Administration simultaneously imposes more rules and makes continual appeals to the faculty for more support in its efforts to cope with permanent emergency. It pleads with the faculty for more "elbow room," more discretionary space in which to make the hard decisions needed when money runs short and students run amuck. That same Administration is right now conducting time-and-motion studies of faculty work and "productivity." Simultaneously, both faculty and Administration make spasmodic efforts to give the students some voice in the governance of the institution. But those efforts are always too little, too late, too grudging.

Besides, as soon as the students get some power, unseemly things happen. Admit the Blacks on campus and they demand their own autonomous departments. Give the students limited power to initiate courses and they bring in Eldridge Cleaver and Tom Hayden. The faculty sees student initiative as a revolting mixture of Agitprop and denial of professional prerogatives. The Administration sees it as a deadly threat to its own precarious standing within the University and before the public. The politicians see it as concession to anarchy and revolution. The result is more rules and less trust all around—more centralization, bureaucratization, and force on one side, more despair and anger on the other.

Under these conditions, the organized system must strive to extend its control and reduce the space in which spontaneous and unpredictable actions are possible. The subjects, on the other hand, come to identify spontaneity and unpredictability with all that is human and alive, and rule and control with all that is inhuman and dead. Order and liberty stand in fatal opposition. No positive synthesis can emerge from this dialectic unless those who now feel themselves pushed out and put down are admitted as full participants. But that is not happening. More and more, we are seeing in this country a reappearance of that stage in the breakdown of political societies where one segment of the whole—in this case still the larger segment—determines to dominate by force and terror other segments which reject and challenge its legitimacy.

This dynamic largely accounts for the crushing violence and terror that hit Berkeley. When spontaneity appeared in People's Park, it was first met by a re-statement of the rules governing possession and control of land. When that re-statement did not have the desired effect, the University failed to take the next step dictated by rule-governed behavior—seeking an injunction. Nor did it take the step which would have acknowledged itself as being in a political situation—talking on a plane of equality, and acting in a spirit of generosity, with the other parties. Instead, it regressed immediately to the use of physical measures. In the eyes of the Administration, the building of People's Park was an "unjustified aggression," and the right of self-defense was promptly invoked.

Once force was called into play, it quickly intensified, and the University cannot evade its share of responsibility for what followed. He who wills the end wills the means; and no University official could have been unaware of the means necessary to keep that fence standing. But the administrators did not quite understand that their chosen agents of force, the police, would not limit their attention only to the students and street-people, who were expendable, but would turn against the University and the city as well.

Ronald Reagan reached Sacramento through Berkeley because, in the eyes of his frightened and furious supporters, Berkeley is daily the scene of events that would have shocked Sodom and revolutionary Moscow. All this came into intense focus in the behavior of the cops who were on the scene.

The police were numerous and armed with all the weapons a fertile technology can provide and an increasingly frightened citizenry will permit. Their superiority of force is overwhelming, and they are convinced they could "solve the problem" overnight if they were permitted to do it their own way: one instant crushing blow, and then license for dealing with the remaining recalcitrants. All the trouble-makers are known to the police, either by dossier and record or by appearance and attitude. But the police are kept under some restraints, and those restraints produce greater and greater rage.

The rage comes from another source as well. Demands for a different future have been welling up in this society for some years now, and while those demands have not been unheard they have gone unheeded. Vietnam, racism, poverty, the degradation of the natural and manmade environment, the bureaucratization of the academy and its active collaboration with the military and industrial state, unrepresentative and unreachable structures of domination—all these grow apace. It seems increasingly clear to those who reject this American future that the forces of "law and order" intend to defend it by any means necessary. It becomes increasingly clear to the forces of law and order that extreme means will be necessary, and that the longer they are delayed the more extreme they will have to be.

Those two futures met at People's Park. It should be clear that what is happening this time is qualitatively different from 1964 and the Free Speech Movement. The difference in the amount of violence is the most striking, but this is largely a symptom of underlying differences. In 1964, the issues centered around questions of civil liberties and due process within the University. The issues now are political in the largest sense.

V

The appearance of People's Park raised questions of property and the nature of meaningful work. It raised questions about how people can begin to make a livable environment for themselves; about why both the defenders and critics of established authority today agree that authority can be considered only in terms of repression, never in terms of genuine respect and affection. These questions cannot be evaded. Those who honestly and courageously ask them are not imperiling the general happiness but are working for the common redemption.

It is increasingly clear that legitimate authority is declining in the modern state. In a real sense, "law and order" *is* the basic question of our day. This crisis of legitimacy has been visible for some time in just about all of the non-political sectors of life—family, economy, religion, education—and is now spreading rapidly into the political realm. The gigantic and seemingly impregnable organizations that surround and dominate men in the modern states are seen by more and more people to have at their center not a vital principle of authority, but a hollow space, a moral vacuum. Increasingly, among the young and the rejected, obedience is mainly a matter of lingering habit, or expediency, or necessity, but not a matter of conviction and deepest sentiment.

The groups who are most persistently raising these questions are, of course, white middle-class youth and the racial and ethnic minorities. The origins of protest are different in the two cases: the former have largely seen through the American Dream of meaning in power and wealth and have found it a nightmare; the latter have been pushed aside and denied even the minimal goods of the Dream. But the ends of the protest are remarkably similar: both are fighting against distortions and denials of their humanity. Both reject the programmed future of an America whose only imperative now seems to be: more.

The people who built the Park (there will be more People's Parks, more and more occasions for seemingly bizarre, perverse, and wild behavior) have pretty much seen through the collective ideals and disciplines that have bound this nation together in its conquest of nature and power. Having been victimized by the restraints and authorities of the past, these people are suspicious of all authorities and most collective ideals. Some of them seem ready to attempt a life built upon no other ideal than self-gratification. They sometimes talk as though they had found the secret which has lain hidden through all the past ages of man: that the individual can live fully and freely with no authority other than his desires, absorbed completely in the development of all his capacities except two—the capacity for memory and the capacity for faith.

No one can say where this will lead. Perhaps new prophets will appear. Perhaps the old faith will be reborn. Perhaps we really shall see the new technological Garden tended by children—kind, sincere innocents, barbarians with good hearts. The great danger at present is that the established and the respectable are more and more disposed to see all this as chaos and outrage. They seem prepared to follow the most profoundly nihilistic denial possible, which is the denial of the future through denial of their own children, the bearers of the future.

In such times as these, hope is not a luxury but a necessity. The hope which we see is in the revival of a sense of shared destiny, of some common fate which can bind us into a people we have never been. Even to sketch out that fate one must first decide that it does not lie with the power of technology or the stability of organizational society. It lies, instead, in something more elemental, in our common fears that scientific weapons may destroy all life; that technology will increasingly disfigure men who live in the city, just as it has already debased the earth and obscured the sky; that the "progress" of industry will destroy the possibility of interesting work; and that "communications" will obliterate the last traces of the varied cultures which have been the inheritance of all but the most benighted societies.

If hope is to be born of these despairs it must be given political direction, a new politics devoted to nurturing life and work. There can be no political direction without political education, yet America from its beginnings has never confronted the question of how to care for men's souls while helping them to see the world politically. Seeing the world politically is preparatory to acting in it politically; and to act politically is not to be tempted by the puerile attraction of power or to be content with the formalism of a politics of compromise. It is, instead, a politics which seeks always to discover what men can share—and how what they share can be enlarged and yet rise beyond the banal.

People's Park is not banal. If only the same could be said of those who build and guard the fences around all of us.

REFERENCE

KENISTON, K. (1967) *The Uncommitted: Alienated Youth in American Society.* New York: Dell Books.

EPILOGUE

Campus Radicalization: Notes on the Buildup at Buffalo—Carlos E. Kruytbosch

The editors' Introduction to this volume reflected our pessimistic feelings during the winter of 1969–70. The outlook at that time seemed grim, with mounting violence, repression and reaction, feelings of powerlessness, and dissipation of hope.

I

What we overlooked—as it seems did most other observers (including most clearly the Nixon administration itself)—was the depth and rapid spread of "radicalization" of the nation's campuses, large and small. By the spring of 1970 hundreds of thousands of students across the country had witnessed, either as participants or as observers, police gas and clubs used against fellow students on campus. It seems incontrovertible that few things unite students (and, increasingly, faculty too) more than demands to get the police off campus—especially after violent incidents have led them to being redefined as "pigs." Few things are as radicalizing as witnessing the clubbing down of persons with whose cause one sympathizes, regardless of the circumstances which led to the incident. This is the emotional consequence of the law enforcement doctrine of meeting force with superior force. People's Park, Orangeburg (S.C.), Santa Barbara, Kent State, and most recently Jackson State in Mississippi symbolized this literal overkill, and they have evoked proportionally outraged responses. As the father of one of the slain Kent State coeds said, "Have we come to such a state in this country that a young girl has to be shot because she disagrees deeply with the actions of her government?"

As of late May 1970, a few weeks after the enraged response to the invasion of Cambodia and the campus killings, some hope seems to have returned. While the attitudinal about-face of the Nixon administration toward the student movement is viewed with considerable skepticism, it does represent a response. Further, and much more significant, is the apparent resolve of students and many faculty to direct their antiwar efforts into electing congressional representatives pledged to that end in the fall of 1970. Princeton's decision to allow students two weeks off before the election so they can participate in the campaign may be followed by other institutions. Indeed, a sound educational rationale for such a practise can be devised. Just as neophyte doctors and lawyers require practise in the application of theoretical knowledge and techniques, so might theoretical study in the liberal arts greatly benefit from practise in functioning social and political life. Naturally, given the predominant political orientation of students in the liberal arts, there would be severe problems of implementing such programs on a large scale in tax-supported institutions. Some of the experimental "colleges" at my own institution—the State University of New York at Buffalo—have had this character, but they have also sustained severe attacks from the community, and when "push" turned to "shove," the administration indicated that the colleges were not financed from state appropriations but from private endowment funds. In any case, campus power, as exhibited in the nation-wide campus disturbances, in the size of the spontaneous march on Washington; in the strikes ongoing at between 10 and 20 percent of all the nation's campuses, with populous and prestigious campuses disproportionately represented (426 campuses were on strike as of May 10th, according to a College Press Service story); and in the congressional response to the movement, has been clearly demonstrated. Feelings of powerlessness have been at least temporarily abated and the majority of protesters—students, faculty, and others—seem resolved to try once more in the framework of the system—to give it one last chance to respond on the issue of the war.

II

The State University of New York at Buffalo is perhaps not untypical of the buildup of radicalization within a two year period, and the following pages sketch the developments and issues in the increasingly intense dissent. Originally a provincial, "minor league" institution (excepting its virtually autonomous Schools of Law and Medicine) it was taken over by the state of New York in 1962 as one of the "university centers" of the new state system of higher education. Being the largest instant campus of the huge state system, SUNYAB attracted some national visibility. A half-billion dollar new campus was promised. High salaries and promise of prestige and room to experiment attracted "star" professors and bright young men from top graduate schools. Martin Meyerson, emerging untainted from his brief Berkeley stewardship, accepted the presidency in 1966. He deluged the institution with new ideas and programs: SUNYAB was to be a "great" university, a leader in educational reform, research, and relevance to the community as well as a model of democracy in faculty and student governance.

The strains and tensions of rapid growth and unfamiliar, vaguely defined new practices and procedures were fully in evidence. Physical discomforts included cramped space, poor building repairs ("why bother when we'll soon have a brand new campus?"), a disorganized library, impossible parking. Newly instituted faculty government flexed its muscles, but found it had as yet very poor coordination. Student's similarly wrestled with the problems of five student governments. Flocking up to SUNYAB from New York city to take advantage of state scholarships and (relatively) low in-state tuition, students jammed into residence halls and often substandard, overpriced off-campus housing. Based no doubt on impeccable research, *Playboy's* annual assessment of the quality of student life on campuses across the nation emphasized Buffalo's freedom from rules of conduct and dormitory restrictions, and its "big-city swinger" social ambience. Of course, the drug quotient of this life style brought frequent, undesired, and unexpected contacts with the "narcs" of Buffalo and Erie County, not to mention the arousal of intense anxiety and disgust among many of the local citizenry.

During 1968 the principal on-campus targets of a small activist group were military research—particularly a "Project Themis" construction program—and the campus (non-compulsory) AFROTC program. However, downtown trials of local draft-resisters generated considerable militant activity including demonstrations and a few arrests. The budding system of experimental colleges, and president Meyerson's expressed interest in developing forms of student participation in governance, as well as the operating programs for admission of underqualified blacks, more or less pre-empted these areas from radical criticism. Meyerson had also endorsed a demand for a moratorium on construction of the half-billion dollar new campus until satisfactory arrangements were reached for employment of blacks on the work force. In the spring of 1969, aroused by conviction of the draft resisters, campus activists mounted an assault on the Themis construction site and harassed ROTC activities. Other classes were invaded by guerrilla theatre groups, and the administration building was occupied. The response of the administration was two-pronged. A court injunction—one of the first uses of court injunction for this purpose in the country—required persons to vacate the office building. And indeed, after an overnight stay some 100 students filed out peaceably but visibly defiant when confronted by a large force of Buffalo police—their first appearance in force on the campus. Complementing the use of the mailed fist, president Meyerson proclaimed a campus-wide teach-in on the subjects of concern, and he himself met for two hours in dialogue with a small auditorium-full of core activists (during the overnight occupation of the administration building). From all accounts, little "communication" took place at that meeting but the administration could not be accused of "not listening" or isolation.

The Faculty Senate took both issues under advisement. A study committee was to examine and recommend on ROTC. The full Senate approved a new university research policy but excluded, by two to one, a clause which would ban the acceptance of military research contracts. In addition to vociferous heckling from the gallery the activists thus had the satisfaction of seeing nearly one-third of the faculty support their goal. Overall, however, when the hubbub died down, toward the end of the semester many felt that while Meyerson had clearly outmaneuvered the activists, little had been accomplished on the substantive issues, and that the use of the injunction and the advent of the police on campus (albeit without incident) did not augur well for the future. It was also clear that while the activists had not generated much "body support" in their occupation of the administration building, the issue of the military on campus had struck considerable resonance among the student body. Faculty optimism, on the other hand, had been dealt a severe blow by the threat of budget cuts for next fall; a major shift from the virtually open purse of the previous years.

Two important changes were apparent when the students returned in the fall of 1969. Meyerson had taken a two-thirds time leave of absence, his place filled by an acting president (the former executive vice-president) with little image or "presence" among students or most faculty. Secondly, after a trial year the experimental college system was pressing for permanent status on conditions favorable to its independent operation. Two of the "farthest out" colleges—both strongly oriented toward work in the local community—drew criticism from faculty concerned with academic standards and heavy fire from community groups incensed at (among other things) college supported agitation in local high schools. Responding to these pressures the administration cashed in some of its credibility among activists and sympathizers in a half-hearted and unsuccessful attempt to limit enrollment in one of these colleges. Similarly, an administration-supported plan for governance of the college system was vehemently opposed by college advocates on the grounds that it made for domination of the system by traditionalist departmental representatives.

Later in the fall a (successful) black student campaign to increase the medical school quota of black admissions was accompanied by some broken windows and threatening language. The verbal violence in particular prompted the acting president to begin to define his image with the issuance of a "hard" declaration that threats and intimidation would not be tolerated and would be met by firm action. Characteristically, attempts on the part of white activists to make common cause with the black actions were received very coolly, and rejected altogether when agreements with the medical school hove into sight.

In January, Martin Meyerson officially resigned to move up into the Ivy League, accepting the presidency of the University of Pennsylvania. The loss of his prestige on the administration greatly weakened its leadership capability—among both students and a large proportion of the faculty.

In early February a black student boycott of a basketball game to force greater black representation in the athletic department triggered demonstrations of support. A tragi-comedy of errors, misunderstandings, and wild rumors led to escalation of confrontations with the small campus police force and the appearance on campus of the city's tough Tactical Patrol Unit. Melees in and around the Student Union building resulted in extensive injuries to students. A later semi-official faculty investigation of the course of events laid the blame squarely upon the acting president for inadequately ascertaining the gravity of the crisis before resorting to large force.

The campus was thrown into a turmoil; the involvement of the police and other unresolved issues from the previous year became rallying points for demonstrations of unprecedented size. Students marched on ROTC and Themis windows were broken. A campus strike was initiated, supported to a considerable but indeterminate degree by students and faculty. The administration building and some classrooms were picketed, some admissions files were scattered and burned, and some doorways were blocked to non-striking students and employees. As before, the administration obtained a court injunction barring the blocking of buildings. While things had by no means returned to "normal," after several days of relative peace, faculty and students were taken by surprise when they returned to work (or to strike) on a Monday morning to discover the campus occupied and patrolled by 400 Buffalo policemen. The acting president announced he had requested them to protect persons and property, and that they had been brought in quietly early Sunday morning to avoid trouble.

Amidst a deceptive calm during the next four days, there was tremendous activity at departmental levels. Faculty and students in most humanities and social science departments, and many others, passed resolutions demanding immediate removal of the police. Ironically, for the first two days activists refrained from confrontations at least partly in deference to the planned campus appearance of Jerry Rubin (out on appeal bail from his "Chicago Seven" conviction). On the fifth day, however, the sight of phalanxes of blue marching around campus became too much. In the evening the largest crowd of students yet assembled moved to the gymnasium where the cops were quartered. They hurled insults and rocks across the buffer line of a recently organized faculty/student Peace Patrol, but made no physical contact. The police nevertheless moved when the crowd assaulted the nearby Themis construction site with rocks and Molotov cocktails. From then on for several hours it was a running battle between groups of police and students throughout the campus. A major battle where most of the injuries took place occurred when a force of club-wielding police charged from the administration building into students assembled outside. Inevitably, cops and kids clashed, blood flowed, and tensions and frustrations mounted.

Before the confrontation, the Faculty Senate had moved overwhelmingly for immediate removal of police from campus and, while an earlier vote calling for resignation of the acting president was defeated (62 to 38 percent), a later vote of confidence (also introduced by faculty hostile to the administration) was also defeated. Administration legitimacy and credibility was further eroded by the resignation of several high university officials—primarily on the police issue. A meeting of the A.A.U.P. local was called to discuss the collapse of university government.

The problem of accessibility to the administration was dramatized when, on a Sunday morning, nearly 50 faculty members staged a sit-in at the acting president's office. They demanded to know why the police remained on campus despite the Faculty Senate resolutions, and vowed to stay until the police were removed. The acting president declined to talk and within the hour had ordered them arrested for trespassing. Once arrested, furthermore, their cases fell into the hands of a politically ambitious District Attorney who proceeded to file several more serious charges against them, including both civil and criminal contempt. The arrest of the "Faculty Forty-five," less than a half dozen of whom could be labeled radicals, had a radicalizing effect upon the faculty, as well as further legitimating direct action by the students. Even many conservative faculty who maintained that the "forty-five" deserved some punishment for their in appropriate behavior felt that the response was all out of proportion to their act.

Within weeks, two of the principal issues came before the Faculty Senate for decision. Under some prodding, the long delayed faculty investigative committee on ROTC made its report. It recommended the program be phased out and replaced by a new interdisciplinary program of military studies without organizational ties to the Department of Defense. The Senate accepted the recommendation. Similarly, some time later, the Senate approved a plan for governance of the College system which was acceptable to those in the most controversial colleges.

While two of the principal issues appeared settled, the following weeks in late March and April were characterized by both exhaustion and unease. Few regretted the resignation of the acting president in mid-April, but the image of a leaderless campus was thereby reinforced. In addition, community blacklash was rapidly building up. Trials of indicted students and faculty proceeded apace, and new charges mounted as investigations developed. (One professor filed an affidavit on the basis of which another was charged with violation of the injunction.) Coincidentally (perhaps), Leslie Fiedler's long delayed marijuana case came to trial at this time, with its strong overtones of violation of academic freedom and persecution of an advocate of an unpopular cause. A grand jury investigation of the disorders was launched, and a subpoena of confidential faculty files brought in the national A.A.U.P.—also to guard against encroachments upon academic freedom. City fire and health inspectors condemned the off-campus premises of one of the controversial colleges. The Buffalo Common Council considered an ordinance making it a crime to address public officials as "pig." The rate of summonses for hitch-hikers around the campus shot up. Authorities in Albany reviewed their records to see which faculty had not signed their "oaths of allegiance."

In this climate, news of the Cambodian incursion was at first received with what virtually amounted to weariness. It provoked no instant reaction, yet within days (actually on the same day as the Kent State killings) a special edition of the student newspaper reprinted an editorial approved by several dozen college newspapers calling for a national student strike against the Vietnam war. The news from Kent State galvanized the campus into action, for identification was powerful and immediate. Some 2,500 students rallied on campus and began the long march downtown to bring the shootings, the war, and the national strike demands home to the people of Buffalo. However, a strategic police roadblock just beyond a railroad underpass effectively barred the only downtown approach for half a mile in either direction. Following some diversionary barricade building and burning, and smashing of local bank windows, the kids and the cops enacted their ritualistic showdown, exchanging volleys of rocks and tear gas (the first use of gas on SUNYAB students). In repeated confrontations the police forced the students back onto campus. On this and the following night police and roaming bands of students pursued each other around campus. On the third night the police spewed massive doses of tear gas inside the buildings used by the students, which effectively denied them bases for further sallies. On this night, also, several students were treated for birdshot wounds. Police and sheriffs denied using shotguns but students firmly believed otherwise.

A few days before final examinations the acting president announced that students who wished to leave because of the dangerous situation would be permitted to do so without academic penalty. The campus began to empty, and when the activists returned from a weekend March on Washington, they found it impossible to restore the mass momentum of the previous week. Resplendent in its rich spring greenery and heavy with the scent of lilac and ornamental trees, the campus was quiet. That is, almost quiet, for peace was broken by the diesel motor of an air-compressor sandblasting all traces of the last few months' revolutionary slogans from the buildings. Clean slate-grey stone replaced "On Strike," "Free Huey," "Off ROTC."

III

Some important issues have been resolved; many others remain. Who will the new president be, and will he be able to restore a sense of direction? How can fractionated campus government be reconstructed to satisfy both students and faculty (and also a newly organized group of professional staff employees)? How will new state-mandated disciplinary procedures work? Will the renaming of Project Themis solve the problem? Will the "Faculty Forty-five" cases be prosecuted with full severity? Can there be rapprochement with the community? Each of these issues has potential for direct action. But it is clear that they will dwindle into insignificance if, come the November elections, the effort directed by students into anti-war congressional campaigns does not bear fruit.

A Concluding Note from Berkeley
—Sheldon L. Messinger

Like other campuses, Berkeley in May 1970 is in turmoil. What does it mean? Is Berkeley on the verge of radical change? It is difficult to say with any pretense of certainty. On the one hand, insistence that changes are needed is widespread. It is asserted that the university's relations with constituent groupings in the society must change; and it is asserted that relations among the groupings that make up the university must change. Nor is such insistence merely verbal; students and faculty have recently shown a notable capacity to underline their assertions with action. On the other hand, insistence that radical changes are needed is not the same as evidence that such changes will come to pass. Nor does action, even violence, provide a guarantee. The capacity of Berkeley, like other

U.S. universities, to absorb or resist radical demands is, or has been, vast.

Yet, if a precursor of radical change in the university, as in the society at large, is "a challenge to prevailing modes of thought" (Moore, 1969: 6) about its structure and operations,[1] then it might fairly be held that one sign of imminent radical change is present. One need not turn to radical broadsides to find such a challenge; one can turn, instead, to such establishment accounts as the much-maligned analysis of Clark Kerr (1963). Kerr's understanding of the university is not too different, in crucial respects, from that recommended by "radicals." Like them, Kerr seems to agree that the "uses" of the university are increasingly determined from without rather than from within, and largely by those forces with the most money and other forms of power. He also seems to agree that relations among the constituent elements of the university are best understood as the outcome of conflicts in which the most powerful element usually wins. To be sure, Kerr tends to take a benign view of the outcome of these pressures and conflicts. In so doing, he parts company with the radicals and many not-so-radicals. One might put it this way: Kerr argues that the U.S. university is decisively shaped by the other U.S. institutions which it serves, particularly by industry and government, including the military. It is of a piece with, indeed, it is one those institutions. The "radicals" agree. They add that U.S. institutions, including the university, are in many respects inhumane, infused with racism, militarism, and imperialistic designs. And they propose to change these institutions.

The point of these remarks is not to malign *The Uses of the University* or Clark Kerr; neither is it to suggest that, if one looks closely, Clark Kerr himself turns out to be a "radical." Rather it is to suggest that Kerr's analysis, when seen in light of the view that U.S. institutions are racist, militaristic, destructive of the environment, and geared to imperialistic designs, supports a highly critical view of what the university has become and does. What the university—Berkeley, in this case—has become and does is currently under severe challenge. "Reconstitution" is the battle cry.

A second precursor of radical change in society is said to be (Moore, 1969: 6) "the appearance of very sharp conflicts of interest within the dominant classes." This second sign of impending change is also arguably present at Berkeley with reference to the university. What will likely turn out to be the sharpest disagreement has not yet fully developed, but seems imminent: who will bear the costs of educating the masses of young persons—particularly those from the ghettoes and barrios? Such costs are, first of all, financial. It is by no means clear, given the numbers of persons now involved and the competing demands for money, that the struggle can be defused by expansion—the university's "solution" of similar (if less serious) conflicts in the past.

Further, the costs are more than financial, as they usually are. Recent views of the proper role and function of the university do not simply call for "more," although they do that too. In addition, they call for "relevance," meaning, in part, viable connections between what the university is and does, and the creation of a humane social order.[2] Some faculty members—in my impression an already significant and increasing number—are questioning their own work as well as that of their colleagues in this light; and many do not like what they see. Conflict is thus engendered among this portion of the "dominant classes."

Conflict between parts of the "dominant classes" of the university is present as well, as it always has been. Boards of trustees, administrators, and faculty members have never been famous for their cooperative relations. My impression is that conflict between these elements is increasing. Some of the foregoing studies implicitly or explicitly suggest why. Hartnett's survey, for example, might be interpreted to suggest that students, faculty, and even administrators are increasingly drawn from different social strata than the members of boards of trustees. Trustees may know this, formally, but they have few means of learning in depth about the wants, much less the needs, of these persons. And it should be added that knowing, in this case as in others, would not necessarily mean agreeing that these wants and needs should be serviced—especially when other wants and needs must be sacrificed, as they must. This condition would seem to make ever more serious conflict quite likely.

Whatever the value of this particular analysis, of such conflict we have seen much in recent years—and it seems certain we shall see more, and more serious conflict, in the coming months. Both Riesman's and Lunsford's analyses can be read to suggest that administrators will be further drawn into the conflict—and may be torn apart by it.

In assessing the possibility of radical changes in the university, one must consider the measures contending parties are willing to use and are capable of using. Although a few years ago it might have seemed "fantastic" to visualize the use of violence, this is hardly fantastic now. In the society at large, as Moore (1969: 6) reminds us, "loss of unified control over the instruments of violence: the army and the police" has typically been a precursor of radical changes. This assumes that other means of social control—particularly, the authoritativeness of routine arrangements—have proven useless. On a number of occasions since 1964 this last has been the case at Berkeley. During the past month or so, it seems to me, the hold, the authoritativeness, of routine arrangements has proved increasingly weak for a very large proportion of those who make up the university. "No-business-as-usual" has become a fact for much of the university.

One aspect of recent university disturbances, too little noted, might well be called an "escalation to the routine." Such an escalation has marked both particular disturbances at Berkeley and the set of disturbances that have taken place since 1964. Conflict has typically begun, in the past, over some set of arrangements that were seen as, in some sense, "special"—for example, whether students could use the campus as a setting for partisan political activities. But as the conflict evolved, much more basic questions were evoked—for example, whether the administration had the right to make policy regarding use of the campus on any subject whatsoever when the affected parties were not a part of the policy-making apparatus. Put like this, the ways in which decisions are routinely made is called into question, and particular decisions become somewhat less important except as signs of a thoughtless or corrupt or authoritarian decision-making structure.

Over the range of conflicts, the challenge—to routines, to what is taken-for-granted—has become ever more prominent. It is my impression that individual universities may still go through the whole set of issues—from particular to general, from special to routine—but that this evolutionary process is speeded up and truncated. At Berkeley, the particular and the special no longer command attention, except as details seen within a larger framework. Put differently, the authoritativeness of routines and those who uphold them has been progressively undermined; disturbances begin, as it were, by challenging the whole structure of authority and the purposes it embodies. In this situation, it is not surprising that police, and troops, are called.

There is little evidence so far, if any, that the police and the army are reluctant to use force to control dissidence on campus—or off, for that matter. Indeed, the police in particular seem somewhat more than ready to use violence; all reports from the campuses agree about this. On the other hand, "unified control over the instruments of violence" presumably means, in part, that those who "control" these instruments have a unified view about the necessity and wisdom of use. This, at least, seems somewhat shaken by the experiences of the last few years and weeks. There is some evidence, for example, that university administrators have been shocked by the violence of police measures, and by their own inability to exert control over these measures once they authorize police action. Whether this shock will lead—or, indeed, has led—to some reluctance to use force on campus is more problematic. If so, it can be argued, I think, that *"unified* control" may be in progressive jeopardy, for there are others among university governors who show neither shock nor reluctance. One straw in the wind may be changes that are rumored regarding campus police forces at Berkeley (and other campuses of the University of California). Reportedly, discretion has been removed from the campus level and placed at the statewide level—always more sensitive to the demands of state government. Such a development may point to growing distrust among the "governing classes" concerned with the university, to a loss of "unified control."

It can be said, of course, that in a struggle between local and higher officials, the latter are bound to win. Perhaps, but this hardly seems certain; short of Draconian repression it may prove extremely difficult to control the activities of a determined faculty and student body. Moreover, and perhaps more important, it is not at all clear that if force and violence continue to be used, the higher officials will accomplish the goal we might impute to them, namely, to control the social and cultural resources of the university. It seems more likely that they will first engender a mutiny, and if they persist, the destruction of the very prize they seek. We doubt that universities are quite so delicate as some claim them to be—particularly those who oppose noisy dissent; we doubt that they are quite so easily "disrupted" as is sometimes said. On the other hand, they can be disrupted, and in some cases have been, by pitched battles occurring within their gates and, more insidiously, by occupying armies of police and guardsmen. These battles and these intrusions have made it clear at Berkeley, at least, that conventional educational activities can be stopped dead, very dead. It is not only that sometimes one cannot walk across the campus, or sit in a classroom or study, or work in a laboratory. Often one *can,* but one does not *want* to do so. It becomes morally repugnant to do so; one feels physically ill going on with "business-as-usual." It is not difficult to imagine such a state of moral repugnance, reinforced by a sense of physical malaise, becoming quite permanent on the campus.

On balance, then, I should say that although there is as yet scant evidence of loss of unified control over the instruments of violence, it seems possible, at least in the sense relevant to the university. Moreover, there is the possibility that should unified control not be lost, or should it be regained if weakened by conflicts among the governors, the outcome might be mutiny (led by lesser officials) or, ultimately, destruction of the university as we know it. Finally, I suggest that continued use of force and violence on the campus (or off, against "students") may so demoralize the enterprise as to change it beyond recognition. Any of these developments would seem to be among those phenomena presaging radical change in the university—although, to be sure, the direction of change will be quite different under these varying conditions.[3]

A fourth precursor of radical change is said to be (Moore, 1969: 6–7) "the transformation of a more or less atomized and diffuse urban plebs or of a proletariat into a politically active revolutionary mass." The analogy is the transformation of the student body, or large segments of it, into an active mass determined radically to change the university's external and internal relations. To a certain extent, it seems clear, this has already happened. If there is not, as yet at least, any overall fusion of students into one large, angry mass, neither is it apparent that this is required, at least to change particular universities. It has never been quite clear relative to revolutions in society what proportion of the potentially disaffected need be, or are, activated; the situation relative to universities is at least as ambiguous. Given the self-doubts that university administrators entertain—and, we think, increasingly entertain; given conflicts among the governors; given the difficulty of estimating the reservoirs of ill will that obtain among students; given the sheer numbers of students (so that 20 percent, or even five, is a very large number); given the images of organization of the opposition that the governors entertain—partly for propaganda reasons, to be sure, but not only for this reason; given all this and more, it seems entirely possible, even likely, that determined protests, frequently made, can wring significant, perhaps even radical changes from the governors. Although President Johnson's decision not to run for re-election cannot be said to represent a radical change (and was not a change in the university, in any case), that the decision was made, and made in part in response to student demands, is quite suggestive. President Nixon's unclear promises about ending the conflict in Southeast Asia may provide another suggestive instance of the power of dissent.

Perhaps the main question about the massification of students, and
their political activation, is, however, whether reforms—including the
end of the war in Southeast Asia—will blunt the trends in this direction
that now seem in train. One popular interpretation of "student discontent"
is that the draft, leading to participation in the most unpopular war in
American history, is the main fuel. What if the war were to end? Or the
draft to end? Would this do it? Would the blandishments of the society
at large regain their appeal—their full appeal, that is, for they continue
to appeal to many? It is impossible to say with any certainty, of course,
but I think this interpretation too narrow. Something much larger and
more profound seems to be happening. Even if this is not so, the disposition of the government to end the war in Southeast Asia (which is itself
uncertain) does not, at this juncture, seem part of a policy to restructure
the role of the United States in world affairs in any other ways. And it is
this role that will determine further Viet Nams and Cambodias—or, at
least, so many students and others believe.

Nor are foreign entanglements all there is to be considered. The
distribution of privileges and rewards within the United States has been
and remains a central concern of student "radicals" and others; and the
role of the university in supporting the extant distribution is under attack.
Reforms in this area, at least effective reforms, seem even more remote
than in the area of foreign wars.

It can be argued, of course, that most university students stand to
benefit from the current structure of privileges and rewards—unlike the
war in Southern Asia. This seems patently so, and it serves to divide
elements of the student movement: many black student "radicals," for
example, seem much more concerned with getting "in" than they are
with opting out in defiance of business-as-usual. It may follow that the
revolutionary zeal of the students will be easily diverted or subdued once
current pressures for war work are abated. I do not think this will happen;
but it is clearly possible.

It is extremely difficult to say *why* I do not think it will happen; I may
be expressing little else than a kind of wishful—and partly fearful—
thinking. (Or should I say "feeling"?) But my sense is that current
disaffections among students and others is not specific, that is, not related
to any particular set of events or relationships. I have the sense that,
instead, it is quite general and flows from the very structure of the society
at large and the ways of being in the world that this structure recommends
or insist upon, or cuts off. (This is not to say that particular events and
relationships do not exacerbate and make actual the underlying revolutionary potential.) I believe that disaffection for things as they are, and
promise to remain, is very, very widespread among the young, including
the younger-than-college-age population; this disaffection is shared, furthermore, by articulate elements of older age groupings. As the younger popu-
lations move to the university and from there to the society at large, I
expect dramatic and, perhaps, radical changes. These may be brought
about by collapse from within.

I think, indeed, that collapse from within is a very real possibility:

collapse of the routines of the society at large and, especially the university. In the latter setting (although here my view may be biased by my experience at Berkeley), the collapse has already begun. (As noted before, I think that such a collapse may be moved along, in part, by outside efforts to shore up the structure through force and violence.) Students, particularly the best students, will no longer easily accept curricula and assignments that they have no hand in fashioning; the claims of "tradition" and "expertise" and "for your own good" are no longer compelling. Equally important, those who in the past would have automatically made such claims—faculty members—have been led, in many cases, to examine their own positions; and in some cases, they have discovered they have no good reasons to support their claims, or what may be worse, only reasons they can no longer accept.

Such a situation makes for a great deal of anxiety. Anxiety, bred of uncertainty, is perhaps the dominant effect in the university today.

NOTES

1. I have drawn the outline of my argument from the seminal article, "Revolution in America?" by Barrington Moore, Jr. As his title suggests, Moore attempts to assess the prospects of revolution in American society at large; I attempt to assess the prospects of revolution in U.S. universities, particularly Berkeley. I have been led, therefore, to interpret rather freely the criteria Moore employs.

2. The call for "relevance" seems to have (at least) two meanings. On the one hand, it appears to be a demand for greater attention to social needs— and, implicitly, an assertion that much of the academic enterprise is "irrelevant" in the sense of "trivial." On the other hand, and more recently, it appears to be a demand for greater attention to the social needs of particular social groupings, e.g., poor or black persons. Put this way, the assertion, often explicit, is that much of the academic enterprise is all-too-"relevant"; it serves the "power structure" and disserves others. Conceivably—and in my opinion— both assertions are probably true.

3. It should be clear that a sharp move to the "right" is just as "radical" as a sharp move to the "left." Moore does not explicitly consider this possibility, exploring, rather, the prospects of radical changes consistent with demands from the "left."

REFERENCES

MOORE, BARRINGTON, JR. (1969) "Revolution in America?" *The New York Review of Books* 12, 2 (January 30): 6–12.

KERR, C. (1963) *The Uses of the University*. Cambridge: Harvard University Press. Also Torchbook edition (1966), New York: Harper & Row.

ABOUT THE AUTHORS

FREDRIC BEISSE is an Instructor and Research Assistant in the Department of Computer Science, University of Oregon. The article in this volume was completed while he was a Research Fellow at the Center for the Advanced Study of Educational Administration at the University of Oregon. His current research interests include computer applications to problems in educational research.

ALEXANDER BUSCH is planning officer on the staff of the West-German Wissenschaftsrat (Council for Science and Higher Education).

BURTON R. CLARK is Professor of Sociology and Chairman of the Department of Sociology, Yale University. He is the author of *Adult Education in Transition* (1956), *The Open Door College* (1960), and *Educating the Expert Society* (1962). A forthcoming study, *The Distinctive College: Antioch, Reed and Swarthmore,* will be published by the Aldine Publishing Company in 1970.

ROBERT DUBIN is Professor of Sociology, School of Social Science and Professor of Administration, Graduate School of Administration, University of California, Irvine. He is author of *Theory Building, Human Relations in Administration, The World of Work,* and co-author of *Leadership and Productivity, The Teaching-Learning Paradox: Comparative College Teaching Methods,* and *The Medium May be Related to the Message: College Instruction by TV.* He is editing a forthcoming *Handbook of Industrial Sociology* and is engaging in an international study of attachment to work.

TROY DUSTER is Associate Professor of Sociology and Associate Research Sociologist with the Center for Research and Development in Higher Education, University of California, Berkeley. He is the author of *The Legislation of Morality,* and is presently completing a monograph comparing university control in the United States and Sweden.

JERRY G. GAFF is Assistant Research Psychologist at the Center for Research and Development in Higher Education, University of California, Berkeley. He has written articles on higher education, has authored *Innovations and Consequences: A Study of Cluster Colleges* and is co-author of a forthcoming monograph *Faculty Characteristics and Faculty Influence on Students.*

RODNEY T. HARTNETT is Research Psychologist in the Higher Education Research Group at Educational Testing Service. He has published numerous articles dealing with higher education and is currently preparing a second report based on the trustee data presented here.

CARLOS E. KRUYTBOSCH is lecturer in organization at the State University of New York at Buffalo. He has published several articles on administration in research organizations and universities. He is currently preparing a report on research organization in the university and is engaged in a national survey of researchers in universities.

TERRY F. LUNSFORD is Research Specialist in sociology at the Center for Research and Development in Higher Education, University of California, Berkeley. He is the author of *The "Free Speech" Crises at Berkeley, 1964–65,* and of several published articles on student protest and institutional change. He has just completed a report of *Administrative Perspectives in the Large University,* based on a survey of 526 executives at 69 major U.S. campuses.

T. R. McCONNELL is Research Educator at the Center for Research and Development in Higher Education, and Emeritus Professor of Higher Education, University of California, Berkeley. He is the author of *A General Pattern for Amercian Public Higher Education,* and numerous articles in professional journals. With associates, he is conducting studies of faculty governance at selected institutions, and summarizing the work of the Center on various aspects of governance.

SHELDON L. MESSINGER is Professor of Criminology and Research Sociologist at the Center for the Study of Law and Society, both at the University of California, Berkeley. He is co-author of *Schizophrenic Women, C-Unit: Search for Community in Prison,* and *Civil Justice and the Poor.* His monograph, *Strategies of Control,* based on study of the California prison system, will be published by Aldine in 1970.

KENNETH P. MORTIMER is a Research Associate and Assistant Professor at the Center for the Study of Higher Education at The Pennsylvania State University. He is co-author of the research monograph *Academic Government at Berkeley: The Academic Senate* and is currently writing and conducting research on the subject of faculty involvement in institutional policy making.

C. MICHAEL OTTEN is an assistant professor of sociology at San Jose State College, San Jose, California. Prior to teaching at San Jose he was a research assistant at the Center for the Study of Law and Society, University of California, Berkeley. He is the author of the forthcoming book *Authority, Students and Society: The Berkeley Experience.* The book covers a century of the University of California's experience in governing students. It will be published by the University of California Press in the spring of 1970.

TALCOTT PARSONS is Professor of Sociology at Harvard University. Among his publications are *The Structure of Social Action; Social Structure and Personality; Sociological Theory and Modern Society;* and *Politics and Social Structure.* He is currently President of the American Academy of Arts and Sciences and one of the senior participants in its program, The Assembly on University Goals and Governance.

GERALD M. PLATT is a lecturer on Sociology in the Department of Social Relations at Harvard University. He is co-author of *The Wish To Be Free: Society, Psyche, and Value Change,* University of California Press, 1969. He is also co-principal investigator with Talcott Parsons on a National Study of the American Academic Professions.

DAVID RIESMAN is Henry Ford II Professor of Social Sciences at Harvard University. He is a member of the Faculty Committee supervising the Undergraduate Social Studies Program, he serves on the College's Committee on General Education, and teaches a General Education course on American Character and Society. He is co-author with Christopher Jencks of *The Academic Revolution* (1968) and is currently working with two colleagues on a book about two new public colleges.

JOHN H. SCHAAR is Professor of Political Science at the University of California, Santa Cruz.

MARTIN TROW is Professor of Sociology in the Graduate School of Public Affairs, University of California, Berkeley. He is currently Director of the National Survey of Higher Education sponsored by the Carnegie Commission on Higher Education. He is co-author of *Union Democracy* and of *The British Academics* (forthcoming).

ROBERT C. WILSON is Research Psychologist and Coordinator of Research on Student Development at the Center for Research and Development in Higher Education, University of California, Berkeley. He has published numerous research articles in the fields of organizational effectiveness, creativity and gifted children. He is the author of *The Gifted Child in Portland.* He is co-author of two forthcoming monographs, *Effective University Teaching and Its Evaluation* and *Faculty Characteristics and Faculty Influence on Students.*

SHELDON S. WOLIN is Professor of Political Science at the University of California, Santa Cruz. He is the author of *Politics and Vision;* co-editor, of *The Berkeley Student Revolt;* and author of several articles in the field of political theory.